A GENERAL HISTORY OF EUROPE

EDITED BY DENYS HAY

EUROPE
1780–1830

FRANKLIN L. FORD

LONGMAN

LONGMAN GROUP LIMITED
London

*Associated companies, branches and representatives
throughout the world*

© *Franklin L. Ford, 1970*

First published 1970
First issued in paperback 1971
Fourth impression 1975

ISBN 0 582 48203 8 cased
ISBN 0 582 48346 8 paper

*Printed in Great Britain by
Western Printing Services Ltd, Bristol*

For

Stephen and John

Contents

XIII. INTELLECTUAL FERMENT IN A REVOLUTIONARY AGE

Maps

I

Introduction

This volume, like its companions in the present series, is concerned specifically with European history. It deals, to be sure, with a period which saw Europe's influence spread across the world in mounting waves, a period, too, when non-European forces were beginning to work back with increasing effect upon the old continent and its principal islands. Nevertheless, it would be folly for such a book to make any pretence of global coverage—especially in view of the fact that many European developments of the period must themselves be passed over, or treated only briefly. An American, despite inherited attitudes and attachments, must look at Europe somewhat from the outside; but he is better qualified to do that than to try to write *world* history as seen through European eyes.

Having accepted the limits of the commission, we can concentrate on a central problem of interpretation. It is the problem of the relationship between Europe before and Europe after the general crisis of the revolutionary-Napoleonic era. Was the quarter-century which began in 1789 in fact the great historical watershed we generally assume it was? Or were the deep, underlying strands running from the eighteenth into the nineteenth century so important that we should dismiss any notion of a deep cleavage between one and the other as merely the product of over-emphasis on exciting events?

Obviously, the only way to attack the question of continuity versus change, in any period, is through thoughtful attention to the 'before', the 'after' and the 'in-between'. Hence, this is a book of narration, but narration interspersed with reflections and preceded, as well as followed, by examinations of European society around 1780, and then around 1830. The chronicle of public events—of treaties and battles, legislative enactments and executive decisions—is not ignored. Neither is the record of European thought and artistic accomplishment. If there exists a topical emphasis, it falls on relationships among groups of people, variously defined in legal, economic, honorific and political terms. Here, it seems to me, the central issue can be most usefully addressed. Was European society at the end of our period only superficially different from what it had been five decades earlier? Or were the differences so fundamental as to mark the coming of a new age? It is a subsidiary thesis of the ensuing chapters that public events, ideas and man's essays at beauty in colour or form or sound or language have all contributed to, even as they have reflected, the patterns and movements of society in general.

One of the most difficult balances to maintain in a book about Europe, 1780–1830, is that between emphasis on France and adequate coverage of other regions or states. There are dangers on both sides. It would be a crippling error to view this period as above all a dramatic segment of French history, in which the other peoples of Europe were obliged or privileged, depending on the historian's nationality, to play their parts. Perhaps less apparent, however, is the opposite form of distortion, which would result if one denied the power and importance of the French engine, at once destructive and creative, in this epoch of the European past. We shall therefore pay close attention to the France of Louis XVI, of Robespierre, of Napoleon and of the restored monarchy after 1815. We must also, however, try to keep the British Isles and the Germanies, the Low Countries, the Iberian kingdoms, Italy, the Austrian Habsburg lands, Russia, Poland, Scandinavia and the Balkans before us.

Because the half-century here examined was so filled with great innovations and violent reversals, there is a temptation to visualize the eighteenth century in excessively quiet colours. By the same token, we sometimes speak of 'the nineteenth century' as though things *settled down* after 1815. Actually, of course, the Old Régime was far from static. It had seen the rise and fall of kingdoms, churches and social groups, amid a vociferous tumult of argumentation and questioning. Every state in Europe was in important respects far different in the 1780s from what it had been in 1715, to say nothing of 1648. Similarly, one has only to think of Germany and Italy, France and Britain, Russia and Austro-Hungary, as they existed by the 1890s, to realize how much was to change in the three-quarters of a century *after* the fall of the Napoleonic Empire. It is worth emphasizing the importance of movement within the periods before and following the developments treated in this book, for we shall only confuse our thinking if we conceive of those developments as sandwiched between two glacial masses of relative immobility. Europe has never been quiet, never truly static.

Our task of comprehension calls for a quite different approach. It involves examining the very end of the pre-revolutionary era, the great crisis itself and then the emerging outlines of the post-Napoleonic European world. We should recognize that we are analysing one slice cut from the annals of a civilization as self-critical and changing as it has been proud and traditionalistic. Our aim is to determine, if possible, whether this slice represents something special. When we have finished, we must try to decide whether the years between the beginning of the 1780s and the end of the 1820s saw a break between an old world and a new one too striking for any historian to ignore, or whether they simply witnessed the temporary disruption of a European system which resumed its earlier characteristics with remarkable speed and completeness, once the storm had passed.

II

The Sources

No historian concerned with Europe in the age of the Revolution, Napoleon and the Restoration should complain of special difficulties or claim unique advantages in the matter of sources. He may sometimes envy the medievalist's concentration on a relatively small number

BIBLIOGRAPHY. An essential guide to older works either containing or identifying documentary sources is P. Caron and M. Jaryc, editors, *World List of Historical Periodicals and Bibliographies* (rev. edn., Oxford, 1939). A more specialized listing of memoirs, correspondence and other materials will be found in F. M. Kircheisen, *Bibliography of Napoleon* (London, 1902). For national selections of central importance see Caron's and his successive collaborators' several *Bibliographies des travaux publiés . . . sur l'histoire de la France depuis 1789*, beginning with a volume covering the years 1866–97 (Paris, 1912); J. B. Williams, *A Guide to the Printed Materials for English Social and Economic History, 1750–1850* (New York, 1926); and Germany's magisterial 'Dahlmann-Waitz', *Quellenkunde der deutschen Geschichte*, launched by F. C. Dahlmann in 1830 but revised by various continuators down to the 10th edition, edited by H. Heimpel, H. Geuss *et al.* (Stuttgart, 1965). Papers having to do with international relations are catalogued by D. H. Thomas and L. M. Case, *Guide to the Diplomatic Archives of Western Europe* (Philadelphia, 1959), while H. Temperley and L. M. Penson, *A Century of Diplomatic Blue Books, 1814–1914* (Cambridge, 1938), combines a listing of the Foreign Office's Parliamentary papers with evaluations of such key figures as Castlereagh and Canning. A number of valuable chapters on statistical materials relevant to the eighteenth and nineteenth centuries have been assembled by D. V. Glass and D. E. C. Eversley, editors, *Population in History: Essays in Historical Demography* (Chicago, 1965). Among important studies of newspapers and periodicals as historical sources should definitely be included Aspinall, *Politics and the Press, c. 1780–1850* (London, 1949); the first volume of the official *History of 'The Times': The Thunderer in the Making, 1785–1841* (London, 1935); René de Livois, *Histoire de la presse française* (Lausanne, 1965); and K. Schottenloher, *Flugblatt und Zeitung* (Berlin, 1922). Finally, although the work is itself one of great substantive value, R. Williams, *Culture and Society, 1780–1950* (New York, 1960), deserves mention for its author's suggestions for the use of literary sources in the writing of social history.

of documents. On occasion he may wish that, like the analyst of very recent history, he could look at motion pictures and hear recordings of his human subjects—or even interview them in person. Conversely, he may take comfort from the greater range of published sources bequeathed by the period 1780-1830, as compared with earlier times, permitting himself a modicum of self-congratulation over the undeniable increase in both the quantity and the statistical exactitude of official records during his period. Essentially, however, the source problems he confronts are those faced by all students of history.

His chief problems are best characterized by two terms which are only superficially paradoxical: incompleteness and profusion. No matter how many pieces of information are available to the scholar, he is bound from time to time to feel that the few indispensable ones are precisely those he lacks. There will always be gaps in the fullest documentation. On the other hand, the researcher cannot escape some consternation as he scans the lists of materials which might, given limitless time and invincible eyesight, be brought to bear on any question of interpretation. Total comprehension of the past, like total recall, eludes us.

It need hardly be pointed out that this volume is not based on extensive work in primary sources. By its very nature, such a book must draw upon specialized studies which in turn are founded on documentary inquiry. Some of the most important of these monographs, as well as certain more discursive essays and syntheses, are cited with appreciation in the Bibliographical Note (pp. 392-4) and in the chapter bibliographies. Even a general history, however, profits from some direct reference to primary materials, both for the concrete details they provide and for the sense of the period which they, and only they, can offer. In any event, the reader deserves to be reminded of the various bases on which our knowledge rests. For each major category of evidence a few examples can be singled out.

First in order of generality are wide-ranging collections of texts, such as H. T. Colenbrander's *Gedenkstukken der algemeene geschiedenis van Nederland van 1795 tot 1840* (The Hague, 1905-22). These twenty-two volumes bring together precious data on almost a half-century of Dutch history from archives and private holdings not only in the Netherlands, but also in England, France and other countries. Another vast assemblage of different sorts of papers, in this case bearing on one aspect of a national history, is the *Collection de documents inédits sur l'histoire économique de la Révolution française* (Paris and other cities, 1906-), edited by numerous experts under the auspices of a special commission of the Ministry of Public Instruction. This series, which already runs to over 100 volumes, is still being extended. Marc Bouloiseau, for instance, is now editing for it the *Cahiers de doléances du Tiers état du bailliage de Rouen pour les Etats généraux de 1789*, in four volumes, two of which have already appeared (Paris, 1957; Rouen, 1960).

Few undergraduate students, of course, will have much need for these huge, detailed agglomerations of material. Many shorter publications, however, offer the chance to get acquainted with history through original documents, under careful editorial guidance. The Historical Seminar of the University of Bern, for example, has been issuing a series of paperbound source books, *Quellen zur neueren Geschichte* (Bern, 1944–), averaging fewer than 100 pages apiece and valuable for the well-selected texts they include. To illustrate, the very first item in the series is entitled *Vom Ancien Regime zur Französischen Revolution* and contains the electoral regulations for the Estates General of 1789, sample petitions of grievances—or *cahiers*—addressed to that body and the full Constitution of 1791. Other numbers are *Europa Politik zu Beginn des 19. Jahrhunderts* (Heft 2); *Napoleonische Friedensverträge* (Heft 5); and *Das Ende des Alten Reiches* (Heft 10). A useful volume assembled by an American scholar, J. H. Stewart, is the 800-page *Documentary Survey of the French Revolution* (New York, 1951). For Great Britain, the best and newest selection for the period we are interested in is *English Historical Documents*, vol. XI, under the general editorship of D. Douglas. This particular volume, prepared by A. Aspinall and E. A. Smith (London, 1959), comprises 587 items from the years 1783–1832.

An era of revolution, war and repression was inevitably a time of expanding governmental action in almost every European nation. State papers thus represent a major class of sources, subdivided by nationality, by originating agency and by type of activity involved. Legislative records are a rich but exceedingly uneven source of information, being limited to countries which enjoyed a degree of parliamentary rule, limited also to certain time spans even in some of those lands. In the case of Great Britain, there is no need to elaborate on the importance of William Cobbett's 36-volume *Parliamentary History of England*, containing actual speeches in the House of Commons down to 1803. The First Series of Thomas Hansard's *Parliamentary Debates*— 'Hansard' as we still know it—runs from 1803 to 1820 in 41 volumes and was kept up to date on an annual basis after 1812, when Hansard took over Cobbett's interest in the enterprise. The New (now considered Second) Series covers the ten years of George IV's reign, to 1830, in 25 volumes. Much less familiar, since they deal with the legislature of a short-lived Italian satellite of the revolutionary France, are the 11 volumes on the *Assemblee della repubblica cisalpina* (Bologna, 1917–48), edited by C. Montalcini, A. Albert, *et al.* More significant as a national body, but far more difficult for the reader of western European languages to get at, was the Diet of Hungary, though certain of its debates were summarized in German for the benefit of Habsburg officials in Vienna.

As might be expected, legislative documentation for France in this era is particularly voluminous. Beginning with P. B. Buchez and P. C. Roux, who edited the still useful though haphazard *Histoire parlementaire* in 40 volumes (Paris, 1834–38), and continuing with the *Archives parlementaires*, Série 1: 1787–99, edited by J. Mavidal, E. Laurent, *et al.* (Paris, 1875–), the publication of such records has proceeded to a point of almost incredible specificity. For example, the Institute for the History of the French Revolution has launched a *Recueil des documents relatifs aux séances des Etats généraux, mai-juin 1789*, the first volume of which, edited by G. Lefebvre and A. Terroine (Paris, 1953), deals entirely with preparations for the Estates General and with one day's session, that of the opening on May 5!

In the publication of administrative, as in that of legislative, records, intense concern with France (a concern by no means limited to French historians) has given the archives of revolutionary and Napoleonic executive bodies a tremendous quantitative lead over all rivals. Important segments of British ministerial records have been reproduced, of course, as appendices to various special studies. As will be noted later, the personal papers of many public figures of the time, whether German or Russian, Austrian or Spanish, help us to gain partial entry into various cabinets and council chambers. Certain collections of eighteenth-century papers, including the nine different series of the *Acta Borussica* (Berlin 1892–1936) on the Prussian administration, contain scattered items for the period after 1780 as well. Yet despite the need to retain some degree of European perspective, the massiveness of the French documentation must again be acknowledged. It constitutes a phenomenon which was visible from the time F. A. Aulard began publication of the 28-volume *Recueil des actes du Comité de salut public* (Paris, 1889–1951). Leaving aside editors of papers from the files of individual prefectures and local governments, the briefest catalogue for France would have to honour the following among Aulard's successors: E. S. Lacroix and R. Farge on the Commune of Paris, 16 vols. (Paris, 1894–1914); A. Debidour on the Executive Directory, 4 vols. (Paris, 1910–17); and C. Durand on the Napoleonic Council of State (Gap, 1954).

Public records, broadly defined, include many special items such as published census reports, which became standard in some European countries during the late eighteenth and early nineteenth centuries. Governmental appointments, promotions and reorganizations were regularly announced in such publications as the royal Bavarian *Regierungsblatt* (1805 ff.). Papers of both official and private origin can frequently be combined to good advantage. We should note as well the rapidly growing body of business archives, often published in connection with the histories of famous old commercial or industrial concerns. In their collection, *Les patrons, les ouvriers et l'état: Le régime de l'industrie en France de 1814 à 1830* (Paris, 1912), G. and H. Bourgin showed the use that could be made of the texts of prefectural and police reports on labour conditions, together with the proceedings of the *Conseil des Manufactures*.

At the mere mention of the phrase 'documentary sources', the category most likely to spring to mind is undoubtedly that of diplomatic papers. It was to such documents or 'diplomas' (whence the name) that the learned archivists of the seventeenth and eighteenth centuries preferred to turn when compiling their pioneer editions. Many of the magisterial figures of nineteenth-century historical writing, from Leopold von Ranke onward, tended to view ambassadorial reports, cabinet instructions to envoys, drafts and final texts of treaties as at once the richest and the most reliable sources for any student of the past. The faith of these historians in the 'primacy of foreign policy' was daily reconfirmed by the very nature of their favourite materials. Modern scholarship has tended to be more reserved in its enthusiasm for this admittedly clear, but often thin and lifeless, stream of observations and opinions. Perhaps the decline of secret, round table diplomacy in our own century has influenced our attitude towards its functions and worth in other times. More likely, the recognition of influences acting upon all governmental policy decisions in ways seldom clear to the diplomatic reporter have diminished the reverence once felt for those neatly tied bundles of foreign office dispatches.

Whatever its cause, however, no such reaction can, or should, rob diplomatic papers of their residual value, especially for the study of an age mired, like our own, in international conflict—an age which produced such famous diplomats as Talleyrand and Castlereagh, Capo d'Istrias and Czartoryski, Metternich and Canning. The number-less minutes, drafts, instructions and dispatches published in the past century-and-a-half, whether in separate volumes or as documentary appendices to monographic studies, remain indispensable aids to research. The same is true even of such hoary collections of treaty texts as F. de Martens and F. de Cussy, *Recueil manuel et pratique des traités* (Leipzig, 1846–57) in seven volumes, or single-nation compilations such as L. Neumann, *Recueil des traités et conventions conclus par Autriche . . . depuis 1763*, vols. I–IV relevant for this period (Leipzig, 1855–58). An illustration of the value of ambassadorial reports for more than just the reconstruction of diplomatic manoeuvres will be found in *Gesandtschaftsberichte aus München, 1814–1848*, edited by A. Chroust (Munich, 1935–51). In these dozen volumes we have, from the separate points of view of the French, Austrian and Prussian envoys to Bavaria, a running analysis of general conditions within that south German kingdom during the first half of the nineteenth century.

It is not always easy to draw a clear line between official sources and other, overlapping categories. Individual correspondence is a case in point. The letters of important public figures generally range all the way from the level of significant state papers to that of trivial, albeit revealing, personal notes to friends and relatives. An example of this variety is found in the six volumes of *Correspondence of King George the Third*, edited by Sir John Fortescue (London, 1927–8). Though the collection ends at 1783, early in the period here discussed, it is now being supplemented by A. Aspinall's projected five-volume edition of *The Later Correspondence of George III*, vol. I of which has appeared (Cambridge, 1962). The correspondence of Napoleon I began to receive serious editorial attention with the 32 volumes published in Paris, 1858–70. Today the number of the Emperor's letters in print exceeds 40,000. A useful selection of some 750 of these items, translated, is J. E. Howard's edition of *Letters and Documents of Napoleon*, vol. I, *The Rise to Power* (London, 1961). Much of the official, as well as personal, correspondence of Austria's leading statesman between 1809 and 1848 appears in the eight-volume collection, *Aus Metternichs nachgelassenen Papieren*, edited by his son, Prince Richard von Metter-nich-Winneburg (Vienna, 1880–4). More recently, an excellent new edition of letters and other state papers of Freiherr vom Stein, *Briefe und amtliche Schriften*, has begun to appear under the editorship of

W. Hubatsch, assisted by the preparations of the late E. Botzenhart. Six volumes, one of them in two parts, have been published so far (Stuttgart, 1957-), carrying the Prussian leader's career through his reform ministry, that is to 1808.

Not all worthwhile correspondence comes from the files of rulers and leading ministers, of course. The Swiss burgher, Peter Ochs, for example, left a precious picture of social and political developments in his native Basel during the revolutionary period in his *Korrespondenz*, ed. G. Steiner, 3 vols. (Basel, 1927-37). A different type of commentary, by an important English economic theorist but not a major politician, emerges from the letters which fill ten volumes of *The Works and Correspondence of David Ricardo*, edited by P. Sraffa and M. H. Dobb (Cambridge, 1951-55). Often we profit from the observations of a relatively obscure individual who was nevertheless well placed to comment upon a scene or a movement of great significance. Thus an unparalleled view of the Italian liberal refugees in London, forerunners of subsequent revolution and unification, is afforded by Giovanni Berchet's *Lettere alla marchesa Costanza Arconati*, vol. 1: *Febbraio 1822–Luglio 1833* (Rome, 1956). Another important example is Liddell Hart, ed., *The Letters of Private Wheeler, 1809–1828* (London, 1951) for which we are indebted to one of Wellington's infantrymen.

As shown by the examples of Metternich, Stein and Ricardo, correspondence is frequently published as only one element in a collection which also includes the subject's essays, notes, speeches and other personal papers. Or again, letters may be printed in company with their writer's more or less artfully constructed memoirs. As a means of checking and verifying memoir literature, correspondence has obvious value; but one should be wary of editorial techniques designed to make the letters, supposedly 'primary' sources, appear to corroborate the assertions of the memoirs. The danger of misinterpretation because of omissions is a real one. All the same, it is quite common to find the correspondence published in combination with memoirs the most valuable portion of the edition, sometimes revealing more, one suspects, than either author or editor intended. This is true of one of the key sources for Russian imperial policy and Polish affairs in the early nineteenth century, the two volumes of *Memoirs of Prince Adam Czartoryski and His Correspondence with Alexander I*, edited by A. Gielgud (London, 1888). It is especially true of Paul Léon Talleyrand's *Mémoires du Prince de Talleyrand* (Paris, 1953-55), since the letters contained in these seven volumes are seemingly authentic, while the original manuscript of the memoirs was hidden by the Prince's heirs and first collaborators and has never been recovered.

With respect to the memoirs of most statesmen, the special pleading is too obvious to constitute much of a threat. That is to say, the student knows the circumstances under which the writer may have fallen from power, or the actions and policies he clearly seeks to justify. Armed with that knowledge, a careful reader can treat the apologetics for what they are, while making good use of assertions which either corroborate other accounts or are inherently probable in the absence of any apparent motive to falsify. Thus, the six volumes of *Memorias de Don Manuel Godoy* (Paris, 1839–41) are a transparent defence of his own record by Charles IV's chief minister from 1794 until 1807; but they also provide a wealth of reflections by a Spanish courtier and administrator who was as shrewd in most matters as he was unscrupulous in some. Another minister, a Prussian associated with both reform and repression for a dozen years until his dismissal in 1819, was K. A. von Hardenberg, whose five-volume set of *Denkwürdigkeiten* (Leipzig, 1877) was edited by Ranke. We are still as indebted to the *Mémoires du Général de Caulaincourt*, three volumes edited by J. Hanoteau (Paris, 1933), for their portrait of Napoleon and his policies from Tilsit in 1807 to the collapse in 1814, as we are to the 56-volume *Collection des Mémoires relatifs à la Révolution française*, edited by S. A. Berville and others (Paris, 1821–7), for a long series of personal accounts. Or, to turn to still another quarter of Europe, the memoirs of General Makrygiannēs, *Strategou Makrugianne Apomnemoneumata* (2nd edn., Athens, 1947), have proven indispensable to specialists in the history of the Greek fight for independence in the 1820s.

Direct, undoctored jottings in current diaries are naturally more difficult to find in print than are re-worked memoirs, at least as regards prominent and controversial figures. It is a curiosity of the revolutionary era that so few private diaries seem to have survived from it and that fewer still among those which have been found have appeared worth publishing. Perhaps the eighteenth century's epistolary tradition, with all its volubility and frankness, remained strong enough so that letters to friends still satisfied the need for expression of many individuals who in a later period would have been diarists. That is pure conjecture. In any case, it should be remarked that travel notes sometimes took the form of a daily journal. Among the liveliest, and most valuable, of such notes were those of the English agronomist, Arthur Young. *Travels in*

France during the years 1787, 1788 and 1789 (Cambridge, 1929), edited by C. Maxwell.

Characteristic of the years we are discussing was a tremendous upsurge of interest in, and production of, periodical literature of all kinds. Newspapers, in particular, took on an importance scarcely dreamed of earlier in the eighteenth century. The decades after about 1760, it is true, had witnessed a very considerable increase in the number, scope and influence of journalistic publications. Nevertheless, it took the public excitement of the revolutionary crisis itself to make the reporter what we now concede him to be: the representative of a Fourth Estate. Accentuating this development was the improvement of printing itself, signalled by the London *Times*'s adoption in 1814 of the rotary principle on a flatbed steam press.

At one extreme stood the solemn official bulletins, containing legislative enactments, foreign news and announcements of public events. The French *Moniteur universel*, though born in the supercharged atmosphere of November 1789, nevertheless retained this character throughout the stormy years that followed. It can now be read conveniently in the 32 volumes of the *Réimpression de l'ancien Moniteur* (Paris, 1840–5). Another French publication, the *Journal des débats*, founded in 1789 to report proceedings in the Assembly, became increasingly formal until in 1805, renamed the *Journal de l'Empire*, it became as clearly a governmental sheet as was the *Gaceta de Madrid*, that decorous reflector of views at the Spanish court regarding European affairs in general. Other papers, though extensively employed for the issuance of official manifestos, managed to be something more than governmental puppets. The sedate old *Wiener Zeitung* and London's *Daily Universal Register*, founded as such in 1785 but renamed *The Times* in 1788, expressed in cautious tones some of the tensions in Austria and England respectively during tempestuous years of foreign struggle and domestic economic strain. More openly dedicated to the strong expression of opinion was *Der Rheinische Merkur*, which Joseph Görres of Coblenz made into a powerful mirror, and magnifier, of anti-French feeling in western Germany by the end of Napoleon's reign. Finally, at the opposite extreme from the *Moniteur* or the *Gaceta de Madrid* were the combative, abusive, often obscene tabloids which writer-editors produced in every trouble spot where such polemics dared appear. In Paris alone, the early Revolution was punctuated by the drum fire of Camille Desmoulins's pastiche of humour and libel, the *Révolutions de France et de Brabant*, Marat's vicious *Ami du Peuple* and Hébert's foul-mouthed but effective *Père Duchesne,* to mention only three leading specimens of the art.

Pamphlet literature retained its already long-established place in popular affections and hence its significance as a source for historians. Even at their worst, the countless folds and broadsides hawked on European street corners during this epoch remind us of the era's passionate interest in topics which in retrospect might appear ephemeral. At their best, of course, pamphlets were powerful tools for shaping attitudes about key issues. Publications such as the Abbé Sieyès's *Qu'est-ce que le Tiers état?* (1789) or the first instalment of Tom Paine's *Rights of Man,* which appeared separately as a booklet in the spring of 1791, must be treated not only as sources but as major events of history in their own right.

The monthly or quarterly magazine of the period, more substantial in format than a newspaper and more regular in date of issue than a pamphlet, was in most of Europe less likely to be a political organ than a literary review, a scholarly journal, or a collection of fashion notes and other women's features. As such, it retains great interest for the cultural and social historian. Generally speaking, the student of public affairs and institutions will have to seek his data elsewhere. England, however, represents an important exception in this regard. There the journal of opinion had enjoyed an assured place since the first triumphs of *The Spectator* in the early eighteenth century; and since 1758 parliamentary debates had been summarized in the *Annual Register,* edited until 1788 by Edmund Burke. The years just after 1800 saw the founding of the *Edinburgh Review* (1802) and the *Quarterly Review* (1809). The former mixed literary criticism with political statements—successfully, to judge from its quickly acquired circulation of 10,000, a huge figure for the day—while the latter was founded to fight back with more conservative arguments. A special, highly personalized, but nonetheless significant publication was William Cobbett's lively and aggressive *Political Register,* which appeared (for certain periods under titles such as *Weekly Political Register* and *Weekly Political Pamphlet*) from 1802 until 1835. (To have fathered what might, under various definitions, be considered either a magazine or a very particular kind of newspaper or even an uncommonly long and regular pamphlet series is nothing if not characteristic of the inexhaustible Cobbett.)

Before leaving popular media, we should remark two other categories, less familiar perhaps than printed news and comment, but scarcely less illuminating. One is the political caricature, especially prized in the era before photography had assumed its place as the handmaiden of journalism. Cartoons ranging from the light and clever to the gross and brutal were sold in profusion, either separately or with accompanying squibs about questions of current interest. The pictures were tacked up in private homes, handed about in cafés and pubs and often, at last, carefully filed or pasted into scrapbooks. Some of them were even reproduced on chinaware, including dinner plates. Thus, it has been possible for M. D. George to catalogue over 17,000 such prints in the British Museum and to edit two volumes of selected reproductions, *English Political Caricature: A Study of Opinion and Propaganda*, vol. 1: *To 1792*; vol. 11; *1793–1832* (Oxford, 1959). Comparable collections have been published for France, exploiting the holdings of the Bibliothèque Nationale's Cabinet des Estampes. Germany, the Low Countries, Austria, Italy, Spain have all contributed smaller but still welcome shares to this fund of graphic evidence.

The second category to be noted here is that of popular jingles set to music. Some of these were printed, either with notes or with references to traditional tunes for accompaniment. Many more have been saved for us by collectors with a penchant for jotting down lyrics, if that is not too exalted a term for some of these verses. A useful compilation of 90 items has been published by C. B. Rogers, *The Spirit of Revolution in 1789: A Study of Public Opinion as Revealed in Political Songs* (Princeton, 1949). The range and the confusion of sentiments expressed in the French jingles reproduced by Rogers help us to get at the reality behind more formal documents such as the *cahiers* mentioned above or the edited texts of parliamentary speeches.

At the other extreme from the doggerel of pub and marketplace stands the body of written work produced by leading thinkers of the period. It is never easy to use such material for purposes of historical reconstruction; for a philosophical treatise is by its very nature partly normative, that is, concerned with things as they should be. To that extent it offers a potentially deceptive picture of things as they are, or were. One theorist may emphasize the dark side of the contemporary scene, hoping to shock his countrymen into supporting reform. Another may cheerfully stress the hints of his preferred utopia already present in the existing situation, in order to minimize the difficulty of going the rest of the way. Still a third may attempt frankly to reach it by satire, exaggeration, overstatement. Allowance made for all these possible refractions, however, we can scarcely afford to forego the insights afforded us by the writings of deeply thoughtful men.

It might appear at first glance that metaphysicians such as Immanuel Kant and Georg Wilhelm Hegel could tell us little about their Germany or their Europe in the late eighteenth and early nineteenth centuries, respectively. Yet in his *Critique of Judgment* (*Kritik der Urtheilskraft*, 1790) or his *Conflict of Faculties* (*Der Streit der Facultäten*, 1798), to cite only two examples, Kant expressed in terms which were anything but abstract his fascination with the revolutionary drama spreading outward from France. Similarly, dispersed through Hegel's writings on law, power, freedom and history are references to the lessons he felt could be drawn from the Napoleonic experience and applied especially to the Prussia of his day. Likewise, it is possible to read the British fathers of modern political economy, from Thomas Malthus through the more engaged, and engaging, David Ricardo to that tireless crusader for reform, Jeremy Bentham (who both antedated and outlived Ricardo), not only as prescribers but as describers too.

Some quite ponderous works composed between 1780 and 1830 were intended as tracts for the times, with no pretence made of preaching to the ages. Johann Gottlieb Fichte's *Addresses to the German Nation*, delivered in Berlin during the winter of 1807–8, while they range over great expanses of history and religion, express a most specific set of reactions to conditions in Prussia under French occupation. To take another instance, the historian Karamzin's *Memoir on Ancient and Modern Russia*, translated and analysed by R. Pipes (Cambridge, Mass., 1959), spoke for unyielding conservatism in the face of foreign and domestic pressures for change under Tsar Alexander I. Whatever their importance as a gospel for modern conservatives, Edmund Burke's *Reflections on the Revolution in France* (London, 1790) illuminate, by both avowal and denunciation, the attitudes which divided British opinion concerning events across the Channel. A number of the prolific Count Joseph de Maistre's treatises, perhaps most notably his *Considérations sur la France* (Basel, 1797), reveal the mixture of political and religious advocacy in the thinking of an anti-revolutionary Savoyard nobleman.

From the theoretical disquisition, used as an 'intellectual' source, it is only a step to any of several other classes of literature. One such consists of travel books. Arthur Young's journals have already been mentioned (pp. 11–12, above), but we have available an army of other, often more stylish, works of description based on their authors' journeys through places of general interest. Here, as elsewhere, it is impossible to do more than suggest the range of such accounts. An invaluable item in the immense library of travel records left by several centuries of Englishmen is William Coxe's three-volume *Travels into Poland, Russia, Sweden and Denmark* (Dublin, 1784). Another work in three volumes, by a knowledgeable Frenchman who was shortly to become ambassador in Madrid, is Jean François Bourgoing, *Nouveau voyage en Espagne, ou tableau de l'état actuel de cette monarchie* (Paris, 1789); and of course there is Goethe's *Italienische Reise* of 1786–88 (Munich, 1925). No student of Russian conditions at the end of Catherine II's reign should ignore the *Journey from St Petersburg to Moscow* by A. N. Radishchev, who paid for the frankness of his agrarian portrayal with a long exile in Siberia. Radishchev's famous exposé, first published in 1790, has been translated by L. Wiener and edited by R. P. Thaler (Cambridge, Mass., 1958).

Travel literature is at least ostensibly based on observations of the existing world. When the historian turns to works of fiction as descriptive sources, he clearly faces the task of sifting factual matter from what he knows to be primarily creations of imagination. He must reckon from the first with the familiar truth that some of the greatest pieces of drama or prose fiction are the least valuable sources of history, precisely because an element of their greatness is their transcendent, timeless quality, their perception of the human condition in many different climes and ages. It is also true that historical significance need not correspond to the author's degree of personal proximity to the people and events embodied in his plot. For example, whatever Jane Austen's novels may reveal about the speech and manners of a restricted segment of English society around 1800, they remain serenely indifferent to the thunderous events occurring at the time. On the other hand, two of Heinrich von Kleist's greatest dramas, *Die Hermannschlacht* (1809) and *Prinz Friedrich von Homburg* (1810)—though the first treats the struggle of Teutons against Romans in antiquity, while the second is laid in the court and camp of Brandenburg's seventeenth-century Great Elector—manage to express in passionate terms the patriotism and the call to martial discipline which Napoleon's rule awakened in Germany. These plays are fascinating not only for the literary historian but also for the analyst of political propaganda.

It should be remarked that certain later works of literature, based in part on their writers' own memories, in part on the accounts of others who lived through the events described, contain a great deal of solid history. The portrayal of Napoleonic warfare at the beginning of the *Charterhouse of Parma* by Stendhal (Marie Henri Beyle, 1783–1842) reflects the insight of a great literary artist who had witnessed some of the Emperor's battles and who knew countless veterans of others. His characterization of the petty tyrannies of Restoration Italy in the same novel is if anything still more significant. Tolstoy's *War and Peace*, viewed simply as the Russian epic of 1812 (though written in the 1860s), contains brilliant and informed characterizations of such central figures as Speransky and Kutuzov. With Anatole France's great novel about the Terror in the French Revolution, *Les dieux ont soif* (Paris, 1912), we are too far from the events discussed to speak any longer of a strictly primary source. The author, however, was born in 1844, and the conversations of his youth supplied living documentation for his eventual work of social characterization.

Poetry as a document poses difficult problems, not the least of which is the historian's uneasiness, even sheepishness, at seeking to extract literal data from works of verbal music and fantasy. Nevertheless, naturalism and anti-intellectualism in Wordsworth, lyrical glorification of the German middle ages in Wackenroder, impatience with formal aesthetics in Chateaubriand, burning national and cultural pride in the Hungarian Alexander Kisfaludy, all are important characteristics of the era here dealt with. Precisely because poetry depends for its effect on more than mere literalism, it often conveys a sense of the past, of rapport with the mood of an earlier time and place which no other medium can duplicate.

Still more elusive than poetry, but at least comparable in its power to transmit the tone of a vanished epoch, is music. Who can listen to a Gregorian chant without added appreciation of the medieval scene, or a composition by Lully without a haunting sense of having walked in the courtly surroundings of Louis XIV? Political songs have already been mentioned; but these we scarcely prize for their musical quality, even when we think we are sure of the tunes. Quite different is the evocative force of Haydn's stately 'Lord Nelson Mass' of 1798, Beethoven's martial Fifth Symphony, a wistful song by Franz Schubert (died 1827) or the lavishly romantic *Symphonie fantastique* written by Berlioz in 1830. Each is at once a thing of beauty in its own right and a source of cultural history.

The pictorial and plastic arts, for obvious reasons, speak to us in more explicit terms than do the voices of poetry and music. Through the genius of a Thomas Gainsborough we actually see the English upper-class types of the late eighteenth century. Jacques-Louis David, he of 'The Tennis Court Oath' and 'The Coronation of Napoleon', was an active participant in some and a graphic recorder of many more great scenes of the Revolution and the Empire. Francisco Goya conducts us from the eighteenth-century courtiers of Charles III's Spain and the cartoons (designs) he executed for huge rococo tapestries, through the changing aspects of the revolutionary era, to the horrors of the Napoleonic invasion and the French occupation of Madrid. Géricault's 'Raft of the Medusa' or Delacroix's 'Massacre of Chios' (the former inspired by a shipwreck in 1819, the latter by an incident in the Greek war of independence) take us straight to the centre of romantic sensibility and melodrama.

As for architecture, the most imposing of the historian's material sources, the age we are examining produced at least its share of contributions to the European mass of monuments and buildings. Berlin's Brandenburg Gate, completed in 1791, was a proud tribute to the Prussian military tradition of Frederick the Great and his ancestors, though the first victorious troops to march under it were the French regiments of Napoleon in 1806. Paris, of courses, bristles with the emperor's own memorials in stone and masonry, dominated by the Arc de Triomphe. In the pleasure palaces of the grounds surrounding the Escorial near Madrid, we can observe the luxury and the imitation of France which marked the Bourbon monarchy in Spain. No one could pretend to have grasped the full meaning of classical revival and Philhellene (pro-Greek) enthusiasm in Germany without having considered the buildings of the Prussian Schinkel and the Bavarian Klenze, erected during the first decades of the nineteenth century. Limited allowance made for Canova, this was an arid season for sculpture. Artifacts and furniture, however, Empire candlesticks in silver, the pottery of Wedgwood, the furniture designs of Chippendale and, later, the interior decoration of Germany's *Biedermeier* period, help us in our effort to rediscover 'how it was then'.

Even this brief tour of principal source categories has necessarily omitted the mass of still unpublished documentation which in countless libraries, archives and family collections awaits the researcher who has the requisite time, interest, patience and resources for travel. The study of manuscripts has no place in a general history. Their existence, however, is signalled by the printed selections here reviewed, as by much of the monographic research on which our generalizations are founded. The student who wishes to form some impression of the volume and range of government documents may refer to the printed inventories of the Archives Nationales in Paris, the Haus-, Hof- und

Staatsarchiv in Vienna, the Archivo Histórico Nacional in Madrid, the Public Record Office in London, and so on. He may also get an idea of less official unpublished sources by examining the catalogues of the Cabinet des Manuscrits of the Bibliothèque Nationale and corresponding listings for a number of French provincial cities, or by consulting the various reports of the Historical Manuscripts Commission and the successive *Catalogues of Additions to the Manuscripts* in the British Museum.

When all available materials have been brought together, of course, the result is not yet history. The analyst may pore over contemporary descriptions to his heart's content, dissect statistical reports, listen to music, look at paintings, tramp through historic neighbourhoods—and the final, indispensable steps still lie before him. He will still have to select, to interpret, in short to give meaning to his evidence. In so doing, he assumes a degree of personal responsibility which no one need bear so long as the data remain unevaluated and unorganized; but it is a responsibility he cannot evade. The relationship between sources and history is one of reciprocal dependence. Source materials await the application of individual judgment, as to their accuracy, adequacy and relevance. On the other hand, no history can be better than its sources. Who cares, after all, how brilliantly the causes of an event may be explained, or how sensitively its implications may be weighed and correlated, if the event itself turns out never to have occurred?

III

Society and Culture in 1780

The preceding volume in this series, M. S. Anderson's *Europe in the Eighteenth Century, 1713–1783* (1961), concludes with the assertion that by the 1780s modern European history was, in a real sense, about to begin. Modernity, of course, was not something which suddenly burst on a bewildered Europe. However one defines its symptoms, they did not appear everywhere in the same guise or at the same rate. What the above remark by Dr Anderson expresses is rather the powerful

BIBLIOGRAPHY. Much valuable material on social and cultural subjects is to be found in political narratives of the period, some of which are cited in later chapters. Among studies devoted to special aspects of the present topic, three demographic surveys, in addition to the volume edited by Glass and Eversley (*see* Bibliography, p. 4), are especially important: M. R. Reinhard, *Histoire de la population mondiale* (Paris, 1949); W. Köllmann's more detailed treatment in Part III of *Raum und Bevölkerung in der Weltgeschichte* (2nd ed., Würzburg, 1956); and C. Cipolla, *The Economic History of World Population* (Baltimore, 1962). Comparative studies of parallel groups in different countries include *The European Nobility in the Eighteenth Century*, edited by A. Goodwin (London, 1953), and E. Dolléans, M. Crozier et al., *Mouvements ouvriers et socialistes* (Paris, 1950). Each volume of the latter collection supplies chronology and bibliography, and each ranges far beyond the history of labour movements narrowly defined.

Analyses of French society are understandably abundant. P. Sagnac, *La formation de la société française moderne*, vol. II: *1715–1788* (Paris, 1946), remains particularly significant, as does F. Olivier-Martin, *L'organisation corporative de la France d'ancien régime* (Paris, 1938). An invaluable new treatment of a neglected subject, the administration of feudal estates, is R. Forster, *The Nobility of Toulouse in the Eighteenth Century* (Baltimore, 1960). See also G. V. Taylor, 'Non-capitalist wealth and the origins of the French Revolution', *American Historical Review*, LXXII (1967). Works on Great Britain less sweeping than G. M. Trevelyan, *English Social History* (4th ed., London-New York, 1958), include the revised editions of G. D. H. Cole and R. Postgate, *The British People, 1746–1946* (London, 1961), P. Mantoux, *The Industrial Revolution in the Eighteenth Century* (rev. edn., London, 1961), and C. Maxwell, *Country and Town in Ireland under the Georges* (rev. edn., Dundalk, 1949). Q. D. Lewis sense of change which any historian must feel as he approaches the late eighteenth century. Nor is this simply a matter of hindsight, of awareness that a great political and military cataclysm was impending. Even if we limit ourselves to the vantage point of 1780, looking about us in imagined ignorance of coming events, we see evidence of dislocation and transition.

One piece of such evidence is statistical: Europe's population, after five centuries or more of relatively slow and periodically interrupted increase, jumped from an estimated 140 million in 1750 to 187 million by about 1800. This phenomenon carried with it a host of implications for the narrative of the period, and we shall have occasion to refer to it in various connections.

There was another sign of transition, less obvious perhaps than demographic data, but no less significant. This was a growing confusion in the *terms used to describe society*. The analysis of social structure, to be sure, is always beset by difficulties. In the Europe of 1780, however, these difficulties were particularly acute; for while old terms betrayed their inadequacy, no new vocabulary had as yet been developed to replace them.

Social Stratification

Let us begin by distinguishing three separate categories: (1) *orders*, (2) *status groups* and (3) *classes*. All three can be found in the structure of late eighteenth-century European society, though only the first would have been easily recognizable to a man living at the time. In most countries of continental Europe, an *order* was a category defined by law. Nobility, bourgeoisie, clergy and peasantry constituted the

treats an important aspect of popular culture in her *Fiction and the Reading Public* (London, 1932). The Spanish situation is described with welcome clarity by R. Herr, *The Eighteenth-century Revolution in Spain* (Princeton, 1958). W. H. Bruford, *Germany in the Eighteenth Century* (Cambridge, 1935), and F. K. Lütge, *Deutsche sozial- und wirtschafts-Geschichte* (Berlin, 1952) are useful introductions. E. M. Link, *The Emancipation of the Austrian Peasant, 1740–1798* (New York, 1949), while perhaps too favourable to Maria Theresa, gives an excellent summary of agrarian conditions and Joseph II's projects to improve them. For Russia, see D. S. Mirsky, *Russia: A Social History* (London, 1931), J. Mavor, *Economic History of Russia* (2nd edn., London, 1925), and J. Blum, *Lord and Peasant in Russia* (Princeton, 1961), together with more specialized contributions such as R. Portal, *L'Oural au XVIIIe siècle* (Paris, 1950), and G. Sacke, 'Adel und Bürgertum in der Regierungszeit Katharinas II. von Russland', in *Revue belge de philologie et d'histoire*, vol. XVII (1938).

four largest and most widespread of the traditional orders; but it should be noted that each of them was subdivided into a multitude of *corps* or *corporations*. Thus, a particular corps might comprise all the noblemen of a specific province, or the bourgeoisie of one town or the chapter of a particular cathedral. Although much of the relevant law was archaic and much of the phraseology inadequate to express the social realities of the day, contemporary arguments went on employing 'orders' as units of social organization.

The nobility offers a case in point. Europe's noblemen comprised several million individuals whose material circumstances ranged all the way from great affluence to genuine poverty, whose individual social prestige might be as high as that of a duke or as low as that of an ignorant bumpkin. With respect to its collective identity, the nobility existed *only* as a legally recognized order. Every genuine member could produce proof that his title had been rightfully acquired, whether by inheritance, by purchase, by free conferral or by occupancy of an ennobling public office. If a man had such proof, he was endowed with noble rank and the privileges, usually including tax exemptions, which went with it. If not, whatever his wealth and power, a commoner he remained.

As a non-noble, he might belong to another order, the bourgeoisie. The modern confusion between the terms 'bourgeois' and 'middle-class' has tended to obscure the fact that in the eighteenth century, bourgeoisie meant something very specific. A bourgeois (burgess, burgher) was not just any townsman. He belonged to the corporation that monopolized political rights in his municipality, in fact *was* the municipality under law. Hence, he was one of a privileged minority of Europe's town dwellers. Like the nobleman, he had documentary evidence—in his case, the official roll of burgesses—to prove it. Those of his neighbours who had not won places on that roll, through time in residence, formal admission to the corporation and payment of set fees, were not bourgeois. They were simply inhabitants.

The two other great orders descended from the middle ages could not boast even the theoretical solidarity of the nobility and the bourgeoisie. The clergy, splintered since the Reformation, now encompassed Scottish Calvinist ministers as well as Italian cardinals of the Roman Catholic Church, Orthodox priests in Russia as well as Lutheran pastors in Germany, Methodist preachers as well as Anglican bishops. As for the peasantry, it had no institutional form at all, save in certain western European villages, where the peasants had some share in local government, or in Sweden, where they actually elected (bourgeois) deputies to a fourth estate in the national legislature. Yet the clergyman and the peasant, like the noble and the bourgeois, still seemed to contemporaries to be identified by order before all else.

The reader will have perceived the chief reason why orders cannot provide our only units for social analysis, namely, that they did not take in all of society. It is important to know whether a particular European of 1780 was a nobleman, a bourgeois, a clergyman or a peasant—but there is an excellent chance that he may prove to have been none of the four. Hence, we must introduce terms and subdivisions which are more modern in origin. One such concept is that of the *status group*, as defined by the great German sociologist, Max Weber. While orders must be thought of as defined by law, status groups are categories representing degrees of social honour. There was, of course, some overlapping. Any nobleman was apt to be treated with more respect than were *most* bourgeois, and certainly more than any peasant. Similarly, any burgess enjoyed a kind of prestige not shared by even the wealthiest non-bourgeois of the same town. In general, however, orders were both too formal and too sprawling to be usefully thought of in terms of shared status.

The nobility, to return to this key example, was crisscrossed by innumerable status distinctions within its own membership. The contrast between the restricted British peerage and the horde of Polish gentry was one such distinction. Even between clergymen of the same denomination, a Catholic archbishop and a village priest, for example, the social distance was practically immeasurable. The bourgeoisie or legal *citizenry* of a given town, be it Geneva or Frankfurt or Toulouse, extended from the prestigious heads of senatorial families to obscure shopkeepers and artisans who clung to an empty franchise as their only claim to status of any kind. As for the peasantry, how could one compare the self-respect of the French *laboureur*, virtually a free-holding farmer, with that of his own hired hands? It would be still harder to relate him to the Austrian serf, struggling under the system of *Leibeigenschaft* (literally 'bodily possession'), or to one of the millions of Russia's 'bonded people'.

In some of their aspects, status groups took account of distinctions which had no place in the original conception of an order of men. One of these sprang from religious variations. In an officially Catholic country, such as France or Spain or the Habsburg domains, non-Catholics of all ranks suffered not only from legal disabilities but also from varying degrees of social discrimination. The same was true of both Catholics and dissenting Protestants under the Dutch Calvinist theocracy or under the Established Church of England. To all this must be added the age-old discrimination against non-Christians, primarily Jews.

Still other ingredients went into that elusive but powerful concept, status. Education, or the lack of it, was such an element. From the humble qualification of being able to read and write, which guaranteed the scribe, the schoolteacher, the parson some degree of local respect, up to the levels of erudition or literary skill which gave an entrée into aristocratic circles, learning had a distinct value of its own. Partly for that reason, leisure, or the time to acquire education, was as prized by those who enjoyed it as it was envied by the less fortunate. But leisure was important for other reasons as well. Not to have to work to feed and clothe oneself had for centuries been the hallmark of 'the noble living nobly', in the language of the Old Régime. Hence the wealthy merchant gazed down proudly on his fragile slippers and his uncalloused hands as badges of honour more impressive even than his bank account.

The mention of a bank account suggests one other distinction which deserves attention in its own right, namely, degrees of wealth. It is obvious that wealth or poverty, both directly and through their bearing on leisure and education, helped to determine social status. Such is the independent power of economic variation, however, that we need to introduce still a third type of category, *class*, defined as a collection of individuals who share comparable *material* circumstances. Stated thus baldly, the notion assumes nothing about religion, legal titles, education or any other factor except the economic one. It was not a conception familiar to the eighteenth century; and had it been explained to the people of 1780, it would have outraged their assumptions about the structure of society.

Yet nothing in the social evolution of their own epoch had been more apparent, and for conservative onlookers more infuriating, than the emergence of 'the rich' as a stratum which cut brutally across older lines of legal order and social status. Traditionalists could not object to the familiar sight of wealthy nobles or churchmen, or even merchant princes of the type familiar to the later middle ages and the Renaissance. But what was one to make of an English *nabob*, back from India with bulging pockets, an Austrian profiteer in arms or grain, a French speculator in luxury imports or royal tax revenues? Some of the oldest

feudal coats of arms, it is true, had also been regilded by their possessors' fortunate investments or marriages to new wealth. But other
great fortunes belonged to men too recently successful to claim any
aristocratic distinction. Such a man might buy a title for himself and
his descendants, but for the present his power lay simply in riches.
Wealth thus became another independent variable. By this I mean
only that it is not enough to know of an individual that he was, let us
say, a nobleman, a communicant of his ruler's faith and a member of
an old family of the neighbourhood. We still want to know whether he
was rich or only comfortable, needy or possibly even destitute. Of a
merchant, we may be less interested in learning whether or not he was
a registered bourgeois of his city than in discovering the size—and,
equally important the nature—of his private fortune.

The usefulness of class analysis extends to all economic strata.
'Middle class', as we have already seen, is not the same as the 'bourgeoisie'. The latter is narrower, in legal and political terms, but covers
a much wider economic range. The former, while restricted to people
neither wealthy nor depressed, is elastic enough so that for certain
purposes it can be extended to take in substantial farmers as well as
townsmen. Finally, the notion of a 'lower class' reminds us that the poor
under the Old Régime, whatever their religion and regardless of whether
they suffered want in cities or in villages, constituted a reservoir of
bitterness and potential violence. What could people such as these care
about the other, finer distinctions so dear to lawyers and social climbers?

The Social and Political Elite

With the three concepts of order, status group and class in mind,
we can appreciate the combination of differences which separated the
Europeans of 1780. That means we can talk of actual groupings and
then note some national or regional variations within them.

At the top of the social pyramid, in country after country, were
to be found the large landholders, led by royalty itself. The special prestige of landed wealth stemmed partly, no doubt, from its association
with noble functions and with noble pastimes. Still more important,
however, was the idea of the land as a source of income theoretically
unsullied by commercial bargaining, a dignified form of property
which permitted even a commoner to 'live nobly' on the labour of
others. Living nobly did not necessarily mean living on one's lands as a
manorial lord. Those lands might just as well support one at court or

in some town house. Mere possession of large parcels of land, however, remained in itself the highest mark of social success.

In the cities, of course, the plutocracy existed in the midst of leisure, comforts and opportunities for amusement unmatched by any but the very greatest country seats. As already remarked, few owners of urban homes were without rural interests as well, and intermarriage combined with the comings and goings of wealthy town- and country-dwellers to produce a substantial mingling between them. Yet the magnate who clung to the city and its concerns remained different in his style of life from the true country gentleman.

Certain other elements helped to make up Europe's ruling group. Higher state officials—judges, fiscal administrators, career military officers—were in general recruited from both the urban and the rural upper classes. Yet the officialdom, in its training, its professional interests and its direct voice in public affairs, was clearly distinguishable from men who devoted their full energies to the life of the manor or the private counting house. The same was true of the higher clergy. It was heavily dependent on the landed nobility for its leading personnel in Catholic countries and in England, rather more on the urban patriciate in Protestant lands on the Continent and on a mixture of both in eastern Orthodox regions. Everywhere, however, it was set apart by its special powers and responsibilities. Lastly, the ruling aristocracy included the most influential members of the professions: lawyers consulted by public authorities, medical doctors residing at court, professors in certain universities.

These, then, were the directors of Europe under the Old Régime: the holders of wealth in land and money, the wielders of judicial and military power, the formulators of religious policies and the custodians of specialized knowledge. Together they formed an élite which clearly overlapped the order of nobility but which had long since been expanded to take in certain rich or talented commoners as well.[1] In terms of status, the very concept of an aristocracy sprinkled with titles and blessed with leisure meant that this was the top stratum of social honour. It coincided in large measure with the highest economic class, though certain of the ecclesiastics and scholars—and even a few of the government officials—remained men of only moderate affluence, while some rich Jews and other religious dissenters remained outside the charmed circle. The question soon to be posed by events

[1] M. Reinhard, 'Elite et noblesse dans la seconde moitié du XVIIIe siècle', *Revue d'histoire moderne et contemporaine*, vol. III (1956).

was brutally direct: could this aristocracy rooted in the medieval past, modified by centuries of social and political adaptation, control the newer demands and discontents of European life?

Rural Producers, Urban Consumers

Turning from the ruling to the subordinate groups in late eighteenth-century Europe, one at once encounters the producers and purveyors of food. Most of the continent's tremendously long coastline bristled with ports which lent shelter and manpower not only to warships and merchant vessels but also to the far more numerous fleets of fishing craft. Like fishing, hunting remained a full-time occupation in the wooded areas of Scotland and Scandinavia, Poland and the Balkans, Bohemia and Germany, Switzerland and France. Human survival, however, depended primarily on products extracted from the soil, either directly in the form of crops or indirectly in the form of domesticated meat animals. In the total population, farmers retained an immense numerical preponderance which the first effects of the eighteenth-century population rise had only accentuated. In Spain, for example, where the population is estimated to have grown from 7·4 million in 1747 to 10·4 million in 1787, there were at the latter date just four cities with more than 100,000 inhabitants (Madrid, Barcelona, Valencia and Cadiz), while only four others exceeded 50,000. The Spanish case may have been extreme, but it was not un-characteristic. In one country after another, it was the growing number of farm folk that still impressed observers in the 1780s.

About no other element in pre-revolutionary European society is it quite so difficult to generalize as about farmers, particularly because during the preceding 50 to 100 years age-old differences had been sharpened and in some instances new ones introduced. Prosperous and independent freeholders were to be found scattered across most of north-western Europe, though their numbers, except in France and western Germany, had been declining as a result of avid consolidation of property by the wealthier classes. On the other hand, even those among western farmers who had lost the independence of peasant proprietorship had never appeared more fortunate in relation to the sinking multitude of eastern European bondsmen. The latter had paid, in both personal freedom and economic wellbeing, for the policies adopted by their rulers out of deference to privileged aristocrats.

Despite this bewildering variety of conditions Europe was in 1780, as it is today, one of the world's most fertile and productive regions. Threatened by periodic blights and freezes, hampered by tariffs and by local or national export restrictions, the stream of food nevertheless poured towards the cities. The marketers of food thus formed one of urban society's largest occupational groups. It was a group not only populous but also elaborately subdivided by specialization. Even now the housewife in many a European town makes a daily round of shops which would bewilder the supermarket trade. She picks up bread from the bakery, milk and cheese from the dairy, vegetables from the greengrocer, bacon from the grocer (or the *charcutier* in France), perhaps a roast from the butcher or seafood from the fishmonger. In making this tour, though she is not likely to think about it, she is re-enacting scenes from the life of her eighteenth-century ancestors. The author once perused a list, dated 1785, which gave the occupations of 132 heads of families in a southwestern German village. Of this number, 68 were primarily engaged in selling foodstuffs to the remaining 64 and, of course, to one another!

Other townspeople included petty functionaries—constables, collectors, sextons, clerks—as well as school teachers and members of the lower clergy. Service personnel formed a major category: household servants, coachmen and wagoners, innkeepers, restaurateurs, pedlars. Craftsmen and shopkeepers, under guild control, sold clothing and utensils to those of their fellow citizens who could afford to buy from experts instead of having to rely on household industry. Finally, certain larger cities contained a growing number of day labourers who worked for wages, using materials and occupying premises supplied by their employers—in other words, factory workers. Industrial labour, as distinct from the traditional journeymen who assisted in small guild enterprises, could be found concentrated only around certain mining establishments, a still very limited number of private plants and a variety of state manufactures. It must be emphasized that in this period the 'putting-out' system, under which weavers, for instance, took home yarn issued them by an industrial entrepreneur and were paid when they brought him back finished cloth—meanwhile often working their own farm plots—was far more prevalent than was the central organization of a London brewery, a French cannon shop or a Russian iron works in the Urals. Nevertheless, an early proletariat, composed of both insecure journeymen and industrial labourers of the newer type, was becoming an increasingly important feature of the urban scene.

Needless to say, the social structure of Europe included some groups which were essentially unproductive. Soldiers, for example, were a

regular component of the population of any garrison town and an irregular one of other places through which troops passed from time to
time. Their demands for billets and supplies, not to mention their
characteristic amusements, might disrupt the life of an otherwise stable
community; but in general the professional military was accepted as
essential to stability itself. Other groups, such as entertainers and prostitutes, attracted a similar mixture of distaste and tolerance on the part of
society's consciously respectable elements. The same could not be said
of the beggars, the vagabonds, the mentally ill, who were hounded into
jails or driven from one locality to the next as fast as the constables could
overtake them. In such circumstances, despite the savage penalties provided by law, the criminal population was large, counting among its
numbers not only the petty thieves and cut-purses of the town but also
the murderous gangs which preyed on all but the best-policed highways.
For despite the crowded humanity of its cities and its more heavily
peopled farming areas, Europe still had great regions of loneliness, regions
where an unexpected sound or flash of light might be either a source of
comfort or a cause for terror, but never a matter of indifference.

Regional Variations

These were a few of the most widespread features of European society
in the last years before the crisis broke. It has seemed best to begin at
a general level, because in spite of the local peculiarities which lend
variety and colour to the scene, the fact remains that we are considering
a civilization in terms not only of its diversity but also of its shared
characteristics. Without this reminder, one might become so impressed
with the differences between the cities of Sweden and Spain, between
the farms of Holland and those of the Ukraine, as to forget how much
all these had in common when contrasted with the life of China or
India or Equatorial Africa.

Britain

Needless to say, even the swiftest tour through late eighteenth-century
Europe showed a traveller countless departures from the pattern
just sketched. If he started in England, for example, he at once encountered a major exception to the prevalent definition of nobility:
the division between the peerage (dukes, marquesses, earls, viscounts
and barons), on the one hand, and on the other, the gentry. In Britain,

only the former were styled 'noblemen' or classified as such by law, though baronets and knights were clearly equivalent to the lower ranks of the continental *noblesse*. Also, though England had its bourgeoisie, technically defined, the old town corporations were rapidly being swamped by the large, vigorous army of newer merchants and manufacturers, an army containing many representatives of the gentry and not a few younger sons of the peers themselves. Nowhere else was the aristocratic prejudice against money-making weaker, nor the alliance of land and trade quite so strong.

Since Parliament stubbornly refused to authorize a national census until 1801, detailed population figures for Great Britain are difficult to come by; but it is clear that the island kingdom shared in the demographic revolution. England, Wales, and Scotland together had perhaps 9 million inhabitants in 1750, and this number had grown to about 11 million by the end of the century. Even in 1780 many English cities were growing faster than urban centres on the Continent. This was especially true of the northern factory towns, such as Manchester; and had it not been for London's phenomenal climb towards the one million mark in just this period, the southern region would have been completely left behind in the population boom.

This precocious development of cities was not solely the result of an early swing towards factory production. Also involved was a crisis affecting the agrarian poor of England and Wales, the peasants who had once eked out their meagre wages as occasional farm workers by growing subsistence crops and grazing a few animals on village common lands. As more and more of these commons were enclosed by parliamentary enactment (the eighteenth-century peak was reached in the decade 1770–80 with 642 such Acts 'dividing, allotting and enclosing'), the gentry and other substantial freeholders acquired tracts large enough to permit efficient exploitation through rapidly advancing agricultural techniques. For peasants and other marginal farmers, however, enclosures meant expulsion or restriction to tiny plots which could not feed them and their families. Their only choice lay between full-time employment as hired hands or migration to the cities. Ugly as the latter unquestionably were, they offered escape to thousands, soon millions, who apparently felt that escape was necessary. Recent studies of the problem have therefore revised the older view that the false lure of factory wages seduced misguided rustics away from an idyllic, or at least wholesome, rural existence into one of sooty degradation. The actual alternatives seem to have been at once grimmer and less flattering to country life.

North of England, the Scottish scene—both in the improving agricultural regions of the Lowlands and in the Highlanders' wild retreats—offered a set of bewildering contrasts. A nobility which reached its summit in the Scottish peers, sixteen of whom were selected by the rest to sit as representatives in the British House of Lords, also included an array of rural lairds and clan chieftains. The tightly knit Presbyterian church structure, at its worst, made possible the petty tyranny of a haughty regiment of clergy and lay elders. At its best, it supported an uncommonly strong and practical system of education. Thus, a vigorous and relatively well-taught population provided skilled labour for an expanding industry while, at the other extreme, many indentured miners were bound to their pits under conditions of virtual slavery. Despite economic progress, Scotland's high percentage of unproductive terrain made it particularly difficult for this partner in the United Kingdom to absorb the population increase of the eighteenth century. In growing numbers, Scots were therefore setting forth to conquer the outside world—including England.

On 'John Bull's other island', the social pattern differed from the European norm primarily because Ireland was viewed by its English rulers as a trophy of conquest, and exploited accordingly. Ulster Protestants enjoyed relatively high status, when contrasted with their 'papist' neighbours in the North and the overwhelmingly Catholic population in the South. Under the small English bureaucracy, however, and the much larger English army, no Irish subject, regardless of his religion, could lay claim to much independence or distinction. Much of the country's income was enjoyed by great lords, mostly resident in England, and by the Anglican hierarchy, also largely absentee in character. Catholic priests, with the surviving Irish gentry and burgesses, for the time being retained their position only at the price of docility. The introduction of the potato had recently added a cheap and comparatively dependable food to the diet of the poor, while linen weaving was beginning to show promise as a putting-out industry; but the bulk of the population, growing from 2·7 to 4·2 million between 1771 and 1791, lived a rude agrarian existence, and a precarious one at best.

Iberia and Italy

The traveller who sailed southward from the British Isles to the Iberian Peninsula found in Spain's 10 million people and Portugal's nearly 3 million an entirely different set of variations in the European picture. Important characteristics of Spanish society resisted strongly the efforts of King Charles III's reform ministers, as Portuguese traditions had earlier done when challenged by the Marquis de Pombal's vigorous ministry. In Spain's case, much the more important for Europe as a whole, the aristocracy comprised the great *señores* (119 *grandes* and 535 *títulos de Castilla* in the census of 1787). It also included the *caballeros*, each appointed by the crown to life membership in one of the four great crusading orders which enjoyed the income from almost 800 localities earlier reconquered from the Moors. In addition there were an estimated 500,000 individuals, many of them only poor *hidalgos* (sons of someone), who nevertheless claimed the legal status of nobility. When to this figure, itself staggering for a population the size of Spain's, is added the further one of 200,000 ecclesiastics, over half of them monks and nuns, the overloading of the social distribution on the side of privileged, nonproducing groups becomes apparent.

Of the peasant proprietors, who constituted something over 20 per cent of the Iberian farm population at the century's close, many held plots too small to distinguish their possessors very sharply from the depressed mass of *peons*. An urban middle class existed, to be sure, and was actually increasing in size and influence. The Mediterranean cities of Barcelona and Valencia in the east, the north coast centres of Bilbao, Santander and La Corunna, together with Lisbon in Portugal, all witnessed the emergence of a new expansionist breed of businessmen. However, while these capitalists were sufficiently numerous and articulate to frighten the older élite, the mass of illiterate peasants and shepherds could generally be counted on to join their traditional 'betters' in opposition to any radical change.

From Iberia our attention moves naturally to Italy, where Spanish influence had been paramount in the sixteenth and seventeenth centuries. Italian society in the 1780s was as variegated as the Italian political map was confusing. The three surviving city republics of Venice, Genoa and Lucca, despite their decaying commerce, were still ruled by the haughtiest of patricians. Savoy and Piedmont, on the other hand, had relatively few towns but numerous proud families of mountain nobility. Or to take another example, fully one-third of the Papal States' sparse population consisted of members of the clergy, while in Rome itself an indolent aristocracy enjoyed the support, in pensions and appointments, of the Holy See.

In the Papal States, in the Kingdom of Naples and on the island of Sardinia, the Italian peasantry doubtless fared as badly as did the

Spanish. In parts of the north, on the other hand, the rural economy compared favourably with that of any other area in Europe. Increased hardships resulting from Italy's population rise—from an estimated 11 million at the beginning to 18 million by the end of the century— did not oppress all parts of the peninsula equally. Tuscany in particular, with Peter Leopold von Habsburg as its grand duke since 1765, had received an impressive series of reforms: equalization of tax burdens, abolition of legal restrictions on agricultural modernization, the ending of legal serfdom, efforts to reduce the number of clergymen. Not all these reforms could be pushed to their theoretical limits, and some were destined to be reversed in the reaction after Leopold left Florence for Vienna and the imperial crown in 1790. Tuscany's lower classes, however, would never again be even remotely comparably to those of the south—the *Mezzogiorno*—in poverty, nor its nobility so vulnerable as that of Rome to the bitter epithet, 'vain swans on a lake of misery'. To a somewhat less striking degree than Tuscany, the Austrian province of Lombardy also stood out favourably against the general Italian background. Under the mild supervision of distant Vienna, native Lombard officials compelled the upper classes in Milan and the rich Po Valley to accept many of the urban and agrarian improvements already decreed in Florence. In this instance, Italian commoners reaped undeniable, if largely unappreciated, benefits from foreign rule.

France

Pushing northward into France, the observer on tour entered what he would doubtless have considered the heartland of western Europe, a nation of 25 to 26 million, two-and-a-half times as populous as either Spain or the United Kingdom. Blessed with uncommonly plentiful and varied natural resources, supporting fewer nobles than did Spain, boasting a higher percentage of land-owning peasant proprietors than did Great Britain, France could not fail to impress visitors fresh from poorer lands. It too, of course, had its famines, its marginal peasants, its beggars and criminals; but to a contemporary traveller the French monarchy must have seemed a veritable giant of mobilizable power.

Yet not all of France's special characteristics could be described in such favourable terms. Given the obvious wealth of the kingdom, the public bankruptcy which always seemed just around the corner was more humiliating, more suggestive of duplicity and fraud in high places than equally inept financial administration might have appeared in a less richly endowed nation. The nobility, albeit less inflated than in several other areas of Europe, was quite large enough (perhaps 400,000 individuals) to enrage vigorous commoners who could not secure access to it. More serious, this same *noblesse*, as one of its most brilliant descendants was sadly to reflect, still enjoyed social pre-eminence over a non-noble population which seldom looked to it for administration at the local level, no longer respected its fighting ability and had long since ceased to feel markedly inferior to it in economic terms. The French nobleman's privileges fanned the resentment of neighbours who felt no need for his protection.[1]

In these circumstances, the most portentous feature of the French situation was the aristocratic resurgence which the nation shared with most of the rest of Europe in the decades preceding 1789. The ministerial reform efforts of the early 1770s had been repudiated when Louis XVI came to the throne in 1774. In the 1780s the law courts (the preserve of the *noblesse de robe*), the army and navy, the civil administration and the church hierarchy were once more in the grip of the higher nobility to an extent unmatched throughout the previous hundred years. The famous army ordinance of 1781, for example, required that every officer candidate have behind him four generations of nobility. From 1783 to the Revolution, every French bishop was a nobleman. Clashing with the increasing freedom of religion and with the progressive collapse of obstacles to commercial and industrial enterprise, the counter-offensive of the privileged orders at the social and political level represented an ominous paradox.

The Low Countries

Across France's northern border lay the Flemish and Walloon (French-speaking) provinces of the Austrian Netherlands, the future Belgium. Here the ruling group included a fairly small cadre of officials sent from Vienna to Brussels, a large number of Belgian administrators, a stratum of strongly Frenchified native nobility, the prelates of the Catholic hierarchy and the burghers who controlled such cities as Ghent, Bruges and Antwerp. Because cities contained an uncommonly high proportion of the 3 million people in this compact region, the urban oligarchs were especially proud and influential. Their influence, however, was no more progressive than that of titled noblemen in many other lands.

[1] A. de Tocqueville, *L'Ancien Régime* (Oxford, 1949), pp. 27–36.

It was the guilds, in fact, that led Belgian resistance to the Habsburg Emperor Joseph II's attacks on special privilege, as we shall see in Chapter v.

As he proceeded up the Atlantic seaboard, our traveller entered the Dutch portion of the Netherlands, resembling the Belgian in its heavy urban development but different in being officially Protestant (Calvinist) and politically independent of foreign control. The United Provinces, led by the richest of them, Holland, had suffered political confusion and relative economic decline since their seventeenth-century apogee of commercial success, naval power, colonial expansion and diplomatic influence. The very question of aristocratic leadership was at issue in the 1780s. The patricians of the regent families, who monopolized seats in the various town councils as well as in the provincial estates and the national Estates General, found themselves faced by increasing opposition from other commercial elements, scarcely inferior in terms of economic class but discriminated against under the existing social and political arrangements. Roughly a third of the total population of the United Provinces, nearly 700,000 out of 2 million, were Catholics and, as such excluded from government appointments, army or navy commissions and high commercial posts, such as those in the Dutch East India Company. Another 10 per cent were Jews or dissenting Protestants (Mennonites, Quakers, etc.), who shared the Catholics' disabilities. Finally, although the little country's commerce and banking still constituted a formidable complex, business had unquestionably suffered from foreign, especially British, competition. The number of poor journeymen and able-bodied unemployed both angered and depressed the Calvinist oligarchs, with their firm conviction that poverty, like illness, was somehow indicative of bad character.

Scandinavia

Still farther north, in Lutheran Scandinavia, the two kingdoms of Sweden and Denmark-Norway recalled the Dutch experience in that since the seventeenth century both had fallen from positions of considerable power. Sweden's warlike past had left the nation with a turbulent nobility; but under the imperious rule of Gustavus III, king since 1771, the nobles found themselves treated with suspicion at court and forbidden to initiate public proposals through the *Rikdsdag*, or diet. Weak in industry (since 1730 even its famed iron works had been cautiously limiting their own production), Sweden had seen once flourishing market cities, such as Wisby, shrivel in size and decline in wealth. Peasant farmers, who made up the vast majority of the Swedish ruler's 2 to 2·5 million subjects, were working hard to improve production by clearing and enclosing larger plots, introducing new crops such as potatoes and turnips and adapting for their own use the new agronomic theories coming out of England. A major problem for agriculture, however, as it was for industry, was that a large share of the capital needed for improvements had to come from foreign countries. The result was that the Swedish economy was especially sensitive to international disturbances over which Sweden itself had no control.[1]

If the approximately 800,000 Norwegian people, stretched thinly along their immense Atlantic coastline, seemed less advanced economically and less diversified socially than the Swedish, the compact realm of Denmark, also with a population under 1 million, was much closer to the central currents of European life. With its handsome capital, Copenhagen, its busy shippers and merchants, its numerous small craftsmen, seamen and fisherfolk, its relatively prosperous farmers and its still haughty nobility, Denmark proper (as distinct from its crown's possession, Norway) showed a close family relationship with the Low Countries and with certain of the German principalities.

The German Lands

The Germanies themselves—the loose structure of the Holy Roman Empire hardly constituted a single 'Germany'—presented a social range which came close to mirroring that of Europe in its entirety. The nobility included princes who were vassals of the emperor at Vienna, but were themselves suzerains of their own territorial nobles and virtually sovereign rulers of their subjects. In addition, especially along the Rhine and in south-western states such as Württemberg, there were about 1,000 imperial knights and barons, holding fiefs of only moderate size but intensely conscious of their own 'immediacy', that is, their direct fealty to the emperor without any intervening allegiance to a local prince.

Eastern Germany—Saxony, Mecklenburg and, above all, Brandenburg-Prussia—had its own special type of nobility, the Junkers, who profited from large estates employing elaborate staffs of overseers and exploiting the labour of serfs, near-serfs and technically free tenants to grow rye and other grains. East of the Elbe, though personal *servitude*

[1] G. Utterström, *Jordbrukets Arbetare* (Stockholm, 1957). English summary.

was declining, peasant proprietors of independent farms were exceedingly rare. In Prussia, the eighteenth century had seen the Junkers acquire not only increased economic power over the peasantry, but also an ever tighter grip on high military appointments. At the same time, they had succeeded in invading the upper levels of the civil service, partly through appointment to bureaucratic posts, partly through intermarriages with non-Junker families of the administrative élite. Frederick II 'the Great', forty years on the throne in 1780, had worked to harness the Junkers for military and civil service in this way, while he condoned their growing exploitation of the lower classes. He assumed that social stability and a loyal aristocracy could be bought for this price; but by the time he died in 1786, it was clear that the Prussian monarchy faced a peculiarly tough and arrogant alliance of privileged elements within its realm.[1]

Far different from the Prussian scene was that to be found in Hamburg, Frankfurt-am-Main, Nuremberg or any of the approximately fifty other free imperial cities, each with its ruling cast of senatorial dynasties. Still different was the pattern in the large southern duchy of Bavaria, south-western states such as Baden, Württemberg and Hesse-Darmstadt, or the north German possession of the British royal family, Hanover. Each of these and some 250 smaller principalities had its landed nobility, its public bureaucracy, its merchants and shopkeepers. In each, however, the small farmer, often a landowner in the Rhineland and the south-west, but just as often a poor tenant or serf even there, was the predominant social type.

Comparable in importance to its varieties of class structure was Germany's diverse religious geography. In officially Catholic Bavaria, the aristocrat who was also a communicant of the Church of Rome quite naturally stood at the top of the status hierarchy. The same distinction was assured the Lutheran patrician in Frankfurt and his Calvinist equivalent in Bremen. In the sprawling Prussian kingdom, on the other hand, the situation was complicated by the fact that a ruling family which professed to be Calvinist presided over some 6 million subjects, the majority of whom were Lutherans but who also included many Catholics in Prussia's Rhenish outposts, as well as its recently won south-eastern province of Silesia. Small wonder that Prussians viewed religion as a less important status factor than did Frenchmen or Dutchmen or, for that matter, Bavarians.

[1] H. Rosenberg, *Bureaucracy, Aristocracy and Autocracy: The Prussian Experience, 1660–1815* (Cambridge, Mass., 1958).

Switzerland

In the thirteen cantons of the Swiss Confederation, religious differences between the Catholic and Reformed churches were compounded by the confrontation of German, French and Italian ethnic groups within this small country. A landed nobility and numerous clergy survived in Switzerland, most notably in the Catholic forest cantons of Schwyz, Uri, Zug and Unterwalden. Among the three most populous urban cantons that of Bern contained the most exclusive patriciate, absolutely closed to newcomers since 1651 and by the 1780s limited to just sixty-eight families. Basel, half of whose inhabitants qualified as citizens or burghers, was ostensibly more democratic; but even here the top positions in the social hierarchy and in the government as well were in the grip of the leading members of the merchants' guild.

Geneva was still an independent republic outside the Confederation. Its French-speaking population of 25,000 made it larger than any of the technically Swiss towns, and it contained a much more complex society. Scaling down from citizens who could hold office, through burghers who could only vote, to *habitants* and *natifs* who could do neither, the Genevan social structure appeared almost a caricature of local distinctions in eighteenth-century Europe. More important, it served as a microcosm from which much could be learned about the stresses of the period we are examining.

Austria and Habsburg Central Europe

Still north of the Alps, its German Austrian provinces forming part of the Holy Roman Empire, lay the bulk of the Habsburg domain, with a total population of about 27 million. Austria proper, in many of its social traits, resembled Bavaria and other south German regions. Its landed nobility and its Catholic clergy were numerous, its farmers divided between small proprietors and the much more numerous dependent peasants on large estates, its urban development unimpressive by western European standards. The great exception to this last was, of course, Vienna, which contained not only a sizeable bourgeoisie and a mass of poor inhabitants, but also the aristocracy of court and administration. Unlike the German gentry of the rural areas, this ruling élite in the capital was an international amalgam of titled lords and high officials: Germans, Bohemians and Hungarians, with smaller delegations of Italians, Belgians, Croats and Slovenes.

38

The Habsburgs' Slavic states—Bohemia and Moravia, Slovenia, Croatia, Polish Galicia—supported some of Europe's wealthiest land-lords on the backs of some of its most miserable peasants. Empress Maria Theresa, who died in 1780, had agreed with her enemy, Frederick the Great, in at least one thing, namely that a loyal nobility was essential; and despite honest efforts at reform on her own estates she had allowed a multitude of farm labourers under seigneurial control to be reduced to what was, under various technical names, a state of serfdom. Her son, Emperor Joseph II, was committed to easing the lot of the agrarian masses, but the resistance of the privilege orders was as furious as it was oppressive. The dreaded Bohemian *robot*, for example, a system providing for several days of compulsory service by the bondsman for his lord each week, has become in numerous languages a byword for soulless labour.

Hungary was famous for its numerous, proud and warlike aristo-cracy, the Magyar nobles who filled the Hungarian Diet and controlled local government in the *comitats* or country councils. Natural growth, combined with immigration by Serbs and Germans, had swelled the Hungarian population from 1·5 million in 1700 to over 6 million by 1780. Yet this figure still amounted to less than a fourth of the French population. Consider then the fact that the Hungarian nobility was roughly equal in size to that of France! Only a few of these Magyar lords moved at the cosmopolitan level of great magnates such as the Esterházy family. The rest stayed at home, profiting from shares in their country's grain raising and horse breeding. The small bourgeoisie, largely confined to a few towns, notably the twin Danubian cities of Buda and Pest, was scarcely a major element of Hungarian society. As for the peasants, the high productivity of the area helped many of them, probably a majority, to live somewhat better than did Poles and Czechs; but in general they shared the weary life of their eastern Euro-pean neighbours.

The Balkans under Ottoman Rule

The social conditions of the Balkan Slavic peoples and of their Albanian and Greek neighbours to the south are by no means easy to reconstruct. Few natives of the region could write, and those who could, primarily Orthodox clergymen, were not much given to descriptive chronicles. Foreign visitors generally recorded only superficial impressions of a handful of cities. Such documents as do exist, furthermore, have all too frequently been interpreted by Balkan historians in the light of their nationalist resentment against the former Turkish rulers and used to paint a picture of unrelieved misery. Actually, the surviving data indicate that the lot of Europeans under Ottoman rule, while certainly not enviable, compared favourably with that of the corresponding classes elsewhere on the Continent.

The Turks exercised their rights in the Balkans in a far from uniform manner. In Albania and Montenegro, for example, the native mountaineers paid only nominal tribute to Constantinople and saw little of their Ottoman masters. The port city of Dubrovnik (Ragusa) on the Dalmatian coast, a genuine trading centre, sent financial payments to Constantinople but otherwise was free to pursue its Adriatic rivalry with Venice. The Rumanian principalities of Moldavia and Wallachia had their own nobility, the *boyars*. These no longer chose the princes or *hospodars* of the two states, now selected by the Sultan exclusively from a few Greek families called *Phanariotes*; but the boyars did represent an indigenous Balkan aristocracy. In Greece, on the other hand, while an élite of clergymen and scholars certainly existed, it would have been difficult to identify a native Greek aristocracy. (The only Greek-speaking nobility, apart from the faraway Phanariotes, was that of the Ionian Islands, which were under Venetian rather than Turkish control.)

Seen in the broadest terms, the society of the Ottoman-governed Balkans revealed two or three characteristics of particular interest. One was the sharp distinction between urban and rural populations. The million or more Turks whose ancestors had settled in Europe since the fourteenth century were concentrated in towns such as Athens, Salonika, Belgrade, and in a number of smaller centres, supporting themselves as civil servants, garrison troops, craftsmen and merchants. In the last-named profession, they were joined by Jews and, in some areas, by Greeks. The countryside, on the other hand, was left almost completely to the indigenous Bulgars, Serbs, Rumanians and so on. Hence there usually existed between any Balkan city and its own hinterland not only the difference in ways of life encountered everywhere in Europe, but also ethnic and even linguistic differences of still greater moment.

Another Balkan peculiarity was the set of almost exclusively financial obligations imposed upon the peasantry under the Ottoman form of feudalism and of the manorial base beneath it. On a fief, whether it was a large *ziamet* or a smaller *timar*, the *spahi* or landlord received a regular tithe (theoretically just 10 per cent of each tenant's produce), while the Sultan's government claimed a head tax or capitation. Forced labour, on the Bohemian or even the Prussian model, was remarkably rare in the Balkan version of the lord-tenant relationship. For this reason, among others, modern researchers have tended to revise the once black picture of lower-class existence under the Turks.

One more circumstance casting doubt on that picture was the protection which the Sublime Porte accorded the Orthodox clergy. Since the conquest of Slovenia and Transylvania by the Austrians at the end of the seventeenth century the Turkish possessions had contained few Catholics. Nevertheless the Orthodox establishment, directed by the Patriarchate of Constantinople, was still encouraged as a purveyor of anti-western sentiments and a defence against the missionary zeal of Rome. The result, ironically enough, was that the Orthodox clergy within this Muslim empire enjoyed more security and higher social status than did any but the most elevated ecclesiastics in Christian lands.

It would obviously be ridiculous to over-react against old horror stories and suggest that the Balkan peoples lived under a benign foreign master whose rule they should have cherished. Capricious ferocity and periodic extortion had in fact become increasingly characteristic of the Porte as its international position deteriorated and as Ottoman administration decayed. Yet the traveller moving northward into Poland might have been forgiven the thought that there were definite advantages for the mass of a population in having something other than an unrestrained native aristocracy.

Poland

In one sense, such a judgment would have been unfair. A segment of the Polish nobility, reacting to the humiliating loss of territory to the first partition eight years before, had by 1780 managed to give considerable impetus to a campaign for both constitutional and social reforms. For the moment, there seemed to be some hope of welding the huge mass of *szlachta* or gentry (perhaps numbering as many as 750,000 in a population estimated at 9 million) into a more responsible aristocracy. In the event aggressive neighbours refused these reformers the time to show what might be done, but it must be said that the purely internal obstacles confronting them were enormous from the start. Nowhere else in Europe did one perceive such a ludicrous exaggeration of noble privilege. It was apparent in the defencelessness of a peasantry denied even the sporadic relief offered the lower classes by the central governments of many other nations. It was apparent too in the virtual collapse of the once considerable Polish bourgeoisie. (The extent to which many Polish towns, like certain Hungarian and especially Transylvanian ones, depended on a combination of German burghers and Jewish merchants offers an interesting parallel to the Turkish-Jewish-Greek domination of urban centres in the Balkans.) With its Catholic clergy demoralized by political conflicts and disciplinary lapses, its public order constantly threatened by rebellious confederations of nobles, and many of its cultured aristocrats more at home in St Petersburg or even Paris than in Warsaw, Polish society presented a baffling challenge to its would-be rejuvenators.

Russia

In distant Russia, the traveller doubtless expected, and assuredly found, some particularly sharp departures from western and central European conditions. This rapidly expanding empire, its population already nearing 25 million, incorporated a huge peasantry, a relatively small industrial labour force concentrated in a few Muscovite cities as well as in the Ural iron region, and a still smaller, highly conservative merchant class. The Russian nobility was itself divided, according to occupation and domicile, into the great families of courtiers and magnates, the 'service nobility' of the imperial administration, the provincial gentry and, of course, the military officers' corps, many of whose members were by this time also serving as local administrators (especially after retirement from active duty). The sprawling mass of Orthodox clergy included types as diverse as the easygoing, often ignorant village priests, on the one hand, and on the other, the better trained, celibate 'black monks' who monopolized the higher ecclesiastical posts. All these social distinctions were further complicated by regional differences: between the still partially nomadic Ural branch of the Cossacks, for example, and the farmers of the Ukraine and White Russia, or between both these elements and the coastal Balts and woodland Finns of the northern frontier. No other realm we have considered, not even the Habsburg possessions, displayed quite the ethnic and economic heterogeneity of 'all the Russias'.

Some of the most revealing characteristics of the Russian situation stemmed from the position of the bonded peasantry. Because of the prevalence of legal servitude, a tsar or reigning tsarina disposed of millions of 'souls', as they were termed with unconscious irony. Hence, instead of describing his gift to a favourite courtier or successful general as such-and-such a tract of land, the successor of the Tatar khans would say: 'Let him be given so-and-so many thousand of my souls'. The bonded peasantry on the Romanovs' own estates remained the largest single block of subjects, but by the end of the eighteenth century the number of *pomyetschèkè* peasants, those bound to noble lands, had probably risen to at least 10 million. Directly tied to the status of agrarian labour was one final peculiarity of Russian society: the effort to build industry by simply ascribing serfs owned by the crown or certain great nobles to particular mines and factories. Unlike their counterparts in the West, early Russian entrepreneurs did not try to attract workers from the countryside, nor did they sweep up the unemployed of the cities. Rather, they contracted to have adequate numbers assigned on a regimented basis; and the 1782 census listed 75,000 such possessional serfs working for private manufacturers alone. All in all, an observer who strayed any distance from the cosmopolitan, French-speaking court of St Petersburg knew that he was on the very fringe of 'Europe'.

The Cultural Scene

Thus far we have centred our attention on distinctions defined by legal order, by status honour, by varying degrees of economic security and comfort. Before ending our survey of social structure we should do well to ask how these distinctions were reflected in other facets of European culture. The latter term should be understood here in its broadest sense. That is, it includes not just the highest flights of human intellect and artistic taste, but also the humbler forms of expression and communication and enjoyment which together characterize a particular civilization. This extension is necessary precisely because the life of Europe in 1780 was so strongly marked by the division between a high culture, the shared possession of the wellborn, the wealthy, the educated of all countries, and a host of lower cultures embodying the ethnic variety and the local traditions which were no less European than was the cosmopolitanism of privileged groups.

For the upper classes there were really two international languages. Latin had by no means lost its place in scholarship and education, where it permitted learned treatises to be discussed and academic lectures to be understood by men speaking a score of different native tongues. Amid the linguistic confusion of central Europe in particular, it served as an important administrative tool. For example, German and Czech officials in Vienna agreed with many Magyars in Budapest that Latin should continue to be the official language of Hungary. Another of its major uses lay in the rituals and the communications of the Roman Catholic Church. Lastly, though no longer the sole medium of diplomacy, it was still used for certain international agreements.

Latin's successful rival as a diplomatic language was French, more flexible than any ancient prose could be, but at the same time, after a century-and-a-half of rigorous purification, more precise and orderly than any other modern tongue had yet become. English, Spanish, Italian and, increasingly, German were recognized for their literary contributions; but only French was essential to qualify one as a cultured individual. This fact will help to explain the extraordinarily swift and general impact of French events, beginning in 1789, on the literate of Europe.

The vernacular tongues, on the other hand, were in many cases all but ignored by the upper classes of the very nations in which they were spoken. A familiar personification of this tendency was Frederick II of Prussia, who spoke and wrote almost exclusively in French, maintaining until the end of his life a contemptuous indifference towards German writers of the calibre of Goethe and Schiller. Local dialect, with its mysterious slang and peculiarities of pronunciation, was apt to be even less attractive to the man of education than was the literary form of his native language. There were some exceptions—Herder and Goethe, both masters of High German, found a special charm in the archaic Swabian and Alemannic expressions of Alsace, for example. Neither the Cockney speech of London, however, nor the *argot* of the Parisian streets had comparable admirers. Was the Florentine gentleman, with his beautiful Italian, the *lingua toscana*, really using the same language as the Calabrian peasant's mixture of vulgarized Latin, Spanish, Arabic, Levantine and other Mediterranean words? In Greece, the scholar used the debased but still recognizably classical *katharevousa*, while the masses spoke the demotic blend of uninflected Greek, Turkish and Slavic roots. In the Balkans generally, the church Slavonic of the Orthodox clergy was a mystery to a Dalmatian fisherman or a Macedonian farmer. Beneath the contempt of educated men, the future national languages of eastern Europe survived only by word of mouth. The first book in Bulgarian, for example, would not be printed until 1806.

As in language, so in formal education, the lines of cleavage followed boundaries of class and, as earlier remarked, helped to determine lines of status. Certain Catholic and Orthodox seminaries, as well as a number of Protestant universities, admitted and supported prospective clergymen recruited from the humbler levels of society. Otherwise, however, education above the elementary level was the almost exclusive preserve of the aristocratic and the well-to-do. Universities were only beginning to free themselves from the desiccated and inert state in which most of them (outside Germany) had existed during the eighteenth century, but they alone could provide the qualifications for admission to the professional corps of scholars. Furthermore, their importance in training civil servants would soon rival their older function as finishing academies for young gentlemen.

Education below the university was somewhat more accessible to the needy, through parish and charity schools. The demand for working hands on family farms and for apprentices in family shops nevertheless prevented most of the sons and virtually all the daughters of farmers or tradesmen from learning even the rudiments of numbers and spelling. Any numerical analysis of the European population in 1780 would almost certainly show a vast majority to have been illiterate. The more prosperous segments of the urban middle class provided some secondary education for their children (again with heavy preference shown to boys); but for more sophisticated instruction in languages, the classics, history or mathematics, it was necessary to rely on private tutors whom only a relatively small minority of the population—nobles, patricians and some rural gentry—could afford.

In view of this very narrow base of systematic training, the scholarly and scientific achievements of Europe's high culture in the late eighteenth century seem particularly impressive. It is important to keep in mind that the Scottish economist Adam Smith, the French chemist Antoine Lavoisier, the Italian physicist Count Volta, the Prussian philosopher Immanuel Kant, and the other great intellectual figures of the time belonged to a tiny élite. It was by no means an élite confined to the richly or nobly born (Smith was the son of a minor customs official, while Kant's father was a saddler in Koenigsberg), but by virtue of training and interests a small, select fragment of the population it remained.

Belles lettres offered a career which was easier than scholarship for poor men to enter, if only because it demanded less formal preparation. Germany's Schiller and Scotland's Robert Burns were both of humble farm stock, while Caron de Beaumarchais, author of *The Marriage of Figaro* and *The Barber of Seville*, had begun life as the son of a Parisian watchmaker. Equally representative of the literary calling in their day, however, were Goethe, the wealthy patrician from Frankfurt, and Harrow-educated Richard Brinsley Sheridan, witty playwright, member of Parliament, friend of some of Britain's most influential politicians. Two great compatriots, respectively the fathers of modern Italian comic and tragic drama, illustrate the contrasts which were possible. Carlo Goldoni began his career as a strolling player from Modena. Count Vittorio Alfieri came of one of the Piedmontese nobility's richest families. But perhaps more significant in this connection is the fact that even the low born among the writers here referred to, with the single exception of the tragically shortlived Burns, eventually acquired means and social recognition. Schiller was paid and honoured as a history professor by the enlightened Duke of Saxe-Weimar from 1789 until the poet's death. Beaumarchais became a brilliant figure at the French royal court. Goldoni too was invited to Paris and there given a pension by Louis XVI. The ruling aristocracy of the Old Régime knew how to flatter writers, though in some cases, including that of Beaumarchais, it did not even attempt to make them stop ridiculing the established order.

In the other arts, with one major exception, the high culture of the waning eighteenth century was more notable for elegance than for power or originality. Architecture seemed locked in the stiff neoclassical formalism exemplified by the Panthéon in Paris (completed in 1781) and by Berlin's Brandenburg Gate (begun seven years later). The suffused colours and fantastic lights of rococo interior decoration sought to make the most of the hard, regular spaces provided by formal domes and rectilinear building shells; but the resultant effect was generally one of display, as distinct from sensitivity or taste.

Formalism and insipidity characterized painting as well, at least on the continent, blanketed as it was by representations of idealized Greeks and Romans or inhumanly pretty aristocrats at play. The English painters, Gainsborough, Reynolds, the much younger Romney, at least retained contemporary costumes and recognizable types in their portraits, together with superb mastery of technical detail. England, for once in her history, was pre-eminent in a field of graphic art—while potters like Wedgwood and furniture designers like Chippendale, Hepplewhite and Sheraton made her a leader in the useful arts as well.

One of the most striking things to be noted about pre-revolutionary European painting in general is not the absence of talent, but rather the extent to which prevailing canons of style suppressed the talent of men who would soon display it in full measure. The Jacques-Louis David of 1780, while already thirty-two years old, suggested little of the vigorous interpreter of great events to come (though as early as 1785, his 'Oath of the Horatii' announced a vivid new school). And who could have detected the depth of tragic feeling, the versatility, in short the genius, of the mature Francisco de Goya in his first sedate designs for tapestries and his portraits of the Spanish court?

The great exception to this impression of relative aridity is music. Much that was inconsequential was being composed, of course, with the full approval of a large part of Europe's aristocracy, the custodians of 'high culture'. In musical composition, however, to a degree unmatched by any other art form, creative genius seemed to gain discipline and precision from a set of formal requirements, yet soar above them to achieve heights of true originality. The sonatas and symphonies of Haydn, exquisitely tooled for the music room or concert hall, nevertheless wove together Croatian peasant tunes from the master's boyhood. With Mozart, European music reached a level of combined craftsmanship and feeling scarcely approached before and seldom equalled since. A modern Protestant philosopher writes of this Austrian Catholic genius: 'He has heard the harmony of creation as providence in coherent form of which darkness is also a part, but in which darkness is not eclipse'.[1] The child prodigy who grew into such a composer of light and darkness was no bland purveyor of rococo self-satisfaction.

Opera deserves special mention because the late eighteenth century saw it well on the way to becoming in northern Europe, as it had long been in Italy, a polished form which was yet meaningful to large sections of the general public. Gluck's most influential works, such as *Orpheus* and *Alceste*, belong to the 1760s; but the old gentleman was still alive in 1780, and the fame of his dignified, intricate technique was at its peak. In the Low Countries and France, all across the Germanies to Vienna and even St Petersburg, the opera was settling in as a feature of city life. With Grétry of Liège, whose *Richard-Coeur-de-Lion* flattered royalty and aristocracy alike, Belgium found its most widely admired composer of the early modern era. With less pomposity, the Italians Cimarosa and Paisiello (the latter a precursor of Rossini in setting *The Barber of Seville* to music) sustained their country's mastery of the form.

[1] K. Barth, quoted in G. Clive, *The Romantic Enlightenment* (New York, 1960), p. 39.

It bears repeating that despite the use of folk tunes by Haydn and others, despite the fascination which popular stories and vernacular idiom held for the younger generation of German writers, what we have been looking at must be thought of as essentially an upper-class culture. As such, it was the possession of a thin, cosmopolitan stratum running across the top of European society. In its literacy, its opportunities for travel, its dress, its food and drink, its shared enjoyment of wit in the salon and high stakes at the gaming table, the 'upper crust' gave a deceptive impression of stability and uniformity. Below it were the forces of localism—and discontent. Popular poetry, for example, with its scurrilous rhymes about easily identified lords and ladies, politicians and clergymen, found a graphic counterpart in the crude cartoon literature of the streets. Strenuous dances, coarse foods, heavy beer and poor wine cheered the life of Europe's poor, in so far as it was cheerful at all. In the distance between such pleasures and those of the ruling élite lay a warning scarcely recognized by men content to answer: 'It has always been this way'.

A concluding observation takes us back momentarily to the realm of folk literature. Dependent though they were on transmission by the spoken word, Europe's vernacular languages nevertheless cherished classics of their own, poems and songs and tales which the next century would rejoice in committing to print. If such humble favourites had any common characteristic which might have been assigned social significance, it was their glorification of the rebel, the hunted victim but also the resister of the *status quo*. From the pirates and highwaymen of Scottish ballads and England's rediscovered Robin Hood to the defiant heroes of the Serbian epics, from the south German legends which inspired Schiller's angry play, *The Robbers*, to the Greek *klephtika* or 'outlaw songs', this theme runs through the popular culture of Europe. It is not to be ignored by a student of the coming upheaval.

IV

The European State System

The phrase 'state system', as applied to Europe before 1789 has several advantages over the expression, 'international relations'. Many of the entities engaged in eighteenth-century diplomacy and warfare were either too tiny or too sprawling to be considered nations as the term is used today. In treating this welter of political units—some already recognizable as nations, some supranational empires and some smaller jurisdictions carried over from the past—we need to be aware that *states* alone constituted the pieces on the chessboard. Only rarely did public affairs under the Old Régime offer whole peoples the occasion to become involved or to identify themselves with their leaders in a manner suggestive of national commitment. The notion of a *system* might be misleading, if it were taken to indicate a rational, self-adjusting relationship among individual states. Such a relationship most assuredly

BIBLIOGRAPHY. There exist a number of manuals which summarize the diplomatic history of Europe under the Old Régime. The newest, and from the French point of view the best, is G. Zeller, *De Louis XIV à 1789* (Paris, 1955); vol. III, part 2 of *Histoire des relations internationales*, ed. P. Renouvin; but M. Immich, *Geschichte des europäischen Staaten-systems von 1600 bis 1789* (Berlin-Munich, 1905), has yet to be surpassed for balanced compactness. The first volume of A. Sorel's *L'Europe et la Révolution française* (Paris, 1885), despite its title, is a critical analysis of the eighteenth century's diplomatic mores. For a penetrating discussion of the industrial revolution's effects on war, see J. U. Nef, *War and Human Progress* (Cambridge, Mass., 1950). A. Vagts, in his *History of Militarism* (rev. edn., New York, 1959), though particularly concerned with technical problems, does not overlook civil-military relations. Several studies of military theory are identified in footnotes to the present chapter; but immediate mention should be made of the classic work on naval questions, A. T. Mahan, *The Influence of Sea Power upon History, 1660–1783* (Boston, 1890). A good analysis of how foreign offices operated is D. B. Horn, *The British Diplomatic Service, 1689–1789* (Oxford, 1961). For a thoughtful treatment of legal and philosophical aspects, see F. H. Hinsley, *Power and the Pursuit of Peace* (Cambridge, 1963).

did not exist. But if we mean simply that there was a definite list of monarchies, principalities and republics, each one occupying a specified territory or series of territories and each expected to observe certain formalities while asserting its own interests, then we may safely refer to a system. One other feature is implied by the term: a rough hierarchy of states, grouped by degrees of size, power and hence ability to affect the course of European events. By visualizing several such orders of magnitude, we can better understand the characteristic duels among sovereigns in the 1780s, as well as the disruptive impact of the quarter-century that followed.

The Major Powers

The late eighteenth century knew five major powers: Great Britain, France, Austria, Prussia and Russia. Against any of these a smaller neighbour was virtually defenceless unless supported by another of the Big Five. By the same token, it required several of the latter, acting in concert, to extort concessions from any one of their peers.

Great Britain, though obviously a major power, could lay claim neither to a strategically central location nor to overwhelming numbers. Its standing army was small and scattered over posts from Dublin to the West Indies, from Quebec on the St Lawrence to Calcutta in the Ganges delta. Yet through its commercial and industrial strength, shielded by naval superiority, the United Kingdom was assured an influential voice in any European dispute it chose to enter. The very dispersion of its colonial empire, like the intangible quality of its financial resources, gave British power a resilience which could frustrate more massive opponents. Whether or not George III's inherited domain on the Continent, the German Electorate of Hanover, should be viewed as an asset was more problematical. Whenever Britain sought diplomatic or military access to central Europe, Hanover seemed a most useful possession. When the Electorate's vulnerability to attack by continental enemies threatened to embroil or humiliate the island kingdom, London rang with indignant criticism.

Across the channel, the French monarchy no longer threatened all Europe as it had a century earlier under Louis XIV's haughty motto: *Nec pluribus impar* (Not unequal to many). However, with its large army, its natural wealth and its geographical position, which permitted direct assaults upon a variety of possible opponents, France remained the Old Régime's most dreaded land power. Its potential naval strength denied even England's governors the right to complacency. Despite colonial losses during the first two-thirds of the eighteenth century, the French still commanded important bases overseas: Pondichéry in India, Gorée in Equatorial Africa and such valuable islands as Martinique in the Caribbean. Even in the years following the humiliating peace of 1763 with England, the French king had (a) finally secured direct possession of the Duchy of Lorraine (closing the previous gap between his older dominions and Alsace on the Rhine), and (b) acquired Corsica from a Genoese republic worn out by futile efforts to subdue the rebellious island.

On a simplified political map, the great continental rival of France might appear to have been the Holy Roman Empire of Germany. A closer look, however, would reveal the true nature of that crumbling monument to medieval statecraft. With its elective emperor in Vienna (the crown had been in the Habsburg family almost continuously for three-and-a-half centuries), its ponderous Diet in Regensburg, its supreme court in Wetzlar and its periodic paper levies for common defence, the *Reich* still maintained a pretence of unity. But it was only a pretence. From the eight electoral principalities[1] down to the tiniest county or free city, the more than 300 states in the Empire acknowleged only formal allegiance to the Kaiser—and behaved as though they owed no allegiance at all.

For the real *loci* of power in central Europe, therefore, we must turn to two monarchies, each a member of the Holy Roman Empire because of major possessions within the latter's boundaries, but at the same time endowed with important territories outside those boundaries. One was the Habsburg complex, which for convenience must be called Austria. Its ruler, Joseph II, was Holy Roman emperor by election. By inheritance he was archduke of Austria, duke of Styria and Carinthia, count of Tyrol, king of Hungary and, quite separately, of Bohemia, margrave of Moravia and overlord of Slavic possessions which stretched from Polish Galicia in the north to Slovenia and Croatia in the south. In addition, Lombardy in Italy and the Austrian Netherlands acknowledged his rule. This immense array of peoples comprised a population larger than that of France, with an awesome potential in terms of military manpower. The main obstacles to the full realization of that potential were obvious: a profusion of scattered commitments and the difficulty of

[1] In 1780 these included the kingdom of Bohemia (ruled by the Habsburgs), the electorates of Brandenburg, Saxony, Hanover and Bavaria, the archbishoprics of Mainz, Trier and Cologne.

1. *Europe in 1780*

welding Hungarian cavalry, Croatian infantry and other diverse elements into a single army under commanders of varying backgrounds.

Smaller, but no more compact, were the possessions of the rival Hohenzollern monarchy, the other protagonist in the German dualism. At his death in 1786, Frederick II was an elector of the Holy Roman Empire, in his role as margrave of Brandenburg. He was also grand duke of Silesia, annexed by conquest forty years earlier. Outside the Empire, he was king of (technically 'in') Prussia, including the western Polish lands snatched in 1772. His realm further included west German territories: the small but rich duchies of Cleves and Mark in the Rhineland, the principalities of Minden-Ravensberg on the Weser and East Frisia on the North Sea coast. Far to the south, he was sovereign prince of Neuchâtel, a member of the Swiss Confederation. Finally, through relatives, he controlled the collateral fiefs of Ansbach and Bayreuth in central Germany. All that held the Prussian kingdom together was the Crown itself, seconded by a large bureaucracy and an army which had won great prestige through its victories over Austria in the 1740s and still more through its success in withstanding the French-Austrian-Russian coalition of 1756–63. By the end of Frederick the Great's reign both the bureaucracy and the army had become calcified to an extent which threatened their high reputation, but Prussia's right to consider itself a great power was beyond dispute.

Under the German-born Catherine II, the fourth reigning tsarina in half a century, Russia too was a major factor in European affairs. Since Peter the Great's death in 1725, the vast empire of the Romanovs had been extended northward into Finland at Sweden's expense, westward by virtue of the Polish partition of 1772, and southward through concurrent victories over the Turks. Its right to sail ships in Turkish waters, to intervene in the Rumanian principalities and, within vague limits, to speak on behalf of Christians throughout the Ottoman realm, had been acknowledged at Kuchuk Kainarji in 1774. In the 1780s Catherine was entitled to congratulate herself on results achieved by her own ruthless will, by the stamina of Russian troops and by the high ability of General Suvorov, the 'Scourge of Islam'. The voice of St Petersburg had never been stronger.

Lesser Powers

A number of states which had been major powers in an earlier Europe had declined markedly by the end of the eighteenth century. The most catastrophic plunge had been that of Poland. Once the centre of a great Slavic realm, the Polish kingdom was now locked in social paralysis, crippled by the losses of 1772 and bereft of natural boundaries for defence against further Prussian, Austrian and Russian depredations.

Still more rapid, though destined to have a less abrupt and dramatic conclusion, had been the decline of Ottoman power. Only a century before, in 1683, the Turks had swept all the way to the walls of Vienna. With the raising of that siege, however, had begun the long Austrian counter-offensive down the Danube, a reconquest from the Christians' point of view, but from the Porte's a torment matched only by more recent defeats at Russian hands. Eaten by political corruption at the centre, this great empire was being hacked at on all sides, Persian and North African no less than Balkan and Caucasian. Its only hope lay in the restraints imposed on its European assailants by other great powers.

Not all the fallen mighty of the past shared the extremity of Poland's and Turkey's peril. Many others had simply slipped, with varying degrees of awareness of the change, to the second rank. Spain, with its poorly equipped armies and sluggish fleets, could no longer be seriously compared with the feared and respected kingdom it once had been. More and more clearly, Spain's ability to act in the diplomatic-military arena had been shown to depend on its old enemy—but since 1700 its Bourbon dynastic ally—France. Such prestige as it still could claim rested on gigantic colonial possessions in Latin America, the Caribbean and the Pacific. As the 1780s opened, it was seeking, like France, to capitalize on Britain's colonial troubles both for revenge and for territorial profit.

The neighbouring Portuguese had never recovered great power status since their period of subjugation to Spain in the late sixteenth and early seventeenth centuries. Though restored to independence in 1640, they had suffered heavy naval and colonial losses at Dutch hands, only to become dependent on England in the eighteenth century. Yet Portugal retained considerable importance, not only because of the British alliance but also because of its own overseas holdings in the East Indies and the Indian subcontinent (notably Goa), on both coasts of Africa south of the equator and, above all, in South America, where Brazil already promised to dwarf its mother country.

The United Provinces constituted the third of these former colonial giants, sunk to intermediate rank by the 1780s. Like the Spanish and Portuguese, the Dutch controlled large and scattered holdings: the lion's share of the East Indies, Ceylon off India, the Cape Settlement in South Africa, even a slice of Guiana on the South American coast. Unlike their old Iberian rivals, however, they had shown the commercial and financial capacity to translate these distant resources into economic strength in Europe. The reason for this capacity's not being fully realized lay in the threat Great Britain posed for the United Provinces, whether as an enemy in war or as an ally who remained an implacable trade rival. This external frustration was the most important source of Dutch social tensions, already referred to in Chapter III. The loss of genuine independence might be hidden by ostensible sovereignty, but it was a felt loss none the less.

Not so prominent in the world of commerce and colonies, but in earlier days, under Gustavus Adolphus and Charles XII, even more potent than the Dutch as a military factor, Sweden now retained only scraps of its former Baltic empire. On the German coast, despite Prussian resentment, the Swedes still held the island of Rügen and a sliver of Pomerania. A large part of Finland was also ruled from Stockholm, but Russian pressure was a constant danger on this flank. King Gustavus III scarcely bothered to deny that he hoped to take back from the tsarina the southern Finnish districts lost in 1721 and 1743. What restrained him, apart from uncertainty about Russia's strength, was the probability that in any Baltic struggle Sweden would be attacked by its old Scandinavian rival, Denmark. The latter kingdom, even taking account of its control of Norway, would be no match for the Swedes in a land campaign. With either Russia or Prussia as an ally, however, the Danes held the key to the 'northern question'. Furthermore, given their position at the mouth of the Baltic Sea and a navy capable of harassing any fleet in those waters, they loomed large in the strategic calculations of ministers as far away as Paris and London.

Another order of geographical considerations made little Switzerland more important to the European power balance than it could possibly have been on the basis of population and wealth alone. Its internal religious divisions, combined with a prudent distrust of involvement beyond its frontiers, generally prevented the Swiss Confederation from taking a decisive stand in any major international dispute. On the other hand its Alpine passes, invaluable to an ally but difficult for an enemy to seize from the stubborn militia of the cantons, retained great military significance. It would have been hard to imagine a more startling evidence of aggressive self-confidence than a direct blow at Switzerland.

In Italy several states qualified as intermediate powers. One was the kingdom of Naples, comprising the foot of the Italian boot and the island of Sicily. Like Denmark in the north, this realm looked out upon a maritime bottleneck of critical importance. Unlike the Danes, however, Naples lacked naval forces capable of disputing the passage of the central Mediterranean against a major fleet. Under the influence of Queen Maria Carolina, daughter of Maria Theresa, it looked increasingly to Habsburg Austria for support and less to King Ferdinand's Bourbon father, Charles III of Spain. Some such bulwark seemed necessary in any case, and the problem of naval defence made even far-away Britain a possible alternative.

The other Italian monarchy, though named Sardinia, was less important for its possession of that island than for its ruler's patrimony on the mainland: Piedmont, Nice and the mountainous duchy of Savoy. King Victor Amadeus III, though his dominions had a sizeable military nobility and a record of past adventures abroad, was generally as conservative in foreign affairs as he was in domestic matters. The only danger that the House of Savoy might disrupt the intricate Italian situation lay in its long-standing ambition to annex the little republic of Genoa.

Not all the rulers of Europe's middle-sized monarchies were kings. The peaceful but strategically located grand duchy of Tuscany in north central Italy was a case in point. Germany possessed two others, each ruled by a duke who was also an elector of the Holy Roman Empire. One was Bavaria, stretching northward across the upper Danube from the Alps. The other was Saxony, with its beautiful capital of Dresden on the Elbe, its burgeoning industrial districts and its crucial, if dangerous, location between Prussia and the Habsburgs' Bohemia.

While monarchy was eighteenth-century Europe's predominant political form, references to the United Provinces and Switzerland remind us that it was by no means the only one. We should feel no surprise, therefore, at finding yet another oligarchy, Venice, among the secondary powers. The Most Serene Republic had been successful in maintaining its hold on the upper Dalmatian coast of the Adriatic and on the Ionian Islands between Greece and southern Italy only because of Turkish distractions elsewhere. In the late eighteenth century, it simply re-enacted the pageantry of former power, each year remarrying its Doge to a sea which had ceased to be an avenue to riches and had become instead a perilous arena for Venetian war galleys and merchantmen. Nevertheless, while no longer the imperious city of the past, Venice exploited its ancient prestige and its proverbial diplomatic cunning to create an impression of influence in Italian and Mediterranean affairs.

The 'Swarm of Gnats'

In addition to the five great powers, we have now identified a dozen kingdoms, duchies and republics of lesser, but still appreciable, importance. It is still necessary to recognize a third category, a host of individually insignificant polities, some of them isolated as enclaves in the territory of larger states, others grouped into what amounted to buffer zones between strong neighbours. Together, these relics of Europe's morselized past still accounted for a substantial fraction of the continent's total area and contained several million of its inhabitants.

This 'swarm of gnats', as an exasperated younger Pitt once called them, could be subdivided into several basic types. First, there were the ecclesiastical principalities, ranging from the Papal States of central Italy (comparable in size, though not in power, to several units discussed earlier), through Avignon in southern France, also a possession of the Pope, to the prince-bishoprics and archbishoprics in the Holy Roman Empire. Second, we should note the smaller secular principalities. The Germanies alone contained about 200 such microcosms, not to mention the 1,000 or more fiefs of all but independent imperial knights (see above, p. 36). Some were as considerable as the duchies of Württemberg and of Mecklenberg or the margravates of Baden and of Hesse-Cassel, while others were as minute as Reuss and Saxe-Weimar. The closest equivalents elsewhere were the Italian duchies of Parma and Modena-Reggio. Third and last, an important classification was that of free cities. Most of these acknowledged a flimsy allegiance to some distant ruler—Dubrovnik on the Adriatic to the Turkish sultan, for example, or Bremen, Hamburg, Frankfurt, Nuremberg and their lesser German counterparts to the Holy Roman emperor. Genoa, in northern Italy, on the other hand, claimed total independence. So did Geneva, not yet a member of the Swiss Confederation. The distinction, however, was academic—all maintained garrisons, conducted diplomatic correspondence and acted as free agents in foreign affairs.

Diplomatic Theory and Practice

This array of jealous polities, from great powers through intermediate ones to the often tiny states just referred to, shared a set of institutions which provided for the exchange of views, the collection of information about one another, the application of pressure by threat or bribery, the conclusion of alliances and the settlement of conflicts. The diplomatic machinery of eighteenth-century Europe was one of the most highly developed bureaucratic features of the age. Every government had some kind of specialized foreign office and reserved a major share of the time of its ruling councils for the discussion of foreign affairs. Every government also had representatives and correspondents stationed abroad, though their number and rank, like their pay, varied enormously among states of differing sizes. Thus, while the king of France or the empress of Russia each maintained a score of ambassadors from Lisbon to Constantinople, plus a number of envoys to lesser courts, a petty German prince was likely to have formal representation only in the larger states directly adjoining his own, and possibly at Vienna and Berlin.

The origins of late eighteenth-century diplomatic practices would have to be sought ultimately in Greco-Roman antiquity. The direct line of development, however, starts in the Christian middle ages, specifically with heralds as official messengers and with the papal nuncios of the Catholic Church. Two subsequent periods had seen lasting expansions in the scope of diplomacy, together with increases in its technical complexity. One was the fifteenth century, when the Renaissance Italian states, led by Venice, had carried ambassadorial reporting to an unprecedented level of both volume and sophistication. The other was the late seventeenth century, when the France of Louis XIV had awed Europe not only by its armies but also by its elaborate machinery for espionage, persuasion and intimidation. The use of codes and ciphers for secret communications, though already known for centuries, had acquired new precision and intricacy at Versailles. Diplomatic protocol had been subjected to explicit rules of the type so dear to Louis's etiquette-conscious court. And it was the Sun King's government that had perfected the 'circular', a uniform set of instructions dispatched to every representative accredited to a foreign government which was involved in a given issue, so that the French point of view could be presented simultaneously and in identical terms to a whole array of foreign capitals.

As a result of the demonstrated virtuosity of Louis's government in this field, eighteenth-century diplomacy was marked by what one authority calls simply 'the French system'.[1] It did not necessarily follow,

[1] H. G. Nicolson, *The Evolution of Diplomatic Method* (London, 1954), third lecture.

of course, that France retained its earlier leadership in actual practice. Prussian diplomacy under Frederick the Great had earned a great reputation for diligence and cynical astuteness, though like military and civil administration, this branch of Hohenzollern government had declined in efficiency by the 1780s. The British, while dependent on fewer specialized professionals than were the French, displayed at least equal ability in the complex peace negotiations of 1782–83 and a clear superiority in responding to the critical developments in the United Provinces during the period 1784–87. Nevertheless, titles, documents, the organization of foreign offices and even the arrangement of their archives tended almost everywhere to follow the French model.

Regardless of nationality, Europe's foreign service personnel had certain common characteristics more significant than the momentary success or failure of any particular government. We are speaking now not of the various spies, informers and part-time commercial agents, but rather of the ambassadors and ministers, the councillors and secretaries who enjoyed diplomatic rank, observed diplomatic protocol and claimed diplomatic immunity from local regulations. Despite the occasional appearance of a gifted commoner, there was no more solidly aristocratic calling. Foreign ministers and ambassadors were generally noblemen of high rank. Charles James Fox, as Britain's secretary of state for foreign affairs in 1782 and again in 1783, was an exception but scarcely an extreme one, for he was from childhood onward unquestionably a member of the ruling élite.[1] It might be added that his three successors in the foreign secretaryship during the remainder of the century were Earl Temple, the marquis of Carmarthen—later duke of Leeds—and Lord Grenville. Subordinate posts were normally filled by gentlemen and often by young heirs to great titles. Even republics, the United Provinces or the free city of Frankfurt, for example, customarily reserved diplomatic appointments to members of their oldest and haughtiest patrician families—in part, no doubt, because ambassadors were expected to pay their own way, using private means.

A professional group thus constituted had certain definite advantages in the conduct of negotiations. Formed by comparable educations, speaking the same language in both the literal and the figurative sense, aware of class and status interests shared across boundaries and across the conference table, the diplomats of the Old Régime communicated with an ease and an understanding which the twentieth century has

[1] G. O. Trevelyan, *The Early History of Charles James Fox* (London, 1880), is a masterful treatment of this governing aristocracy.

come to envy. Their common desire to uphold the structure of privilege imposed not so much generous restraint toward opponents (consider the fate of Poland!) as a prudent reluctance, in most cases, to push issues to violent conclusions. Total struggles were known to be risky and total decisions, unpredictable. In their caution and their suspicious understanding of one another, these practitioners sought to avoid a holocaust.

As is so often the case in history, the potential weaknesses of the system were inherent in its strengths. Men who spoke each other's language would have found it hard to understand the common people of their respective homelands, had they cared to make the effort. They were soon to experience the difficulty of comprehending, to say nothing of manipulating, mass emotions of a diffusion and an intensity wholly strange to the cool world of dynastic calculation. In viewing war as a subordinate arm of policy, they were unprepared for an age in which militarism and militarists would make a handmaiden of diplomacy itself. Finally, because they believed in the underlying stability of the state system, such men could scarcely imagine a nation or a ruler prepared to wipe out the cluttered network of frontiers they knew so well.

Armies and Navies

Not that the eighteenth century had been either peaceful or static in terms of military development. Many of the strategic and tactical issues soon to be tested in violent action had already been agitated by several generations of theorists.[1] With relatively few exceptions, however, the soldiers of Europe's Old Régime, like its diplomats, remained deeply conservative, satisfied with the limitations and the narrow range of operational choice imposed by the methods of early modern warfare.

It was assumed, for example, that the best armies were limited in size, recruited on the basis of long-term enlistments and composed of professionals whose lack of emotional identification with the governments they served was viewed as irrelevant. Britain's King George III found it objectionable that regiments of German hirelings should fight in North America against rebellious colonists who claimed the 'rights of free Englishmen', but his own ministers overrode the royal scruples. Ireland and Switzerland continued to supply mercenaries to states

[1] See the excellent chapter on 'Armies and navies' in Anderson, *Europe in the Eighteenth Century*, pp. 130–51.

all over Europe. During the 1780s, over 40,000 Swiss citizens were regularly in service with a half-dozen foreign armies. France maintained the largest Swiss contingent, some 15,000 strong; but Spain and the United Provinces each had several thousand of these businesslike specialists from the cantons. Even countries with elaborate laws demanding enrolment of their citizens for militia duty in fact relied very little on citizen soldiers. Russia required its peasantry to provide one conscript from each specified group of households; but since the men thus called to duty had to serve at least twenty-five years, they were fully as professional and as divorced from their civilian countrymen as any mercenaries could have been.

For half a century or more, a technical debate had been in progress over the relative advantages of two methods of arranging troops for combat. One of these orders of battle was the reigning system of thin lines, dependent on the fire power of their disciplined ranks. The theoretical alternative was to rely on more massive columns or phalanxes whose effectiveness would depend on the shock effect of a bayonet charge. The line formation, its champions argued, had proved itself in countless battles, notably those of the 1740s, 50s and 60s in which Frederick the Great's Prussian infantry had cut larger enemy units to pieces and broken cavalry charges by steady musket fire. On the other side were the still more recent successes of Suvorov's Russian columns against the Turks in battles decided at close quarters after furious mass assaults.

In France, where the debate over the *ordre mince* (line) and the *ordre profond* (phalanx) reached its highest verbal intensity, the 1780s ended with no decision yet agreed upon.[1] The brilliant Comte de Guibert refused to believe that the alternatives were mutually exclusive, arguing instead that movements in both line and column could be combined with dashing cavalry actions and supported by the improved, mobile field artillery developed by General de Gribeauval. In practice, however, this synthesis was to be without effect until the next decade, when a new France at last began to heed the prophets of the old army. In the meantime, on drill fields from Potsdam to Dublin, regiments practised the sinister minuet of manoeuvres in line and volley firing by long ranks of standing or kneeling soldiers. Only a few experiments with irregular advanced lines of skirmishers revealed any awareness in

[1] A recent study of this topic is R. S. Quimby, *The Background of Napoleonic Warfare: The Theory of Military Tactics in Eighteenth-Century France* (New York, 1957).

Europe that across the Atlantic red men fired prone from shrubbery and white men who had learned from the Indians crept to battle along creek beds or behind stone walls.

Old assumptions about naval warfare had been subjected to only a few challenges during the eighteenth century. In the 1780s the short-barrelled naval cannon, or carronade, had just begun to swell the fire power of British ships at close quarters with an enemy. War galleys dependent on oarsmen had gradually disappeared from all except a few stretches of Mediterranean coastal waters, while the launching in 1782 of the big French man-of-war, the 118-gun *Etats de Bourgogne*, announced a new scale of magnitude in shipbuilding. Despite such changes in equipment, however, the criteria of sea power and the tactical rules for its use remained essentially what they had been for the preceding 200 years.

In terms of naval strength, Great Britain, with her 174 ships of the line in 1783 and her much larger number of supporting vessels, towered over all potential rivals. It is true that France's eighty ships of the line could mount a considerable challenge, especially if joined by Spain's sixty to seventy; but the battle of The Saints in 1782, when Rodney and Hood defeated De Grasse off Martinique in the West Indies, served to underline the danger of facing the British at sea. To be truly vulnerable, the Royal Navy would have had to be crippled by an especially heavy desertion rate or by a more protracted interruption of its supply of timber for hulls and masts than any opponent had yet managed to inflict upon it.[1] As for other fleets, the Dutch and Portuguese had long since abandoned any pretence of independent naval power; while Catherine II's Russia, though its thirty to forty ships of the line in the Baltic and another twenty or more in the Black Sea made it a newcomer of considerable importance, could not seriously affect the balance of forces outside those restricted waters.

Traditional Rivalries: Britain and France

There is no need here to recount every minor diplomatic exchange and military clash of the 1780s. We should, however, pay attention to a few episodes which may be grouped about the two most important rivalries involving European states before the revolution: the English–French and the Austrian–Prussian–Russian. Sometimes these zonal

[1] R. G. Albion, *Forests and Sea Power: The Timber Problem of the Royal Navy, 1652–1862* (Cambridge, Mass., 1926).

conflicts overlapped, but the principal axis remained distinct in each case. The various issues involved, the alignments formed and the characteristic modes of action adopted, will provide the basis for comparisons and contrasts with later episodes. The same observations may also help to explain the conditioned reflexes of conservative governments during the ensuing era of upheaval. In most countries, after all, it was statesmen formed by the old diplomacy who would have to confront the changes produced by its temporary collapse.

When the decade opened, the chief issue exercising the chancelleries of western Europe, and momentarily those of the German-Slavic East as well, was the lonely position of Great Britain. To the long revolt of the North American colonies, begun five years before, had been added a no more portentous but, from London's viewpoint, a far more dangerous renewal of the world struggle between the United Kingdom and the Bourbon monarchies of France and Spain. In 1778, encouraged by American victories in the Hudson Valley, the Comte de Vergennes as French foreign minister had committed his government to a fresh assault on its old British enemy. The following year, Spain had accepted a French promise of territorial prizes, including Florida and Gibraltar, and had joined the alliance against George III.

So far as European observers were concerned, battles in remote places with names like Cowpens and Savannah appeared less significant than Vergennes's determined effort to organize naval and mercantile opposition to England on the part of the entire continent. The French minister found his opportunity in the angry disagreements between London and most other capitals over definitions of contraband, blockade and freedom of the seas. His Majesty's government insisted that shipbuilding materials and in some circumstances even foodstuffs, especially cereals, were liable to seizure by the Royal Navy if they were found aboard any ship bound for a French or Spanish port. Those neutrals who faced a threat to their trade in timber and grain from northern Europe entered particularly sharp protests; but the British continued to take prizes on the Admiralty's own terms. Paris and Madrid, meanwhile, were loud in their protestations of respect for the rights of neutrals everywhere at sea.

Still, most trading nations were reluctant to be drawn into open hostilities against England; and France, as a belligerent, could scarcely assume the leadership of a band of neutrals. In this situation, the initiative of the empress of all the Russias proved decisive. Catherine II had begun in 1779 by expressing as much indignation over Spanish attacks on some of her grain ships as over British searches and seizures. The latter, however, proved far more numerous than the depredations by the Bourbon navies; and as the months passed, Vergennes played skilfully on the tsarina's gratitude for his friendly role in earlier Russo-Turkish negotiations. Gradually, St Petersburg swung towards the provisions urged by France: (1) free passage for neutral vessels except through an effective blockade; (2) rejection of 'paper blockades' not actively sustained by naval units covering a definite zone; (3) limitation of contraband to mean only weapons and munitions. On 28 February 1780 (Old Style—that is, on the Julian as opposed to the modern Gregorian calendar, which made this same date 11 March), Catherine sent a formal declaration to London, Paris and Madrid, containing the above stipulations and adding:

> Her Imperial Majesty, in making these points public, does not hesitate to declare, that to maintain them, and to protect the honour of her flag, the security of the trade and navigation of her subjects, she is preparing a considerable part of her maritime forces.[1]

Within barely six months after this manifesto, Russia, Sweden and Denmark-Norway were linked by an agreement to arm their merchantmen and to coordinate convoy arrangements for the purpose of enforcing their definition of neutral rights. In January 1781 'Their High Mightinesses', the States General of the United Provinces, joined the growing League of Armed Neutrality, only to find themselves singled out by England for a full-scale naval war. Later in 1781 first Prussia and then the Holy Roman emperor acceded to the system. A nervous Portuguese government followed suit in July 1782. Finally, in February 1783, when preliminary peace treaties had already been signed by the former belligerents, the kingdom of Naples swung grandly, if somewhat irrelevantly, into line.

How significant Catherine II's League of Armed Neutrality really was has long been a subject of debate. Except for involving the Dutch in active hostilities, it can scarcely be credited with much influence on the course of the fighting. Its direct value to Britain's enemies should certainly not be exaggerated; for the Americans were little interested in noncontraband shipments from neutrals, while neither timber nor grain seems to have reached France and Spain in sufficient quantities to make much difference in the war capabilities of either nation. The

[1] J. B. Scott, ed., *The Armed Neutralities of 1780 and 1800* (New York, 1918), p. 274.

League did, however, express European resentment concerning British naval supremacy and its uses. This first effort to organize the whole continent against England held an augury of future undertakings by rulers bent on conquest instead of mere neutrality. For the time being, however, the League's greatest importance doubtless lay in reinforcing the feeling of the British themselves that they were perilously isolated in a world of enemies and unfriendly neutrals. It was that feeling, combined with the economic strain of almost seven years of war and the discouraging course of events in America, which in February 1782 led 193 members of the House of Commons, just one short of a majority, to vote for an immediate peace.

These parliamentary proceedings doomed the ministry of Lord North, who resigned the following month after twelve years in power. They also led to the launching of formal peace negotiations in Paris. The news of Rodney's and Hood's naval victory in April (*see above*, p. 63) helped to offset British gloom over Cornwallis's surrender to the French and Americans at Yorktown the previous autumn. Nevertheless, the new ministry of Lord Rockingham faced a number of unpalatable choices in dealing with France, Spain, the United Provinces and the United States. At the outset, England's councils were divided. Charles James Fox, who as secretary of state for foreign affairs was charged with the European settlement, favoured practically unlimited concessions to the Americans, in order to get them out of the war and thus to weaken France. The secretary of state for home and colonial affairs, the earl of Shelburne, on the other hand, still hoped to escape with only a qualified grant of domestic independence to the thirteen colonies, which he for a time believed might still accept English leadership in matters of trade and foreign policy. The fact that each of these strong-willed politicians had his personal agents in Paris during the period of early soundings only added to the confusion and apparent unreliability of British peace offers. Not until Rockingham died in July could Shelburne assume what amounted to the premiership, as first lord of the treasury, and by naming his own men to the two secretaryships take control of all aspects of the negotiations.

The hostile coalition, on its side, also revealed conflicting interests which British diplomacy now set out to exploit. The American spokesmen, led by Benjamin Franklin, John Adams and John Jay, were intent on securing full recognition of the former colonies' independence, plus as much land and freedom of action as the new nation could obtain on its western frontier. Vergennes, while seeking maximum gains from

England in the West Indies and perhaps elsewhere, felt no enthusiasm over the prospect of an independent power on the North American mainland. He especially hoped that the United States might be left insecure enough, and sufficiently bitter against the British, to make French protection and supervision a continued necessity. Spain had its own territorial demands, specifically Florida and Gibraltar, though a four-year siege of the latter stronghold had proved insufficient to dislodge the British from the Mediterranean gateway. From Madrid's point of view, everything depended on French refusal to reach a separate agreement with England before the latter accepted the Spanish list of war aims in its entirety. Yet how could Vergennes, with his government in desperate financial straits, be expected to prolong hostilities on behalf of what was beginning to appear an expression of unrealistic Iberian pride? As for the Dutch, about the most they could hope was that their unfamiliar Bourbon allies would help them to escape undamaged from the grip of British sea power.

The outcome was a classic example of cold diplomatic bargaining. It required some concessions by an England unaccustomed to making any concessions at all. Considering the military odds, however, it was an achievement for which Shelburne deserved something better than the parliamentary revolt which swept him from office only weeks after the preliminary treaties were signed. The solution he had worked out involved several steps. First, with respect to the newborn United States, he belatedly adopted the thesis of Fox, deciding that it would indeed be necessary to pay the price required to deny France any further hope of using the rebellious colonies for its own purposes. Britain therefore granted the Americans a separate treaty (November 1782) which recognized their full independence, acknowledged their claim to the Northwest Territory all the way to the Mississippi and guaranteed them generous fishing rights off Newfoundland. Then Shelburne turned to the Bourbon monarchies. In the general preliminaries signed at Paris in January 1783 and confirmed by the treaty of Versailles the following September, he conceded to France Senegal in Africa, Tobago in the West Indies and certain fishing privileges in the North Atlantic. For the rest, Vergennes secured only a mutual return of territories occupied during the war. Spain received Florida and the Mediterranean island of Minorca, but not its dearest prize, Gibraltar. The United Provinces, thus abandoned, were unable to arrange a settlement until well into 1784, when they yielded to Britain both Negapattinam, near India's southern tip, and trading rights in the rich eastern island chain, the Moluccas.

In some respects, no doubt, Lord Shelburne was building better than he knew. By his much-criticized generosity to the Americans, he left the United States free to reject French tutelage and to grow by slow stages towards another kind of partnership with England. Though His Majesty's government yielded some non-essentials to the Bourbon kingdoms, thereby isolating the hapless Dutch, the general restoration of occupied territories left Great Britain in possession of all its key strategic bases abroad. They were soon to be needed more desperately than the men of 1782 and 1783 could possibly have foreseen.

The sequel, so far as Anglo-French relations were concerned, had two separate themes. One was continued rivalry, now transferred to the Dutch internal struggle, to be considered in the next chapter. Here it is enough to say that the political crisis within the United Provinces following 1784 was also a major test of great-power diplomacy. The republican opponents of Stadtholder William V had the support of France, with whom the States General concluded a treaty of alliance in 1785. Both Prussia and England, knowing that Louis XVI's government was in no condition to face a general war, were eager to upset this arrangement by restoring the stadtholder to power on terms which would eliminate French influence from the Hague. The young British minister there, James Harris (later rewarded with the title of earl of Malmesbury), proceeded with great skill and persistence, among other things arranging financial aid for the Dutch Orangists from George III's civil list. It was not until the summer of 1787 that the pro-French Patriots themselves supplied a pretext for armed intervention by insulting the princess of Orange, wife of the stadtholder and sister of King Frederick William II of Prussia. London and Berlin promptly agreed that a Prussian army should launch what proved to be a bloodless invasion, and on October 10 Amsterdam capitulated. Within six months, the triumphant William V formally repudiated the French treaty in favour of an Anglo-Dutch agreement, and before the end of the summer a treaty was signed in Berlin making Prussia the third party to this new Triple Alliance.[1]

The other trend in French and English relations produced a move towards economic understanding which showed how swiftly eighteenth-

[1] A. Cobban, *Ambassadors and Secret Agents: The Diplomacy of the First Earl of Malmesbury at the Hague* (London, 1954). The same author cites the figure of £89,100 as an extraordinary charge on the civil list for aid to the Orangists in 1787, 'British secret service in France, 1784–1792', *English Historical Review*, vol. LXIX (1954), pp. 234–7.

century diplomats could shed national hatreds when they chose to do so. The trade agreement signed in Paris on 26 September 1786, and commonly called the 'Eden treaty' in honour of William Eden, its British originator, marked an unprecedented experiment in commercial cooperation between the two kingdoms. The final mover on the French side had been the once seemingly irreconcilable Vergennes, on the British, William Pitt the Younger, prime minister since December 1783. Both sought peace and commercial recovery for their nations after the dangerous struggle which had ended only three years before. Both of them, the ageing Frenchman with only a year to live and the twenty-seven-year-old Englishman near the beginning of his long ministry, were groping towards something beyond the jealous mercantilism which for so long had dominated their governments' trade policies.

The treaty provided for a reciprocal lowering of tariffs on manufactured goods and foodstuffs, including beverages. A significant exception was silk cloth, which the French had hoped to see included; but the grain, wine and brandy of France could now enter the United Kingdom under tariffs lower than those charged on similar imports from any other country. Conversely, Britain's hardware, cottons and industrial products in general could invade the French market on a scale never before permitted. It was unfortunate for Vergennes's posthumous reputation that France was already gripped by an economic crisis, shortly to be intensified by a series of bad harvests. Under such conditions—with no great surplus of food and drink to sell in Britain, and with many sectors of French industry at least temporarily suffering from foreign competition—it was easy to leap to the conclusion that France was being ruined by the pitiless 'English mechanics'. Free trade enthusiasts might insist that reciprocity would eventually bring compensating benefits to the French economy, but history refused them the time to prove it. Both the treaty and the arguments it spawned were about to be swept away by a quarter-century of Franco-British hostility unparalleled by any the Old Régime had known.

Traditional Rivalries: Austria, Prussia and Russia

While Britain and France were moving from armed conflict to a mixture of diplomatic fencing and shortlived economic understanding, the powers of eastern Europe pursued their several aims with unswerving devotion to the law of the jungle. The joint seizure of Polish lands in 1772 had suggested a degree of community among Austria, Prussia and

Russia which was thoroughly belied by their subsequent actions. Joseph II, Holy Roman emperor since 1765 and after the death of Maria Theresa in 1780 sole ruler of the vast Austrian patrimony as well, inherited his mother's determination to recover Silesia from Prussia. In addition he hoped for various other gains which the house of Hohenzollern was certain to resist. In Berlin the elderly Frederick II sought to protect his Silesian prize and to increase his recent Polish acquisitions by ingratiating himself with Russia, while checking Austria wherever possible. As for Catherine II, though she would not yield the slightest advantage to the two German powers with respect to Poland, her attention was increasingly directed southward towards the Ottoman empire. On this Balkan–Black Sea front, Austria might appear at any given moment as either a valuable ally or a serious rival. Prussia's importance, as seen from St Petersburg, no longer loomed so large as in the days when Russian interest had been riveted on the Baltic region.

In 1780 a visit by Joseph II to Russia set the stage for the next year's signing of a defensive agreement between Austria and Catherine's empire. This treaty has been called the 'second diplomatic revolution', though it scarcely marked a reversal comparable to the Austrian-French alliance of 1756. From Frederick the Great's point of view, the second 'revolution' did have drastic implications precisely because of the earlier one, in the sense that France, where Joseph II's sister Marie Antoinette now sat as queen, was also still a formal ally of the Habsburgs and thus a potential foe of Prussia. The nightmare of isolation continued to haunt Berlin.

It was Empress Catherine who seized the first fruits of the new alliance. Promising Austria immense rewards in the Balkans, claiming for Russia itself the western Caucasus, the Crimean peninsula and the left bank of the Dniester, her 'Grand Plan' of 1782 was also called her 'Greek Plan' because it invoked the vision of a restored Byzantine empire under a Romanov *basileus* or emperor. If the project were carried out, the tsarina's three-year-old grandson, named Constantine not quite by accident, would rule Greece, Macedonia and Bulgaria from the city of his namesake, once the latter had been liberated by the Christian allies.

In the event, Russia settled for much less. Joseph II was not eager to alienate France by an all-out attack on the Bourbons' old Turkish client. Furthermore—and this was a recurrent theme of the period—he was reluctant to weaken his position against Prussia by becoming heavily engaged in the south-east. In 1783, therefore, the Russians struck alone. Announcing that conditions in the Crimea demanded intervention on behalf of the Tatar khan, technically a vassal of the sultan but actually a protégé of the tsarina, a Russian army occupied the entire peninsula. At this point Catherine was prevented by Turkish appeasement from pursuing the Grand Plan any further. Under pressure from Vergennes's envoy in Constantinople, the Porte wrote off the Crimea with unexpected speed and early in 1784 signed a treaty ceding it to Russia. For the time being, the tsarina halted Black Sea operations, sardonically thanking her embarrassed ally, the emperor in Vienna, for his 'measured behaviour' and 'benign prudence'.

These phrases contain a special irony in view of Joseph's actual conduct in several other areas. A ruler of considerable intelligence and humane impulses where domestic reforms were concerned, he proved himself as ambitious as he was unpredictable in foreign affairs. Though not quite the ruthless expansionist portrayed by later generations of Prussian historians, he was prepared to agitate conditions in western Europe and in the Germanies at the same time that he continued to listen to Russian blandishments in the East. Hence, an inordinate amount of diplomatic excitement was whipped up in widely scattered capitals by his various projects during the 1780s.

At the very beginning of his personal reign, for example, he launched an attack on existing treaty arrangements in the Low Countries. Ever since 1715 Dutch troops had occupied seven fortified towns on the southern frontier of the Austrian Netherlands, facing France. This 'Barrier' was intended to help prevent any resurgence of French aggression in the style of Louis XIV, and the original agreement had been an integral part of the transfer of the Belgian provinces to Austrian control. In 1781, however, the emperor brusquely announced that the Barrier was no more and ordered the Dutch garrisons to leave his territories at once. Protests from the Hague were brushed aside; and the United Provinces, already at war with England, felt compelled to abandon the old forts.

Shortly thereafter, in 1784, Joseph repeated the same tactics against the beleaguered Dutch, abruptly informing them that 'his' River Scheldt was no longer closed to trade, as it had been ever since the Peace of Westphalia in 1648. This time the States General did not yield. The French government, as unenthusiastic as the Dutch over the prospect of commercial competition on the part of Antwerp, advised Vienna that there must be no unilateral repudiation of existing agreements. Prussia automatically joined the opposition to Austrian demands.

Furious over the reverse, Joseph II nevertheless accepted a modest Dutch indemnity for damages to certain of his Belgian subjects' ships which had been fired upon by shore batteries—and the Scheldt remained closed.

The Austrian Netherlands during these years occupied the emperor's thoughts in still another connection, this one primarily German in its implications. Joseph had already tried once, in 1777-9, to annex part of the big duchy of Bavaria when the last direct Wittelsbach had died without legitimate offspring. That attempt had been blocked by Prussia and Saxony. In 1784 it became generally known that Austria had formulated a new project: a simple exchange of Bavaria for Belgium (minus Luxembourg and Hainault, which would go to France if it supported the transaction). Joseph would be rid of the remote and troublesome Netherlands, while the annexation of Bavaria by Austria would create a massive south German state which could easily outweigh Prussia in the councils of the Holy Roman Empire. The elector of Bavaria was quite willing to move from Munich to Brussels. He was, after all, not a native Bavarian but a Rhinelander (having formerly been ruler of the Palatinate) and was easily dazzled by the promise of a Belgian realm renamed the 'kingdom of Burgundy'. The trouble was that like his predecessor, this lazy, voluptuous prince had no legitimate children; and the next Wittelsbach in line, the duke of Zweibrücken, was a grown man who made clear his preference for the Bavarian succession.

In this situation, the attitudes of the other continental powers became decisive. Russia's empress sent Joseph II vague good wishes and a cool refusal to help. For France, the choice was anything but simple. A weak Belgium under Wittelsbach control might well be an easier neighbour on the north than the Netherlands had been during three centuries of Habsburg rule. Luxembourg and Hainault constituted a tempting bribe, as the Austrian party of courtiers around Queen Marie Antoinette pointed out. Vergennes wavered, but his fundamental caution, fortified by dislike for the notion of a great south German power, inclined him to oppose the scheme. That, in effect, is what he did by suavely insisting that the other German states must give their approval.

Prussia's Frederick II saw the chance to win his last contest with the Habsburgs. In gambling on either Russian or French support to cancel Prussian influence, Joseph II had actually defeated his own purpose; for he had frightened and enraged a series of German rulers who would otherwise have been suspicious of any initiative from Berlin.

Instead they rallied to Frederick's call for resistance to the threatened destruction of the Empire. The League of Princes was ostensibly instigated by the margrave of Baden, but its act of association was signed at the Hohenzollern court in January 1785. Prussia, Saxony and Hanover were joined by a dozen lesser principalities in a formal declaration of intention to uphold the duke of Zweibrücken's rights, that is, the *status quo* in Bavaria. Vergennes now had his excuse to withhold any French endorsement of the exchange, and a further embittered Joseph II had his answer. Hope for an Austrian-Bavarian merger was dead beyond hope of resuscitation. The family compact between Versailles and Vienna was at best extremely weak.

One might suppose that Joseph had been thwarted on enough occasions to make him reject any further adventures abroad. That such did not prove to be the case was in part a result of the emperor's restless temperament. It must also be said, however, that his next undertaking stemmed partly from events which he had not set in motion. This final act in the confused melodrama of pre-revolutionary diplomacy and warfare opened in 1786, when Catherine II put forward a new set of designs for a joint assault on the Ottoman Porte. She had an excellent opportunity to do so, for Joseph went along on the tsarina's famous tour of the Crimea and the Dnieper Valley. As a matter of fact, her imperial guest returned to Vienna unconvinced that Russian plans contained anything of value from his point of view; but the prospects, as seen from Constantinople, were unnerving.

Had the Turks been aware of the lukewarm Austrian attitude, they might have felt less anxious to seize the initiative in the summer of 1787. Instead, fearing the worst and hoping to catch its menacing opponents off guard, the Sublime Porte suddenly presented Catherine II's government with an ultimatum demanding immediate cessation of Russian interference in the khanate of Georgia. When this was rejected, Ottoman forces attacked Prince Potemkin's inadequately prepared army, with the result that five years of savage warfare opened amid unaccustomed Turkish victories. By 1788 Catherine II faced another danger, a Swedish assault launched against Russian holdings in Finland, only about 150 miles from her capital of St Petersburg itself. This attempt at collaboration between Gustavus III and the sultan seems to have frightened the tsarina more than any other episode in her tumultuous career.

The Turkish-Swedish alliance, however, enjoyed only brief success. In the north, Gustavus III was soon distracted by Denmark's entry into the war against him; and though the Danes accomplished little or nothing in a military way, Sweden felt compelled to accept a *status quo* peace with Catherine in 1790. Meanwhile, Austrian intervention and the strengthening of Russian armies had already turned the tide on the Ottoman front. Unenthusiastic as he had been at first, Joseph II realized that he had no choice but to honour the treaty of 1781 and join the fighting if he hoped to retain any voice in Balkan affairs. Consequently, by the spring of 1789 a large Habsburg army swept forward into Serbia towards Belgrade, which it captured that autumn, while the Russians, now led by the gifted Suvorov, began a relentless campaign to occupy the Rumanian coast of the Black Sea.

As the decade of the 1790s began, the final collapse of the Ottoman empire in Europe and its division between the Austro-Russian allies seemed imminent. One more time, however, the balance wheel of eighteenth-century diplomacy swung back to restrain the rush towards a 'total solution'. Denied French support, as so often before, the Austrian government kept looking nervously over its shoulder at the danger of a Prussian attack. The threatened revolt in Hungary and the actual one in the Netherlands further weakened the hand of the new Emperor Leopold II. Early in 1790, therefore, a Turkish-Austrian truce was concluded; and the following year, Vienna signed the treaty of Sistova, abandoning Belgrade and all other conquests save for a small segment of Bosnia. Russia fought on until January 1792, then at Jassy accepted the Dniester as its new frontier, returning the Rumanian principalities to Turkish rule. All things considered, the sultan could count himself lucky.

By the time these agreements were reached, events in France already promised to make western Europe once more the focus of attention. The shift, be it noted, was neither instantaneous nor complete. The Polish situation in particular would continue to engage Prussian, Austrian and Russian avarice until the denouement of 1795. Nevertheless, Europe was about to experience a series of unprecedented shocks from a force whose like had never been seen before: a nation in arms.

The European States in 1789

The last years of the Old Régime, far from being wholly aimless or static, had witnessed a series of highly important shifts in the European state system. To understand the setting for the revolutionary crisis, it is essential to bear in mind those shifts, at least in so far as they helped to determine the posture of each of the five great powers in 1789. Great Britain, dangerously isolated only a half-dozen years before, had survived that predicament and now had a working alliance with Prussia and the virtually monarchical United Provinces. Prussia benefited in turn from this Triple Alliance, especially as a makeweight in dealings with Vienna and St. Petersburg. Russia, engaged in the latest of its successful wars of expansion, was able to command Austrian support when needed, yet was basically strong enough to play its own game from the Baltic to the Black Sea. Austria, oscillating between its German-Belgian involvements and its secular struggle with the Turks, seemed tempted to intervene everywhere yet able to succeed nowhere without the concurrence of a major ally.

It was France, however, that had suffered most in these years of the Bourbon twilight. Despite the outward appearance of recovered prestige in 1783, a tribute to the sophisticated intelligence of Vergennes, the threat of financial disaster had combined with the conflict of factions at court—'Austrians' versus 'Anglophiles', 'expansionists' versus 'immobilists'—to leave Louis XVI's government practically impotent in foreign affairs. Within a half-dozen years after the treaty of Versailles, mighty France had abandoned its Turkish protégé twice (in 1784 and 1787), deferred to Frederick the Great in the matter of the Bavarian succession, allied itself with Sweden only to refuse Gustavus III any help in Finland, evaded the claims of another ally, Austria, for protection against Prussia after 1788 and allowed London and Berlin to manoeuvre the Dutch into an unforeseen alliance.

Coupled with undoubted strength, this posture of aloofness might have had much to recommend it. But in the French case each new disengagement seemed to suggest not strength but a nervous admission of weakness. The diplomatic record, in fact, supports the view that the French Revolution erupted in a country whose government was already paralysed. It also helps to explain the reluctance of France's enemies in the next few years to believe that anything very serious was going to happen to them.

V

Domestic Politics in the 1780s

In the previous chapter, we discussed the relations among European states as though each of them actually had been the kind of unit shown on a solid-colour map. Even in treating diplomatic history, such simple and concrete language can be deceptive if not carefully used. To say, for example, that Prussia was openly hostile to Austria is not really to say, though it does suggest, that every Prussian was simultaneously

BIBLIOGRAPHY. By all odds the most satisfactory survey of this period in European politics is R. R. Palmer, *The Age of the Democratic Revolution*, vol. I: *The Challenge* (Princeton, 1959), dealing with the years 1760–91. This remarkable work of synthesis has contributed both factual points and interpretive insights for which the present writer is deeply indebted. In part because of the interest stirred up by the late Sir Lewis Namier's theories, the past quarter-century has produced a number of important studies of British politics, including H. Butterfield, *George III, Lord North and the People, 1779–1780* (London, 1949), R. Pares, *King George III and the Politicians* (Oxford, 1953), and I. R. Christie, *The End of North's Ministry* (London, 1958); but G. S. Veitch, *The Genesis of Parliamentary Reform* (London, 1913), has by no means lost its importance. Although the situation in Ireland is partly illuminated by the above studies, additional mention should be made of R. B. McDowell, *Irish Public Opinion, 1750–1800* (London, 1943). For the Low Countries, P. Geyl, *De Patriottenbeweging, 1780–1787* (Amsterdam, 1947), and S. Tassier, *Les démocrates belges de 1789* (Brussels, 1930), are basic analyses of the Dutch and Belgian crises. The bibliography of the French Revolution will be taken up separately in Chapter VI; but two works of widely differing emphasis must be included in any pre-1789 survey: H. Carré, *La fin des parlements, 1788–1790* (Paris, 1912), and C. E. Labrousse, *La crise de l'économie française à la fin de l'ancien régime* (Paris, 1944), the latter a profuse and sometimes confusing, but nonetheless important study of prices and profits. The affairs of Germany's remaining assemblies of estates are recounted in F. L. Carsten, *Princes and Parliaments in Germany from the Fifteenth to the Eighteenth Century* (Oxford, 1959), while the specific problems of Prussia under Frederick William II appear in H. Brunschwig, *La crise de l'état prussien à la fin du XVIIIe siècle* (Paris, 1947). The most general study of the Germanies, however, is F. Valjavec, *Die Entstehung der politischen Strömungen in Deutschland, 1770–1815* (Munich, 1951).

glowering across the frontier at every subject of the Habsburgs. Still, the convention of personifying countries is justified by the nature of diplomacy, the organization of military power and the centralized structure of public finance. Governments did, and for that matter still do, speak for whole peoples in dealing with other governments.

The situation is abruptly altered when we turn to questions of domestic politics. Here states can be treated no longer as individuals in a many-sided competition. The point at issue becomes precisely the extent to which a particular government does in fact represent the population under its authority. The two arenas are not altogether separated. Foreign policy is obviously affected by internal affairs, while successes or failures abroad may influence profoundly a struggle for power at home. This overlapping area, however, constitutes only a small part of an exceedingly complex picture. Many other elements in a given political situation derive from the internal experience of the state concerned and have little or nothing to do with international relations.

Unrest and Reform: Material and Ideological Pressures

What is the first, the strongest and the most enduring impression imparted by a general view of Europe in the 1780s? Clearly, it is one of agitation, of a turbulence scarcely suggestive of the 'good old days' later generations are inclined to see in the period which precedes any great upheaval. Just as clearly, this turbulence can be explained only by a combination of separate causes, some of them operative for years or even generations past, but now especially active in a noisy decade.

One such cause sprang from fundamental changes in the physical

Rather surprisingly, in view of the immense outpouring of later works on the Habsburg version of enlightened despotism, it is still impossible to dispense with two treatments both of which are over fifty years old: P. von Mitrofanov, *Joseph II: Seine politische und kulturelle Tätigkeit* (Vienna-Leipzig, 1910), and H. Marczali, *Hungary in the 18th Century* (Cambridge, 1910). With respect to Russia, Scandinavia or the Iberian kingdoms, there is no need to mention titles not cited in other chapters or in the Bibliographical Note. Because of Poland's special significance, however, note should be taken of C. Dany, *Les idées politiques et l'esprit public en Pologne à la fin du XVIIIe siècle* (Paris, 1901), and the much more recent J. Fabre, *Stanislas-Auguste Poniatowski et l'Europe des lumières* (Paris, 1952). The geographically restricted but historically very important Genevan crisis occupies several chapters in the *Histoire de Genève des origines à 1798*, published by the Société d'Histoire et d'Archéologie de Genève (Geneva, 1951).

conditions of European life. As we have already seen, the eighteenth century had witnessed a marked rise in population, a rise which quickened its rate as the century went on and which, down to the 1780s, had been heavily concentrated in rural areas. The economic and political implications of such a phenomenon were tremendous. In good years more farm hands and the simultaneously advancing agricultural techniques had the effect of driving down commodity prices in the urban markets. In bad years, on the other hand, the unconquered threat of famine might still return to the countryside. Either way the peasantry in many regions saw the much-touted 'agricultural revolution' as a process of deterioration, and felt correspondingly bitter towards groups ranging from noble landlords to townsmen in general, and government officials in particular.

Though the general population growth had yet to make its full influence felt in most cities, such increases as had already occurred were adding to the political strains in urban centres. The master craftsmen and old patricians who had for centuries managed town affairs found themselves challenged by a combination of technical developments and new social configurations. They had to face the resentful demands of manufacturers whose methods and ambitions could not have been fully accommodated by the regulated guild system, even if that system had been flexible enough to offer all of the 'new men' personal membership. In addition, as one local study after another has shown, the 1780s witnessed an unprecedented increase in the numbers of factory workers in cities all the way from Manchester and Paris to Brno in the Habsburgs' Moravia and to Prussia's Silesian capital, Breslau. Many of these workers were beginning to seek political rights for which the old distinction between burghers and other residents made no provision. Finally, as remarked in Chapter III, the guilds had their own dissatisfied lower class, the numerous journeymen who could not look forward to admission as masters unless long-standing restrictions disappeared.

In an atmosphere of agrarian and urban discontent, ideas of reform could set up unexpected reverberations and thus in themselves become a second, distinct source of political unrest. Much has been written about the political theories of the Enlightenment, the intellectual ferment which Europe had been experiencing since the late 1600s; but it is still hard to determine the precise influence of critical analysis on the course of public events. One thing seems abundantly clear: philosophical criticism of the existing order was at once more widely distributed over the entire social spectrum and less direct in its effects than was believed by many nineteenth-century historians. For them the Enlightenment was a weapon consciously adopted by middle-class agitators to achieve the destruction of the Old Régime.

By the 1780s the diffusion of numerous theories had combined with the altered circumstances of daily existence to make political argument a major activity for thousands if not millions of Europeans. Newspapers and journals of opinion, many of them far more audacious than their readers' grandparents would have believed possible, kept springing into print under the noses of censors even in authoritarian states. The penetration of reformist ideas below the 'literacy line' in society is by definition all but impossible to document. The known popularity of certain street corner orators, however, and the slogans memorialists tell us were shouted by mobs in a score of cities even before 1789 suggest that poor and uneducated people had seized upon catch phrases which crudely echoed the thoughts of philosophers and journalists. At the other extreme, countless gentlemen of wealth and title prided themselves on their familiarity with such ideas, and many a discussion overheard in an elegant private salon would have been judged seditious in a humble tavern.

Had the Enlightenment produced a coherent programme of political change pointing towards possible revolution? Once again, a simple answer eludes us. The century-old contractual theories of John Locke, for example, might be used to explain the overthrow of a lawless ruler, but they were also available to men in England's Parliament or Hungary's Diet who feared the actions of the populace. Montesquieu's *Spirit of Laws*, published in 1748, was critical of any monarchy which suppressed the established orders, but its message was assuredly not one of incitement to mass rebellion. Voltaire was generally anti-aristocratic and always anti-clerical, but his form of political realism demanded a heavy reliance on royal power. Rousseau was in the 1780s better known for his views on religion, education and morals than for his confusing espousal of popular sovereignty as the ultimate basis for legitimate authority. In the latter regard, the author of the *Social Contract* had yet to become a patron saint of democracy; and it has been well said that the Revolution made Rousseau, rather than the opposite.

Yet despite all qualifications and reservations, there is no denying that the Enlightenment had bequeathed to the late eighteenth century a number of specific arguments and, still more important, a penchant for radical, probing criticism. Locke *had* declared that a government might forfeit its right to rule. Montesquieu *had* examined the nature of tyranny and conceded the danger that aristocrats might become selfish oligarchs. Both Voltaire and Rousseau, together with dozens of their contemporaries, *had* pointed fingers of scorn at a series of traditional institutions. Even the most unpolitical of the *philosophes*, Beccaria in Italy, Lessing in Germany, Hume in England, had cast doubt, respectively, on brutal treatment of accused wrongdoers, on religious oppression and on the irrational nature of many hallowed beliefs. All these men were dead by the 1780s, but Jeremy Bentham and his fellow Utilitarians in England were currently demanding that all behaviour, presumably including that of rulers, be judged in terms of its usefulness to mankind in general. At the same time, a race of publicists far more extreme than the departed giants of Enlightenment—Tom Paine, Brissot de Warville in France, Karl Friedrich Bahrdt in Germany and many others—produced a flood of invective at once impassioned and sarcastic. At the very least, it must be said that for the period we are examining no belief, no custom, no human relationship could claim immunity from criticism on grounds either of immemorial age or of divine sanction.

To the compound of physical changes and reformist ideas must be added a third source of agitation: the American Revolution. Whether or not the colonists' struggle for *independence* was also a *social* upheaval continues to be a matter of sharp controversy. In any event, for most sympathizers in Europe, including numerous Englishmen, the important aspect of the American drama lay in its specifically political implications. The actors were no band of noble savages, but recently transplanted Europeans who were able to put forward their own *philosophes* in Franklin, Jefferson, Adams and others among the Founding Fathers. They had succeeded, with the help of several European autocrats to be sure, in defying the mightiest naval and commercial power of the day. Still more important, they were demonstrating that free men could frame, modify and reframe a structure of responsible authority through the action of a startlingly new device, constitutional conventions.

It is difficult to say just how many European troops survived the fighting in America, but the figure almost surely exceeded 60,000 and may have been as high as 100,000 (there were 30,000 Hessians and other Germans alone). After peace came, perhaps a third of these men (an estimated 40 per cent in the case of the Germans) decided to stay in the new country, but the rest went back to their homes across the ocean full of stories about their experiences. All over Europe, enthusiasts extolled the triumphant colonists, often in terms which represent more good will than accurate information. Frederick II of Prussia, it is true, wrote sourly to his minister at the Hague in May 1783: 'I am very much persuaded that this so-called independence of the American colonies will not amount to much'.[1] The cynical old king's judgment, however, was scarcely typical. The Italian dramatist, Alfieri, in his *American Free* (1783) wrote of

> The raging storm,
> Which is bringing salvation and liberty to us.

A year earlier, the Russian social critic, Radishchev, had composed an *Ode to Freedom*:

> To you my inflamed soul aspires,
> To you, renowned land . . .

And from Holland, though written in French, came an anonymous epic, *America Delivered*, whose author cried:

> Venerable Congress, of a people free and good,
> You have cemented the glory and union; . . .
> Clear-headed scrutinizers of our vain prejudices . . .[2]

Not all discussions of American achievements, of course, were uncritical. John Adams and Thomas Jefferson, from their respective diplomatic posts in London and Paris, felt compelled to defend various provisions in the new constitution of 1787 against sharp attacks by European thinkers. Many of the latter expressed disapproval of the strong presidency and branded the United States Senate an aristocratic upper house. Many more denounced the Order of the Cincinnati, a hereditary fraternity of ex-officers in the Continental Army, as an American nobility in the making. The very intensity of such debates nevertheless testified to the importance of the New World for the politics of late eighteenth-century Europe. Furthermore, the criticisms just noted suggest the democratic tone which entered many of these debates.

From America's revolutionary war it is only a short step to a fourth cause of discord on the Continent and in Great Britain as well. This was the general course of foreign affairs, which we have already recognized as *one* of the factors to be kept in view when studying domestic

[1] M. L. Brown, Jr., trans. and ed., *American Independence through Prussian Eyes* (Durham, N. C., 1959), p. 201.
[2] Quoted in R. R. Palmer, p. 506 (*see* Bibliography, p. 76). The translations are Mr Palmer's and are quoted here with his kind permission.

politics. With the possible exception of Russia, no European government could preen itself on having given its people much reason for pride. The concessions made by England in 1783, in order to escape the military crisis, had sharp repercussions both inside and outside the halls of Parliament. The French monarchy, greatest of the apparent victors in that year, embarked almost at once upon the series of humiliating abdications of influence summarized in Chapter iv. The loudly denounced commercial treaty with England in 1786, however well-intentioned, only seemed to intensify the French sense of diplomatic misfortune. Defeats at the hands of the British hurt the Dutch leadership's domestic standing in the early 1780s, while Gustavus III's authority in Sweden gained nothing from his rash embroilment with Russia and Denmark in 1788. As for the Habsburg dominions, Joseph II's numerous ventures in Germany and the Low Countries fed the suspicion and resentment which many of his subjects felt towards him on other grounds.

A fifth definable source of unrest was similarly rooted in the official actions of public authorities. It is customary to speak of the quarter-century preceding 1789 as the age of enlightened despots *par excellence*. In almost every European country a strong ruler or minister had made determined efforts to impose reforms, at the same time clamping his own grip more tightly on the reins of power. Joseph II in Austria, Hungary, Bohemia, the Milanese and the Netherlands, Frederick II in Prussia, Pombal in Portugal, Charles III in Spain, Struensee in Denmark, Gustavus III in Sweden, Grand Duke Peter Leopold in Tuscany, Turgot and Maupeou in France, Shelburne and, for a time, the younger Pitt in England, can all be said to have satisfied the above definition, however widely they may have differed in their conceptions of Enlightenment and in the consistency with which they sought to enforce its dictates.

The important point to bear in mind here is that by the 1780s almost everywhere, save perhaps in Spain and Tuscany, enlightened despotism was in trouble, its limitations exposed to a public criticism couched in terms which reforming autocrats themselves had taught their peoples, its promise dimmed even in the eyes of many former enthusiasts among Europe's intelligentsia. The resistance was complex and highly variable from one country to the next, as we shall shortly have cause to note. A régime might be denounced as too despotic or too enlightened—that is, too unmindful of traditional interests—or both. One ruler might appear too vacillating to carry through his own projects: another, too hypocritical to act on the principles he claimed to embrace; still another, too impetuous and unrealistic to operate the complicated engine of state. Above all, however, there was a spreading conviction, the more easily expressed because 'enlightened' authorities had in many places relaxed the rules of censorship, that the best-intentioned autocrat could not be trusted to dispense final wisdom from on high.

The nature and the range of opposition must not be oversimplified. The diversity of liberal and in some cases democratic demands in itself constitutes a sixth distinct cause of confusion and acrimony. The proponents of change were deeply divided by their backgrounds, immediate aims and opinions concerning the best way to proceed. At the base of all the confused agitation lay popular demands for relief, demands which retained an unpredictable, volcanic quality disturbing even to many of the exponents of reform. Among the educated group, these exponents included middle-class agitators, who almost everywhere tended to emphasize constitutional reform. There is no doubt that they took economic freedom and opportunity very seriously as well, but the campaign to secure legal safeguards against capricious tyranny was commonly viewed as the necessary first step towards economic liberty.

It would be a great mistake to envisage all such reformers as businessmen. Their number would have been far smaller, and their influence considerably weaker, if among them there had not been many lawyers and civil servants. We shall have to return to the role of public administrators as agents of innovation in many countries during the revolutionary and Napoleonic eras. Here it should be enough to call attention to the significance of what one historian has described, referring to Germany, as 'the encouragement by the civil service (*das Beamtentum*) of politically progressive strivings in the period after 1789, but also in definite ways before'.[1] Furthermore, as already mentioned in connection with the diffusion of the Enlightenment, Europe's aristocracy itself produced a number of reformers. The Yorkshire landlords who demanded English parliamentary changes, the Marquis de Condorcet and the Comte de Mirabeau in France, Count Ignace Potocki in Poland, Baron Radishchev in Russia, these and scores of other critics of the old order were men of anything but humble origin. The general agitation of the 1780s was characterized by that extremely wide social range which throughout the western world has often marked progressivism.

The half-dozen separate factors we have now identified might appear

[1] F. Valjavec, p. 83 (*see* Bibliography, p. 76).

more than adequate to explain the specific conflicts to which we shall turn in a moment. But there is still a seventh element which must be included in our reckoning, if the nature of these struggles is to be fully understood. This is the hardening of conservative resistance to all the pressures for change, whether these came from governments or from liberal agitators. Without such resistance, there would have been many reforms effected in one country after another, doubtless with varying degrees of strain; but there would scarcely have been the series of outbursts which culminated in France.

For several generations it has been fashionable to explain the birth of modern conservatism as a natural reaction to revolutionary violence and hence, since it supposedly *followed* such violence, to treat it as a product of the 1790s and the early nineteenth century. According to this view, the revolutionary crisis of 1789 and after was a sudden attack on unsuspecting traditionalists who naturally, if tardily, sprang to the defence of old values. In direct repudiation of the sequence envisaged thus, R. R. Palmer has argued persuasively that the conservative reaction, far from beginning in the 1790s, had in fact set in well before the 1780s and that it reached a new level of intensity in that decade.[1] He asserts that revolutionary violence, when it came, was directed not against a static eighteenth-century situation but against a widespread campaign to push the Old Régime backward towards the renewed acceptance of privileges, viewed by their proponents as essential to orderly existence. Privileged groups do indeed appear to have created the rhetoric of modern conservativism in reaction not against the 'Great Revolution', but against pre-revolutionary reforms.

As we go from country to country in the pages that follow, this resistance to non-violent, often officially sponsored change will appear in a variety of forms. Generally speaking, however, its propagators all over Europe will be seen to have belonged to several groups: (1) the nobility of birth, (2) the hierarchies of established churches and (3) other constituted bodies of the old corporate system—assemblies of estates, judicial bodies such as the French *parlements*, town governments, guilds. Not *all* members of such bodies, it bears repeating, agreed that change should be opposed, much less that it should be reversed. We have already observed that individual reformers in the opposite camp were recruited from every order of society. Nevertheless,

[1] *See* Bibliography, p. 76. Palmer's interpretation of this development is central to his entire volume, but is set forth with particular emphasis in pp. 55–82 and 308–17.

without the resistance of organized conservatism, a force which had very considerable intellectual resources of its own, the ensuing narrative would have been far simpler than it in fact is.

England and Ireland

When the 1780s opened, disturbances in the British Isles seemed particularly menacing to the established order. Both the unsuccessful course of the war in America and the increased taxes it required gave rise to widespread charges of misgovernment. Demands for reform arose from sources as different as Yorkshire landowners and radical spokesmen in Parliament's home borough, Westminster. The demands of all groups concerned tended to split along separate lines, one economic or, more precisely, financial, the other political, being directed towards efforts to make the House of Commons responsive to the views of a larger fraction of the population. For a number of Whig politicians, including Edmund Burke, what came to be known as 'economical reform', especially the elimination of wasteful public expenditures, seemed both desirable in itself and advisable as a means of diverting the pressure for parliamentary reform *per se*. Such agitators as Christopher Wyvil and Sir George Savile, on the other hand, insisted that better financial administration would be an illusory gain so long as Parliament itself remained unrepresentative and corrupt.

The parliamentary reformers called for annual elections, the addition of as many as 100 county members to the Commons (thus increasing the influence of the shires relative to the boroughs) and, above all, a thorough revision in the list of boroughs sending members to Westminster. Since that list had not been brought up to date since 1678, some adjustment seemed necessary if only to give seats to the many cities which were springing into new importance in the late eighteenth century. On the other hand, these critics argued, there was need to eliminate numerous 'rotten boroughs' which had become depopulated over the years, so that some were now scarcely more than manorial villages, but which still chose members of Parliament. An M.P. selected by a single landlord, whether directly, on the basis of the lord's owning most of the local property, or indirectly, through bribes and instructions given the handful of remaining voters, did not impress the reformers as much of a bulwark against royal and ministerial influence.

Certain leading Whigs, among them Shelburne and Fox, adopted the cause of parliamentary reform, to the indignation of Burke and others among their party colleagues. Despite the distrust which the more advanced reformers felt towards these political leaders, the latter's opposition to the king and Lord North seemed by 1780 to ensure political changes. It appeared all but inevitable that major concessions would be extorted from both George III and the House of Commons as then constituted. That very year, however, two developments combined to frighten moderates out of the alliance. The first was the summons to an extra-legal General Association, issued in February by a handful of town and shire spokesmen who had assembled in London under the aegis of the Westminster radicals. The very thought of such an association's dictating to Parliament led most of the regular Whigs to abandon the entire movement—Shelburne was the only prominent exception.

Then, a few months later, came a second shock: the Gordon riots. Though actually unrelated to the constitutional question, this fiasco seemed to prove that revolutionary violence was too near the surface of English life for political changes to be safely discussed. Lord George Gordon, the unbalanced son of a Scottish duke, considered himself the appointed oracle of opposition to both the Pope in Rome and the North ministry in England. Becoming incensed over a slight measure of relief extended to Catholics in 1778 (the elimination of religious provisions from the oath of allegiance demanded of military recruits), he proceeded to make himself the centre of anti-popish agitation in the poorer neighbourhoods of London. On 2 June 1780 Lord George appeared in Parliament with a plea against religious toleration; and the crowd outside—which he periodically ran out to harangue—shortly became a raging mob. For almost a week, London was terrorized by uncontrolled looting and burning. Not only Catholic homes but also those of unpopular officials were attacked. The emptying of several prisons only increased the general panic. By the time volunteer citizens' companies finally restored order, portions of the city resembled a smoking battlefield.

While the Gordon riots completed the destruction of the broad coalition which had briefly supported some democratization of British politics, the drive against corruption continued on the two established fronts. In 1782 Burke's Economic Reform Bill became law, improving the accounts kept of public funds and working a small reduction in the annual budget by eliminating certain useless offices. At the same time, the twenty-two-year-old William Pitt, just elected to the House of Commons, moved a bill to modify parliamentary representation. It failed to pass in 1782, as did similar bills in the ensuing two years; but in 1785, now as prime minister, Pitt made his strongest bid for electoral reform. His proposal sought to eliminate thirty-six rotten boroughs, give representation in the Commons to expanding cities such as Birmingham, Manchester and Leeds, and simultaneously broaden the county franchise to include not only forty-shilling freeholders but also copyholders of land worth that much per year and certain lessees as well. Even this modest project could not get by a hostile-to-indifferent House; and with its defeat, Pitt abandoned the cause of parliamentary reform. Henceforth, he tried to make public administration increasingly honest and efficient, but in general he was content to hold power as a king's man who used 'treasury influence' to the full in marshalling political support for his ministry. Though other reformers below the ministerial level kept up the fight throughout the 1780s and on into the 1790s, their fate became bound up with English reactions to the French Revolution and thus must be treated in a later chapter.

In the same stormy period when the British Parliament found itself confronted by rebels in North America and rioters in London, it had also to face hostile agitation in Ireland. For political purposes, it should be remembered, 'Ireland' at this time meant essentially the 450,000 Anglicans or Anglo-Irish—a mere 10 per cent of the total population—plus a small number of Catholic and Presbyterian landowners. The mass of Catholic peasants, in particular, occupied a place in the thinking of Anglo-Irish leaders not much more elevated than that of Indians and Negroes in the nascent American republic. The Anglo-Irish Protestants' sense of being suspended between the British government above and a huge disenfranchised majority below conditioned every phase of the parliamentary struggle between the two islands in the 1780s.

During the course of the American war, marked as it was by rumours that a French invasion army would receive a welcome from the Irish Catholics, London agreed to the organization and arming of a local militia. This was composed of upper- and middle-class Protestants, who took the name of 'Irish Volunteers'. By 1780 the Volunteers had developed in numbers and in popularity to a point where leaders in the Irish Parliament, notably Henry Grattan and Henry Flood, could use the militia as a source of pressure upon His Majesty's government. That very year London granted an initial concession, a substantial reduction in export restrictions bearing on Irish trade. More than commerce, however, was now at stake. The Irish Parliament, though securely in the grip of the Anglican minority (Catholics could not even vote for its members until 1793), had for almost 300 years been subject to an English viceroy, the lord lieutenant. Furthermore, the Dublin body was subordinate to the commercial, diplomatic or military decisions of the British Parliament in Westminster. To escape this inferior status and to achieve equality with the British Parliament under the crown, Grattan and his fellow agitators mobilized protest meetings attended in the aggregate by tens of thousands of armed Volunteers.

Distracted by other military commitments, Lord North yielded. In 1782, the Irish Parliament was declared equal to the British, though still responsible to the lord lieutenant. Their immediate aim achieved, the Anglo-Irish abruptly ceased to protest and resumed a conservative role. Grattan's Parliament, as it was called, still rested on a House of Commons a majority of whose members were named by fewer than 100 Anglican aristocrats. Somewhat grudgingly, it did agree to grant the Irish Catholics a few small economic and legal concessions after 1782, but scraps from the table could scarcely do more than whet the appetite of the stirring masses. Meanwhile, the Volunteers had shifted their field of agitation and were demanding both a broadened electoral franchise and the elimination of Ireland's swarm of rotten boroughs.

In Ireland, as in England, parliamentary reform met total defeat. A Grand National Convention of the Volunteers in Dublin agreed in 1783 to support Flood's proposal for an expanded *Protestant* franchise, but the Irish Parliament voted the bill down by a ratio of two-and-a-half to one. The National Convention itself disbanded in 1785, amid numerous arrests and mounting censorship of anti-government publications. Meanwhile, the Irish battle lines were shifting, and no amount of repression could permanently conceal the change. Irish Catholics and disenfranchised Protestants, who had benefited not at all from Grattan's victory in 1782, were destined to become a revolutionary force beside which the memory of the Volunteers would seem pale indeed.

The United Provinces

Across the Channel, a different kind of revolution was beaten down in the Dutch United Provinces. While the immediate background of the crisis was the unsuccessful war with England, ending in 1784, the basic issues were deeply embedded in two centuries of Dutch history. The first stages of resistance to the House of Orange were marked by collaboration between the patrician regent families and the more radical

Patriots, in an effort to curb the powers of the Stadtholder, William V. Both elements felt that foreign affairs had been mismanaged and suspected that the cause was official corruption resulting from William's intervention in civil affairs. Both objected, in particular, to the stadtholder's efforts to control the choice of public officials by town councils and provincial assemblies of estates. Nevertheless, the conservative members of the opposition were early alarmed by the threat of popular agitation. Democratic orators, such as J. D. van der Capellen, a nobleman from the rural province of Overyssel, proved almost as harsh towards the merchant dynasties of the big cities as towards the House of Orange. No sooner had a Free Corps of armed burghers been formed, to offset William V's control of the army, than the division within the Patriot movement became apparent. The mutual suspicion between conservatives and radicals threatened to drown all consideration of common purposes in the National Assembly of Free Corps, meeting at Utrecht late in 1784.

During the next two years, what amounted to a three-way deadlock prevailed among (1) most of the regents, who sought to withstand the the stadtholder's claims to executive control yet avoid concessions to the populace; (2) the Patriots, who demanded election of officials by all burghers in the future; and (3) William V, who stubbornly refused to appeal to the democratic forces against his patrician enemies, though he had good precedents for doing so. The final test of strength began in Utrecht, where in 1786 the Patriots simply deposed the town council and replaced its membership with popularly chosen councillors.

As recounted in the previous chapter (p. 62), the outcome was decided by outside forces. The Patriots considered themselves pro-French, and France did in fact appear to support their cause. The stadtholder, on the other hand, could claim the sympathy of his brother-in-law, who in 1786 became King Frederick William II of Prussia, while Britain's minister in the Hague, Sir James Harris, was sparing no effort to rebuild a strong Orangist party tied to England. In the summer of 1787, sporadic fighting was already in progress between the rebellious Free Corps and William V's troops. The stadtholder's consort made an effort to race from Nimwegen to the Hague, in the hope of gaining Orangist support there; but her coach was stopped by Patriots and forced to turn back. In Berlin, her royal brother denounced this 'outrage' and, after what amounted to a peremptory ultimatum, sent a Prussian army corps across the Dutch frontier. Within a matter of weeks, the entire revolt was over, the Free Corps melting away before the regiments from Germany. The stadtholder assumed virtually royal prerogatives, guaranteed in 1788 by the treaty with England and Prussia. The regents might grumble over the prince's victory, but they could breathe more easily with the agitation suppressed. As for the Patriots, their turn was still to come, with intervention by a different France in 1795.

The Austrian Netherlands

Another major complex of revolts occurred in the dominions of Emperor Joseph II. The sharpest test took place in the Austrian Netherlands and especially in the big province of Brabant, with its active assembly of estates at Brussels. (There had been no Estates General since early in the seventeenth century.) Relatively prosperous and until the 1780s generally complacent, the Austrian Netherlands reacted first with consternation, then with anger, to Joseph's drive to modernize the Habsburg empire. By denouncing persecution of Protestants, suppressing several monasteries which he considered useless, and extending to the Low Countries the rest of his campaign against church privileges, the 'revolutionary emperor' infuriated Belgium's Catholic hierarchy. By ruling that guild monopolies and employment restrictions should end, he alienated the town oligarchies. By seeking in 1787 to abolish manorial courts, he turned the landed nobility against him.

At first, Belgian opposition to the emperor was marked by less social cleavage than had appeared in the Dutch rising. It appeared essentially conservative yet broadly based, for the defence of native tradition against the foreign innovator had the support of abbots and bankers, barons and professional men, village priests and master craftsmen. Such disagreement as existed among the rebels until the end of the 1780s was ostensibly confined to questions of tactics. Thus, the wealthy H. Van der Noot, favouring reliance on foreign aid, moved to Holland in 1788 and there sought support from the Anglo-Dutch-Prussian allies. The Brussels attorney, J. F. Vonck, took a different course, organizing from his secret headquarters in Brussels itself a patriotic Society for Hearth and Altar.

Early in 1789 the long impending storm broke at last. Against a background of popular demonstrations which Vonck's society had helped to launch, the estates of Brabant curtly announced that no further monetary tribute would be sent to Vienna. Joseph II took several months to decide on a course of action, then in June dissolved the estates and abrogated Brabant's ancient charter of provincial rights. Unfortunately for Habsburg security measures, August brought a revolution in Liège, a prince-bishopric of the Holy Roman Empire which literally bisected the Austrian Netherlands. Belgian rebels by the thousand were now able to organize companies and to drill on independent Liègeois soil, then cross back into their own homeland to confront the depleted Austrian garrisons. Before the end of 1789, in a bewildering display of military weakness, Austrian power simply evaporated in the Netherlands. One after another the Belgian provinces proclaimed their independence.

Only now, with foreign control apparently ended, did the familiar conflict between local conservatives and democrats come to light in Belgium as well. Under Van der Noot, the nobles, prelates and town fathers who dominated the assemblies of estates hardened in defence of traditional privileges, which were what they had been upholding against Joseph II all along. Around Vonck, on the other hand, tended to cluster the reformers who declared that their countrymen were free to remodel Belgian society in whatever way the majority of the people might see fit. Quickly reconvening in December 1789, the estates of Brabant seized the initiative by proclaiming themselves the sovereign authority in that province and shortly thereafter secured the accession of the other provincial estates to a loose federation of quasi-independent units concerting their policies through the hastily revived Estates General. The opposing party of Vonckists denounced the reactionary direction of these steps; but cautious as Vonck's programme of democratic reforms may seem in retrospect—he was far from espousing a truly broad franchise—it was too radical for the majority of Belgians, including the deeply religious peasantry. Aided by a veritable 'white terror', the Estates Party by March 1790 completely crushed the Vonckists, imprisoning some of their leaders while others fled abroad.

From his exile in France, Vonck warily opened negotiations with Habsburg representatives. The democratic spokesmen turned to the new Emperor Leopold II as they had never turned to his deceased brother, Joseph. Paradoxically, decisive albeit unintentional support for Leopold's effort to retake the Netherlands came from the quarrelsome and inept Estates Party leaders, who swiftly demonstrated their inability to give Belgium either peace or justice. In so doing they sapped the country's resistance to Habsburg rule; and late in 1790, when the emperor ordered his troops back in, the Austrian forces resumed control as swiftly as they had abandoned it a year before. Leopold kept his word by letting the banished Vonckists return. Further than that he would not go, for he feared the unfolding crisis in France too much to antagonize conservative forces anywhere in his empire. Time was to prove that he might well have been less deferential to the conservatives, who were little inclined to view the French innovators as allies. Instead it was the Belgian democrats who, having returned full of gratitude towards the Habsburg monarch, only to find that he contemplated no basic reforms, soon concluded that real help could come only from the side of revolutionary France.

Habsburg Central Europe

In other parts of the Habsburg empire, Joseph II's innovations stirred up variations on the Belgian theme of conservative resistance. Seeking to convert the serfs under his rule into a free peasantry, attacking the fiscal and judicial privileges of the nobility, brusquely curtailing the prerogatives of the Catholic clergy, suspending aristocratic assemblies all the way from Bohemia's Diet to Milan's Council of Sixty, he seemed bent on destroying the very foundations of social hierarchy. Finally, in February 1789, he took what seemed to traditionalists the culminating step in this direction, proclaiming a uniform land tax to be paid by nobles and non-nobles at the same rate throughout all his dominions save the Netherlands and Lombardy. When Joseph died a year later, at the age of only forty-eight, he bequeathed to his brother, Leopold II, a general crisis in Bohemia, Austria, the Tyrol, not to mention the more distant troubles in Transylvania, Belgium and the Milanese. What added a note of panic to conservative protests was the apparent danger that a popular revolt might be touched off by imperial policies. With Czech peasants and the oppressed Vlachs of Transylvania beginning to stir beneath the rule of local masters, the problem of different levels of discontent was appearing in the Austrian empire as clearly as it had in Ireland and the United Provinces.

Nowhere was the Habsburg crisis clearer than in Hungary. There the spokesmen for the aristocracy had first sought to oppose the emperor's will in the national Diet, only to have him respond by refusing to convoke that body. The Magyar nobles could still express themselves through the county assemblies or *comitats*. Joseph, however, treated their protests with angry contempt, transferring Hungary's sacred crown of St Stephen from Pressburg to Vienna in 1784, ordering that German should become the country's official language, sending in non-Magyar officials to execute his commands. He even proposed to sweep away the *comitats* in favour of a system of German-style administrative districts or *Kreise*.

To an outside observer, many of the Emperor's judicial and economic reforms appear to have had much to recommend them; but throughout his realm they simultaneously infuriated the upper classes while exciting the lower ones. The former organized secret societies, created armed bands in defiance of imperial prohibitions and in 1790 at last compelled Joseph, literally on his deathbed, to permit the Hungarian Diet to reassemble at Pest. Unfortunately for his successor's repose, this action, while it averted an open revolt by the nobility, did nothing to allay the fears and hatreds of the farm population. Like the Vlachs in Transylvania, the Hungarian peasants began a series of risings in the spring of 1790, attacking numerous manors and invoking the memory of the late Emperor in denouncing the landlords who controlled the Diet.

The outcome again revealed Leopold II's eagerness to pacify his riotous empire, even at the cost of concessions to his brother's old opponents. At the same time, it showed the effects of the peasant rebellion on the Hungarian Diet, now grudgingly resigned to some of Joseph II's less extreme reforms. An Austrian army corps marched in during August 1790 and with the aid of the Magyar nobles managed to restore order in the country. Simultaneously, the Diet abandoned its maximum demands and accepted a new *Diploma*, or charter, by which Leopold acknowledged the sanctity of many old customs, though he insisted on enforcing the permanent abolition of personal bondage, as decreed in 1781. Despite this and a few other reservations, the document must be considered a victory for the conservative opposition. The new emperor had in effect agreed to the survival of a system which his brother had sought to revolutionize from above.

Poland

A very different case, having a very different sequel, was that of Poland. It would not be accurate to speak of a Polish revolution in this period, if by that term is meant a violent repudiation of an existing government. In another sense, however, the work of the famous 'Four Years' Diet' which opened at Warsaw in October 1788 was directed toward such fundamental departures from the existing situation that it seems scarcely enough to call them reforms. Many of the issues raised elsewhere in the present chapter are discernible here too, albeit modified by the peculiar nature of the old constitution of Poland and by the acuteness of the nation's external peril.

From the outset, despite the sense of crisis which pervaded the country after the staggering losses of territory in 1772, many of the lower nobles were hostile to constitutional change. It was equally clear that among Poland's neighbours, Russia in particular was opposed to any strengthening of the kingdom and generally ready to aid all local opponents of a stronger and broader political system. On the other hand, a remarkable circle of aristocrats, including Prince Adam Czartoryski and Ignace Potocki, joined King Stanislas Poniatowski in his desire to offer Polish subjects a new basis for loyalty and confidence. Nowhere else in Europe does the American Revolution, for example, seem to have had greater intellectual and emotional appeal—not surprisingly, since one Polish hero, Pulaski, had given his life in that struggle while another, Kosciuszko, had come home to tell about it. When Catherine's war against Turkey in 1788 temporarily reduced the threat of Russian intervention, the Polish king and his fellow innovators seized the opportunity to convene the Diet in Warsaw on terms which made it virtually a constitutional convention.

Almost from the start of its deliberations, the Diet was split into something like parliamentary parties. The aristocratic Republicans were pro-Russian in foreign affairs because they opposed any reduction in Poland's 'Golden Liberty', which is to say, noble privileges. The Moderates, who represented the king most directly, hoped to make a number of specific changes without giving Russia a pretext for military action. The Patriots were more radical both in their demands for a sweeping social advance and in their defiance of outside powers. The enactments which the king finally incorporated into the Constitution of the Third of May (1791) represented most clearly the Moderates' position, but the Patriots too had reason to rejoice. The Diet voted, for example, that landless nobles should no longer attend provincial assemblies, where the 'barefoot gentry' had previously turned up by the thousand to do the bidding of this or that great lord. Another statute, sponsored by the brilliant orator, Niemcewicz, defined and extended citizenship in cities chartered by the Crown. In addition, it gave twenty-one such royal towns places in the Diet, where burghers would at last take their places beside noblemen. Still a third decision abolished the paralysing rule of unanimity in votes of the Diet, thus ending the notorious *liberum veto* by which irresponsible squires had often blocked major pieces of legislation. As proof of his unselfish determination to strengthen the central government, King Stanislas put aside his own family pride and supported the institution of a monarchy which, instead of being elective as in the past, would be hereditary in the German house of Saxony.

An air of inescapable pathos surrounds this final effort at regeneration on the part of the old Poland. Very late, though they hoped it was not too late, some of the eighteenth century's most generous and intelligent aristocrats tried to redefine Polish freedom and give it meaning for an enlarged segment of the population. At the same time, they sought to balance this freedom with enough organized authority to assure their country a chance of survival. That neighbouring monarchs, in concert with unreconstructed elements in Poland itself, moved quickly to destroy the kingdom in 1793–5 does not prove the worthlessness of the Four Years' Diet. On the contrary, their action was in part a tribute to the prospects for a Polish revival, were the new constitution allowed time to prove itself.

Reform and Reaction in Other Countries

We need not give equal attention to the political narratives of all the European states in a decade which was of course more eventful for some than for others. In Russia, though Catherine II's Charter of Nobility (1785) was a recognition of aristocratic status more nearly comparable to that of western Europe than any previously known in that empire,[1] there were no domestic tests or conflicts during the 1780s. Radishchev's *Journey from St Petersburg to Moscow*, a searing exposé of peasant suffering, was completed, it is true, in the same year as the Charter of Nobility; but it was not published until 1790. The subsequent excitement over the book really belongs to the record of foreign reactions to the French Revolution. For the time being, the tsarina simply made her deal with the nobility, and the millions who paid the price were silent.

In the Germanies, a wide range of local conditions prevailed. A few principalities, notably Württemberg, retained assemblies of estates which continued to bicker with their rulers, over finances in particular. Popular agitation for democratic reforms flared up periodically in ecclesiastical states such as Cologne and Mainz, as well as in Frankfurt, Nuremberg and several other imperial cities. Even Prussia, that

[1] M. Beloff in A. Goodwin, ed., pp. 172–89 (*see* Bibliography, p. 20).

regimented 'Sparta of the North', showed signs of internal tension. A combination of economic troubles and the unpopular administration of Frederick William II's favourites, Woellner and Bischoffwerder, produced a mounting chorus of criticism, especially from bureaucratic and commercial groups. Yet it does not appear that Germany as a whole was threatened by revolution in the 1780s. The most that can be said is that liberals and a small number of radical democrats were beginning to object to the system of small tyrannies (*Kleinstaaterei*) in terms which suggested that a revolutionary crisis originating outside the Empire might find a welcome from some elements within it.

Sweden's situation seemed potentially much more explosive than any to be found in the German lands. The aristocrats whose prerogatives of the Freedom Era had been swept away by Gustavus III in 1772 still nursed their hatred of the king. In 1786, when the crown proposed to create a paid standing army, the *Rikdsdag* followed the initiative of the nobles and refused to vote the requisite taxes. Two years later, when Gustavus threw what forces he had into the assault on Russia, a number of Swedish barons actually opened negotiations with the tsarina against him. Early in 1789 the four-house *Rikdsdag* convened once more. This time it became deadlocked through disagreement among the separate chambers, and Gustavus saw a chance to strike another blow at his titled enemies. Expelling all nobles from the session, he issued, and the remainder of the Diet willingly accepted, an Act of Union and Security. Though certain high offices and court positions were still reserved to the nobility, a remarkable degree of civil equality was henceforth guaranteed all subjects of the Swedish crown. Commoners were assured the right to own land, to be tried in proper courts and to hold offices below the few reserved to noblemen. Three years later, the king was to pay with his life for his treatment of the aristocracy, but for the time being he had given his throne a broad popular base.

In several other countries reforms imposed from above produced less furor than in Sweden, either because the reformers moved more cautiously than had Gustavus III or because they succeeded better in linking social changes to economic advance. In Denmark, after twelve years of reaction against the fallen Struensee, the able Count Bernstorff came to power in 1784 and within four years succeeded in practically wiping out what was left of serfdom. In Portugal, where the ferocious Marquis de Pombal had been ousted in 1777, the nobles were able to reduce the pace of innovation to a crawl; but at least there was no violent reaction in the 1780s. Spain under Charles III and his gifted set of ministers—Campomanes, Floridablanca, Jovellanos—was enjoying its first real agricultural and industrial expansion since the sixteenth century.[1] As mentioned earlier, the Spanish monarchy joined the Italian grand duchy of Tuscany as one of the two realms which for the time being appeared to show the clearest margin of gain on the balance sheet of enlightened despotism.

Before turning to the massive problem of France, we should fit one last, small piece into the surrounding mosaic of European politics. This involves the little republic of Geneva, the violence that flared there and the bitterness it left behind. Despite an earlier struggle in the late 1760s, the government of this independent city state remained in the hands of the office-holding citizens and the less exalted, but voting, burghers. The disenfranchised residents, or 'natives', at last revolted in 1781, demanding admission to the ranks of bourgeois voters. At first, the campaign for electoral reform appeared successful. The General Council, or town meeting, actually decided to admit to the status of burghers some 460 natives who were third-generation residents. The more aristocratic Small Council of Twenty-five rejected this concession and appealed to Geneva's 'guarantor powers', France and the two Swiss cantons of Bern and Zurich, to uphold the existing governments. In response, a French-Swiss army besieged the city for three weeks in 1782 and ultimately occupied it, though with a minimum of bloodshed. Secure once more, the patricians of the Small Council asked the guarantor powers to draft a pacification, called by its opponents the 'Black Code'. Not only did two-thirds of the newly enfranchised natives lose their rights as bourgeois, but the burghers' own General Council was stripped of all real power. The Small Council and its creatures, the four syndics, now ruled as an unrestrained oligarchy. In Geneva, however, as in Ireland, the Low Countries and various petty German states, hatred of the existing order left an ominous legacy to the coming years, when revolution moved from small arenas to an undeniably major one.

France

Since the French Revolution itself will receive special attention in Chapter VI, the only question still to be raised here concerns the place of France in European politics on the eve of that crisis. The point at issue is whether or not there was anything about the French situation

[1] R. Herr (*see* Bibliography, p. 21).

which long before 1789 marked it as peculiarly tense. In short, was the crisis in France unique from the earliest moment it can be seen developing, or was it simply another variant of the unrest we have been observing in many other lands?

The beginning of the pre-revolutionary crescendo is frequently dated from the publication in 1781 of Jacques Necker's *Compte rendu*. The choice of that event has some validity, for the printed report of the recently dismissed controller-general of finances did bring into view the royal deficit, at a time when the expenses of the American war had just been added to the endemic evils of fiscal confusion and sweeping tax exemptions. It is reasonable to see in the ensuing uproar sardonic proof that injustice and inefficiency may be tolerable for generations, until they begin to be discussed publicly, explicitly and, above all, statistically. At any rate, a mounting wave of suspicion that both economic and diplomatic affairs were being administered by incompetents loomed large in the acrimony which enveloped French public life. After 1781, for example, popular resentment towards Marie Antoinette became more and more intense. A queen who was both a spendthrift and an Austrian seemed to epitomize financial knavery on the one hand and to personify an unpopular foreign alliance on the other.

In certain respects, however, the crisis had begun to unfold as early as 1774, when Louis XVI had opened his reign by overriding Chancellor Maupeou and giving back to the parlements, the great regional law courts containing well over 1,000 aristocratic judges, all the powers taken from them in 1771. Just two years after Maupeou's fall, the king had also dismissed the Baron de Turgot as first minister, thus seeming to obliterate any hope that the worst inequities of the old society might be alleviated by energetic, royally sponsored reforms. In a very real sense, the predicament in which Louis found himself by the mid-1780s had been prepared by his own timidity and incomprehension a decade earlier.

Wherever the opening of the *general* crisis is placed, one can scarcely avoid dating the specific final one from 1786 and the decisions taken that year by the controller-general, Charles-Alexandre de Calonne. Calonne was intelligent enough to recognize that only by making the wealthy and the wellborn pay a fairer share of the state's revenues could he attack an annual deficit which had climbed to 110 million *livres*, tripling the figure of just ten years before. He was also vain enough to believe that by avoiding the brusqueness of Turgot he could induce noblemen and Catholic church leaders to consent to a new, equitable land tax and to the elimination of many regional differences in payments. The body from which he proposed to obtain this consent was to be not the Estates General, which had last met in 1614-15, but instead a smaller 'assembly of notables', handpicked by the government to discuss and approve the new measures.

The notables, mostly titled lords and high prelates with a few wealthy bourgeois added, came together in Paris early in 1787—and flatly rejected Calonne's pleas. They asserted that the privilege of exemption from taxes was sacrosanct and advised the royal administration to cut expenditures in place of trying to increase revenues. Calonne was beaten, despite a belated public appeal which only reinforced the sensation Necker's *Compte rendu* had earlier created. The notables went home, leaving the new controller-general, Loménie de Brienne, archbishop of Toulouse, to deal with the stiff-necked judicial magistrates of the parlements. The latter had to register (that is, verify and accept) any royal edict, fiscal or otherwise, in order for it to be executed by lower officials. Thus, during the long coma of the Estates General, the *parlementaires* (by this time all privileged noblemen of the robe and owners of their offices as private property) had grown accustomed to a quasilegislative role, negative though it was. Brienne did secure the parlements' overdue assent to ending the *corvée*, the enforced peasant labour to maintain roads and bridges, which would henceforth be kept up by workers paid from public funds. However, he could not induce the courts to register his watered-down version of Calonne's tax reform. The king and his finance minister wavered between sternness and appeasement, first banishing the Parlement of Paris to Troyes during the summer of 1787, only to recall it to the capital that autumn. Then, in May 1788, the government announced that the thirteen parlements would no longer exercise the power of registration, which would henceforth be vested in a single Plenary Court, to be made up of judges newly appointed by the Crown.

For the next four months France was in turmoil. What was taking place has been justly called an aristocratic revolt, centring in the resentful parlements and in certain surviving or revived provincial assemblies of estates. It should also be pointed out, however, that a wide range of public opinion was for the time being strongly favourable to the opposition. The parlementaires in particular managed to appear as spokesmen for the rights of all subjects against a corrupt court and a pack of ministerial despots. Faced with a campaign of resistance which was mounting in intensity and spreading in geographical scope, the

Crown once more backed down. In July Louis XVI pledged himself
to convene the Estates General the next year. In August Brienne
resigned and Necker was called back as finance minister. In September,
the Plenary Court was abandoned, and the parlements triumphantly
resumed their old functions.

To modern eyes it may seem strange that the French aristocracy
should have congratulated itself on having compelled the king to re-
convene the Estates General. At the very time when the government was
preparing the formal summons to the great assembly, there was mounting evidence of popular discontent which might become dangerous to
all vested interests, including those of parlementaires and other noblemen, if it found an institutional outlet. By the autumn of 1788, an
extremely bad harvest was evoking the spectre of rural famine, while
raising bread prices in the towns to almost unheard-of levels. These in
turn contributed to an industrial depression which had been developing
for several years, partly as a result of increased English competition, but
even more, it would appear, as a cyclic function of previous over-
expansion in certain areas of manufacturing. Now, the food crisis on the
farms merged with the urban difficulties to form an especially ominous
combination. Demands for higher wages inevitably followed the increasing cost of bread, and beleaguered employers, faced with rising
labour costs, defended their capital in the only way known to the eighteenth century: by laying off workers. Food scarcity and spreading
unemployment added a desperate quality to the political and social
grievances already felt by masses of Frenchmen. State taxes and
manorial dues alike began to appear not just burdensome, but literally
intolerable. The implications of all this, however, were scarcely visible
to aristocrats who hailed the Crown's surrender in the summer of 1788
as an unqualified victory for the established orders of the realm. The
sequence which would unroll from the opening of the Estates General
the following May lay hidden in the mists of the future.

Was the French case then recognizably different from the others we
have examined? Looking back from our vantage point, we can find
good reasons for saying that it was. If we call to mind the list of general
sources of unrest which were suggested at the start of this chapter—
(1) economic strains resulting from demographic and technological
change; (2) the political ideas stemming from the debates of the
Enlightenment; (3) the direct influence of the American Revolution;
(4) frustrating reverses in foreign affairs; (5) the policies of often well-
intentioned but seldom energetic or consistent public administrators;

(6) demands for change advanced by a variety of liberal or democratic critics; and (7) the stiffening of conservative resistance—we note that *all* were represented to a marked degree in the developing French crisis.[1] As so often before and since, every wind blowing across Europe seemed to converge on France.

In two other respects France's situation has impressed subsequent observers as peculiarly acute. First, this was, despite its size, the most centralized nation in all of eighteenth-century Europe, a nation quickly responsive to events taking place at its centre, Paris. In creating such a centralized structure, as Tocqueville pointed out more than a century ago, the old monarchy itself had prepared the stage for a national revolution. The second difference between the French crisis and any of the others we have discussed lay in a unique combination of power, prestige and physical location. Any major development in France was bound to be felt almost immediately everywhere else in Europe. On the other hand, no foreign monarch who found such a development unsettling could reverse the tide of events merely by sending in a small military force, as Frederick William II had done in Holland, Leopold II in Belgium and Hungary, or Louis XVI himself in Geneva. If outsiders proposed to intervene in France, they could do so only at the cost of a European convulsion.

Thus *we* reason and reflect, looking back at 1789 across the tumultuous quarter-century which was about to begin. From all that has been said, however, we should be prepared to sympathize with the many contemporaries who thought they saw elsewhere, especially in Great Britain and in the Habsburg dominions, revolutionary portents at least as serious as any then visible in France. This appeared to be equally true whether the threat of revolution was visualized as chiefly concerned with legal, financial and social privileges or was supposed to relate to the distribution of political power within the state. If the former, then the Austrian empire of Joseph II was a likely testing ground. If the latter, there seemed to be little need to look beyond England, that home of constitutional strife in the preceding century.

We may understand the problem most clearly by asking ourselves

[1] In addition to C. E. Labrousse (*see* Bibliography, p. 76), monographs devoted to special aspects of causation in the French case include D. Mornet, *Les origines intellectuelles de la Révolution française, 1715-1787* (Paris, 1933), and D. Echeverria, *Mirage in the West: A History of the French Image of American Society to 1815* (Princeton, 1957).

what a European living in the 1780s conceived a revolution, any revolution, to be. What model did he have, given the historical lessons available to him? Was revolution essentially a popular rising in vast reaches of the countryside, a *jacquerie* like the German Peasants' Revolt in the 1520s or Pugachev's rebellion in Russia during the 1770s? Or was it more likely to be an outburst of urban mobs, swept along by a religious passion or aimless frenzy, as in the Paris of the St Bartholomew's Day massacre or in the London of the Gordon riots? Was it best represented as a struggle for regional independence, on the pattern of Dutchmen against Spain in the sixteenth and seventeenth centuries or of Americans against Britain in the eighteenth? Or was it, first and foremost, an internal political contest—and if so, should it be expected to recall the aristocratic *Fronde* of Louis XIV's boyhood, the English parliament's assault on Stuart absolutist claims or conversely, a palace coup such as Sweden's King Gustavus III had engineered as recently as 1772?

Many intelligent men before 1789 realized that a revolution need not always assume just one of these guises and that two or even three different kinds of revolution might be interwoven. It is unlikely, however, that anyone visualized a revolution which would incorporate elements of *all* the known precedents, bringing together the rural *jacquerie* and the violence of town mobs, mingling aristocratic, liberal and absolutist political claims, reawakening separatist impulses in outlying provinces which would bedevil the revolutionaries themselves. It was precisely because Europe's turmoil in the 1780s involved so many levels and lines of conflict that the situation proved bewildering to onlookers. And because the French Revolution, when it came, proved to be a whole cluster of revolutions, it has remained, in the words of an American scholar, 'one of the few events of modern history towards which, even today, a man may entertain a feeling of awe'.[1]

[1] C. Brinton, *A Decade of Revolution* (*see* Bibliographical Note, p. 392).

VI

The Upheaval in France

By the autumn of 1788, as we have seen, the royal administration in France had bowed to the demands of privileged opposition groups. Louis XVI's promise to convene the Estates General was greeted by such groups as an admission that the traditional social structure of the kingdom must be reconsecrated in defiance of the Crown's own

BIBLIOGRAPHY. Certain works of interest here live on as monuments of historical literature, though long superseded by more careful research. Two such are T. Carlyle, *The French Revolution*, ed. C. Fletcher (New York, 1902), first published in 1837; and J. Michelet, *Histoire de la Révolution française*, written between 1848 and 1851 (rev. edn., Paris, 1952). Others among the now classic studies retain their interest primarily because of their authors' strongly expressed viewpoints. Thus, A. Aulard, *The French Revolution: A Political History, 1789–1804* (London, 1910), is the English translation of the most thorough treatment in what might be called the 'official' terms of the Third Republic. J. Jaurès, *Histoire socialiste de la Révolution française* (Paris, 1922–24), as the title indicates, takes an entirely different point of departure. More extreme even than Jaurès in his attack on Aulard from a Marxist angle was the work first published in 1921 by the formidable A. Mathiez, *The French Revolution* (New York, 1962). Beside several general works to be noted in the Bibliographical Note, *see* M. Göhring, *Geschichte der grossen Revolution* (Tübingen, 1950–51). In the present chapter's footnotes will be found references to a number of valuable monographs; but a selected handful of other works on special topics should be cited at once. C. Brinton, *The Jacobins* (New York, 1930), was recognized from the day of its appearance as a pioneering application of historical sociology. Another American, R. R. Palmer, has written a comparably significant study of the Committee of Public Safety, *Twelve Who Ruled* (rev. edn., Princeton, 1958). A more recent handbook, masterfully summarizing the expressions of opposition to successive regimes between 1789 and 1804, is J. Godechot, *La contre-révolution* (Paris, 1961). Finally, notice should be taken of D. Greer's invaluable statistical summary, *The Incidence of the Terror during the French Revolution* (Cambridge, Mass., 1935). A cogently argued interpretation, that not a modern capitalist class but an older-style bourgeoisie 'won' the struggle, is presented by A. Cobban, *The Social Interpretation of the French Revolution* (Cambridge, 1964).

projects for reform. Events were to show that the view of this as simply a struggle between the government and its conservative critics was both superficial and extremely misleading. We can easily recognize other sorts of conflict developing in the months before the Estates assembled, if we remind ourselves of the different social categories introduced in Chapter III.

From Estates General to National Assembly

We have observed that, whatever eighteenth-century theorists liked to believe, legally defined orders were far from being society's only meaningful divisions. But even if orders *had* occupied this unique position, the relations among them in late 1788 and early 1789 promised tension and acrimony enough. The leaders of the clergy (First Estate) were well aware of past occasions when the nobility (Second) and commons (Third) had joined forces to make the Church bear the brunt of financial contributions to the Crown. The lay nobles, on the other hand, looked enviously at the riches of the ecclesiastical establishment, while at the same time denouncing the pleas of non-nobles for progress towards legal equality. Above all, spokesmen for the Third Estate, including a host of busy journalists, were demanding recognition of the fact that over 97 per cent of all French subjects were neither clergymen nor nobles. The Abbé Sieyès, for example, in his famous pamphlet, published early in 1789, *What is the Third Estate?* answered his own question in a word: 'everything', and added: 'What does it ask? To be something'. Specifically, these voices urged that the number of deputies accorded the Third Estate should be equal in number to those of the other two estates combined.

The king and Necker conceded this point with deceptive speed, announcing that in the elections set for March and April 1789 the First and Second Estates were to choose 300 delegates apiece, while practically all other adult males, voting through a complicated system of district and subdistrict electoral assemblies, would name some 600 representatives. The 'doubling of the Third', however, still did not settle the question whether voting in the assembly of Estates itself was to be by head or by order. If the former, then the commons had indeed won a great victory; but if each of the three Estates was simply to agree, as in the past, on how its single, corporate vote should be cast, then to have more delegates would constitute no advantage. Despite mounting pressure to clarify this point, the government refused to make a decision in advance. Meanwhile, since the parlements roundly denounced the claims of the Third Estate, the aristocratic judges lost their earlier popularity with bewildering abruptness. Instead of seeming to be tribunes of resistance to despotism, they now impressed more and more Frenchmen as reactionary exponents of the nobility's interests.

These rifts in the original opposition to the royal tax programme were clearly recognizable at the time, because they were taking place within the acknowledged system of orders. How much more confusing, then, were the clashes along what we should consider more specifically economic, honorific and political lines. Through the lists (*cahiers*) of grievances drawn up by the various electoral assemblies to guide their chosen representatives, poor men cried out against manorial dues, ground rents, low pay and high prices. Late April 1789 brought the Revolution's first outbreak of mob violence in Paris, the *affaire Reveillon*, which entailed two days of rioting in the Faubourg Saint-Antoine, with twenty-five deaths at the time and three subsequent executions. This outburst, it should be noted, was touched off not by antimonarchist or antinoble passions but by the public statements of Reveillon and another rich manufacturer in favour of lower wage scales. It was, in short, an expression of class hatred in the modern sense.

At the same time the status consciousness of various groups was being exacerbated by such arguments as those over ceremonial arrangements in the approaching Estates General. The commons ended by agreeing to march first (the least dignified position) in all processions, to occupy the lowest seats at any joint session of the three chambers and to wear simple black suits and tricorns, in contrast to the high clergy's brilliant robes and the nobility's plumes and satins. Yet at the very time when these provisions were being more or less sullenly accepted, a curious and significant reversal of status was becoming discernible. Responding to this change, the Count de Mirabeau and the Abbé Sieyès, along with certain other nobles and clergymen, decided to stand for election to the Third Estate, as the most 'honourable' segment of society. Even within the Third, however, status rivalry embittered the spring elections. In countless towns the enrolled bourgeoisie, which had long controlled local affairs, resented, and was resented by, the other inhabitants who now found themselves able to vote under the new national franchise.

Conflict of an explicitly political nature also began to emerge at the very outset of the Revolution, though its outlines were naturally indistinct until a legislative forum was created. Through the pamphlet wars and public speeches of the winter of 1788-9, there took shape a rough division not unlike the split within the Polish Diet then meeting in Warsaw (*see above*, p. 94). Men differing widely in birth, occupation and economic position found themselves allied either in defence of what they considered the ancient constitution of France, or in support of moderate reforms, or in agitation for fundamental changes in society and government. Thus the interplay of orders, classes and status groups was more pregnant with implications for the future than any single level of conflict would have been alone, not least because that very interplay was producing still another element: parties in the broadly political sense.

Despite confusion and recriminations, the spring elections did manage to produce the requisite lists of deputies to assemble at Versailles, where deliberations opened on 5 May. The roughly 600 deputies of the Third Estate were clearly dominated by lawyers, constituting over half their number. Other major groups of commoners included government officials (many of them also lawyers by training), merchants, investors and representatives of the liberal professions, especially medicine. Farmers and workmen were apparently to be represented only by their social and economic betters. The nobles included some individuals, such as the Marquis de Lafayette, who were willing to consider reforms but very few not bound by their constituents to reject any basic social change. Deputies of the First Estate were divided between prelates on the one hand and, on the other, a large number of parish priests, many of them quite radical in outlook.

From the first it was clear that until the voting issue was settled there would be no way of determining what kind of legislative body had been called into being. Charged by the Crown with the responsibility for deciding this question, the three Estates fell into six weeks of apparent deadlock. The clergy and the nobility (though the vote in the First Estate was only 133 to 114) favoured separate deliberations and final voting by order. The Third insisted with growing vehemence on a merger of the three chambers and voting by individual deputies. Finally, on 17 June, the commons adopted the title of 'National Assembly' and bluntly invited the other two orders to join them.

In one of his characteristic oscillations between severity and surrender, the king first yielded to the court party led by his brother, the Count d'Artois, and tried to coerce the Third Estate. On 20 June he ordered that the commons be locked out of their meeting hall, only to learn that they had adjourned to a nearby tennis court (the game was then played exclusively indoors) and had there pledged themselves not to dissolve until they had written a new constitution. In response to the Tennis Court Oath, which had finally enlisted the more cautious members of the Third on the side of defiance, Louis directed the commons to stop all talk of a National Assembly and to proceed with deliberations as one of the three established orders. The deputies, though avoiding explicit disrespect, simply ignored the royal command. On 27 June, by which time a clear majority of the clergy and about fifty of the nobility were sitting with the erstwhile Third Estate, the king suddenly gave in, appealing to the remaining noble and ecclesiastical deputies to join what thus emerged as a single body. The Estates General had become the National Assembly.

The Declaration of the Rights of Man

In his famous work on 1789,[1] Georges Lefebvre suggests that while an aristocratic revolution had been necessary to bring the Estates back to life, what was happening between early May and late June amounted to a second revolution, this one engineered by the lawyers, civil servants and businessmen of the Third Estate. Even these two revolutions might yet have been undone if the upper and middle strata of society alone had confronted the power of the Crown. Lefebvre argues that although Louis XVI remained unclear about the best course of action and was probably most concerned with avoiding bloodshed, a royalist *coup d'état*, using the army to arrest some and disperse the rest of the deputies at Versailles, was a genuine possibility at the beginning of July. On 8 July Mirabeau rose before the Assembly to point with alarm to the military forces, perhaps as many as 20,000 soldiers, then pouring in to reinforce the regular garrisons of the Paris-Versailles region. On the 11th, while demands that these regiments be sent away still echoed in the wake of Mirabeau's speech, the king suddenly dismissed Necker as controller-general, replacing this most popular of his ministers with the Baron de Breteuil, a member of Queen Marie Antoinette's circle of courtiers. Necker was known to have opposed the royal attempt at repression preceding the Tennis Court Oath, and his displacement was greeted by many as a signal that the National Assembly and its supporters in the capital were about to be crushed by armed force.

The result in hungry Paris was anxiety which quickly turned to violence. For two days, 12 and 13 July, impromptu parades and public

[1] *The Coming of the French Revolution* (Princeton, 1947), *passim*.

meetings helped to whip up feelings of fear and anger. Just how this excitement was channelled into an assault on the Bastille nevertheless remains a mystery, for the impulse to storm the old prison fortress on the eastern edge of the city seemed to arise spontaneously in a number of places and amid various groups of men. At any rate, early on the morning of 14 July a crowd began to form outside the Bastille's main gate and negotiations designed to preclude any army action against the populace were opened between self-appointed civic leaders and the commandant. The latter, with only about 100 men under his command, was inclined to make concessions, perhaps even to surrender the fort itself: but the crowd, growing in size and increasing its armaments with each passing hour, became impatient. When desultory attacks on the outer courtyard drew fire from the garrison, a murderous onslaught developed. Before it was over, perhaps as many as 125 of the crowd were dead; but the Bastille was taken, soon to be demolished and its stones distributed far and wide as sacred relics of freedom. The commandant and several of his men were killed after surrendering. All the prisoners were released from the cells, which had been expected to yield up a number of political martyrs but in fact proved to contain just five convicted criminals and two pitiful lunatics.

Thus, to the aristocratic and middle-class revolutions, a third, popular revolution had lent its shock effect. The very next day, 15 July, the king spoke to the Assembly at Versailles, announcing the re-appointment of Necker, promising the dispersal of the extra troops and explaining, perhaps quite truthfully, that they had never been intended for anything beyond the maintenance of order. Even now, however, there was still the possibility of a reversal in the course of events if all revolutionary activity remained limited to Paris and a few other cities; for the countryside might offer the nobility a base for counter-offensive action. Hence, again according to Lefebvre, a fourth revolution may have been a prerequisite to sustain the momentum created by the other three. This wave entailed widespread risings in rural areas.

There had been certain earlier attacks on manor houses, with the express aim of destroying leases and other documentary records of peasant indebtedness. In addition, raids on grain convoys by desperate villagers had been reported in various parts of France for several months past. But in late July and August peasant risings assumed a new intensity, seemingly explained by the fear that either an aristocratic reaction or an invasion by brigands, or both, would drench the countryside in blood unless local vigilantes armed and struck first. This was the 'Great

Fear' of 1789, a complex agrarian panic which greatly increased the incidence of château burnings—and thus worked back upon the deliberations at Versailles.

It was in such circumstances, with the royal government apparently cowed and with both town and country folk engaged in sporadic violence, that the National Assembly took its first major legislative steps. One of these comprised the resolutions voted on the night of 4 August, together with the acts subsequently passed to give them legal force. The other was the Declaration of the Rights of Man and of the Citizen.

It is not quite accurate to say that the night of the Fourth of August 'abolished feudalism', since *feudal* relations in the technical, medieval sense of relations between knightly vassals and their superiors or suzerains were scarcely at issue. What the Assembly did do was to abolish the legal basis of the *manorial* system, as well as countless noble, ecclesiastical, corporate and provincial privileges. As speaker after speaker rose to renounce on behalf of his order or his locality some ancient right or exemption, the structure of the old society seemed to crumble before men's eyes. Consider only the most striking features of that society which were now declared at an end: peasant dues based on personal subjection to a lord; all differences between nobles and commoners in matters of taxation as well as in judicial penalties; regional variations in tax rates; seigneurial as opposed to public tribunals; the ownership of public offices as private property, including the immensely valuable seats in the parlements and other sovereign courts; all church tithes and the annates previously sent to the Vatican; even the guilds' old restrictions on freedom to pursue a trade or craft. Some of these measures were reworded more cautiously in the days that followed; and the Assembly showed its concern for property rights by voting that officeholders should be paid for their lost offices and landlords compensated for the sacrifice of any income not based on earlier serfdom. Nevertheless, it is difficult to escape the conviction that after 4 August the *ancien régime* in France was dead at its roots.

To this assault on old arrangements, the Assembly added a positive catalogue of principles to be followed in the making of the new constitution. The Declaration of the Rights of Man was formally adopted on 26 August, after several weeks of debate. When the Declaration announces in Article 1 that 'men are born and remain free and equal in rights', in Article 2 that 'these rights are liberty, property, security and resistance to oppression', and in Article 3 that 'all sovereignty rests essentially in the nation', it seems an abstract manifesto of liberalism.

However, critics who have dismissed it as only that have missed the hard, specific quality of many of the other articles. For the framers also had in mind a list of problems with which eighteenth-century Frenchmen were only too familiar. They stipulated, for example, that 'every citizen may ... speak, write and print freely' (Article 11); that 'no man may be indicted, arrested or detained except in cases determined by law' (Article 7); that 'only strictly necessary punishments may be established' (Article 8); that every man must 'be presumed innocent until judged guilty' (Article 9); and that 'all citizens have the right ... to have demonstrated to them the necessity of public taxes [and] to consent to them freely' (Article 14). These points struck at particular abuses.

The incident which completed the initial drama of 1789 was the march on Versailles of 5 October. That day a large crowd of women formed in Paris, shouting for bread but also demanding that the king give his approval to the decrees of 4 August and to the Declaration of the Rights of Man. The women, accompanied and to an unascertainable extent perhaps led by male agitators, made the five-hour walk to Versailles and there invaded the Assembly's meeting place. In due course a delegation of marchers was admitted to the royal palace itself; and after some temporizing, Louis announced his acceptance of the August legislation, as well as his determination to rush food supplies to Paris. Still the crowd would not break up, but instead spent the night before the palace gates. In the cold, wet dawn of 6 October rioters burst into the great courtyard, insisting that the royal family move to Paris, where the king could be protected by his people—presumably against his courtiers. Once more Louis XVI yielded, this time loading Marie Antoinette, the Dauphin or crown prince and himself into a coach which the now jubilant mob escorted back to the capital. Ahead of it ran the cry that 'the baker, the baker's wife and the baker's boy' were on their way. With the royal family ensconced at the Tuileries in Paris, the National Assembly decided that it too should move into the capital. Henceforth, the political centre of France would be not Versailles, with its elegant parks and stately halls, but a great city of teeming streets and immense explosive power.

The Monarchical Experiment

For the next three years, French politics witnessed an effort to find both freedom and stability under constitutional monarchy. It was an effort which disintegrated progressively over the second half of this period and which, even at the beginning, was beset by a host of difficulties. Quite aside from the task of devising new foundations of government (the National Assembly was called the 'Constituent Assembly' with increasing frequency after its move to Paris), royal officials and elected deputies shared a common concern with a number of individual problems. These included feeding the kingdom, reordering its local administration, buttressing its financial position, regulating the status of the Roman Catholic Church in France, creating dependable armed forces and conducting relations with foreign states. On the degree of success achieved by the Crown and the Assembly in attacking such issues, as well as on the shape of the emerging constitution, would depend the fate of what has been called 'the monarchical experiment'.[1]

Louis XVI is best known to history as a good man because of his lack of cruelty and his freedom from personal vices, but a bad king because of indecisiveness and inconsistency which on occasion produced effects indistinguishable from those of conscious deceit. In 1789, in 1790 and, indeed, well into 1791 he still possessed some considerable political assets. The aura of consecrated royalty was not quickly dispelled. Popular hatred of many of his advisers and even of his queen seldom extended to him personally. 'If our father, the king, only knew' was a common expression in the mouths of even his angriest subjects. Not one of the hundreds of *cahiers* of grievances drawn up for the Estates General had been an antimonarchical document. Yet the facts of power and the tides of opinion were such that in all probability only a royal genius, and perhaps not even he, could have ridden out the stormy transition from theoretically absolute to expressly limited monarchy. He would have had to assume the role of arbiter, above parties and special interest groups. In particular, he would have had to repudiate, or at least very sharply reduce, his special concern for the nobility and a privileged church. How could poor, phlegmatic Louis XVI, with his gift for showing stubbornness or docility at just the wrong times, comprehend his demanding situation?

The Assembly too faced dilemmas and difficult choices. In the debates of August and September 1789 a clear party division emerged with respect to constitutional principles. J. J. Mounier, a lower court judge from Dauphiné in south-eastern France, chief framer of the Tennis Court Oath and leading member of the first committee on the constitution, was the spokesman for what might be called the moderate

[1] C. Brinton, *Decade*, pp. 1–63 (*see* Bibliographical Note, p. 392).

wing. That is, he and his supporters favoured a set of checks and balances which reflected their admiration for the British system as earlier portrayed by Montesquieu, as well as for the new government of the United States. They urged that the king be recognized as an important factor, that an absolute royal veto over legislation be written into the constitution, and that the future lawmaking body include in addition to a democratic lower chamber, an upper house or senate, not hereditary but reserved to the wellborn and the rich.

Opposing these views stood a faction led by the Abbé Sieyès, one of the three members of the clergy chosen as deputies of the Third Estate the previous spring. As a speaker in the Assembly, Sieyès brushed aside arguments that the royal veto might actually protect popular interests against aristocratic machinations. He did not trust the king and asserted flatly that no good could come from diluting the sovereignty of the people by surrendering great executive authority to a monarch. In addition, he denounced Mounier, quite unfairly, for wishing to save a privileged nobility by instituting an upper legislative chamber. While many other speakers took the floor during the months of debate, the conflict between Mounier and Sieyès brought the issues into particularly sharp focus.

The formal outcome was embodied in the constitution which went into effect only in 1791. The basic decisions, however, had actually been reached before the end of 1789. On 10 September, for example, the Assembly overwhelmingly endorsed the one-house legislature favoured by Sieyès. The next day, embracing a compromise arranged by a group around Lafayette, the deputies voted to give the king no more than a suspensive veto, which would permit him to delay legislation for a maximum of four years. When these decisions were announced, Mounier resigned from the constitutional committee in disgust and soon afterward went home to Dauphiné, the first step on his road to exile.[1]

The prickly question of the franchise was finally settled by classifying as a citizen every male twenty-five or more years old who had lived in one locality for a year and was not a domestic servant, but then stipulating that only those who paid taxes equivalent to three days' wages could vote as 'active' citizens in the lower or primary electoral assemblies. This provision reduced to 'passive' citizenship about one-fourth of the 6 million or more men who would otherwise have qualified as voters. In addition, it was initially decided that payment of direct

[1] On this important, but neglected figure, see J. Egret, *La Révolution des notables: Mounier et les monarchiens, 1789* (Paris, 1950).

taxes worth *ten* days' wages was required to entitle an active citizen to be an elector in the higher assemblies which would choose all important elective officials, including national legislators. Finally, national deputies would be recruited only from payers of taxes worth a silver mark

2. *The French Republic by Departments (1790)*

(54 livres), or as much as ten times the amount set for electors in low-wage areas. Despite certain changes introduced by the Constituent in its last weeks, the above provisions governed the election to the new Legislative Assembly, the only national body chosen under the Constitution of 1791.

Between the National Constituent Assembly, from June 1789 to its dissolution on 30 September 1791, and the Legislative Assembly, which convened the very next day and lasted until September 1792, the change of personnel was complete; for the Constituent had voted to make its own members ineligible for places in the Legislative. Even earlier, many familiar figures had left the political arena, whether by choice, as in the case of Mounier and that of Necker (who resigned from his ministerial post in the late summer of 1790), or by death, as when Mirabeau succumbed to a long illness in April 1791. For the moment, however, it seems best to consider this period of limited monarchy as a whole, noting the handling of the urgent problems mentioned above, the growing opposition to measures adopted and the circumstances under which the monarchy finally collapsed.

There is not much to be said about the food crisis, though it impinged on the political situation on many occasions, obviously including the October Days of 1789 when the women marched on Versailles. For months thereafter, all the government could do to stave off massive riots was periodically to release stored grain and to send emergency shipments into Paris and other large cities. Then, with the excellent harvest of 1790, the threat of famine receded, not to return in full force until after the monarchy's fall and the establishment of the Republic.

To administer the distribution of food and other matters affecting public order, a system of local administration was urgently needed in place of the welter of provincial and municipal régimes doomed on the night of 4 August. The new structure, as elaborated in 1790, provided for eighty-three *départements*, each named for a geographical feature of its area—Seine–Inférieure, Basses–Pyrénées, Haut–Rhin—in direct repudiation of the historic names of provinces such as Normandy, Béarn or Alsace. Each department comprised several districts, each district two or more cantons and each canton a number of communes. At every level, from the municipal or rural council and mayor of a commune up to the council, the directory and the syndic-procurator-general of a department, popularly elected officials were charged with administration. It soon became apparent that merely establishing such institutions did not make skilful officials out of illiterate farmers and previously humble townsmen. The system created in 1790 nevertheless provided the units from which the departmental, district and local hierarchy of modern France would be fashioned by Napoleon.

More pressing in 1789–92 than administrative needs or even food shortages was the issue of national finances. 'Patriotic loans', emergency taxes, dramatic appeals for public contributions of jewellery and precious metals, all failed to halt the flight of capital abroad. The difficulty of collecting taxes from a population inclined to see in the Revolution an end to taxation itself is shown by the fact that only one-third of the revenues due by the end of 1791 had actually been paid a full year later. Desperately seeking an escape from this fiscal crisis, the Assembly had long before, in November 1789, voted that ecclesiastical property could be disposed of for the good of the nation. In due course, as more and more nobles fled the country, the confiscated belongings of emigrants were added to those of the clergy as *biens nationaux*. The latter, amounting to as much as 25 per cent of the land in some departments, in turn formed the backing for what quickly became the new paper currency of France, the *assignats*. In theory the assignats were notes given to creditors of the government, who could use them to buy confiscated land. Actually, however, by August 1790, when it authorized the issue of additional assignats worth 800 million livres, the Assembly not only tripled the amount in circulation but also made the notes legal tender, that is, currency in the full sense.

The new medium of exchange proved, despite later abuses and inflation, a more successful answer to the government's financial needs than most economic historians used to be willing to admit.[1] The liquidation of the *biens nationaux* also had important political results, in that countless middle-class farmers and businessmen, who had bought confiscated property at relatively low prices, found themselves the beneficiaries of a revolution they could not afford to see reversed. These developments, however, also involved tense relations between the constitutional monarchy and the Catholic Church. The Assembly, in seizing church lands, had accepted responsibility for supporting at least the secular clergy (monks and nuns were strongly urged by the state to renounce their religious vows). On 12 July 1790 the Civil Constitution of the Clergy became law, providing for the selection of priests by district electoral assemblies, the abolition of the old episcopal dioceses in favour of new ones corresponding to departmental boundaries, and payment of bishops and priests by the government. All papal jurisdiction in France was terminated. Within a year, Pope Pius VI formally condemned the Civil Constitution and, indeed, the entire Revolution. In France itself, while many 'constitutional' clergymen accepted their new relationship to the state, 'refractory' priests were now classified as public enemies and in some instances, with the support of pious laymen, behaved accordingly.[2]

[1] S. Harris, *The Assignats* (Cambridge, Mass., 1930), defends the wisdom and relative success of the revolutionary currency issues.
[2] P. de La Gorce, *Histoire religieuse de la Révolution française* (Paris, 1912–23), esp. vols. I and II.

Along with all its other problems, the French government had serious military and diplomatic worries. The Constitutional Assembly, by removing the army and navy from the king's authority, had created a situation in which military advancement depended on a curious mixture of elections and seniority. The creation of the National Guard, a militia in which every man who claimed to be an active citizen must enrol, further confused the organization and distribution of armed power in the country. Many regiments, embittered by the irregularity of their pay, were demoralized by mingling with the civilian demonstrators in garrison towns. In August 1790, for example, the three regiments at Nancy in Lorraine, two of them French and the other Swiss, joined forces with a disorderly mob in a wild mutiny put down by other troops only after a pitched battle which killed 400 men of the loyal units alone. A parallel naval mutiny occurred the next month at the Atlantic port of Brest. The emigration of nobles inevitably decimated the corps of trained officers, while even the veteran commanders still willing to serve France were in despair at the disorder confronting them.

The military confusion helps both to explain the indecisiveness of the National Constituent Assembly in foreign affairs and to emphasize the bravado shown by its successor when it declared war on two major powers in 1792. Early in 1790, for example, Spain demanded French help against England in the Nootka Sound dispute over rights of navigation and settlement on the Pacific coast of North America. Louis XVI felt compelled by the old family ties between French and Spanish to offer naval aid. The Assembly, however, amid speeches to the effect that treaties not originally approved by the people through their representatives could not be viewed as binding, postponed a decision until the Spanish despaired of French assistance and yielded to the British terms. In the course of the debates that spring the French Assembly soared away from the question of Nootka Sound to renounce all warfare designed to reduce the liberties of other peoples. This was unquestionably the high point of revolutionary pacificism, which would give way to a frankly crusading spirit only by degrees. Even in September 1791, when the expiring National Assembly voted to annex the former papal principality of Avignon in southern France, it insisted that this was not a conquest but the welcoming of fellow Frenchmen who had revolted against a foreign tyrant. Still, the very nature of the distinction suggested certain ambiguities for the future.

The crux of the foreign situation appeared to the National Assembly, and still more alarmingly to the Legislative after it, to be the threat of invasion by the armies of anti-revolutionary monarchs. In late August 1791, King Frederick William II of Prussia and Emperor Leopold II held a personal meeting at Pillnitz in Bohemia. At its close they issued what both seem to have considered a cautious assurance that while concerned about the safety of Louis XVI, neither of them would move against France without the concurrence of England and the other powers. The French, however, found little comfort in a statement which implied that, in certain circumstances, they *might* be attacked. It was also known in Paris that Leopold's son, who became Emperor Francis II on his father's death early in 1792, was much more bellicose than his predecessor. Quite apart from foreign threats, culminating in the new Austro-Prussian alliance of 7 February 1792, some of the most eloquent political leaders in France were becoming convinced that war could both unite the nation and strike down its enemies abroad. Men such as General Dumouriez, a foe of Austria, and the Girondin chieftains, Roland and Brissot de Warville, demanded action against foreign tyrants. The Girondin party, which had not yet split off from the mass of Jacobin deputies, was in fact the most consistently aggressive influence in the Legislative Assembly throughout the period which ended on 20 April 1792 with the declaration of war on Austria and Prussia.

The Fall of the Monarchy

With the outbreak of formal hostilities, the monarchical experiment entered its final stage. Although that experiment had almost from its inception alienated many aristocrats and ecclesiastics who rejected the changes taking place, a still more potent source of political dissatisfaction lay in the opposite conviction, namely, that the Revolution was not being pushed far enough. In particular, the network of local political clubs that took their lead from the Society of Friends of the Constitution in Paris and their famous nickname from the old Jacobin monastery in which it met, provided an ample hearing for radical critics of limited monarchy. Not only in their clubs but through the press, the speeches of orators such as Robespierre and the discussions of communal councils, the more extreme Jacobins kept up a running fire upon 'aristocrats', clericals, pro-Austrians and other alleged enemies of France.

By the summer of 1791 the acridity of the political atmosphere belied the official agreement between the king and the National Assembly over the constitution then being completed. It was in this tense situation, on the night of 20–21 June, that Louis XVI took the fateful step of attempting to escape from the 'protection' of Paris. Slipping out of the Tuileries with his family, the king was driven eastward in a heavily curtained coach, only to be recognized and stopped at Varennes-en-Argonne. It has never been clear whether the flight to Varennes was intended only to place the monarch among loyal troops in Lorraine or whether Louis meant to claim asylum in Luxembourg with the Austrian forces of his imperial brother-in-law. In any case, the king was brought back to Paris and temporarily shielded from public wrath by the rather lame announcement that he had been kidnapped but happily rescued from his abductors.

Despite this official version, for many knowledgeable people the flight to Varennes doomed the constitutional monarchy even before its constitution was promulgated. Loyalist army officers, for example, began to emigrate in sharply increased numbers. Radical politicians in general and the more extreme Jacobins in particular became openly republican, hinting broadly that the king should be viewed as a traitor. For one more year, however, the appearance of parliamentary-royal compromise was maintained. The Legislative Assembly, elected that summer and convened on 1 October, had no aristocratic-clerical wing, such as had survived in the National; but it did have a moderately conservative group on the right, called the *Feuillants*, while a clear majority in the centre still rejected the anti-royalist demands of the Jacobin left. The latter, be it noted, was deprived of Robespierre and several of its other parliamentary spokesmen by the self-denying ordinance which prevented deputies in the National Assembly from coming back to serve in the Legislative.

It was in local government, above all in the forty-eight wards or *sections* of Paris, that the republican agitators found their alternative field of action. As the assembly of one section after another fell under Jacobin control, conservative elements became either too frightened or too discouraged to take much part in Parisian politics. On 30 July 1792 Danton's own section announced that it would henceforth disregard the distinction between 'passive' and 'active' citizens. This obvious effort to attract support from residents too poor to meet the property requirement for voting was an unabashed repudiation of the Constitution. The next day, another important ward assembly voted to march to the Legislative Assembly on 5 August and invited other sections to join it in demanding that Louis XVI be stripped of his royalty.

The violence that marked the end of the monarchy came in two waves. During the night of 9–10 August, a new revolutionary Commune elected by the sections threw the members of the established Paris Commune out of their meeting room in the city hall, placed a Jacobin in command of the National Guard and launched an armed mob in the direction of the royal residence, the Tuileries. In the early morning hours, though the king had fled to the protection of the Legislative Assembly and had ordered his Swiss guards to withdraw, the crowd smashed into the palace and in a frenzy of rage massacred the Swiss troops, numerous courtiers and even some of the servants. The Assembly, terrified by the slaughter, took the king into protective custody, turned executive power over to a committee of six ministers led by Danton and ordered that a new legislature under the name of the National Convention be elected by a wide manhood suffrage (though domestic servants were still denied the vote).

Before the Convention could be constituted, a second orgy of violence drowned the expiring monarchy in blood. News of military defeats in the north and east kept coming in, to merge with rumours of aristocratic treason at home—rumours which produced so many arrests that the prisons were bursting with suspects. During the first week of September, with the tacit complicity of the revolutionary city government, mobs began a series of gruesome murders of prison inmates. Jail after jail was broken into and emptied of suspected aristocrats and monarchists, as well as many petty criminals. Most of those dragged from their cells were butchered on the spot. The September Massacres, claiming over 1,000 lives by the very lowest estimate, foretold the coming of the Terror.

The Birth of the Republic

A total of 782 deputies having been elected, the Convention was called to order on 21 September 1792 and immediately declared the monarchy dissolved. Seventy-five veterans of the National Assembly, including Robespierre, and over twice that many ex-members of the Legislative were returned. It was among the hundreds of 'new men', however, that some of the most extreme revolutionaries were to be found: Danton, the Cordeliers Club's leader, for example, and the radical editors, Marat and Desmoulins. The right, as previously represented by the *Feuillants*, had been swept away in the elections. The new right comprised the group around Jacques Pierre Brissot, often called *Brissotins* or even Brissotin Jacobins, but more familiar to history as *Girondins* because many of their spokesmen came from Bordeaux in the Department of the Gironde. That the Girondin faction, which had been the war party of the previous spring and had not fully detached itself from the Jacobins until the summer of 1792, should now appear conservative was proof of the direction in which the political tide was running. Across the assembly, in the high seats on the far left which gave them the nickname of 'The Mountain', sat Robespierre, Danton and their Jacobin cohorts. Between these two positions stretched the expanse of initially uncommitted deputies, 'The Plain', for whose support Girondins and Jacobins would soon be locked in mortal combat.

The proclamation of the Republic on 22 September 1792 seemed to many a positive action, freighted with joy and fraternal optimism. Under the slogan, 'Liberty, Equality, Fraternity', the French people were invited to take their future in their own hands, at the same time offering aid to all other peoples who might strive for freedom. No clearer expression of the messianic sense of a new dispensation can be imagined than the French Republican Calendar. Henceforth, time would be measured from the birth of the Republic, the first day of the Year I. Since that date falls near the average autumnal equinox, it was easy to divide the year into quarters roughly equal to astronomical seasons. Each month was allotted thirty days, divided into three ten-day weeks and given a name which referred either to its characteristic weather or to its place in the cycle of farm life. The five days thus left over each September (six in a leap year) were called *Sans-culottides*, in honour of the long-trousered enemies of aristocracy, and were reserved for patriotic festivals. The months' names, chosen by Fabre d'Eglantine, have considerable beauty and rationality, since the same ending was used for the three months of each season (see next page).

Unlike the metric system of weights and measures—grams, metres, litres, etc.—adopted by the National Assembly in 1791, the Convention's calendar failed to win general, continuing acceptance. Perhaps this was because, unlike the metric system, which brought much-needed order out of the previous chaos of varying measures and introduced convenient decimal divisions, the new years and months had to compete with well-established, internationally recognized notions of time. In any case, the Republican calendar was formally abandoned by Napoleon in 1806, two years after he became emperor.

Far grimmer questions lay before the revolutionaries in the winter of 1792–3. The negative side of founding a republic was the liquidation of the monarchy, which in turn involved a decision about the person of the king. Throughout Louis XVI's trial for treason, which occupied the Convention that December and January, numerous Girondins and deputies of the Plain urged imprisonment or submission of the entire matter to a popular plebiscite. They were defeated by the implacable orators of the Mountain, in particular Robespierre and the young Saint-Just. On 15 January 1793 overwhelming majorities voted for the

Republican Month	Reference	Equivalent on Gregorian Calendar[1]
Vendémiaire	Vintage	22 September—21 October
Brumaire	Mists	22 October—20 November
Frimaire	Frost	21 November—20 December
Nivôse	Snow	21 December—19 January
Pluviôse	Rain	20 January—18 February
Ventôse	Wind	19 February—20 March
Germinal	Buds	21 March—19 April
Floréal	Flowers	20 April—19 May
Prairial	Meadows	20 May—18 June
Messidor	Reaping	19 June—18 July
Thermidor	Heat	19 July—17 August
Fructidor	Fruit	18 August—16 September
Sans culottides		17 September—21 September

king's guilt and against any appeal to the people. The next day, 361 of the 721 members present, a majority of precisely one vote, favoured immediate execution, though thirty-nine others endorsed the death penalty subject to various reservations. On 21 January the king died calmly under the blade of the guillotine on what is today the Place de la Concorde. He was followed to the same scaffold by Marie Antoinette some nine months later.

To ask how the Convention was transformed from a new constitutional assembly into a long-term legislature, controlled by mobs outside and by dictatorial executive committees within, is in effect to ask how the republican experiment evolved into the Terror. To answer that question in turn demands an understanding of several forces which were sweeping France beyond the reach of moderate parliamentary solutions. One of these, no doubt, was the brutalizing effect of bloodshed itself. The beheading of the king, only a few months after the

---

[1] Gregorian equivalents are for 1792–93. Differences in the placing of leap year's extra day caused fluctuations in these equivalents for some subsequent years.

September Massacres, seemed to herald a departure from ordinary humanity, whether to soar above it or to plunge below. 'Politics', in any familiar sense of the term, was on its way to becoming a hopelessly inadequate label for public affairs in France.

In 1789 defeat in the struggle for power had meant silence for a time and possibly retirement. In 1791 it had been more likely to mean emigration or exile. By the later months of 1793 it meant almost certain death under the great knife which Dr Guillotin had hoped would humanize the cruel executions of the Old Régime. A statistical analysis of over 14,000 executions between March 1793 and August 1794 shows that in each of the first seven months of that period about 500 death sentences were carried out. Then the monthly figure began to mount rapidly, finally reaching a high of over 3,500 judicial killings in January 1794.[1] While such statistics, like the infinitely greater human toll exacted by mass terror in our own century, are all but incomprehensible, it is important to bear constantly in mind the fact that the chill of death, like the heat of believing one's opponent was surely a traitor who must die, conditioned almost everything a Frenchman might say or do under the reign of 'Madame Guillotine'.

The apprehension born of war against foreign powers fed the demand for the extirpation of secret enemies at home. On 1 February 1793 'throwing down the head of a king as a gage of battle', the Convention added England, Spain and the Dutch United Provinces to a list of foes which already included Austria, Prussia and Sardinia. As we shall see in Chapter VII, the hostile coalition concerted its efforts very poorly. Nevertheless, after General Dumouriez had overrun Belgium, an Austrian counter-attack swept back into Brussels. Early in April Dumouriez himself, as ambitious as ever but now frightened by the Convention's suspicious questions, slipped across his own battle lines and became one more *émigré* in the Habsburg camp.

From then until August 1793 the Republic's armies were on the defensive almost everywhere. It was on 23 August that the government formally announced the *levée en masse*, the general mobilization which was one of the most important symbolic acts of the Revolution. 'Young men will go to the front,' read the decree, 'married men will forge arms and transport foodstuffs; women will make tents, clothes, will serve in hospitals; children will tear rags into lint [for gun wadding]; old men will have themselves carried to public places, there to stir up the courage of the warriors, hatred of kings and unity in the Republic.' The tre-

[1] D. Greer, *Terror*, p. 165 (*see* Bibliography, p. 103).

mendous hammer of revolutionary France began to rise over an older Europe it soon would shatter into unfamiliar fragments. Meanwhile, however, the French nation itself was gripped by hatred and uncertainty.

Its rulers during this period included members of the Convention, of course, and of its judicial arm, the Revolutionary Tribunal. Executive authority, however, was centred in the Convention's Committee of General Security and Committee of Public Safety. Danton was a member of the latter from the day it was formed, 6 April 1793; but when Robespierre was added to it in July, a new leader began his march towards primacy. Another of the Committee's important figures was Lazare Carnot, already concentrating on the military measures which were to earn him the title, 'Organizer of Victory'. One more agency which wielded such great influence that it was actually a major organ of the national state was the reorganized Commune of Paris, where the violent and abusive journalist, Hébert, was the dominant force. It was these bodies that formed the true government of France, despite the new Constitution of 1793, ostensibly democratic but suspended for the duration of the war and never in fact put into operation.

Internal Threats to the Republic

The most serious issues confronting the Republic, apart from foreign attack, were (1) economic difficulties, (2) counter-revolutionary uprisings and (3) the vicious struggle among groups represented in the Convention, in other words, among the revolutionaries themselves. Poverty remained endemic. Official plans for seeing that humble sansculottes and poorer peasants shared in the distribution of the confiscated lands of aristocratic émigrés did not significantly alter the pattern set by the sale of the earlier, ecclesiastical portion of the *biens nationaux* —citizens already prosperous gobbled up the newly available property.[1] Added to this source of lower-class resentment were the mounting inflation of the assignats and severe new food shortages, traceable to uneven distribution which was made worse by military requisitions in some areas.

The response of the government involved in particular two measures, both designed to bring relief—albeit at the cost of repudiating the Revolution's earlier devotion to a free market economy. The first of

[1] The best regional study of this phenomenon is G. Lefebvre, *Les paysans du Nord et la Révolution française* (Bari, 1959).

these measures, the so-called *maximum*, actually developed out of a long series of partial expedients dating from 1792; but the comprehensive Law of the Maximum was passed only in September 1793. It fixed commodity prices all over France at local levels set by adding one-third to figures taken from 1790, while wages were limited to the norms of 1790, plus one-half. Secondly, a ration-card system was instituted to control the distribution of meat, the coarse 'equality bread' and other foodstuffs. These steps were frankly authoritarian and, in eighteenth-century terms, distinctly illiberal; but they served the French war effort by saving the assignat as a viable currency for the time being, and they almost certainly prevented paralysing hunger riots.

Meanwhile, another internal crisis, this one involving the government's hold on a number of key areas in France itself, added peril to the war situation. Revolts against the Jacobin Republic, generally supported by its foreign enemies and partially dependent for leadership on French royalists and other émigrés who had slipped back into the country, broke out in 1793 from the Channel to the Mediterranean. In March the poor farmers of the Vendée in western France, with the connivance of certain ruined noblemen and a number of 'recalcitrant' priests, erupted in a furious rebellion which expressed a combination of monarchist, clerical and socio-economic motives.[1] It was followed that summer, especially after the fall of the Girondins enraged their supporters outside Paris, by risings in Normandy, Bordeaux and the big city of Lyon, much of whose National Guard joined forces with a royalist brigade under one Count de Précy. Almost simultaneously, the Mediterranean ports of Marseille and Toulon revolted. In the former, enemies of the government executed numerous Jacobins and launched a military assault on the Convention's forces in the region. At Toulon, local insurgents opened the gates to a landing party of British, Spanish and Sardinian troops put ashore on 28 August from Admiral Hood's warships.

The Committee of Public Safety struck hard at all these monarchist, Girondin and 'federalist' (i.e. anti-centralist) elements. Army officers who had been born noble were abruptly deprived of their commissions —an obvious, if costly, precaution—while political agents of the Convention, called 'representatives on mission', were sent into the provinces to coordinate the work of military units and Jacobin committees in crushing resistance. One by one, the defiant cities fell to the

[1] P. Bois, *Paysans de l'ouest* (Le Mans, 1960); also C. Tilly, *The Vendée* (Cambridge, Mass., 1964).

republican armies. Bordeaux, like Rouen and Caen in Normandy, capitulated without heavy fighting. Other places had to be taken by storm: Marseille in late August 1793, Lyon in October after a two-month siege, Toulon only on 18 December in an attack which won young Captain Napoleon Bonaparte prompt promotion to the rank of brigadier general. The very names of these three municipalities were stricken from the rolls of the Republic. A wrathful Convention re-baptized them, Marseille as Ville-affranchie (Freed City), Lyon as Ville-sans-nom (Nameless City) and Toulon as Port-la-Montagne (Port of the Mountain).

Only in the stubborn Vendée and inland Brittany did rebellion sputter on. Even after their great defeat by republican forces at Chollet in late October 1793, and despite the massacre of thousands of dissi-dents which was organized at Nantes by Representative-on-Mission Carrier, the embittered Vendéans and the Breton guerrillas called 'Chouans' kept up a series of intermittent raids. Distracting as this long struggle in the west was to prove, it is worth noting that the *general* complex of uprisings against the Republic, like the most extreme danger from foreign invasion, had been overcome by the end of 1793.

The Peak of the Terror and Robespierre's Fall

Why then did the Terror, with its denunciations, mass trials and staggering total of executions, not subside at that point? Part of the answer doubtless lies in the force of panic become vindictive. Though the régime had won some great victories, the popular fear of enemies both within and outside France's borders took months to lose its hysterical intensity. Equally important was the political struggle to the death among the principal revolutionary leaders. To appreciate the growing fanaticism with which that struggle was pursued, one must read countless speeches, including those of Robespierre before the Convention and those of Prosecutor-general Fouquier-Tinville before the Revolutionary Tribunal. One should also bear in mind that this was the era during which Hébert's Cult of Reason was officially pro-claimed in place of Christianity (November 1793), only to be replaced at the festival of 8 June 1794 by Robespierre's Supreme Being, an un-commonly pitiless god of anger.

Among the countless individual condemnations, we can distinguish four successive purges which punctuated the crescendo of the Terror. The first struck down thirty-one Girondin leaders, including Brissot and Mayor Pétion of Paris, who were arrested on 2 June 1793 by vote of the Convention and beheaded the following October. Though the alleged moderation of the Gironde had been under growing attack from the Jacobin Mountain and Parisian demagogues such as Hébert and Marat (the latter assassinated by Charlotte Corday soon after the June crisis), it was the treason of Brissot's friend and military collaborator, General Dumouriez, which had provided extreme patriots with the chance to brand all Girondins enemies of the Republic.

With its former opponents in the Convention delivered to the guillotine, the Jacobin leadership became increasingly hostile to the noisy group around Hébert and their ceaseless agitation within the Paris city government. Some members of the Committee of Public Safety appear to have been sincere in their distrust of these radical 'ultras' who periodically denounced the Committee itself as lukewarm in its devotion to revolutionary principles. Others in the national administration may have felt nothing more elevated than political jealousy. Whatever the motives involved, the Convention was suddenly advised by the Robespierrists that the ultras were not patriots at all, but conspirators who intended to turn the Paris mob against the central government. Indicted before the Revolutionary Tribunal on 17 March 1794, Hébert and nineteen of his associates were executed within a week.

Danton had spent the winter in close collaboration with Robespierre. Despite his own misgivings about the uncontrolled ravages of the Terror, in a sense *because* of those misgivings, he had been in full accord with the crushing of the Hébertist extremists. It is nevertheless clear that even before the Parisian ultras were denounced, the leaders of the Mountain had marked the Dantonists too for destruction. On 30 March Saint-Just, young, handsome, icy—'the angel of the Terror', as he has been called—presented to both of the great Committees a report prepared by Robespierre and designed to show that Danton had been guilty of secret machinations against the Republic, conspiracy with England, pro-Girondin sympathies and a host of other crimes. That night a number of alleged Dantonists were arrested, and the next morning a thoroughly frightened Convention bound these newest culprits over to trial. Before the Revolutionary Tribunal, Danton's powerful oratory seemed for a time to be swinging popular feelings and perhaps the court itself his way, but a rumour was hastily launched to the effect that the defendants were plotting a general insurrection. Convicted on 5 April, Danton, Camille Desmoulins and a dozen others were rushed to their deaths on the scaffold.

The Revolution was now devouring its own at a bewildering rate. Girondins, Hébertists, Dantonists had disappeared in turn, and most members of the Convention were uncertain who might be next. For over three months after Danton's fall, however, Robespierre, in appearance still the fastidious little lawyer who had come to Paris from Arras in 1789, ruled the Convention and its agencies with a certitude that belied any notion that he too might fall. In the best tradition of Greek tragedy, it was actually a gesture of supreme self-confidence which led to Robespierre's undoing. On 22 Prairial of the Year II (10 June 1794), he forced through the Convention a law which subdivided the Revolutionary Tribunal into four panels for the swifter handling of cases, set up a vague category of criminals known simply as 'enemies of the people', denied the accused parties all right of counsel and gave the two committees (Public Safety and General Security) the power to indict even a deputy of the Convention without need for formal action by that body.

At a time when the guillotine was taking more than 1,000 lives per month, the Law of 22 Prairial could be passed because no one dared speak against it. This very prevalence of fear, however, produced the secret plot which finally destroyed Robespierre. The deputy Fouché, who knew that he was himself suspected of Hébertist leanings, concerted the action with several apprehensive members of the Committee of Public Safety. These included not only Carnot but also the ferocious Collot d'Herbois, who had the special advantage of being the Convention's presiding officer. When Saint-Just rose to speak on 9 Thermidor (27 July), he held in his hand a new list of victims, but he never was able to read their names. Instead he was drowned out by an uproar of hostile shouts. From the pandemonium there finally emerged an indictment of Robespierre himself, together with a number of other officials accused of sharing his misuse of public power for selfish ends. During the night that followed, it still appeared that a popular insurrection by the sans-culottes of Paris might save the Jacobin chieftains, especially since Robespierre was not actually imprisoned and could have harangued the populace before the city hall. He declined to do so, however, possibly because he felt sure that he could win a triumphant acquittal before the Revolutionary Tribunal—and the crowds slowly melted away. Meanwhile, Robespierre's enemies in the Convention seized the excuse to change the charge against him and his followers to one of insurrection against the Republic. The vote outlawing the Robespierrists also eliminated the need for a formal trial, and they were seized after a brief scuffle in which the Incorruptible himself either was shot, or shot himself, in the jaw. Next day, with Saint-Just and twenty of their associates, he was guillotined.

The fall of Robespierre marked the beginning of the end of massive Terror, but the end itself was a bloody one. Almost 1,400 people were executed in July, first by Robespierre's régime before the 27th and then by his foes in the hectic days which followed. The Thermidoreans, as the new masters of the Convention were called, did not willingly abandon wholesale decapitation as an instrument of rule; but they could not long disregard an unmistakeable shift in public opinion. Once the Paris Commune had been liquidated and the Jacobin Club in the capital destroyed, indictments before the Revolutionary Tribunal shrank to a relatively insignificant number. (The court itself was abolished within a year.) Numerous former outlaws, including Girondins who had survived in hiding, were pardoned. By early 1795 not only political trends but also social developments—the revival of wigs and colourful dress, the reappearance of an argumentative press and a libertine theatre, the renewed toleration of prostitutes, even the return of certain avowed aristocrats—all showed that the more (or less) than human demands of the Republic of Virtue had lost their force.

The Republic, despite considerable easing of the tension at home and a series of reassuring military victories in the Low Countries and the Rhineland, still faced severe difficulties. Late in 1794 the *maximum* was repealed in a spirit of loosening controls, and a new inflation began at once. The following spring two bread riots shook Paris, with the indirect result that the Convention wiped out the last veterans of the Mountain, beheading six deputies, exiling Collot d'Herbois and several others. In July 1795 the suppression of a new, British-backed revolt by the Chouans in the west led to over 700 official executions, while the rebels in turn butchered about 1,000 republican prisoners. Finally, on 5 October, a rising of monarchist elements in Paris, known to history as the Thirteenth Vendémiaire, had to be put down by cannon—the 'whiff of grapeshot' which brought the Convention's artillery commander, Bonaparte, to public notice.

By the time this final insurrection was crushed, the Convention was nearing the end of its stormy three-year life. Its deputies, however, did not propose to fade out of politics. The Thirteenth Vendémiaire was in part a demonstration against the provision in the newly adopted Constitution of 1795; for the rightist rebels in that affair, though they welcomed the now restored property qualifications for voting, were outraged by the provision that two-thirds of the first Council of (250) Ancients and the Council of Five Hundred should be chosen from among members of the Convention. In October the latter assembly held its final sessions, then dissolved itself to make way for the bicameral legislature and for a five-man Directory to exercise executive control.

The Government of the Directory

It is instructive to consider the origin and nature of this Directory, if only to place it in the evolution of executive power from Louis XVI through the several revolutionary régimes to the Emperor Napoleon. The five members, who had staggered terms so that the two Councils would elect a new director each year, had more direct authority over internal, military and foreign affairs than any previous executive save, briefly, Robespierre but less than Napoleon would have later, since in 1795 control of public finances was assigned to another group of five men, the Treasury Commission. The Directory's power over the administrative hierarchy, in particular, was direct and virtually unlimited. The original five members: Barras, Carnot, La Révellière-Lépeaux, Letourneur and Reubell were all veterans of the Convention. All had voted for the execution of the king, and all took office hoping for the support of a wide spectrum of republican, including Jacobin, opinion. But not one of them was any longer an idealist, as the next four years would demonstrate.

The story of the Directory, from 1795 until its overthrow in 1799, is heavily dominated by military and diplomatic events, and for that reason, much of it belongs to the next chapter. As for domestic affairs, the Directory's performance was no better than might have been expected from a series of middle-class republican politicians. Certainly, however, it was better than the orgy of graft and corruption portrayed by many historians whose hearts have lain either with Louis XVI or with Robespierre or with Napoleon—and who have agreed on almost nothing except their condemnation of this interim régime.

By the mid-1790s there was no denying that military success was essential to the government's prestige, a significant hint of things to come. In Director Carnot France possessed an able builder and supplier of armies. In Hoche, Jourdan, Masséna and Bonaparte, it found a set of energetic generals. Not only on distant battlefields but also in France's own western provinces, where Hoche crushed the last concerted onslaught by Vendéans and Chouans in 1796, the military proved equal to its many opponents. Meanwhile economic troubles continued. The assignats, despite various attempts to bolster them, persisted in depreciating until the government, after elaborate and unsuccessful manipulations, finally discontinued their use in 1796, redeeming those in circulation at one-seventieth of their face value, payable in coin. Even this stringent conversion was made possible only by the foreign stores of gold and silver captured by French armies in the field. Yet the régime did avert financial disaster, and it ultimately succeeded in restoring some measure of public confidence in the treasury.

Why, then, was Napoleon able to overthrow this government so easily in 1799? Part of the reason may lie in the fact that the Directory was just not very exciting. It did not attract the passionate loyalty of anyone; and especially in a nation at war year after year, the felt need for charismatic leadership can become a political force in its own right. Many of the directors at one time or another displayed a world-weary cynicism with respect to the Directory itself—and if even they did not believe in its merits, who else could? Meanwhile, the dashing young generals on the battlefields of Germany and Italy had the opportunity to appear far more glamorous in the eyes of the public than could any civilian arguing over currency or taxes in Paris.

Above all, the Directory's weakness stemmed from its failure ever to overcome the splintering of French political life which followed the collapse of the Terror. In May 1796 the threat seemed to come from the left, specifically from the protosocialist demands of Gracchus Babeuf's Society of the Pantheon. This 'conspiracy of the Equals', which included a plan for a lower-class revolt, was easily exposed by the government, and Babeuf went to the guillotine.[1] In September 1797 circles loyal to the régime became convinced that right-wing plots were now the great source of danger. A number of conservative politicians and generals, some frankly monarchist in outlook, were rounded up; and two of the directors, one of them the capable but disillusioned Carnot, were packed off into exile. There were many other political crises during the years we are considering, but Babeuf's conspiracy and the fall of Carnot suffice to illustrate the range of challenges faced by the Directory.

The final coup d'état brought together several kinds of dissatisfaction, and in so doing it destroyed the political compromise of 1795. Since the end of 1798 and the creation of the Second Coalition, the alliance of Russia, England and Austria had inflicted a series of reverses upon a

[1] E. Wilson, *To the Finland Station* (New York, 1940), pp. 71-9.

French nation grown unaccustomed to military defeats. At the same time, a combination of economic and financial troubles, some of them quiescent for several years past, flared up once more. In politics, a Jacobin resurgence was bringing demands for a more broadly based republicanism, and the elections of May 1799 produced a majority in the Council of Five Hundred openly hostile to the incumbent directors. The latter were compelled to accept a turnover of membership, with the result that the Directory itself henceforth contained at least two members, Sieyès and Roger-Ducos, who made no secret of their distaste for the existing situation. In a sense, the most acute and the most understandable misgivings were those felt by political moderates who feared either a reactionary uprising or a revival of Jacobin Terror. At the same time, one should not underestimate the extent to which distrust of the populace led such men to heed the demands of certain military leaders for an end to 'civilian mediocrity'.

Here was a situation charged with confusion but also rich in opportunity for an ambitious soldier. Into it stepped General Bonaparte, most lionized of the army's field commanders, known as the hero of the Italian campaign of 1796-7, and now just returned (early in October 1799) from an Egyptian expedition which still touched the imagination of Frenchmen who had yet to learn of its disastrous results. Sieyès, the old constitutional debater of 1789, had the ironic role of conspiring with two of the other directors, Roger-Ducos and the more reluctant Barras, to destroy the Republic as a parliamentary régime. On 18 Brumaire of the Year VIII (9 November 1799), these three, who had been in touch with Bonaparte for several weeks in Paris, announced that they were resigning from the Directory under the threat of a Jacobin revolt. The next day, as arranged in advance, Napoleon appeared before the two legislative Councils and asked for the authority to save the nation. When this manoeuvre miscarried, he did what Louis XVI had failed to do ten years before, simply ordering troops to clear the building. A few hours later, selected representatives of the Ancients and the Five Hundred, using, if not misusing, their right to choose directors, voted emergency powers to three consuls, Bonaparte, Sieyès and Roger-Ducos. In circumstances suggesting a comic opera, the revolutionary era faded into the Napoleonic.

Interpreting the Revolution

When we pause to look back over the entire period from the meeting of the Estates General in 1789 to the Eighteenth Brumaire a decade later, certain aspects of the French Revolution stand out. Some demand only a reflective pulling together of familiar points in the narrative. Others take the form of questions to which no categorical answers can be given on the basis of our present knowledge. But all should help to explain why the Revolution has remained a favourite testing ground for social psychologists no less than for economists, for ethical as well as for political philosophers.

We observed, for example, how a broad coalition displayed its power in the summer of 1789—anti-authoritarian nobles and clergymen joining forces with middle-class reformers in the Assembly and, somewhat less willingly, with popular agitators in the streets of Paris. Thereafter, we saw the revolutionary front undergo two successive changes. The first, which continued until the summer of 1793, entailed a steady *shift* of the parliamentary spectrum towards the left. One by one, through defection or physical destruction, groups which represented conservative, or at least relatively moderate, views on certain issues disappeared (liberal monarchists in the National Assembly, Feuillants in the Legislative, Girondins in the Convention), while on the other side more radical elements increased their strength.[1] Then a second change began, a marked *narrowing* of the revolutionary front itself, as Hébertist ultras and Danton's faction within the Jacobin movement were exterminated by the Robespierrists. When even Robespierre fell, all that remained was a corps of administrators, facing a set of disparate factions—Babouvists, diehard Jacobins, yearners after the constitutional monarchy, impatient soldiers. The Directory was able to preside over the Republic for four years, but it steered no course determined by a national consensus or even by a well-defined minority. In this sense, Bonapartist enthusiasts have some excuse for arguing that by 1799 there was no longer any revolutionary momentum for Napoleon either to reverse or to maintain, that the question was not whether the first consul should *continue* or *suppress* the Revolution, but instead whether or not he should *resume* it.

This problem of revolutionary momentum or energy touches on another matter of some importance, namely, the puzzling record of mass behaviour. What (or who) gave direction to the Parisian crowds that stormed the Bastille, brought the royal family back from Versailles

---

[1] P. Beik, *The French Revolution Seen from the Right* (Philadelphia, 1956), gives twenty-one case studies of men who were moderate conservatives in 1789, including their subsequent careers.

three months later and in 1792 massacred the Swiss guards in the Tuileries? Why did certain town populations, such as those of Bordeaux, Lyon, Marseille and Toulon rally to the standard of federalism in 1793, while many others upheld the Jacobin central government?[1] How near were the Paris *sections* to rioting in order to save Robespierre on the Ninth Thermidor?

These and related questions will yield answers, if at all, only to meticulous local studies aided by every social and psychological insight the historian can bring to bear. Recent interest in the revolutionary mobs has already turned up some important findings. Police records reveal, for instance, that many of the individuals who fought on the celebrated 'days' of the Revolution were quite comfortable shopkeepers and professional men. Hatred born of poverty and panic rooted in superstitious ignorance were by no means the only contributing motives. At the very least, two other, seemingly paradoxical forces may be seen at work. One is the influence of apparently sincere, rational convictions about liberation and progress. The other is the sudden, often unpredictable power of contagious emotions once large numbers of people come together under conditions of nervous strain in an atmosphere alive with rumours.[2]

Since the Revolution was violent, it is not uncommon to find those who deplore it, as a whole, citing its brutality as conclusive proof of its essential wrongness in all respects. Conversely, for some who sympathize with many of the revolutionaries' aims, there persists the tantalizing thought that it should have been possible to stop short of the Terror, whose bloody means ultimately compromised some worthy ends. The figure of Robespierre poses this issue in its sharpest form.[3] Despite his tiresome pomposity and his resolute refusal to let either sympathy or humour soften the pitiless self-assurance of his oratory,

---

[1] An exceptionally interesting local study is R. M. Brace, *Bordeaux and the Gironde, 1789–1794* (Ithaca, N.Y., 1947).

[2] Notable examples of the important work being done in this field include G. Rudé, *The Crowd in the French Revolution* (Oxford, 1959); A. Soboul, *Les Sans-culottes parisiens en l'An II* (Paris, 1958), available also in an abridged translation (Oxford, 1964); K. Toennesson, *La défaite des Sans-culottes* (Oslo, 1959); and R. Cobb, 'The revolutionary mentality in France, 1793–1794', *History*, vol. XLII (1957).

[3] Aside from various sections in the works of Mathiez, for whom Robespierre was the hero of the Revolution, two useful short analyses are J. M. Thompson, *Robespierre and the French Revolution* (London, 1952); and M. Bouloiseau, *Robespierre* (2nd edn., Paris, 1961).

the Incorruptible did embody a sincere belief that the Revolution would be both a failure and a fraud unless it brought a new standard of justice and security to *all* Frenchmen, including the lowest classes. He was correct in asserting that there were many who wished to stop short of that goal, though not all of them for such utterly selfish reasons as he charged. But how could justice and security be given to a people at the cost of hundreds, even thousands of executions per month?

No attempt will be made here to solve all the moral dilemmas implicit in the mixture of enlightened reform and cynical opportunism, of foreign crusade, rapacious conquest and civil war which made up the French Revolution. Whatever might be said on these scores, the dilemmas implicit in violence would remain. A few brief suggestions, however, may help to keep the problem in perspective. One is that the eighteenth century, though it had seen a considerable quantitative decline in cruelty, was still an era in which suffering and death stood close to nearly everyone. The society of the Old Régime had been one which knew not only the physical but also the psychological anguish of unexplained disease, which occasionally broke men on the wheel for having violated religious taboos and which sent mere youngsters to the gallows for petty theft. How then could one who was intent on destroying that society object to the swift decapitation of any number of people he saw as plotters against the emerging nation itself? Throughout history deep conviction, whether religious or social or political, has shown itself capable of triggering human actions which in themselves appear repellent. Tolerance, respect for the rights of individuals, kindness itself all demand a certain degree of good humour, perhaps tinctured with indifference. And whatever else the French revolutionaries were, they were neither good humoured nor indifferent!

At the other extreme from considerations of mass emotion and the violence it supported stands the question of individual roles. Generations of historians have argued, for example, over the nature and even the reality of the choices open to Louis XVI. Should he have struck down the National Assembly when it defied him, or should he have accepted its proposals more wholeheartedly than he did? Could he have made himself a national symbol by leading French resistance to foreign intervention, instead of attempting to flee from Paris? If modern observers have tended to attach less importance to the moderating roles of men such as Lafayette and Mirabeau than once was common, the enigma of Robespierre and Danton, their personal relationship and their respective influences on the Terror, has lost none of its fascination. Or again, if Bonaparte had found no Sieyès to help him in 1799, we may still ask, would an alternative director have served the turn? And if there had been no Bonaparte, would another soldier, Jourdan perhaps, have been jobbed into power?

One factor to consider when seeking answers to such queries is what some political scientists call 'executive discretion'. However intricate the causation of the Revolution's crucial developments, no matter how deep their roots in conditions which had developed over the course of centuries, the fact remains that at every point either one man or a small group of men had the authority to initiate specific responses. In other words, the way in which issues were presented to the public view, the tone in which they were discussed, even the order in which they were taken up depended in part on individual judgments and personal styles. The French monarchy might have been destroyed regardless of who was the king from 1789 to 1792; but if Louis XVI had possessed the supple cynicism of England's Charles II, the ferocity of Russia's Peter I or the cold intelligence of Prussia's Frederick II, the story of its destruction would have been different. There might well have been a Terror without Robespierre, but it would not have been precisely the same Terror. The Directory might still have collapsed in 1799 or thereabout; but without a Sieyès and a Bonaparte, can anyone seriously imagine that it would have collapsed under exactly the same circumstances, or with identical implications? That much we need not concede to historical determinism.

It remains only to consider the essential meaning of the Revolution, as assessed from different points of view. For Edmund Burke, in his *Reflections* of 1790, its meaning lay in what he considered the tragic misapplication of mechanical principles to an organic problem, the tearing apart of a basically sound society by innovators who mistook the body politic for a machine and who thus destroyed what they should have sought to heal. For Count Alexis de Tocqueville, writing in 1856, it lay in a no less tragic perversion of a vision of liberty into a delusive quest for equality, ending in tyranny under a demagogue. For Karl Marx and Friedrich Engels, developing their Communist doctrine in the 1840s and 1850s, it lay in the selfish, though historically 'necessary', seizure of formal control by the entrepreneurs of business, who had already displaced the older feudal class as the possessors of the decisive means of production and who were now ready to reshape the political system and indeed the entire culture in their own interest. For the Italian sociologist, Vilfredo Pareto, writing at the turn of our own century, it lay in the violent displacement of a soft, tired aristocracy by a new élite of ability and ruthless ambition. And so on through a wide range of other theories.

My own concluding estimate calls for a brief reminder of the several categories and levels of conflict we have encountered repeatedly since first approaching European society as it existed in the 1780s. So far as *orders* of men were concerned, their primacy seemed to be vindicated by the convening of the Estates General; but in fact the assault on a structure thus conceived began almost at once. Neither nobles nor clergymen could assert the right to legal privileges after the night of 4 August 1789. The Law of Municipalities (abolishing restricted lists of hereditary bourgeois), the Civil Constitution of the Clergy, the repudiation of a legally recognized nobility, indeed the undifferentiated nature of the title 'citizen', all struck at the very idea of orders so dear to the Old Régime. None of these measures escaped later modification and even reversal; but after the Revolution, Frenchmen would never again accord to human differentiation by order the kind of reverence it had enjoyed for centuries before 1789.

Classes, on the other hand, could no longer be dismissed as a figment of some troubled imagination. The debates over property qualifications for voting and office-holding, the espousal of poor men's interests by Robespierre and other leaders, the institution as well as the subsequent repeal of the Maximum, the attack on existing economic relationships by Babeuf and his followers, the fear of a Jacobin resurgence felt by well-to-do men in 1799, these and other evidences of class struggle abound in the Revolution's narrative.[1]

In the same narrative, *status* struggle also occupies an important place. The glorification of the sans-culottes, the denigration of aristocrats, the decline of leisure and international culture as badges of social honour, these constituted basic elements in the revolutionary overturn of traditional values. By the end of the 1790s, a new status system was emerging, one which attached more significance to wealth than to birth and which emphasized service to the nation, especially military service. These changes, like many others already noted, were themselves destined to be watered down by the compromises of the Napoleonic and Restoration eras. What was true of other categories, however, can be said here as well, namely, that there could be no full return to the Old Régime.

[1] A. Soboul, 'Classes and class struggles during the French Revolution', *Science and Society*, vol. XVII (1953).

Finally, we should now be able to appreciate the importance of *parties* as yet another type of human organization; for neither orders nor classes nor status groups would suffice to explain all of the Revolution's pivotal conflicts. Those categories would not, for example, permit us to distinguish between the opposing factions around Mounier and Sieyès in the National Assembly, nor to differentiate Girondins from Hébertists or Dantonists from Robespierrists in the Convention. No, these were true parties, groupings held together not by a sense of legal or social or economic identity, but rather by certain shared political principles and by the ambition of their members to wield power in the state. The sequence of attempted coups against the Directory after 1795 reflected no less clearly the influence of rudimentary party interests.

The Revolution thus operated at many levels, driven onward by many types of motivation. It destroyed much, and it created much, though sometimes only to destroy again. It crushed old enemies of change and others who had seemed the very prophets of change. It excited generous hopes, and it released blood-thirsty passions. It made of France, for better or for worse, a nation unlike any the world had previously known. In the process, both through the agency of France and through the direct effect of the revolutionary principles, reaching across borders into other lands, it began a transformation of Europe which in turn has transformed the world.

VII

The Revolution Outside France

Several recent historical works have pointed out that the very term, 'French Revolution', misrepresents the European situation at the end of the eighteenth century. There was, so the argument goes, a general ferment of ideas and discontents, not all of which can be explained by a simple theory of contagion from the French source. We are reminded that when Edmund Burke chose a different phrase, '*the* Revolution *in*

BIBLIOGRAPHY. An indispensable two-volume synthesis of the Revolution's European-wide ramifications is J. Godechot, *La Grande Nation* (Paris, 1956), which is concise yet meticulous in its presentation of details. Equally valuable is R. R. Palmer, *The Age of the Democratic Revolution*, vol. II: *The Struggle* (Princeton, 1964). More limited in aim but excellent for statistical reference is D. Greer, *The Incidence of the Emigration during the French Revolution* (Cambridge, Mass., 1951). Among countless national or regional studies, only a few can be noted here. For England, see P. A. Brown, *The French Revolution in English History* (London, 1918); S. Maccoby, *English Radicalism, 1786–1832: From Paine to Cobbett* (London, 1955); and A. Cobban's edition of over 200 documentary extracts, *The Debate on the French Revolution, 1789–1800* (London, 1950). H. W. Meikle, *Scotland and the French Revolution* (Glasgow, 1912) and R. Hayes, *Ireland and Irishmen in the French Revolution* (London, 1932), are well worth consulting for other parts of the British Isles. A clear analysis of the founding of the Batavian Republic will be found in R. R. Palmer, 'Much in little: The Dutch Revolution of 1795', in *The Journal of Modern History*, vol. XXVI (1954). With respect to Germany, Valjavec's work already cited (*see* Bibliography, p. 76) and J. Droz, *L'Allemagne et la Révolution française* (Paris, 1949), have largely replaced G. P. Gooch, *Germany and the French Revolution* (London, 1920), save for readers restricted to the use of English. R. Koser's old essay, however, 'Die preussische Politik von 1786–1806', in his *Zur preussischen und deutschen Geschichte* (Stuttgart-Berlin, 1921), is still useful in connection with the Prussian situation. Switzerland's experience is examined in detail by H. Büchi, *Vorgeschichte der helvetischen Revolution*, vol. I: *Die Schweiz in den Jahren 1789–1798* (Solothurn, 1925). More than just literary reactions in Italy are dealt with in P. Hazard, *La Révolution française et les lettres italiennes, 1789–1815* (Paris, 1910); but this work can be usefully supplemented by C. Lombroso *et al.*, *La vita italiana durante la rivoluzione francese e l'impero* (Milan,

France', it was because his criticisms were aimed at what he knew to be only the most startling instance of a widespread phenomenon. The problem thus becomes one of balance, that is, of giving due weight to international aspects of the crisis without belittling the French drama as a source of examples and also of physical challenges for the rest of Europe. In the present chapter, we shall observe not only the impact of the new France upon other lands but also the ways in which conditions indigenous to those lands helped to determine the type of crisis experienced by each.

First Reactions to the Revolution

The revolutionists lectured other peoples through journalism, tracts and published state papers—the Declaration of the Rights of Man, for example, or the Constitution of 1791—as well as through correspondence between Parisian and foreign political clubs. Many non-Frenchmen also learned of new developments from the written and spoken words of compatriots who had visited France. Arthur Young's account of his travels there, extending up to January 1790 and quickly published not only in English but also in numerous translations, has remained the most famous of such reports. Those of the Russian historian Karamzin, the English surgeon and radical journalist Sampson Perry, the Berlin Opera's director Reichardt, were scarcely less influential at the time. After the French armies began to spill out across Europe, the gospel of the Revolution was directly, not to say forcefully, broadcast; but before that happened, another kind of French invasion had for several years been carrying abroad some strong impressions of events at home. This was the emigration.

From the night in July 1789 when the Count d'Artois, brother of Louis XVI, left Versailles and headed for Brussels, the stream of émigrés became broader almost by the month. They went first to the Low Countries, Rhenish Germany, Switzerland, northern Italy, Catalonia in Spain. Then, when these areas were threatened or actually overrun by the Republic's forces, seemingly safer havens beckoned:

1900). By far the most valuable study of the Habsburg dominions is the volume by E. Wangermann, *From Joseph II to the Jacobin Trials* (London, 1959). As for Russia, C. de Larivière, *Catherine le Grand d'après sa correspondance: Catherine II et la Révolution française* (Paris, 1895), despite its age, deserves attention, as does the much newer biography by D. M. Lang, *The First Russian Radical: Alexander Radishchev, 1749–1802* (London, 1959).

England, Prussia, Austria, Russia, and even European settlements overseas. Eventually their numbers swelled to an estimated 130,000. Their social variety was far greater than the familiar image of exiled noblemen and priests suggests; for the Revolution was an immense civil war in which men of widely differing backgrounds could find themselves impelled to leave their homes in France. Of the 90,000 émigrés whose status has been established, over 27 per cent, it is true, were clergymen, while another 18 per cent were members of the nobility. But note that émigrés belonging to the first two Estates accounted for less than one-half the total figure. The remainder comprised persons identified as upper or lower middle-class (19 per cent), working-class (15 per cent), peasants (21 per cent).[1] Obviously, foreign countries learned about French developments from many different types of informants.

For this and other reasons, the prevailing response to the Revolution on the part of foreigners was anything but unanimous. In nearly every country there were enthusiasts, some of them highly placed, who believed that a new and better age was dawning for mankind. To understand the evolution and in many cases the abandonment of such attitudes, it is necessary to survey European reactions by periods. We shall look first at the years between 1789 and the outbreak of formal hostilities in 1792, then at developments dominated by war and by the French internal Terror through 1794 and finally at the course of Europe's struggle with France under the Directory from 1795 to 1799.

In the case of England, as we saw in Chapter v, the news from across the channel broke upon a political scene already agitated by debates over the need for basic changes at home. Though Pitt, as prime minister, had ceased his own pressure for parliamentary reform several years earlier, eloquent voices were still heard in the land, demanding the reorganization of the legislature and of municipal governments, civil equality for Protestant nonconformists (if not yet for Catholics) and abolition of the trade in African slaves. By an accident of chronology, 1789 fell only one year after the centenary of England's own 'Glorious Revolution', an occasion which had called forth numerous speeches and pamphlets attacking abuses which the reformers insisted made a mockery of the constitutional 'principles of '88'. The names of Horne Tooke, Jebb and Major Cartwright are most familiar in this connection; but those of theorists such as Bentham and Priestley or of prominent politicians including Shelburne and Fox should not be forgotten.

[1] D. Greer, *Emigration* (*see* Bibliography, p. 138).

It was Fox, after all, who greeted the fall of the Bastille as 'much the greatest and the best event that has ever happened'.

In 1791 Horne Tooke and his circle revived the Society for Constitutional Information; and early the next year a Corresponding Society was founded in London for the stated purpose of achieving constitutional reforms. Even after the September massacres of 1792 some English groups went so far as to send formal congratulations to the National Convention in Paris on the founding of the French Republic. At that time, British subjects still felt free to discuss what Sir James Mackintosh, in his *Vindiciae Gallicae* of 1791, had called 'a grand experiment to ascertain the portion of freedom and happiness that can be created by political institutions'. Tom Paine's *Rights of Man*, published the same year, was far more explicit in its scorn for the British monarchy and its adulation of revolutionary France.

Meanwhile, an opposing attitude had been taking form. Burke's *Reflections*, though not published until the autumn of 1790, had begun to crystallize in the author's mind almost as soon as he heard of the October Days and the march on Versailles a year before. The author's understanding of French history was very imperfect, and his knowledge of existing conditions across the channel was, if anything, faultier still. On the other hand, he wrote passionately and sometimes beautifully of the deep roots of institutions, the respect due the past and the perils of ill-considered change. His sense of impending tragedy in France seemed to belie all the hopes of a Mackintosh or a Paine. In the short run, the persuasive force of Burke's famous essay probably influenced British public opinion less than did disgust aroused by the increasing bloodshed in France and apprehension engendered by republican agitation in Ireland. The founding of Wolfe Tone's United Irishmen in 1791 launched a sequence of events which brought mounting alarm to England. At the highest political level, Pitt himself had by early 1792 abandoned his earlier noncommittal attitude and was expressing his anti-revolutionary sentiments in no uncertain terms. In May of that year, the government solemnly directed local authorities to take sterner action against sedition, by which it meant specifically pro-French propaganda. Yet Fox clung to his earlier position: the cataclysm would bring much that was good, whatever violence might occur at the outset. With Britain's two leading statesmen aligned on opposite sides of the great issue, the stage was set for a decisive test. The only thing which could sharpen the question any further would be war between England and France.

In the highly sensitive region of the Low Countries, no less than in the British Isles, the early reactions to the French crisis were clearly conditioned by existing political tensions. As we saw in Chapter v, Emperor Leopold II was able to reoccupy the Austrian Netherlands with his troops in 1790. Although he let the democratic Vonckist exiles return to Belgium, he was in other respects deferential towards their conservative enemies in the Estates party. Whatever the Vonckists might think, the power of religious and social traditions in their country was such that a majority of Belgians seem from the first to have been hostile to revolutionary France. Yet the coming of the Republic's armies meant that more and more would be heard from the vocal minority who insisted that the future of man was being shaped in Paris.

The arrogant behaviour of the stadtholder since his—or more accurately, the Prussian army's—victory over the Dutch Patriots in 1787 had made pro-French sentiment stronger and more widespread in the United Provinces than it was in Belgium. Unlike Leopold II in the Austrian Netherlands, William V had not let Dutch democrats return after his military control was assured. Hence, there were countless exiles sending enthusiastic reports from France to various 'literary' clubs in Amsterdam, Leyden and other cities. Several thousand Dutch volunteers marched northward with Dumouriez in 1792, while anti-Orangists formed Batavian Committees that year in Paris and in Brussels. Both inside and outside the country, the enemies of the stadtholder and of the regent families were organizing themselves.

German reactions to the revolution in France have been more thoroughly studied than have those of most other Europeans, often with heavy emphasis on the responses of intellectuals. We are constantly reminded, for example, that most of the major figures of German philosophy and literature alive at the time greeted the early tidings from Paris with an enthusiasm sometimes approaching rapture. Kant, Wieland, the aged Klopstock, Herder, Hölderlin, Schelling, Hegel, Schiller and, to a lesser degree, Goethe all saluted the new dawn. Exceptions to this chorus included certain important lawyers and scholars, including Niebuhr, the historian of ancient Rome. Friedrich Gentz, after a brief period of supporting the Revolution, read Burke's *Reflections*, which he translated for publication in 1792, and embarked on his own career of conservative advocacy. There can be no doubt, however, as even Gentz's case illustrates, that the stagnation of the empire's political life during the seventeenth and eighteenth centuries had made a large majority of the most thoughtful Germans initially receptive to notions of sweeping change. Dozens of excited journalists whipped up comparable sentiment at a lower level of ideas.

The fall of the Bastille and the subsequent march on Versailles touched off some insurrections in German principalities, especially in the Rhineland, where French influence was most immediately felt. At Trier, in October 1789, the local bourgeoisie met and declared all noble and ecclesiastical privileges abolished. This action was promptly nullified by the arrival of imperial troops whom the archbishop-elector felt compelled to call in. As was to happen in many other cases, the crisis led the elector to reverse his previous reformist policies and to begin a period of reaction which would end only with the coming of the French. Something very similar happened at Mainz in 1790. Here the town deputies in the hastily revived estates of the electoral archbishopric demanded an immediate end to special tax exemptions. As at Trier, the answer was repression. Only a few months later, the dissident liberals of the south-western duchy of Württemberg, in avowed imitation of French ceremonies, assembled on the banks of the Neckar River to plant a 'liberty tree'.

Responses to the Revolution in other German states varied widely. The free city of Hamburg, greatest of the empire's North Sea ports, witnessed a celebration on 14 July 1790 in honour of the first anniversary of the Bastille's capture; and the speeches and poetry recited there in honour of French liberty were printed and widely distributed throughout Germany. In Berlin, on the other hand, many critics of Frederick William II's régime somewhat puzzlingly decided that what was happening in France was a laudable experiment in enlightened despotism, according to the principles of Prussia's own Frederick the Great. Needless to say, after some initial indifference the Prussian royal government, by implication accused of having strayed from those principles, directed a more and more baleful glare at the unfolding drama.

In Switzerland we encounter much the same mixture of official hostility and private enthusiasm expressed by numbers of literate citizens. The already nationalistic Helvetic Society, founded in 1762 to overcome narrow cantonal loyalties, welcomed the centralist tenets of the Revolution. Pro-French clubs appeared at Basel, Zürich, Bern and other Swiss cities. In many places, Genevan fugitives from the Black Code of 1782 fed the agitation, while democratic elements in Geneva itself nurtured their resentment and their plans, after the fashion of similar groups in Holland and Belgium. At the same time, the cantonal governments, supported by much of the religious peasantry, heard of the events in Paris with mounting consternation; and the Federal Diet refused to extend diplomatic recognition to the French Republic when the latter was proclaimed in 1792. Only France's distractions elsewhere postponed a military showdown for six more years.

The regional variation in Italian responses was comparable to that encountered in Germany. The king of Sardinia, father-in-law to both of Louis XVI's brothers, quickly made the larger towns of Savoy into asylums for French royalist émigrés—and incidentally, by so doing, appears to have made the resentful inhabitants more friendly towards the Revolution than they might otherwise have been. In Tuscany, at the other extreme, both Grand Duke Peter Leopold (who did not begin to fear the new situation until after his accession as emperor in 1790) and the court councillor, Manfredini, were outspoken admirers of the experiments being tried in France. In the Papal States, as well as in Naples and Lombardy, official reactions to those same experiments were blankly hostile and the public reaction, largely uninformed. Throughout most of Italy, in fact, including the relatively cosmopolitan republics of Venice and Genoa, even partially informed judgments of French affairs, whether friendly or the opposite, were for several years restricted to a tiny minority of officials, scholars and journalists.

If this was true of Italy, how much general awareness could one expect to find in Spain? The coronation of the new king, Charles IV, took place in late September 1789. There was an eight-day celebration at Madrid marked by an absence of references to contemporary affairs in France which cannot be explained simply in terms of governmental censorship. With understandable awe, the Prussian minister wrote back to Berlin: 'The Spanish people are good, noble and peaceable'.[1] Simultaneously, the highest legislative body in Spain, the Cortes of Castile, opened a two-month session which produced absolutely no challenge to royal authority. However apprehensive the chief minister of state, Floridablanca, may have been about revolutionary contagion— he took the trouble to have the Inquisition ban all foreign newspapers— the general public showed no enthusiasm for the godless innovators north of the Pyrenees.

Apart from shortlived political clubs in Portugal, the only source of potential sympathy for the new France within the Iberian countries appeared to be a handful of veteran reform ministers of Spain's late

[1] Quoted by Herr, p. 241 (see Bibliography, p. 21).

Charles III. Actually none of these men became as excited over the fall of the Bastille and the Declaration of the Rights of Man as did Fox in England or Grand Duke Leopold of Tuscany. Floridablanca himself at first appeared to feel that there was no need to repudiate Spain's own era of enlightened despotism if foreign influences were carefully excluded. Nevertheless, as the king became more hostile to a French government which among other things had betrayed the Family Compact (see above, pp. 116–17), the suspicion with regard to liberal administrators became more marked. In 1791 Campomanes was rudely dropped from the Council of Castile, and Jovellanos was exiled to his native province on the Bay of Biscay. One of Burke's shrewdest insights, to wit, that the Revolution would everywhere make harder the lot of moderate reformers, was coming true in Spain as it was in many other lands.

Little space can be devoted to early reverberations of the French crisis in countries farther from the scene. Even in Poland, where the Four-year Diet completed its constitutional labours several months before the National Assembly's Constitution of 1791 went into effect, the drafters found in the example of France only the most general sort of inspiration. Their specific political prescriptions were derived, as we have seen, more directly from British and American models. While a Czartoryski or a Kollontay might admire the French patriots, Polish conservatives were naturally scandalized by the tidings from Paris. As for King Stanislas, he seems to have read them with a foreboding bordering on dread. Poland, after all, was racing to overcome threats peculiar to its own position, not to join an international revolution.

Austria produced a few enthusiasts. The poet Alxinger reacted like many of his north German counterparts. Joseph II's old minister Sonnenfels held views very close to those of Fox in England until long after his country was at war with France. The bulk of the ruling group, however, was anxious to see that Joseph's autocratic reform programme did not return in a democratic disguise; and the new emperor, Leopold II, was until his death in 1792 increasingly apprehensive about revolutionary threats to his sprawling dominions. Leopold's fears were scarcely borne out by any mass excitement on the part of either Austrian or Bohemian commoners. Only in Hungary, where old claims for national autonomy, for the official use of the Magyar tongue and for Protestant emancipation all became entangled with issues being raised in French terms, did a real crisis show signs of persisting despite the pacification of 1790.

Reactions in other countries naturally varied. In Denmark a remarkably popular reform administration held power under Crown Prince Frederick (his father, Christian VII, having been declared insane in 1784). In Turkish-occupied Serbia, on the other hand, and still more in Greece, the heady news from Paris set small groups of literate radicals to talking heatedly, if for the moment ineffectually, about independence from the Ottoman Empire, itself agitated after 1789 by the administrative reform projects of the new Sultan Selim III.[1] Sweden's autocratic ruler, Gustavus III, who had subdued his own nobility in 1789, roundly condemned the calling of the French Estates General and then went on to denounce the National Assembly in even stronger terms. It was he who, first among European princes, proposed a general crusade against revolutionary France. Ironically, only his murder by a Swedish noble in 1792 prevented this anti-aristocratic authoritarian from seeking allies for a great campaign whose chief beneficiaries, had it succeeded, would have been the old privileged orders of France!

In Russia, finally, the ageing Catherine II, having granted much to the nobles of her own dominions, could lay claim to somewhat greater consistency than could Gustavus III in denouncing the revolutionary changes in France. Like the pope, she almost immediately condemned the National Assembly and all its works; and by the time her *Memoir on the French Revolution* appeared in 1792, she too was talking of a league of monarchs to save Louis XVI. A handful of her highest born subjects showed a fleeting sympathy for the French experiment, but many more shared their tsarina's horror. The great mass of Russians, if we may judge from contemporary accounts, were simply unaware of what was happening in western Europe.

Revolutionary France at War

Who started the long war that began in 1792 between France and much of the rest of Europe? Many parties for many different reasons. In Paris the king appears to have believed that war would *force* other powers to scatter his domestic enemies as a prelude to treating with him in the old way. Marie Antoinette confidently assured her imperial brother in Vienna that the revolutionists would prove both disorganized and cowardly. Noblemen such as the Comte de Narbonne, named war minister in December 1791, and the Marquis de Lafayette, initially

[1] B. Lewis, 'The impact of the French Revolution on Turkey', *Journal of World History*, vol. I (1953).

in command of over half the French forces in the field, saw an international crisis, even after the flight to Varennes, as an occasion for reviving aristocratic leadership. Roland, Brissot, Dumouriez and their fellow Girondins, convinced of the political advantages to be gained by war, accepted what turned out to be a fatal alliance with courtiers of the doomed monarchy. Only Robespierre and certain other Jacobins at first denounced this 'betrayal' and the diversion from the Legislative Assembly's proper tasks they were sure it would entail.

On the other side, it must be said that Austria and Prussia, while ostensibly seeking only to protect the rights of the French ruler, of the pope and of German princes who had lost fiefs in Alsace, coolly planned a direct intervention against the Revolution as such. In this regard, the death of the pacific Emperor Leopold II early in 1792 proved decisive. Thereafter, despite the cautious tone of their earlier pronouncements and their obvious concern over the Polish situation, the German powers hardened in their intent to attack France. Hence the Legislative Assembly's declaration of war against Austria on 20 April—the first of a long series—was perhaps more justified than Robespierre would admit at the time.

What was not justified was the blithe self-assurance with which the Girondin-court coalition approached the test of arms. We have noted earlier the effects of the Revolution on the French military establishment; yet the Assembly was assured that 300,000 men would hurl back the enemy. Actually, fully four months after war was declared, and after Prussia had joined its unfamiliar Austrian ally, French forces numbered only 80,000 men from the channel to Switzerland. Over half the officers in service in 1789 had already emigrated. Before the war was more than a few weeks old, Dumouriez's plan to invade Belgium had collapsed because of poor morale and incompetent or disloyal leadership at various points. No fewer than three full regiments changed to the Austro-Prussian side on the decisions of their officers. By July, when the Allied commander, the duke of Brunswick, issued a contemptuous manifesto against the Revolution, the French appeared helpless to withstand the coming offensive.

The failure of that offensive has been explained by 1792s uncommonly heavy summer rains in northern France, by the inability of the Allies to concert their efforts and by an almost miraculous recovery of will power on the part of the French armies, for whom Lafayette's defection to the enemy in August symbolized the elimination of half-hearted commanders. Doubtless the weather did delay the Germans' advance during critical weeks. The Allies, for their part, certainly did not exploit very effectively such victories as the capture of Verdun in early September. And it seems clear that French troops had gained some seasoning by the time the energetic Dumouriez took charge in the field. On 20 September Brunswick's army, pushing westward into Champagne from Verdun, encountered a large French force encamped on a fog-covered hill at Valmy. The artillery exchange was heavy, the infantry fighting very light; but once it was clear that the previously unreliable French regiments were holding firm, the Allies first broke off the attack, then went into a mystifyingly swift retreat.

The 'miracle of Valmy' was due essentially to unexpectedly stout defence. In the ensuing six weeks, however, with Custine's pursuit of the Prussians into the Rhineland, Dumouriez's long-cherished invasion of Belgium following his victory at Jemappes in November and the French occupation of Nice and Savoy at the king of Sardinia's expense, the Revolution for the first time passed to the offensive. It was unable to maintain this momentum indefinitely, especially after Britain, Holland and Spain entered the war in the spring of 1793. Yet even after the loss of Brussels, Mainz, Alsace and Toulon to foreign foes, combined with widespread anti-Jacobin revolts at home, the Republic fought for its life with a desperate ferocity having nothing to do with the spirit in which the Girondin-royalist ministry had launched the war. By the end of the year, while the Terror gripped France itself, the chilling discipline of Robespierre's régime and the success of Carnot in marshalling new resources through the *levée en masse* had stiffened the armies once more. In December, the Allies left Alsace and retreated again across the Rhine.

What was then beginning, though no one could have been sure of it at the time, was a two-year period of French victories. The Republic's forces, steadily replenished with recruits, kept up merciless pressure on all fronts. During 1794 Pichegru's triumph over the British at Tourcoing in April and Jourdan's and Kléber's over the Austrians at Fleurus in June once again opened the Low Countries to invasion. Belgium was cleared of Allied forces; and by January 1795 Pichegru's veterans entered Amsterdam while Stadtholder William fled to England. At the same time Jourdan had wheeled about and was sweeping southeast through the German Rhineland, taking Coblenz, Cologne and Mainz on the left bank, then Mannheim across the great river. Simultaneous victories over the Spanish in Catalonia and on the Biscay coast were matched by continued pressure on the Austrians and Sardinians in north Italy. It took Hoche and his Army of the West less than one month to crush the ill-conceived English effort in June 1795 to support the Chouan rebels by landing an émigré army on the coast of Brittany.

By that time, the First Coalition was going to pieces. Under the treaty of Basel on 5 March 1795, the Prussians, discouraged about the western front and eager to concentrate on Poland, had withdrawn from the war at the cost of confirming French possession of the entire left bank of the Rhine. Several other north German states followed suit. In July, also at Basel, Spain made peace, ceding France San Domingo in the West Indies. In December, on both the Alsatian and the Italian fronts, the Austrians concluded local armistice agreements with the victorious Republic, though Vienna, like London, insisted that the general struggle must go on.

The Final Partition of Poland

It may be well to pause here for a reminder that, despite the immense scope of the revolutionary crisis, not all the issues confronting the European state system in the 1790s centred about France. Prussia and Austria went on bargaining over possible annexations and exchanges of territory: the Netherlands, Bavaria, Bohemia and perhaps—here the French war did impinge—the lost province of Alsace, assuming it could be reconquered. The Russian-Turkish duel and the struggle in the Baltic area still absorbed the attention of eastern capitals. For that matter, they also involved London, at least until March 1791, when Pitt's effort to make England the sponsor of a Swedish-Prussian-Polish-Turkish coalition to restrain Russia foundered on the suspicious isolationism of a majority in the House of Commons. Beyond question, however, the most important non-French centre of tension was the ill-fated constitutional monarchy of Poland.

Even before concluding peace with Turkey in the first days of 1792, Catherine II had suggested to Berlin that Prussia and Russia should ignore Austrian remonstrances and proceed with a further division of Polish lands. Once the Turkish war ended, the tsarina turned her full attention to the problem. In March 1792, she secured Frederick William II's agreement to the principle that Prussia should compensate itself in Poland for the expenses of the impending war against France, and by late April, the Confederation of Targowice, a league of reactionary Polish nobles, had been formed under her sponsorship—its formal compact was actually signed at St Petersburg. On 18 May over 100,000

Russian troops, ostensibly answering the appeal of Poland's own aristocracy, launched a full-scale invasion. For two months, King Stanislas and his generals, including Kosciuszko, led a brave and, it appeared, not entirely hopeless defence. Then the king's determination simply melted. Abjectly, he rescinded the Constitution of 1791 and awaited the pleasure of Russia and its Prussian ally. Austrian hopes that England might join in opposing a second partition of Poland, which in Vienna's eyes represented dangerous aggrandisement for two major rivals, proved groundless. By the treaty of 23 January 1793 the tsarina took the rest of White Russia and a major slice of the Polish Ukraine, while Prussia received some long-coveted prizes: Danzig, Thorn and Posen.

The third partition proved to be scarcely more than an epilogue. Kosciuszko's patriotic rebels of 1794 were no match for the massive Russian forces under Suvorov. By the following spring, the Polish state had virtually disappeared as a political entity. With the Prussians disengaging themselves from the war against France, Austria no longer dared to stand aside from a final settlement. On 24 October 1795 a treaty among the three great eastern powers obliterated what was left of the Polish kingdom, Russia taking the rest of historic Lithuania and, in the south, Volhynia; Prussia, the Warsaw region; Austria, all of western Galicia including Cracow and Lublin. The death of Poland forms one of those chapters of late eighteenth-century history which must be understood as distinct from the French crisis, but the two were not unrelated. It seems inconceivable that the atypically 'total' denouement in the east could have occurred had the western powers been free to intervene.

Europe Takes Stock

The year 1795, when the Convention gave way to the Directory in Paris and when many of the Revolution's foreign enemies abandoned hostilities, offers a convenient point from which to survey the changes which had been taking place in Europe. Most obvious, aside from Poland's obliteration, had been the extension of French control to include a number of neighbouring areas. Belgium, invaded in 1792, largely evacuated the following year, retaken by Pichegru and Jourdan in 1794, became, under a decree of 1 October 1795, an integral part (nine new departments) of the Republic. To the north, the former United Provinces, after ceding a strip of border territory to French

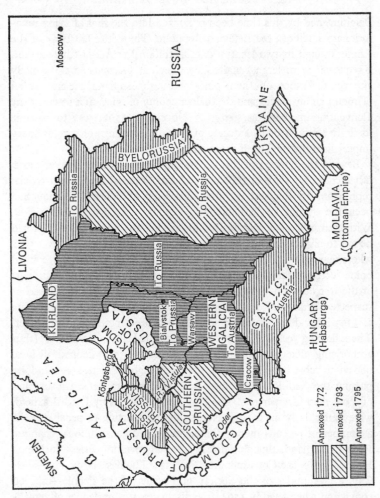

3. *Partitions of Poland*

Belgium, had by this time been organized into the first of many revolutionary satellites, the Batavian Republic. The entire left bank of the Rhine, though its two 'central administrations' at Aix-la-Chapelle and Kreuznach were largely staffed by obedient Germans, was formally annexed to France. On the Alpine-Mediterranean front, the annexation of mountainous Savoy and the former county of Nice, first voted by the Convention in Paris as early as November 1792, was to become 'definitive' by virtue of a decree of 1796. The pattern of revolutionary imperialism revealed itself more and more clearly.

Beyond the borders of this expanding France and its dependencies, other countries showed the strain of war, internal unrest and official repression. In England the first clear sign of political reaction had been the decline in parliamentary support for Charles James Fox. With the outbreak of war against France in 1793 numerous Whigs had begun to shift their allegiance to Prime Minister Pitt; and by 1794 a whole new party of Whig leaders around the duke of Portland, named home secretary that July, had joined forces with the Tories in support of the war effort. Meanwhile, the government was treating avowed or suspected Francophiles with growing harshness. From the beginning of 1793 individual arrests for sedition had been increasing in number. The following year, Parliament suspended the Habeas Corpus Act (thus authorizing detention of prisoners without trial), defined disloyal behaviour more broadly through the Treasonable Practices Act and, by passing the Seditious Meetings Act, outlawed unlicensed assemblies of more than fifty persons. The Scottish courts, led by Lord Braxfield, were particularly harsh, imprisoning or transporting to penal colonies a number of persons merely for having urged constitutional changes. Even in England, though thirteen accused revolutionaries—including Horne Tooke, the Corresponding Society's Thomas Hardy, and Thelwall, a co-founder of the Society of Friends of the People—escaped conviction when tried in 1794, free discussion was in danger of vanishing. The knowledge that, despite Parliament's hasty grant of voting rights to the Catholics of Ireland in 1793, Wolfe Tone and other Irish leaders were in Paris to negotiate with the French government added an element of fear to the outlook of British Tories and Whigs alike.

The government of Spain, soon after Charles IV's accession in 1788, had adopted what now appear to have been unnecessarily stern restrictions on press freedom, incoming mail and public discussion. As in several other Catholic countries, notably including the kingdom of

Sardinia and the Austrian dominions, Spanish administrators revealed a strong tendency to identify Jacobinism with religious dissent, so that foreign residents were compelled to swear allegiance not only to the Crown but also to the Roman Church. It was the war with France, initially greeted with public enthusiasm in 1793, but increasingly unpopular as the military news from the Pyrenees became worse and worse, that first led some small groups of Spaniards to express a limited sympathy for the Revolution. In spite of exaggerated rumours at the time, however, nothing approaching Jacobin Clubs appeared. After the ageing Aranda succeeded Floridablanca as first minister in 1792, Manuel Godoy, duke de la Alcudia and lover of the queen, became the dominant figure, two years later ousting Aranda himself. Godoy, transparently ambitious though by no means unintelligent, was never popular, even after the welcome Basel settlement (*see above*, p. 149) won him the resounding title, 'Prince of the Peace'. But at least the Spanish monarchy had weathered its first clash with the Revolution and could now reverse its foreign policy, actually accepting a French military alliance without apparent fear of revolutionary contagion.

Portugal's royal government, at war with the French since 1793, and in 1796 attacked by the Spaniards as well, hunted down radicals with extreme severity; for these were the 'years of Manique', the dreaded intendant of police. In both Italy and Germany, some states, including Tuscany in 1794 and Prussia, Saxony and Hanover the following year, had withdrawn from the military struggle. Others, such as Bavaria and the Italian kingdoms of Sardinia and of Naples, still remained allies of Austria against the French Republic. But whether at war or not, all continued to feel the menace of French arms and the stirring of dissatisfied elements at home. The latter, be it noted, ranged from lower-class admirers of the Jacobin sans-culottes, through businessmen yearning for the end of feudal privilege, to the sort of idealistic young aristocrats whose advanced views brought them death upon scaffolds in a dozen Italian and central European cities. Within these threatened lands, as in Switzerland, where such men as Peter Ochs in Basel looked to France to destroy the old order, an uneasy peace was maintained only by police vigilance. In Austria and Hungary conspiratorial stirrings began to be uncovered by the brutal régime of Francis II's minister, Baron von Thugut. At Budapest, for example, in May and June 1795, seven alleged 'Jacobins' were beheaded. They included the former Franciscan monk, Martinovics; the writer, Hajnóczy, son of a Protestant pastor; the gentleman officer, Laczkovics; and the learned

Count Jaco Zsigray.[1] Despite the disillusioning shock of the Terror and certain disquieting reports about occupation practices in Belgium, the Rhineland and Savoy, French armies could still count on a welcome from sizeable minorities almost everywhere.

There were some exceptions. In Denmark, for example, the government's pursuit of domestic reforms had kept even the small Jacobin Club in Copenhagen explicitly loyal to the Crown. Sweden, after the bitter anti-revolutionary Gustavus III's assassination, was administered for four years by a pro-French Regent, the duke of Sudermania, under whom the Swedish press recovered its freedom to report news from Paris; but in 1796, young King Gustavus IV attained his majority and promptly swung back, if not quite to his father's vehement hostility, at least to a suspicious isolation. As for Russia, Catherine II never wavered in her hatred of the new French order. She had the social critic, Radishchev, condemned to death in 1790 for having written his indignant *Journey from St Petersburg to Moscow* and his much more emotional *Ode to Liberty*; and despite the commutation of this harsh sentence to exile in Siberia, no further commentaries in Radishchev's vein were permitted to appear. If Catherine refrained from military intervention in the west, while exploiting her Polish opportunities, her government forbade any organized expression of interest in the Revolution. The only republican discussions of any importance took place in absolute privacy between her grandson, the future Alexander I, and his Swiss tutor, the Francophile classicist La Harpe—and even they ended with La Harpe's return home in 1795. When the old Empress died the following year, she was succeeded by her still more violently anti-French son, Paul I, a tsar prepared to join actively in the struggle against the Revolution.

The Emergence of Bonaparte

Even before Russia became involved, that struggle had grown infinitely broader and more complicated than the warfare of the years before the Directory. To understand these changes, it is necessary to recall that by 1795 France had come through the first phase of its military crisis and for the time being had clearly assumed the initiative. The Pyrenean and Flemish frontiers were now stabilized, and since the treaty of Basel with Prussia, there was no fear of a major attack from northern Germany. When Carnot and his fellow directors looked about them, and

[1] C. Benda, 'Les Jacobins hongrois', *Annales historiques de la Révolution française*, vol. XXXI (1959).

began to plan operations against the two principal enemies of the Republic, it was with a sense of considerable freedom to choose their means and their battlefields.

Against England, the war of privateers was to be pushed to the limit, with American help at sea if that could be secured, while Irish rebels such as Wolfe Tone and Napper Tandy were to receive direct support through the landing of an invasion force under General Hoche. Against Austria and its allies, the directors agreed upon three massive land strikes. Jourdan and the army of the Sambre and Meuse should drive along and beyond Germany's Main valley to join Moreau's army of the Rhine and Moselle pushing eastward through Baden and Württemberg. A junction in Bavaria might prove decisive. Meanwhile Bonaparte would advance from Nice along the Mediterranean coast into Italy, in the hope of defeating the Austrian-Sardinian forces and then turning north through the Alps to join the final assault on Vienna itself.

It was a magnificent plan, destined to be adapted and revived several times in the next ten years; but on the first application, all but one feature of it miscarried. The United States would not collaborate against England, instead actually engaging French naval raiders in a three-year undeclared war. In December 1796 Hoche's army, transported from Brest to Bantry Bay, Ireland, was unable to reach the shore because of storms. The following year some 1,400 French troops who had landed in South Wales were promptly rounded up by the English local militia; and Humbert's small landing on the Irish coast in 1798 met no better fate. By this time the Directory's armies in Germany were painfully aware that Austria had finally found a general. Francis II's brother, the Archduke Charles, defeated Jourdan at Würzburg on the Main in September 1796, then turned south to drive Moreau back through the Black Forest to the Rhine. For a number of reasons, including the unforeseen energy of the archduke and the lack of co-operation between the jealous French commanders, the northern arm of the great pincers had been broken.

Against this background, it is easy to see why Bonaparte's Italian campaign seemed so dazzling. Advancing south-east in the spring of 1796, the army of Italy knocked the Sardinians out of the war in a matter of weeks, crushed an Austrian force at Lodi on 10 May and entered Milan five days later. On the 16th, the conquered Milan was proclaimed a satellite of France, the Lombard Republic. Stalled for months by the siege of Mantua, Bonaparte finally took the stubborn city early in February 1797 and reluctantly (since he was eager to invade

Austria) yielded to orders from Paris that he march against Rome. Once satisfied by the terrified pope's cession of Bologna, the Romagna and other territories, the French commander in March wheeled his hardened regiments about once more, driving north into the Austrian Alps to engage Archduke Charles. Here he was frustrated by anti-French revolts in Venetia and the Tyrol, as well as by the failure of the French offensive in Bavaria. Nevertheless, on 18 April the Austrians felt compelled to accept a truce pending final negotiations.

In the six months between this 'preliminary peace' of Leoben and the treaty of Campo-Formio, signed on 17 October 1797, Bonaparte was anything but idle. In May his army occupied Venetia, which he held as a pawn for dealings with Austria. By July he had fashioned two new satellite republics: the Ligurian (Genoa) and the Cisalpine (Lombardy, the Bolognese and the Romagna). All this Austria accepted at Campo-Formio, where Napoleon performed the first of his many prodigies of territorial shuffling. The Habsburgs recognized French annexation of Belgium, the left bank of the Rhine and a former Venetian possession, the Ionian Islands between Italy and Greece. In return, Austria was given the city of Venice and most of its mainland territories, a promise of the archbishopric of Salzburg, with a strip of southern Bavaria, and the secret assurance that France would allow Prussia no territorial compensation for the Rhineland. Since this provision was a direct French betrayal of the treaty of Basel, while the clause touching Bavaria struck at Austria's chief German ally, Campo-Formio can scarcely be said to have been a model of good faith. In any event, the treaty was signed by representatives of Francis II, in his capacity as ruler of Austria. France would still have to negotiate with the Holy Roman Empire in a peace conference to be convened at Rastatt in Baden.

The year 1798 witnessed a whole new series of French tours de force. Early in the year, Rome was occupied, a Roman Republic proclaimed and Pope Pius VI carried off to France, where he shortly died. Simultaneously, the Directory, at the instance of La Harpe and other Swiss exiles in Paris, as well as the Basel revolutionaries around Peter Ochs, recognized the creation of a Helvetian Republic. French armies overran Switzerland to enforce the new order, at the same time annexing the once proud city-state of Geneva to France itself. In May Bonaparte left Toulon with over 30,000 men on his dash to seize Egypt and open the road to India. Landing near Alexandria, he struck at the Mameluke forces of the Egyptian *beys* (vassals of the Turkish sultan) and on 21

July, in sight of the pyramids, he defeated them in a pitched battle. The next day, his army of the East entered Cairo. This was one of the high points in an incredible military career, yet the disaster which doomed the expedition occurred only a few days later. Admiral Horatio Nelson's British naval squadron, after weeks of exasperated pursuit, finally caught the French fleet in Aboukir Bay near the mouth of the Nile and on 1 August 1798 virtually destroyed it. Bonaparte himself campaigned for another year in both Egypt and Syria. Then he slipped back to France, leaving the army of the East under Kléber's command, to survive as best it could without naval support.

In Europe too, from the Directory's point of view, events had by this time taken an alarming turn. In December 1798, while a French army was advancing into southern Italy, a new alliance against the Republic was taking form. This Second Coalition's chief members were England, Austria and Russia; for Tsar Paul was at last ready to strike *his* blow, and Vienna eagerly resumed hostilities only fourteen months after Campo-Formio. Throughout most of 1799 the Allies pressed the French backward on widely separated fronts. Archduke Charles won new victories over first Jourdan and then Masséna on the upper Rhine. From April through June Suvorov's Russian veterans, with Austrian aid, drove the French out of most of northern Italy, while in the south the shortlived Parthenopean Republic was destroyed in a vengeful blood bath by the returning king of Naples. For a time the Russians seemed to be everywhere at once, contributing 17,000 troops to the British expedition against Holland, sending a naval squadron with the Turks to seize the Ionian Islands off Greece. In August Suvorov crossed the St Gotthard Pass from Italy into Switzerland, there to join another Russian force which had recently traversed the Habsburg domains from Poland.

At this point, however, the French, though still weakened by the diversion of Bonaparte's seasoned troops to Egypt, reasserted their capacity for defensive warfare close to home. The Russian-Austrian advance was halted at Zürich, and Masséna, by taking Constance in southern Germany, made an advance across the Rhine too risky for the Archduke Charles to undertake. In Holland the commanders of the British-Russian force, after months of unsuccessful manoeuvring, finally settled for an exchange of prisoners and left the mainland. By the end of October the furious fighting had subsided. Paul I, angry over the alleged greed and inaction of his allies, abruptly called his expeditionary forces back to Russia and left the coalition.

As the century drew to a close, the military situation, viewed from Paris, justified a renewal of confidence. The newborn Consulate had inherited some dangers, to be sure. Especially in Italy, where Genoa was for the moment the only major base under revolutionary France's red, white and blue flag, the Tricolour, another series of victories would be necessary to restore the situation. In Egypt the army Bonaparte had abandoned in order to become first consul fought on without hope of anything better than a negotiated withdrawal. British sea power continued to gnaw at French commerce and communications, while the collapse of the Rastatt Congress early in 1799 meant that the Holy Roman Empire still did not recognize French conquests. On the other hand, the 'natural frontiers' of France—Rhine, Alps, Pyrenees—appeared secure, the first two made so by annexations, the third by the Spanish alliance. Important buffers such as the Batavian and Helvetian Republics had not been torn from the French system, despite the exertions of the Allies. Russia, Prussia and Sweden, meanwhile, were moving towards a new League of Armed Neutrality, at least as disadvantageous to Great Britain as to France. Under the circumstances, First Consul Bonaparte could choose his own battlegrounds, much as the directors had been able to do in 1795.

France and Its Territorial Conquests

Let us now try to form some general estimate of Europe's relations with revolutionary France on the eve of the Napoleonic adventure. Two of the aspects involved, political echoes in various countries and military hostilities, we have been following in alternating sequence through the decade which ended in 1799. Still another factor, however, must also be taken into account, because of its powerful influence on foreign attitudes towards the Republic. This is the record of the French in areas which came under their control through military action.

The picture is by no means a simple one, in part because there were considerable differences between the revolutionary conquerors of 1793–94, for example, and those of 1796–98, in part because even at a single time a wide variety of policies were being pursued in separate regions. Certain areas, of course, after varying periods of exploitation were simply incorporated into the *Grande Nation*: Avignon (1791), Belgium (1795), Nice and Savoy (1796), Geneva and Mulhouse in Alsace (1798). The left-bank Rhineland, annexed but not fully integrated, remained under what amounted to a continuing military occupation. Other areas, Dutch, Swiss and Italian, submitted to the organization of satellite republics under constitutions worked out by local admirers of the Revolution, with the peremptory advice of French officials.

Practically everywhere they went, from Amsterdam to Mainz and from Basel to Naples, the armies of France could count on a welcome from critics of the Old Régime in each locality. Some of those who hailed the invaders as liberators were, as noted earlier, individuals educated to reform under the aegis of the Enlightenment. Others had organized revolutionary clubs which stepped forward to claim political power once the French arrived. There is no question that in encouraging these elements, often reinforced by the return of former democratic exiles, the occupation authorities created a situation which encouraged an unattractive paying off of old personal scores. A newly erected guillotine in Brussels or Geneva could not fail to excite both fear and disgust among established social groups. In addition, the conquerors often imposed constitutional reforms which, although reasonable enough in themselves, struck many of their intended beneficiaries as unnatural importations from abroad. If certain arrangements, notably the creation of neat geographical districts on the model of *départements*, had lasting effects all the way from Holland to the Ionian Islands, many others, including reorganized judicial systems, proved viable only so long as the French forces were on hand to enforce them. This mixture of artificial support for radical minorities and doctrinaire insistence on historically rootless institutional reforms created an impression that Jacobinism bloomed under the Tricolour—long after France had thrown its own Jacobins out of power in 1794.

The religious policies of the Republic in occupied or satellite areas have been the subject of considerable misunderstanding. It is all too easy to assume, for instance, that a France which confiscated the Church's property at home, as early as 1789, *must* have been consistently and violently anti-Catholic everywhere abroad. Instead, the fact is that in only two regions, Belgium and the German Rhineland, did the Roman Church suffer any sustained pillaging of its belongings or mistreatment of its clergy. Belgium was invaded first in 1792 and then again in 1794, precisely when the two most extreme outbursts of anti-clericalism were occurring in France itself. Yet even here, the Convention's decision in 1795 to insist upon the separation of Church and State brought an easing of tension, however unhappy Belgian Catholics might feel about the equality now accorded Protestants and Jews.

Catholic principalities in the Rhineland also witnessed numerous acts of confiscation; but the priests in this region—as distinct from the bishops and other prelates, practically all of whom had fled—suffered much less than their stubborn resistance to the new order might suggest. In Italy the cautious approach of General Bonaparte is particularly striking; for he demanded nothing more than freedom for religious minorities in the big Cisalpine Republic and elsewhere did not challenge the dominant position of Catholicism to even that limited degree. It should be added that his solicitude for Muslim sensibilities when he invaded Egypt revealed this same reluctance to outrage subject populations over questions of faith.

In general, of course, the Revolution did bring with it relief for Protestants and, still more strikingly, for Jews in occupied states. For example, 1797 saw the ghetto gates of Venice and several other Italian cities destroyed in formal ceremonies. A further point which merits some attention is the liberalizing effect of French occupation on *non-Catholic* ruling groups—for bigotry and intolerance had not been monopolies of the Roman Church. The United Provinces, for all their vaunted toleration, had excluded Jews and Catholics from many key positions. The Batavian (Dutch) Republic, on the other hand, became the European state whose degree of religious equality most nearly matched that of revolutionary France itself. Protestant states in Germany west of the Rhine and Protestant cantons in Switzerland also had to extend religious freedom to Catholic and Jewish minorities. In the Ionian Islands it was not the wish to see an end to religious persecution which assured the Russians such a warm welcome in 1799; instead, it was the resentment of the local Orthodox majority against the equality granted Catholics and Jews by the French during their two-year occupation.

Political favouritism, constitutional innovations and antidenominational religious policies all made France some enemies, of course. At the same time, these very features of occupation or satellite status enlisted the support of important local groups. The general impression made by French conquerors might have been more favourable, therefore, and their place in the historical memory of a number of other countries considerably higher, had another factor not assumed overwhelming importance. This was the question of material exactions, including both military requisitions for use in the field and financial tribute to be sent to Paris. The most recent study of the subject fixes the aggregate of such demands for the eight years, 1792 through 1799, at a figure which, though meaningless in itself, represents only slightly more than one-half the French Government's average budget for *one* of those years.[1] Seen in this perspective, the amount involved does not appear crushing. However, the constant demands of the armies and the apparent avarice of the Directory in particular contrasted mockingly with the Republic's gospel of fraternity and a better life for all men everywhere. At specific times and in specific places, the exactions were unquestionably onerous. Finally, they were imposed with little warning, often in arrogant terms which led many an erstwhile friend of the Revolution to complain that the French came as liberators, only to stay as extortionate conquerors.

From the autumn of 1792, when Dumouriez entered Belgium and ordered Tournai to supply his troops with 12,000 rations of bread per day, 6,000 pounds of meat and large quantities of fodder, all to be paid for in assignats, the roll of requisitions and tributes grew steadily longer. Belgium escaped the status of a conquered country when it was annexed by France in 1795; but that same year, the new Batavian Republic to the north was required to pay, for the maintenance of 25,000 French troops, the sum of 10 million *florins* annually until further notice, plus an impossible indemnity of 100 million. About 50 million florins were actually collected over the course of the next two years. (By 1797, be it added, the continuing Dutch contribution had been scaled down to the more realistic figure of 3 million per year in wartime.) In the German Rhineland, meanwhile, though exact computations are impossible, the level of requisitions remained high. Before launching his drive eastward in the spring of 1796, for instance, Jourdan demanded 13,000 metric tons of various cereal grains, huge supplies of meat and one-thirtieth of the civilian-owned horses in his sector of the left bank. As for Italy, most systematically plundered of all the occupied territories, it has been estimated that by the end of July 1796 over 53 million *lire*, then still equated with French *livres*, had been assessed upon Italian states occupied or threatened by Bonaparte, that 32 million had been collected and that some 15 million had already been shipped to France to help buttress the Directory's new currency, the silver *franc*. The formal treaty with the Cisalpine Republic, signed early in 1798, provided for a yearly tribute of 18 million *lire*, to be paid in monthly instalments. That same year, the treasures of Switzerland were opened to the Helvetian Republic's French 'brothers', and

---

[1] Godechot, p. 565 (*see* Bibliography, p. 138). Illustrative figures given in the ensuing paragraph are all derived from Chapter XVI of this work.

Masséna promptly exacted 800,000 francs apiece from Zürich and Basel. Even the Francophile La Harpe was staggered.

Reactions Elsewhere in Europe

Disillusionment with the Revolution on the part of many elements within the geographical limits of French control was matched by shifts of attitude outside those limits. The Terror, the aggressiveness of the French armies and their behaviour in occupied areas, especially when exaggerated by hostile reports, all contributed to the change. There is evidence, for example, that well before Hoche sailed for Bantry Bay in 1796 many Irish rebels, who yielded not a whit of their hatred of the English, had begun to question the benefits of the help from an 'atheistic republic'. The following year, Tyroleans fought Bonaparte in the Alps with a zeal which belied their longstanding grievances against the Habsburgs of Vienna.

The danger of sketching this reaction too simply is that one might conclude that all dissension had vanished within the borders of countries hostile to the Directory. The real point is quite different. Unrest still growled just below the surface of the restored Kingdom of Naples after King Ferdinand overthrew the Parthenopean Republic. In Austria, Bohemia and, above all, Hungary, signs of resentment against Thugut and his police methods were if anything increasing. Most of the German states maintained their nervous measures of surveillance and repression, inevitably accompanied by popular complaints. But at the end of the '90s, none of these quarrels involved such explicit admiration for or rejection of the *French* model as had dominated most local situations just a few years earlier.

This phenomenon of continuing tension in a changing context was nowhere quite so striking as in the British Isles. Early in 1798 fighting broke out in Ireland between the English army and rebel forces containing not only Protestants but also growing numbers of resentful Catholics. Pitched battles were fought by these United Irishmen at Wexford, Ballinahinch, Vinegar Hill, while the reciprocal slaughter of prisoners introduced an element of savagery unmatched on the island for several generations past. With no firm assurance of French aid and with no widespread belief in its desirability, the rebels gambled on victory in their own cause. They failed miserably. Fresh royal forces under the new viceroy, Lord Cornwallis, crushed the United Irishmen, captured the small French landing party under Humbert and arrested

Wolfe Tone, who had come ashore with it. (He killed himself in jail after having been convicted of treason.) Yet neither the Catholic emancipation of 1793 nor the military victories of 1798 had brought Pitt's government a solution of the Irish question. Within three years, the prime minister was to try a very different expedient: the full political union of Ireland with England, Scotland and Wales.

In England itself the behaviour of the revolutionary clubs reflected ever more strongly both disillusionment with events in France and fear of prosecution for sedition. The House of Commons, it is true, under Fox and his younger collaborator, Charles Grey, resumed debates over parliamentary reform in 1796; but confronted by Pitt's stubborn insistence that this was no time for constitutional tampering, Grey's Reform Bill lost in 1797 by a vote of 256 to 91. The response of Foxite Whigs was significant of the temper of the times—they simply withdrew from active political life, beginning the long interruption in liberal pressure for change. Meanwhile, the government moved to tighten still further the bonds of political discipline. Naval mutinies at the Nore and Spithead in 1797, though alarming in themselves, had no apparent link with pro-Jacobin feeling, the sailors being motivated instead by their own bitterness over low pay, poor quarters and lack of medical care. The Tory ministry, however, was taking no chances with any type of opposition. In 1799, despite the Corresponding Society's prudent discussion the previous year of an enlistment of volunteers to fend off any French invasion, that body and several other clubs were suppressed by law. At the same time, Parliament passed the first of a series of Combination Acts against organizations which were seeking to promote higher wages and shorter hours.

The shift of emphasis from the fear of a French landing to that of indigenous rebellion in Ireland was thus matched in England by a swing from primarily anti-Jacobin to more specifically anti-labour and anti-reformist measures. These changes, like the related ones occurring in Germany, the Habsburg lands and Italy, were extremely important. Political, social and economic unrest had by no means disappeared in countries threatened by France. But a transformation in the way such unrest expressed itself had occurred during the decade of turmoil we have been examining.

The French Revolution had begun amid excited applause from Whig reformers in Britain, supporters of the Josephine programme in Austria and the men around Grand Duke Leopold in Tuscany, not to mention the democrats of Holland and Belgium, the Germanies and

Switzerland. Down to 1792, principles enunciated in Paris had exercised a strong appeal over wide areas of Europe. With the coming of war and the Terror, this identification of progressivism with Francophilia began to break down. After Thermidor, the Directory's apparent opportunism at home and rapacity abroad damaged still further the image of France as the 'homeland of all who love liberty'. When the century ended it was possible for an Englishman, a Neapolitan or an Hungarian to feel highly critical of the government under which he lived, yet give that government his support against the French national enemy.

Up to a point this could be taken to mean that 'the Revolution' had already been assimilated as a shared experience and that no single country was any longer its sole sponsor. The issues of 1789 and 1791 and even of 1793-4 in France were in fact destined to become part of a spreading European debate, subject to various formulations in different lands. For the time being, however, the military crisis was blanketing these issues, making identification with the Revolution more and more unpopular as the intensity of conflict with France increased. By 1799 war had become the dominant theme of European life. At just this point, the rulers of France installed a dictator who was going to discipline the Revolution at home, while spreading the war over distances unparalleled since Genghis Khan.

VIII

Napoleon in Power

Bonaparte the Man

At the end of 1799 the soldier who had just become first consul of the French Republic was thirty years old. Born the son of a minor nobleman on the island of Corsica, shortly after Genoa had sold it to France, he was christened Napoleone Buonaparte. At the age of ten, upon crossing to the mainland and entering the military academy at Brienne, he adopted the more familiar French spelling. Commissioned a lieutenant in 1785, he began what promised to be a routine army career; but 1789

BIBLIOGRAPHY. A brilliantly sustained essay, at once reviewing successive historians' treatments of Bonaparte's place in history and presenting its own carefully developed judgment, is P. Geyl, *Napoleon: For and Against* (London, 1949). Another important treatment of the same general problem, A. Guérard's *Reflections on the Napoleonic Legend* (New York, 1923), was followed over a quarter-century later by his *Napoleon I* (New York, 1956). For the most sweeping study by a non-Frenchman, one should consult F. Kircheisen, *Napoleon I: Sein Leben und seine Zeit* (Munich, 1911–34), in nine volumes. The student interested in direct evidence bearing on the emperor's personality and intellect will find a fascinating cluster of source readings in J. C. Herold, ed. and trans., *The Mind of Napoleon: a selection from his written and spoken words* (New York, 1955). On the structure of French government and society, the best general manual is J. Godechot, *Les institutions de la France sous la Révolution et l'Empire* (Paris, 1951). A much shorter sketch, which summarizes many of Godechot's sections, while inserting a series of pro-Bonapartist judgments, is F. Ponteil, *Napoléon Ier et l'organisation autoritaire de la France* (Paris, 1956). Important treatments of specific institutional features of the era include J. Régnier, *Les préfets du Consulat et de l'Empire* (Paris, 1907); C. Durand, *Etudes sur le Conseil d'état napoléonien* and *Le fonctionnement du Conseil d'état napoléonien* (Paris, 1949; Gap, 1954); and E. d'Hauterive *et al.*, *La police secrète du premier Empire*, 4 vols. (Paris, 1908–63). J. Valynseele's two genealogical studies, *Les maréchaux du premier Empire* and *Les princes et ducs du premier Empire, non maréchaux* (Paris, 1957 and 1959) are rather narrowly antiquarian in aim, but they contain much of interest concerning the highest levels of Napoleon's aristocracy. Among the scores of more or less judicious works dealing with religious affairs, four deserve mention here: A. Latreille, *L'Église catholique et la Révolution française*, vol. II: *L'Ère napoléonienne et la crise européenne, 1800–1815* (Paris, changed all that. During the next four years, he alternated between active duty with his regiment and pro-French agitation in Corsica during several home leaves. Then, in September 1793, having attracted the favourable attention of the Committee of Public Safety by writing a strongly pro-Jacobin pamphlet, *Le Souper de Beaucaire,* he was promoted to the rank of captain and placed in command of the artillery facing rebellious Toulon. With the capture of the great port from the royalists and their allies, Bonaparte won his first victory for the Revolution and with it the rank of brigadier general.

He still had far to go, however, on the untraced road to solitary power. Arrested in the Thermidorean reaction after Robespierre's fall in 1794, the young officer spent a month in jail, then was released and ordered to prepare an expedition against the Corsican separatist régime. British naval forces opposed that project, but it seems to have been Bonaparte's own mixture of political curiosity and calculation which made him find excuses for staying around Paris all through the following year. Hence, in October 1795, he was on hand to supply the 'whiff of grapeshot' which scattered the royalist insurgents in the Rue Saint-Honoré. The expiring Convention and then the Directory shared a natural enthusiasm for this energetic soldier, who was shortly named commander of the army of the Interior and then, in 1796, of the 30,000 ragged troops composing the army of Italy. We have already observed his rise during the years that witnessed the brilliant first Italian campaign, the grandiose thrust at Egypt, the abrupt return to France and the overthrow of the Directory on the Eighteenth and Nineteenth Brumaire.

Behold this thirty-year-old Corsican immigrant—for it is difficult to think of him as anything else—first citizen of the mighty and mercurial nation which had slain Louis XVI, Danton and Robespierre, driven out Dumouriez, Lafayette and Carnot! Yet the more amazing portion of his career still lay ahead. Victorious maker of peace and the Concordat of 1801, consul-for-life in 1802, emperor of the French in 1804, victor over the other two emperors, Austrian and Russian, at Austerlitz the following year and then over the once dreaded Prussia, Napoleon at Tilsit in 1807 would spread out before the tsar his plan for a new

1950); H. Walsh, *The Concordat of 1801* (New York, 1933); R. Anchel, *Napoléon et les juifs* (Paris, 1928); and finally, though it deals with Calvinist 'Huguenots' over a long period, to the exclusion of the French Lutheran minority, B. C. Poland, *French Protestantism and the French Revolution* (Princeton, 1957).

European order. Invader of Spain in 1808, in 1810 husband of the Habsburg emperor's own daughter, leader of the Grand Army's gigantic assault upon Russia in 1812, the one-time artillery lieutenant would at last meet defeat on a converging spiral of fronts: Russia, Germany, Spain, southern France and finally the Seine itself. Exiled to Elba in 1814, back to try one more throw of the dice during the next year's 'Hundred Days', defeated at Waterloo, exiled this time to the British island of St Helena in the South Atlantic, he would spend the concluding six years of his life creating the material and suggesting the themes for the Napoleonic legend. It was the legend of a Promethean hero, as he saw himself, chained to a rock by the outraged gods he had defied—and more immediately, according to his version, by the old world tyrants he had challenged.

Let us pass over the legend in favour of the story of Napoleon, as accurately reconstructed as the limits of knowledge and space will allow. For detractors no less than for admirers, that story has exercised an inexhaustible fascination, partly because of its implications for the subsequent history of all the European peoples, but partly too because of its own dramatic form. No other career seems to embody quite so strikingly the dynamism of what Oswald Spengler was later to call 'Faustian man'—tireless in his activity, at once intelligent and un-scrupulous in his choice of means, ruthless in his egoistic will to power. Thus, the personality of the first consul of 1799 is uncommonly sig-nificant for an understanding of the hectic decade-and-a-half we still refer to by his name.

The pale, arresting countenance, with its luminous eyes, sharp nose and tight mouth above a deceptively soft, dimpled chin, is known to us from countless portraits. In an age which saw many elaborate coiffures even for men, Napoleon brushed his hair smooth. That feature, combined with the clean shaven face he preferred to the mus-tachioed bravado of his own Imperial Guardsmen, only added to the classical severity of his appearance. He was short of stature and, from his late thirties onward, increasingly thickset. It should be added, however, that in his time a height of barely five feet was less likely to inspire a sense of physical inferiority than it might in a present-day European.

To reach a confident judgment about his mind is not altogether easy. He was a rapid, voracious, but highly selective reader, preferring history to abstract philosophy, caring little for *belles lettres* as such, despite his not very convincing expressions of rapture over the fraudulent

Scottish folk poetry of Ossian. He was highly articulate, even eloquent in his own writing; and some of his published battle reports, as well as certain much-quoted orders-of-the-day to his troops, played no small part in advancing his political fortunes. As a speaker, he was effective in presiding over commissions and small councils. Yet he could be strangely inept before large audiences, as for example when he faced the Five Hundred in 1799—and having failed to move the legislators with haltingly delivered arguments, had to resort to military force instead. On balance, however, no other great general known to history, with the possible exception of Julius Caesar, has possessed comparable verbal skills. Combined with a powerful memory and a gift for selecting the relevant detail, those skills made Napoleon a highly effective administrator and diplomat.

Certain of his other traits, however, are either baffling or distinctly unpleasant to contemplate. His lavish treatment of relatives—he made kings or princes of four brothers and three brothers-in-law—bespoke a stubborn refusal to admit their marvellously consistent incompetence, a refusal hard to reconcile with his generally cold-blooded demand for efficiency. It seems scarcely adequate to suggest that in his vanity he assumed that there must be great abilities in everyone related to him, even by marriage. The traditional clan allegiance of Corsica may offer a better explanation, but some element of mystery remains. More easily understood, but less sympathetic, was Napoleon's contempt for the highest among human motives: generosity, devotion to an ideal, self-sacrifice, respect for the truth as near as men may see it. He was willing cynically to exploit these motives in people whenever the occasion arose; but there were others—self-esteem, fear, greed, lust— on which he preferred to base his calculations. He was no monster of personal cruelty, as some kings and dictators have been; but he was indifferent to the suffering of individuals or of entire armies. Other men were pawns to be sacrificed, or obstacles to be crushed without pity, all according to the dictates of his literally boundless ambition, his projection of an admittedly remarkable ego.

One thing else was Napoleon: a liar, sometimes calculating and sometimes self-deceived. He often dissembled quite consciously, leaving unblinkable evidence of mendacity in his written instructions to subordinates and in his characteristic disavowals of unpopular acts which he had in fact initiated but the blame for which he let slide on to underlings. To object that self-interest and 'reason of state' have made many other men behave in similar fashion does not alter the case. It is difficult to imagine that anyone with whom Napoleon ever dealt, in any capacity, would have been justified in trusting him completely.

In addition, as already noted, he suffered from that standard malady of the vain, namely, self-deception. He appears at times to have believed absolutely preposterous things about the nobility of his own reasons for taking repugnant measures. During the last half-dozen years of his life, when from St Helena he lectured posterity on his inspired battle against tyranny, he often achieved a tone of real conviction in this apologetic fiction he was writing under the name of memoirs.

His relations with women offer another example of false piety. As promiscuous as most other army officers and high officials of his day, he had his share of erotic adventures, though only one, with the Polish Countess Walewska at Schloss Finckenstein in 1807, deserved to be called a love affair. The others, as a French biographer has remarked, 'smacked of the garrison'. Yet he never had publicly acknowledged mistresses; and especially after he became emperor, his entourage strove to maintain a façade of petty bourgeois respectability, smugly presented as a vast improvement over the open sensuality of eighteenth-century court life.

A military genius, a brilliant executive, an eloquent visionary the mere scale of whose projects captures the imagination, yet at the same time a climber, a perverter of humane values, a deceiver of others and of himself as he exploited men and women for his several purposes—what simple characterization will encompass such a being? It is equally difficult to classify Napoleon Bonaparte in terms of the various historical types with which he has been compared, or with which he compared himself. Should we see him as a latterday Caesar, wrenching the imperial honour from a republic whose armies had carried him to fame? Or ought we instead to consider him a precursor of twentieth-century dictators, claiming to divine the masses' needs by intuition and to serve them without accountability? Was he perhaps something less foreign to his eighteenth-century background, an enlightened despot like Frederick the Great or Joseph II, determined to base his own power and his subjects' prosperity upon rational estimates of the public good? Or was he after all simply an Italian adventurer, a *condottiere* displaced from the Renaissance with a stock of Machiavellian prescriptions for seizing and holding a crown? Doubtless a full picture of Napoleon must include some traits found in all those models, others characteristic of any revolutionary leader and still others peculiar to his own personality.

The Constitution of the Empire

Lacking the means for retrospective research on public opinion, no one can say with confidence just how far Bonaparte's reorganization of the French state, his efforts to force society into a matrix of centralized order, responded to popular yearnings. His admirers naturally hail the steps he took after 1799 to overcome the financial confusion and the widespread brigandage, the chaotic religious situation and the formlessness of legal relationships which they perceive in the era of the Directory. His critics just as emphatically charge that he robbed Frenchmen of their liberty, offering the exhilaration of martial glory, but at the same time restoring social distinctions which belied the very spirit of the Revolution. On one point, all commentators agree, to wit, that Napoleon imposed his will upon the entire mechanism of what became his empire, if not completely—he ended, like most other dictators, by overestimating his control over events—at least sufficiently to leave an arresting impression of energy, ambition and intelligence.

The political structure of his régime first took shape in the Constitution of the Year VIII, promulgated in December 1799 by two commissions set up for this purpose by the old Councils of Ancients and of Five Hundred. The new constitution, fleshed out during the ensuing months in a series of 'organic laws', was superseded in the summer of 1802 by the Constitution of the Year X, after a national plebiscite had approved Napoleon's assumption of the title 'consul-for-life', and finally by a decree of May 1804, commonly referred to as the Constitution of the Year XII, which superimposed the Empire upon the Republic. Despite this succession of documents and the evolution in Bonaparte's own position to which they corresponded, many principles were retained and amplified from 1799 down to the Empire's collapse in 1814.

The pattern of executive power was one of authority dispensed downward through the ranks of the administrative hierarchy, not upward through levels of election as in the revolutionary constitutions. Napoleon, supreme war lord and ceremonial chief of state, was also, by virtue of his tireless scrutiny of governmental operations, the supreme bureaucrat as well. The second and third consuls of 1799, Sieyès and Roger-Ducos, were replaced by Cambacérès and Lebrun when the Constitution of the Year VIII went into effect, but none of the four ever posed as a rival to the real ruler of France. The ministers, including at the outset Talleyrand for foreign affairs, Lucien Bonaparte for interior,

Fouché for police and several less prominent figures, formed no cabinet and were individually responsible to the Council of State. This body, in turn, was under Napoleon's direct control. It was, in fact, his favourite instrument for deliberation and policy-making. Here sat the men whose judgment he trusted most, twenty-nine of them in 1799, always thirty-five or more after 1805, as many as forty-six in 1811, divided into five working sections: war, navy, interior, legislation and finance. They included lawyers and judges, veteran administrators, scholars and generals, some of them returned émigrés, others convinced republicans, but no Jacobin extremists and no nostalgic adherents of the Bourbon monarchy.

The same preference for efficient technicians of not too pronounced political views was apparent in the recruitment of prefects. Handsomely uniformed in their silver-trimmed blue coats and their white trousers or breeches, surrounded by considerable pomp in their own right, charged with immense responsibilities and endowed with great authority in their respective *départements*, these regional officials were nonetheless kept fully aware of their dependence on the minister of interior, who nominated them, and on Napoleon, who appointed and could at any time remove them. Nowhere else was the authoritarian nature of the régime more apparent than in the control from above to which the prefects were subject, instead of being responsible to the departmental councils as in the 1790s. The councils remained, but now only in a consultative capacity.

Just as ministers, councillors of state and prefects were subordinated to the will of Bonaparte, so too were the three branches of the national legislature. The Senate was composed of sixty (later eighty) men, initially selected by the consuls in 1800, but thereafter supposedly kept up to strength by co-optation. In theory, that is, the incumbent senators filled each vacancy by themselves electing a new colleague for life. In fact, however, each such choice was made under the thinly concealed surveillance of the first consul. Many distinguished Frenchmen were so honoured—generals such as Kellermann, for example, and scientists such as La Place and Berthollet—but their vague mandate to uphold conservative interests should not be confused with real power to make laws.

The Legislative Chamber (*Corps Législatif*), whose 300 members were elected for five-year terms by the Senate, was theoretically junior to that body. The minimum age for senators was forty, while legislators could be as young as thirty; and individual salaries were fixed at only 10,000 francs for the latter, as opposed to 25,000 for the former. Nearly all those elected to the Chamber in 1800—277 out of the first 300—were veterans of earlier assemblies; but shrewd observers noted that experience had left most of them not so much self-confident as wearily cynical. Renewed at a rate of sixty members chosen each year thereafter, the body remained an almost invariably obedient sounding board for Napoleon's projects. It had no right to initiate legislation, instead being restricted to enacting laws submitted to it by the government and discussed, supposedly in critical terms, by orators designated by the Tribunate.

This third arm of the Napoleonic legislative complex was grandly described in the Constitution of the Year VIII as the voice of 'national representation'. Yet a tribune was elected to his five-year term by the Senate, scarcely a representative body. He need have reached only the age of twenty-five but had to be drawn from the list of 6,000 national 'notables' (later 'electors'). Of the original 100 tribunes, almost two-thirds had been members of the Ancients or the Five Hundred before 1799. A few of them, including Benjamin Constant, did begin by trying to defeat certain bills before the Legislative Chamber, only to discover that they were risking disgrace, or worse, if they took their duty as critics too seriously. The first consul, as a matter of fact, never did feel any enthusiasm for the Tribunate, despite its rapidly acquired caution. In 1802, he abruptly reduced its membership by half, announcing that the remaining fifty would henceforth limit themselves to the unpublicized discussion of decisions taken by the Council of State.

The conception of 'notables', just mentioned in connection with the recruitment of tribunes, deserves a word of separate comment, for it is characteristic of the precautions against open democracy written into the Constitution of the Year VIII in 1799. The French electorate remained very broad in appearance, including all adult males who were not domestic servants and who had resided in the same district for at least one year. However, the voters of a locality chose just ten per cent of their number as communal notables, who in turn elected ten per cent of *their* group to the list of departmental notables. The latter then picked a final ten per cent of their membership to be national notables, subject to review by the Senate. At each level, communal, departmental and national, both government officials and recipients of various ceremonial honours could be named only from the appropriate list of notables. The fact that men of some wealth and education tended to dominate these lists showed how far France had moved away from the era when radical *san-culottes* had swept the administration before them.

Hand in hand with the carefully controlled selection of legislative and administrative officers went a tightening of the central government's grip on judicial institutions. A law of February 1800 suppressed the elective principle for all judges except the purely local justices of the peace. Hereafter, members of the highest tribunal, the Court of Cassation, would be named by the Senate. Judges of all other civil, criminal and appeal courts would be selected by the first consul, always from among the notables of the region and the level involved.

At the same time Bonaparte appointed a commission of four legal experts whose work, debated in over 100 sessions of the Council of State with the first consul himself often presiding, led in 1804 to the great Civil Code, in 1806 to the Code of Civil Procedure and in 1810 to the Code of Criminal Procedure. These three, together with a more fragmentary compilation of commercial law promulgated in 1807, made up the famous *Code Napoléon*. It was a structure of law designed to favour order and stability in interpersonal relations, reasonably prompt court action, national uniformity as opposed to variegated regional customs, civil equality, freedom of religion and, of course, the power of the state. In criminal procedure, torture was reintroduced on a limited basis, and a jury, selected by the prefect, could convict by simple majority vote. The Code as a whole was an intellectually respectable effort to reconcile the laws of the Old Regime with those of the Revolution, but it was also a powerful instrument of authoritarian rule.

The very fact that Napoleon had a special minister of police, Fouché, until 1802, and then in 1804 resurrected the office under Savary, reveals his concern with repressive action. His personal impulses were clearly expressed after the bomb attempt on his life in a street near the Opera on Christmas Eve of 1800. He first rushed through the deportation to the French penal colony in Guiana of some 130 republican critics, calling them 'the general staff of the Jacobins'. Then, when Fouché identified the real culprits as royalists, the first consul saw to it that these were promptly executed. He did not, however, release any of the men already deported. From that point onward, increasingly harsh censorship was matched by widespread use of police spies and *agents provocateurs* against suspected enemies of the state. More secure than Robespierre had been, and perhaps less convinced of his opponents' wickedness, Napoleon committed many fewer victims to the guillotine. Nevertheless, his régime kept the jails full and the prison ships busily occupied on the dangerous run to South America.

The Internal Economy

Napoleon never showed any great understanding of economic and financial problems nor, for that matter, any strong interest in them except as they touched his conception of national greatness and his struggle against Great Britain. The latter aspect, that of economic warfare, we shall take up in Chapter x. Here it must suffice to point out a few of the major developments within the French economy itself. Progress was made in tax collection, an area where conditions could scarcely have grown worse than they had been before 1800. The greatly increased power of the government, in particular the energetic action of many prefects, made evasion more difficult than it had been during the hectic decade of the Revolution proper. Even so, the great expense of seemingly endless military operations simply devoured available funds, including exactions from occupied foreign lands. The exalted Court of Accounts, ranking just below the Court of Cassation, struggled ponderously, but in vain, to eliminate waste and corruption from the administration of public moneys. War profiteering, often on a massive scale, was endemic throughout the period of the Consulate and the Empire.

By 1805, with the national deficit soaring to new heights, a major crisis developed. It was made worse by the fact that the Bank of France, founded in 1800, had issued paper money so far in excess of its metal reserves that in a space of only a few weeks that autumn its bills depreciated by 15 per cent. The emperor's personal intervention, when he rushed back to Paris from central Europe's battlefields in January 1806, brought several large confiscations of funds from incriminated financiers, the reorganization of the Bank under a state-appointed governor and a temporary restoration of public confidence in the franc. Napoleon's own financial vision, however, remained curiously limited. He stubbornly refused, for example, to resort to official bond issues, because he objected to having *his* credit discussed on street corners. Despite further improvements in record-keeping, despite the long overdue standardization of the national coinage and despite the use of increasingly sophisticated budgetary procedures, the economic structure of his régime was never really secure. In 1810 a new and greater crisis broke, involving poor harvests, an industrial decline after three years of relative boom and a resurgence of monetary problems. The Empire's military and political collapse four years later found this complex of difficulties still unresolved.

The principle of authority was strikingly apparent, though in different ways, throughout the fields of industry, commerce, agriculture and urban labour. A law of 1803 created a hierarchy of local and regional consultative chambers of manufacturers, each composed of six businessmen elected by their peers to deliberate under the chairmanship of the *maire* of their town or the prefect of their department. The textile industry, in particular, enjoyed a somewhat artificial efflorescence because of the trade war against English imports. By the end of Napoleon's reign, France had some 2,000 cotton mills, employing close to 40,000 workers, while linen production occupied an estimated 58,000 home or factory labourers. Iron mines and forges were kept busy by the demands of war, as were beet sugar refineries and the establishments of the young chemical industry. It cannot be shown, however, that French manufacturing as a whole expanded more than it might have under peaceful conditions—nor that it grew as rapidly as it had in the last decades before 1789. Indeed, if one considers many important products, including metals other than iron, one arrives at just the opposite conclusion.

Commerce too had its set of officially supervised consultative boards and local or departmental chambers, culminating at the national level in the General Council of Commerce under the minister of interior. Such institutions had come and gone repeatedly during the Old Régime, but their number and the elaborateness of their graded relationships had never approached the pattern established under the Empire. Napoleon expected French merchants to profit from his victories and their own exertions—but only for the greater glory of France, the strengthening of his war machine and the weakening of current or potential foes. It is possible to paint a fairly rosy picture of Napoleonic commerce if one concentrates on certain inland centres, such as Lyon and Strasbourg, which served as trading hubs for the continental domains of the Empire. There is no question that the era also witnessed a new surge of highway, canal and bridge building. However, the French and captive seaports, Marseille, Bordeaux and Nantes, Rotterdam, Antwerp and Genoa, paid the price in stagnation for the struggle against British naval power. In desperation, many of their entrepreneurs turned to smuggling, often through clandestine arrangements with the English which directly violated Napoleon's sternest orders. As the years passed illicit trade to avoid excise payments spread to the inland trading centres as well. Involving not only private merchants and shippers, but also countless government officials, smuggling became the greatest single instance of corruption behind the Empire's façade of disciplined loyalty.

Agriculture was encouraged by official societies, publications and prizes for successful innovations (the improved sugar beet, improved fertilizers and feed crops, increased output of grains, new veterinary techniques). Wheat, potato and beet production rose swiftly. Flax and hemp, on the other hand, declined, while the effort to raise home cotton was disappointing. Taking all crops into account, and allowing for certain improvements and the reclamation of thousands of acres of additional farm land, agricultural production under Napoleon seems to have no more than held its own in proportion to the growing population. In fairness it should be added that given the insatiable drain of manpower into the armies of the Empire, the fact that agriculture could do even that speaks well for French energy and ingenuity under pressure.

The manual labourer was for Napoleon simply another resource to be organized and exploited. The penal code, for example, established far more severe penalties for collusion among workers than for illegal agreements among manufacturers. From 1803 onward each labourer was required to possess a *livret*, or work book, and to present it to his employer when entering upon a job. This document both identified its holder for police purposes and showed the conditions under which he had left previous payrolls. Nonpossession of a work book was considered evidence of wilful vagabondage. Despite the promising advent of local arbitration boards and the existence of certain fraternities of labourers (the *compagnonnages*, tolerated by the régime for limited social purposes but kept under close official surveillance), French workers remained essentially isolated, at the mercy of their employers and of the state.

Religious Policy

No single area of Napoleonic statecraft has been more hotly argued over than that of religious policy. Part of the problem is that the several lines pursued by the government, though each was clear enough in itself, were never perfectly coordinated. Bonaparte did not destroy the gains made by Protestants and Jews during the Revolution, so far as civil equality and freedom of worship were concerned. Everywhere, however, the familiar pattern of state supervision was in evidence. Each Calvinist synod or Lutheran general consistory met under the eyes of a prefect or his representative. Rabbis, unlike ministers, were not considered salaried public functionaries; but all the Jews of a given district were taxed to pay their clergy. Each local synagogue and each regional Jewish consistory was administered with the participation of wealthy laymen selected from the proper list of notables. Non-Catholics were, in short, both protected and brigaded by the irreligious general who was their ruler.

Napoleon's dealings with the Church of Rome followed a much more tortuous course. His instinct for religious conciliation, which we have already seen at work in Italy and Egypt, led him to open his term as first consul with a series of gestures toward the 'recalcitrants', the French priests who had never accepted the Civil Constitution of the Clergy. On the other hand, he applied himself to effecting a settlement between the papacy and the 'constitutional clergy' who had sworn the required oath to the Republic in the 1790s. On 15 July 1801 a new Concordat was signed, at Paris, between representatives of the Vatican and of the Republic. Henceforth Catholicism was recognized, if not as the state church of France, at least as 'the religion of the great majority of Frenchmen'. The first consul was empowered to name archbishops and bishops, who would swear allegiance to his government; but only the pope could bestow the canonical 'institution' which consecrated them in their sacred functions. Cathedrals, chapels, seminaries and local churches not already secularized were returned to the direct control of the ecclesiastical hierachy.

For the moment, it appeared that Pius VII had won a major victory against the Revolution. In some respects, including his new right to depose bishops who defied him, the pope now enjoyed greater power in France than his predecessors had possessed even under the old monarchy. The proud Gallican tradition of autonomy for a national Catholic church seemed to have been sacrificed to the needs of diplomacy. Actually, however, the first consul was about to launch a long series of impositions which would make the remainder of his reign an increasingly humiliating trial for the Holy See.

As early as April 1802 the Legislative Chamber adopted a set of 'organic articles' purporting to give legal effect to the agreement of the previous summer. Instead, they reversed a number of assumptions which had seemed to underlie the Concordat. No papal legislation could be published in France, nor could any nuncio or legate be sent there without governmental approval. Prefects were to report any disloyal behaviour by churchmen. The latter, indeed, were explicitly equated once more with salaried state officials. The pope protested, to no avail.

Then in 1804 Pius was induced to come to Paris for Napoleon's coronation as emperor of the French, only to have the agreed ceremony in Notre Dame altered without prior notice: at the climactic moment, Bonaparte placed the imperial crown on his own head. Less than two years later, in 1806, the government in Paris announced a new catechism, to be used as the basis for all Catholic religious education throughout the Empire. The seventh lesson in particular, though approved by the docile nuncio to France, Cardinal Caprara, nevertheless outraged more deeply religious churchmen. Every true believer, it stated, must pledge to 'Napoleon I, our Emperor, love, respect, obedience, loyalty, military service ... because God ... whether for peace or for war, has made him the minister of His power and His image upon earth'.

By this time it was clear that Napoleon's conception of the agreement between France and the Vatican was distinctly onesided. For the Catholic Church and for its spiritual head, however, the worst still lay ahead. In 1809, after a long sequence of mounting encroachments upon Rome and the surrounding Papal States of Italy, Napoleon finally proclaimed their annexation to the Empire, under rights derived from 'Charlemagne, our august predecessor'. Pius VII, who had become more and more hostile since the coronation farce, now responded by excommunicating the 'despoilers'. The pope was seized, carried off to Avignon and finally installed as a virtual prisoner at Savona on the Italian Riviera. Rome, officially styled the Second City of the Empire and intended as the seat of Napoleon's future heir, was to be a dynastic and political stronghold, not a religious one. Only in 1814, after five years of exile, was the pope permitted to return to the Vatican, at the behest of Austria and its victorious allies.

Napoleon's treatment of Protestants, Jews and Catholics alike reflected personal indifference to matters of faith, combined with steady insistence on political obedience. Because Catholicism was at once the majority religion of France and an international force, it raised special problems and offered special temptations. In his dealings with it, the emperor showed himself fully alive to the possible value of the hierarchy's support, achieved at first by sweet words but increasingly, as time passed, by coercion. What he could scarcely have foreseen was that his persecution of the papacy would give it a new spiritual appeal, even for Gallican churchmen, and would form the background for an ecclesiastical resurgence in the nineteenth century rivalling that of the Counter-Reformation in the sixteenth.

Education Reorganized

With respect to education, Napoleon's actions were set against a background of disruption inherent in a prolonged civil and military upheaval. Under the Directory, the government had been content to rely on noncompulsory elementary schools, financed entirely by student fees, offering an uninspiring combination of the 'three R's' plus a fourth—republican morality—and staffed by ill-paid teachers who were apt to be ignorant and, in some cases, depraved. Public secondary schools had fared somewhat better, but they also had charged enough to keep many promising students away from their combination of mathematical, literary and historical courses, the last two generally much inferior to the first. After the closing of the old universities in the early 1790s higher education had lagged badly, this despite the revolutionists' efforts to construct a new network to replace that of the Ancien Régime. The reopened medical schools at Paris, Strasbourg and Montpellier, the Museum of Natural History, the Central School of Public Works (renamed in 1795 the *Ecole Polytechnique*), the Observatory, the Normal schools for the training of teachers, and the other special foundations culminating in the National Institute of Arts and Sciences, did not fully replace the universities, the national and provincial academies, the endowed scientific and scholarly centres of the former monarchy.

The Napoleonic reform of education was launched in the spring of 1802. The financing of elementary schools was declared to be henceforth a joint responsibility of local treasuries and of the pupils' parents. The establishment of private schools was at the same time made easier; and the Catholic teaching orders were encouraged to resume full activity. Local secondary schools were reorganized around a utilitarian curriculum emphasizing French, mathematics, history and geography. A more élite echelon of schools for pupils between the ages of ten and fifteen, the *lycées*, stressed all these subjects plus science and certain ancient classics as well, though the inculcation of military virtues constituted an additional, at times it seemed an overriding, aim. The state made clear its direct interest in lyceans by granting over 1,000 scholarships a year to gifted candidates and to needy sons of heroes who had died fighting for France. At what had previously been the university level, a general creation of new institutions waited several more years after 1802, notwithstanding the resurrection of such traditional degrees as the doctorate and the successful launching of a dozen law schools capable of handling some 2,000 students at any one time.

Then in 1806 a much more sweeping project was announced: the establishment of an Imperial University. As developed further by successive decrees down to 1810, this mechanism of state had nothing to do with a 'university' in the older sense. It was a single, monolithic structure, presided over by the emperor's representative, the Grand Master, and charged with the supervision of education throughout the Empire, private as well as public, from the primary grades through the highest levels of training. At the elementary and secondary stages the results proved disappointing, in part because the original time schedule was unrealistic, in part because military demands kept draining the country of adequate teaching personnel. Napoleon had set a goal of 100 lycées by 1813, for example; but when that year arrived there were still not fifty in operation.

In higher education the results, at least on paper, were somewhat better. The overarching university was divided into twenty-seven academies, each responsible for the arbitrarily defined jurisdictional district of a court of appeals. Under the control of each academy and its rector was a faculty of letters. In addition, scattered through various cities not only of France but of North Italy, Switzerland and the Low Countries as well, were thirteen faculties of law, fifteen of sciences, seven of medicine, ten of Catholic and three of Protestant theology, each subordinate to the regional academy. The quality and the numerical strength of these various faculties were from the outset extremely uneven; and in the deteriorating situation of the later Empire, few if any achieved a pattern of operation one might call normal. The elaborate system, however, was sketched for all men to ponder.

Napoleon appears to have treated education as he did every other force within his reach, that is, as something to be centralized and administered from above according to a clear chain of command. There can be no doubt that he wanted his subjects as well trained as possible, in the interests of military efficiency, public service and material productivity. At the same time, he appreciated the importance of schools for the propagation of pride in the nation and loyalty to his régime. We can scarcely be surprised that he went no further towards recognizing the inherent value of free inquiry. At any rate, his other undertakings, both at home and abroad, so vitiated his educational programme as to leave it just one more truncated monument to his sharp, orderly, ungenerous spirit.

The Control of Culture

That same spirit shaped the government's attitude towards information, art and letters. The master policemen, Fouché, and after him Savary, took pains to have their press bureau scrutinize all periodicals. In January 1800, scarcely a month after the Consulate was established, a decree suppressed no fewer than sixty newspapers in Paris and its suburbs, accusing them of being 'in the hands of the Republic's enemies'. Only thirteen political journals were permitted to go on publishing, and even they were threatened with confiscation if they printed articles critical of the public authorities. Napoleon himself scrutinized censors' reports and press summaries with great care. Year by year his régime grew harsher and more suspicious until finally, in 1811, a new decree reduced to just four the number of legal newspapers in the capital—the now entirely official *Moniteur* and three other banal sheets—each one receiving the undivided attention of a censor responsible to the minister of police.

When it came to the production of books, the Napoleonic formula combined monetary rewards to properly admiring authors with the confiscation of volumes the proofs of which revealed hostile tendencies. As a matter of fact, the full development of the official screening machinery, like so many other expanded controls, came rather late in the history of the Empire. Not until 1810 was the Directorate General of Printing and Bookselling created, with a staff of over sixty readers, inspectors and border guards. Long before that happened, however, countless writers had felt the sting of official displeasure expressed through fines and confiscations. One of the first sufferers under the organization launched in 1810 was the famous Madame de Staël, daughter of the former royal finance minister, Necker, and herself one of Bonaparte's early admirers. In the first months of its operation, the new Directorate General called to the emperor's attention her recently completed book, *Concerning Germany*. Enraged at the sympathy the work expressed towards a people whose growing nationalism was already giving him trouble, Napoleon ordered the edition to be seized and the author banished to Switzerland.

Faced with the difficulty of policing the soaring number of French theatres, the government in 1807 at last resorted to its favourite principles of reduction and rigid classification. That year, all but eight of the thirty-three theatres in Paris were ordered closed. Those that remained were distinguished as four 'grand' ones (the *Comédie Française*, the *Opéra*, the *Opéra Comique* and the *Odéon*) and four lesser vaudeville houses. Other cities were simultaneously restricted to one or, in a few instances, two stationary troupes apiece. Both in the capital and in the provinces, each company had to limit itself to a fixed repertory of productions, which even so could be performed only under police supervision.

In art as elsewhere the command principle was the guiding rule, however uneven its application may have been. Early in 1800 Jacques-Louis David was named 'painter to the government' and given authority over all paintings undertaken in France. Two years later, a veteran diplomat, Vivant Denon, was made director general of museums, in effect a minister of fine arts with sweeping powers. After 1804 the Opera was also entitled the Imperial Academy of Music and the Dance, though in these fields even the Emperor could never detect much political danger.

The Reintroduction of Social Hierarchy

One of the several features of Napoleon's rule which have continued to agitate, and often to confuse, observers down to the present day was the so-called 're-aristocratization of France'. That a professional soldier, a general, should feel kindly toward a pyramid of ranks and honorific distinctions, with himself at the top of it, is certainly not surprising. Merely to say, however, that Napoleon left Frenchmen their *civil* or *legal* equality, while abandoning the Revolution's ideal of *social* equality, is to leave several questions unanswered.

To what extent was this phenomenon a matter of restoration of the old pre-1789 aristocracy, as distinct from the creation of new privileged groups? Bonaparte did not wait long before explicitly encouraging the hordes of émigrés, including large numbers of former nobles, to return to France. It is true that an article in the Constitution of the Year VIII pledged the government to uphold 'the irrevocability of the laws against émigrés'. As early as April 1802, however, the Senate acceded to the first consul's demand that this article be annulled and the exiles welcomed back on condition of sworn allegiance to his régime. Unfortunately we have no such detailed figures for returnees as we do for the emigration itself. Nevertheless, the *ralliés*, the old enemies of the Revolution who came home from abroad to live under Napoleon, were henceforth an important element in the French population, prominently mentioned in contemporary records and encountered with increasing frequency on lists of civil and military appointments.

What complicates the picture is the fact that the return of formerly noble *ralliés* did not in itself reconstitute the pre-1789 nobility. It was not uncommon for such a returnee to go on using his title as a social adornment, but he was generally referred to by his fellow citizens as the *ci-devant* (or 'the sometime') marquis, count or chevalier. Furthermore, he recovered no special tax exemption, no privileges in any court of law, no rights of ceremonial precedence at public or religious functions. Even after the Senate's action of 1802, it cannot be said that the old noblesse fastened itself once more on French society. Its members became noblemen in a newer and more meaningful sense only if they were assimilated, as individuals, into the Napoleonic hierarchy of honorific recognition for public services.

It is important to recognize, beneath the titles and ornate uniforms of this hierarchy, a principle of advancement quite foreign to the notions of the Old Régime. This was the requirement that the individual honoured must himself have demonstrated heroism in battle, administrative capacity, diplomatic skill or the ability to make money. There is no way of being sure that, had the system survived for two or more generations, the original rewards for personal achievement might not have become the basis for just one more hereditary caste. At the outset, however, the offer of personal dignity to soldiers, bureaucrats, diplomats and rich men, regardless of their birth, sought to reconcile aristocratic distinctions with the dream of careers open to talent, of 'a marshal's baton in every soldier's knapsack'.

The Constitution of the Year VIII established a somewhat curious mixture of democratic and élitist principles. We have seen that 'notables' were chosen by their peers at the local, departmental and national levels. The result was a graded series of rosters, culminating in the national list of 5,000 to 6,000 names and supposedly identifying the most 'considerable' Frenchmen available for a wide range of legislative, judicial, administrative and even religious duties. Nevertheless, these notables *were* elected and served only for fixed terms. In 1802, when a new law abolished the earlier lists in favour of electoral colleges at the corresponding levels, several features of a more frankly aristocratic nature were added. First, the members of these colleges were chosen for life. Second, the voters of each locality could henceforth choose their primary assembly or *collège d'arrondissement* only from a list of 600 citizens nominated by the government as 'most imposing', which in practice generally meant wealthiest. Third, the consul-for-life could now appoint ten members to each local assembly and twenty to each departmental one, in recognition of public services. Subsequent modifications of the electoral colleges tended to make them only more clearly privileged, predominantly appointive cadres.

In the same year which saw the adoption of this system, Napoleon also realized his aim of creating a standardized set of rewards for military valour, and other civic virtues. This was the Legion of Honour. On 18 May 1802 the Legislative Chamber passed the law which established the new institution, placed it under a Grand Council, with Napoleon as president, and endowed it with lands the revenues from which would provide pensions for all members. The national organization was subdivided into sixteen cohorts, each under its own administrative board. A legionnaire was named, for life, by the Grand Council in Paris, and was originally assured an annual stipend ranging from 250 francs up to 2,000 for a commander and 5,000 for a grand officer. Despite ostensibly strict rules covering the choice of members, including an eligibility requirement of twenty-five years' distinguished service to France, the Legion's size grew at a startling rate. By 1808 its numbers had surpassed 20,000, posing obvious difficulties of a financial nature. Finally, in 1811, the monetary payments were abolished. Nevertheless, titles and decorations of the Legion of Honour remained—and still remain today—public reminders that France counted certain of her sons as far more praiseworthy than the rest.

There were many other examples of honorific designations and attendant financial benefits. The *senatories*, for instance, were endowments of land and income which the ruler could confer for life on especially favoured members of the Senate. There were fifteen of them in 1804, thirty-six just ten years later. Another case of conspicuous distinction, this one copied from the expiring Holy Roman Empire, involved the six 'grand dignitaries' with whom Napoleon surrounded his imperial throne in 1804. They included the emperor's brothers and designated heirs, Joseph and Louis Bonaparte, as grand elector (titular head of all the electoral colleges) and grand constable, respectively; his brother-in-law, Murat, as grand admiral, without duties at sea; his stepson, Eugene Beauharnais, as arch-chancellor of state; and his two previous fellow consuls, Cambacérès as arch-chancellor of the Empire and Lebrun as arch-treasurer.

Most revealing of all these innovations was the Imperial Nobility established in 1808. This, far more than the welcome home extended to nobly born émigrés, more even than the founding of the Legion of Honour, expressed the emperor's repudiation of social equality among his subjects. Each grand dignitary now became a prince of the Empire—'his most serene highness'. Ministers, senators, councillors of state, archbishops became counts. Presidents of departmental electoral colleges, higher judges, bishops, mayors of thirty-seven large cities became barons. Ordinary members of the Legion were henceforth chevaliers. It would be easy to conclude that with this action Napoleon did 're-aristocratize' France once and for all, but we must be careful to note that even in 1808 he did not restore the *order* of nobility as the Bourbon monarchy had known it. Like the *ralliés* from the Old Régime who had come back to France as citizens, the imperial nobility enjoyed none of the legal and financial privileges which had been the very substance of *noblesse* in the eighteenth century. Furthermore, the emperor not only identified honorific titles with specific forms and grades of public service, but also tied the hereditary succession of such titles to financial requirements which would have utterly outraged the earlier possessors of rank derived from birth. A prince of the Empire could be sure that his eldest son would be a duke, able to pass that title on to future generations, only if the father could transmit an estate made indivisible by entail (*majorat*) and yielding an income of at least 200,000 francs per year. The title of count could be inherited only if accompanied by an assured income of 30,000 francs; and the figures for a baron and a chevalier were 15,000 and 3,000, respectively. Napoleon's nobility was intended to remain an 'upper class' in the most modern, most strictly economic sense.

Innovations—Ephemeral and Permanent

Looking back over the whole range of projects and policies, we should ask ourselves to what extent Napoleon's institutional reforms were fundamental and to what extent ephemeral. Many of his innovations clearly failed to take root. The lists of notables and the electoral colleges which replaced them, the solemn fraud of the Tribunate, the archaic role of the grand dignitaries and indeed, save for its one mid-nineteenth-century revival, the hereditary Empire itself were all rejected by later French constitution makers. The imperial catechism for Catholics, like the essentially military organization of the schools and the elaborate censorship of everything from imaginative paintings and foreign books to provincial comedies and speeches made at working-men's social evenings, also proved unable to outlive the reign of Napoleon.

One should be careful, of course, not to assume that everything which proved temporary perished because it had no basic vitality or importance. It would be a mistake to ignore the deep changes in French intellectual life which *might* have resulted had the superstructure of the Imperial University, as constituted by 1810, maintained itself for not four but forty years. Similarly, the imperial nobility of 1808 lasted only until the Bourbons returned to the throne, but its potential effect on social organization became manifest even in that short time. Many of the Napoleonic creations disappeared, in other words, not because they had shown themselves incapable of reshaping society, but because the régime itself was destroyed by military action from abroad before any such reshaping could take permanent effect.

When all is said and done, however, the greatest significance still attaches to those institutional changes which were *not* reversed in 1814–1815; for these continued to affect French life—and in many cases European life more generally—long after their instigator was dead on St Helena. In government, to cite one example, the prefect's combination of wide powers in the execution of policy but clear subordination to the central ministry of interior, where policy was determined, became a hallmark of French administration from 1800 onward. The judicial system was never again staffed by owners of venal offices, as under the Old Régime, nor made dependent on the political election of judges, as during the 1790s. The Code Napoléon, needless to say, remains the foundation of modern French law (even after the recodification since 1958) and of the law of numerous foreign countries.

In other areas of human affairs, the far-reaching influence of the Napoleonic expedients, modified and adapted by later generations, is not hard to demonstrate. The Concordat of 1801, despite occasional challenges, remained throughout the nineteenth century the charter which defined relations between successive French governments on one side and the Roman Catholic Church on the other. Not until 1904 was it abrogated by French legislation aimed at achieving a total separation of church and state. (That same year also saw the abandonment of Napoleon's system of financial support for the Protestant clergy and official supervision over Jewish synagogues.) The organization of lower schools, the prestige of the lycées, the unparalleled centralization of French higher education, all survived the *Université Impériale* when it died with the Empire. So did the technical excellence of the 'Polytechnique' and other specialized *Grandes Écoles*.

Turning to another field, one perceives the aura of official authority which still surrounds such theatres as the Comédie Française and the Opera. Finally, in view of the not very laudatory judgments expressed earlier with regard to the Empire's economic institutions, it is only fair to add that one of those institutions, the local arbitration board (*conseil de prud'hommes*), generally according the workers more of a voice than they had under the Empire, has remained a flexible and a valuable feature of modern French industrial relations. Whether or not all the innovations mentioned here, as well as countless others which might be cited, strike a modern observer as changes for the better, their combined historical importance is scarcely open to question.

Let us return briefly to where this chapter began, to Napoleon Bonaparte himself. His almost frenetic energy and the range of his personal activism help to explain why historians have found it so difficult to agree in classifying and characterizing him. He was in fact at various times an imaginative revolutionary statesman and a demagogic dictator, an enlightened despot after the letter and an unscrupulous outsider come from Italy to make his own and his family's fortune. Yet the figure of the latterday Caesar remains most compelling of all: the successful and eloquent general, quick to smash all republican obstacles in the way of his own drive to power, but then anxious to give the state and society a formal structure which would restrain other ambitious men from aspiring to his high place.

Seen thus, Napoleon appears neither as the betrayer nor as the executor of the Revolution. There is no evidence that he was determined to fortify all the trends of the decade which ended in 1799, nor that he was intent upon reversing them all. He was as anti-Jacobin as he was anti-royalist, being determined to suppress criticism and opposition on both flanks. Whether he revived a specific feature of the Old Régime or perpetuated some characteristic of the Republic he had in effect overthrown, he acted without admiration for the avowed principles of either of those systems. *He*, after all, was now the system.

To some extent, of course, whether one considers Napoleon a 'man of the Revolution' or the opposite depends on how one conceives the Revolution itself. If its essential aims were personal liberty, social equality, dignity of the independent spirit, then assuredly it was betrayed by Napoleon Bonaparte (though liberty, dignity and social equality were scarcely delivered intact into his hands by the régimes which had ruled Frenchmen from 1793 to the Eighteenth Brumaire). If, to take another position, the Revolution's own momentum had been not towards liberty, but towards governmental efficiency and the equality of all citizens before the law and the tax collector, Napoleon can reasonably be portrayed as its greatest continuator.

Even if a judgment of the man's career becomes meaningful only in terms of a judgment of the times, the career itself retains a kaleidoscopic character at once baffling and fascinating. How, but for the immense variety of elements to be found in it, could his record have appealed, after his death, to both anticlerical liberals and conservative French nationalists? How else can we explain the fact that in our own century his political legacy has been claimed by radical democrats, though admittedly it has seemed more often to be the special property of militarists, even of fascists. To adherents of each group, certain of Napoleon's measures have appeared to mark him as 'their' man. This disagreement over his historical significance has beset not only Frenchmen but also foreigners whose countries bear the marks of his passage. It therefore seems natural to turn now to the events of the Napoleonic era in Europe as a whole, to the mixture of collaboration, imitation and violent resistance that filled the age with fury and confusion.

IX

Napoleon and the Nations of Europe

The fifteen-year segment of European history we call the 'Napoleonic era' possessed, like the career of its central figure, a structure at once epic and dramatic. Its story is one of tremendous French victories turning at last to over-extension and massive defeat. The same story features several lulls or pauses in the tumultuous narrative, points at which one is tempted to ask: Why did Napoleon not stop here, consolidate his gains and ask no more of Europe? Whether or not there ever

BIBLIOGRAPHY. Among surveys of diplomatic history, the most up-to-date is A. Fugier, *La Révolution française et l'Empire napoléonien* (Paris, 1954), vol. IV of *Histoire des relations internationales*, ed. P. Renouvin. Also very useful is the sequel to Immich's work mentioned earlier, A. Wahl, *Geschichte des europäischen Staatensystems, 1789–1815* (Munich-Berlin, 1912). Two still older treatments are nevertheless well worth reading for their magisterial style and strongly stated theses: A. Sorel, *L'Europe et la Révolution française* (*see* Bibliography, p. 49), wherein vols. VI–VII present the view that Napoleon fought a hopeless struggle for France's 'natural frontiers' against the tradition-based opposition of other powers; and E. Bourgeois, *Manuel historique de politique étrangère*, vol. II: *Les révolutions, 1789–1830* (Paris, 1898, with many later printings), which stresses Bonaparte's obsession with the Middle East. More specialized studies which deserve mention are H. C. Deutsch, *The Genesis of Napoleonic Imperialism* (Cambridge, Mass., 1938), E. Gulick, *Europe's Classical Balance of Power* (Ithaca, 1955), and O. Connelly, *Napoleon's Satellite Kingdoms* (New York-London, 1965). The authoritative treatment of England's diplomatic role is vol. I in the *Cambridge History of British Foreign Policy, 1783–1919*, ed. A. W. Ward and G. P. Gooch (Cambridge, 1922), though this has been modified in important regards by C. K. Webster, *The Foreign Policy of Castlereagh, 1812–1815* (London, 1931). Numerous biographies, notably J. H. Rose, *Life of William Pitt* (New York, 1924), and P. Guedalla, *Wellington* (New York, 1930), give valuable accounts of the great conflict. The classic *Studies in Napoleonic Statesmanship: Germany*, by H. A. L. Fisher (Oxford, 1903), and the valuable new monograph by R. C. Raack, *The Fall of Stein* (Cambridge, Mass., 1965), may be supplemented by such major works as F. Meinecke, *Das Zeitalter der deutschen Erhebung, 1795–1815* (Bielefeld, 1913); G. Ritter, *Stein: Eine politische Biographie* (rev. edn., Stuttgart, 1958); and F. Stählin, *Napoleons Glanz und* was a real chance of his drawing rein, the times when he appears, in retro-spect, to have had the opportunity—1802, 1807, 1810–11—punctuate the drama of the age, dividing it almost as intermissions divide a pro-duction in the theatre.

In the present chapter, we shall look at the cluster of military and diplomatic events which constituted each of these 'acts'. While doing so, we must bear in mind that save for a single year one nation at least, Great Britain, was continuously at war with Bonaparte's France. The stubborn conflict between these enemies facing each other across the channel might seem to upset the division into subperiods suggested by events on the Continent. Even in the Anglo-French struggle, however, the sequence of European crises and relative lulls revealed itself clearly enough to justify our taking up the account as a whole in chronological segments.

We shall have to do more than merely chart the wars and temporary pacifications between 1800 and the peace of 1815. We must also follow the main internal developments within various European states during successive periods, though we cannot hope to keep all the nations constantly in view. Our goals will be, first, to discern the widening im-pact of the Napoleonic offensive on an entire civilization and, second, to distinguish the variety of responses, country by country, which in due course will help to explain the new map, the new Europe of 1815.

There is another problem, a significant one for the student who tries to place the Napoleonic wars in relation to other campaigns of sweeping conquest, Louis XIV's in the seventeenth century, for example, or Hitler's in the twentieth. This is the question of 'French

Fall im deutschen Urteil (Brunswick, 1952). For eastern Europe, two earlier works may be consulted, M. Handelsmann, *Napoléon et la Pologne, 1806–1807* (Paris, 1909), and S. Tatishchev, *Alexandre Ier et Napoléon, d'après leur corres-pondance inédite, 1801–1812* (Paris, 1891); but the basic treatment is now E. Tarlé, *Napoleon's Invasion of Russia, 1812* (London, 1942). M. Raeff, *Michael Speransky: Statesman of Imperial Russia, 1772–1839* (The Hague, 1957), is a valuable recent contribution. For the chief Mediterranean countries, see M. Artola, *Los orígenes de la España contemporanea* (Madrid, 1959), 2 vols., A. Fugier, *Napoléon et l'Espagne, 1799–1808* (Paris, 1930), and his *Napoléon et l'Italie* (Paris, 1947), together with G. Bourgin and J. Godechot, *L'Italie et Napoléon, 1796–1814* (Paris, 1936), and G. H. Lovett, *Napoleon and the Birth of Modern Spain* (New York, 1965), 2 vols. Finally, two studies of the central figure in Sweden's crucial relations with Bonaparte are F. D. Scott, *Bernadotte and the Fall of Napoleon* (Cambridge, Mass., 1935), and T. T. Höjer's monumental *Carl XIV Johan*, vol. II: *Kronprinstiden* (Stockholm, 1943).

hegemony'—how it was conceived by Napoleon himself, how close it came to being realized under his leadership and, to the extent it ever became a reality, why it finally collapsed. Recurrent struggles for hegemony and, indeed, evolving conceptions of what hegemony is or might be, as distinct from a balance of rival powers, are among the most significant themes of European history.

To the Treaty of Lunéville

As was pointed out in Chapter VII, the French military situation at the end of 1799, when Bonaparte became first consul, revealed the scars of Austro-Russian victories the previous spring and summer. On the other hand, it had improved a great deal as a result of the Allies' withdrawal from Holland, the tsar's disgusted abandonment of the coalition, and Masséna's victories in Switzerland—all events of the weeks preceding the Eighteenth Brumaire. During the winter the enemies of France experienced further reverses. Russia exchanged its recent military partners, Austria and England, for a northern cluster of diplomatic allies, the armed neutrals, Prussia, Sweden and Denmark. Britain bitterly condemned this Russian 'betrayal', while on his side Paul I found cause for resentment against London in the Royal Navy's designs upon the island of Malta. That Mediterranean stronghold, between Sicily and Africa, had a garrison made up of French troops put ashore in 1798 by Napoleon's expedition en route to Egypt. The wily first consul, however, was now issuing hints that he might cede the island to the tsar, who was Grand Master of the Knights of St John, the international Maltese Order. As a result, the Russian government was openly hostile to the British blockade and to the Admiralty's undisguised plans for an assault.

It was Austria, however, which attracted Bonaparte's special attention as he sought an opening series of victories. In part, this was because the Habsburg dominions constituted a land power, accessible to French military action, while any major onslaught against Britain would have to await costly naval preparations. In addition, the determination to strike at the Austrians was a response to the pressure which Habsburg forces were applying on the Italian front. Here the French clung only to Genoa, plus the coast stretching westward to Nice. Early in April 1800 the Austrian forces of General Melas suddenly fell upon and split in two the army which Masséna had just brought into Italy. One set of survivors had to fall back towards Nice, to shield southern

France itself from invasion. The other fragment, under Masséna, dug in at Genoa to face a siege by the Austrians on the land side and by Lord Keith's British squadron at sea. For two months the siege dragged on under conditions of mounting horror for the Genoese population and its French 'defenders', until June 4, when a capitulation on honourable terms was concluded.

While this was going on, the first consul in Paris, with no immediate concern for the unfortunate regiments trapped in Genoa, moved ahead coolly with his own offensive plans. In April General Moreau was given command of a large army and launched across the Rhine into southern Germany, which he succeeded in clearing of Austrian units without a pitched battle. Having taken Munich in July, Moreau concluded a temporary armistice and stood by for orders. Bonaparte himself, meanwhile, reviving the two-pronged strategy adopted by the Directory five years earlier, took command of a new army of Italy and in mid-May led it over the Alps via the pass of Great St Bernard. Sweeping down into the Po Valley, he entered Milan on 2 June, proclaimed the rebirth of the Cisalpine Republic and began operations designed not only to reverse the decision at Genoa, but actually to drive the Austrians completely out of Italy.

It is conceivable that no other battle, until Waterloo, was so crucial for Bonaparte's career as that which decided this second Italian campaign. In order to justify his assumption of control over the French war effort, the first consul *had* to win—and he very nearly lost. Bonaparte had dispersed many of his units to block supposed Austrian lines of retreat, when on 14 June, near the village of Marengo, the energetic Melas appeared with an army of 30,000 Imperials, confronting only about 18,000 French. By mid-afternoon, the battle seemed sure to end in victory for Melas, defeat for Bonaparte. Nevertheless the apparently beaten French regiments kept up a desperate resistance until General Desaix arrived with one of the brigades earlier sent away by Napoleon. Desaix charged immediately, leading 6,000 fresh troops on to the field; and though it cost him his life, he saved the day. The discouraged Austrians, having lost 9,000 killed or wounded as against 7,000 French casualties, asked for an armistice. As for Bonaparte, the 'victor of Marengo' returned to Paris amid scenes of wild enthusiasm.

Before a general peace could be imposed on Vienna the decision of arms had still to be reached in Germany. This was especially true since Emperor Francis II, in return for a subsidy of £2,500,000, had just promised the British government that he would continue hostilities at least until 1 February 1801. French and Austrian diplomats did begin preliminary discussions at Lunéville in Lorraine; but as the summer dragged into autumn, Bonaparte became convinced that another great victory was required. Consequently, early in November he formally terminated the armistice applying to both Germany and to Italy. Moreau's powerful command in Bavaria, numbering fully 120,000 men, began to roll toward the Inn Valley, gateway to Austria. Slowed at first by the tactics—confusing because confused—of the Archduke John, who had replaced his abler brother, Charles, the French finally caught the Austrians in the snow and mud around Hohenlinden and there on 2–3 December 1800 inflicted over 20,000 casualties on their shattered army.

The combination of disasters at Marengo and Hohenlinden left the Habsburgs no choice but to sue for peace. On Christmas Day, with Moreau's invading army only sixty-five miles from Vienna, a new armistice was signed. It was followed some six weeks later, 9 February 1801, by the formal treaty of Lunéville. Under the latter's terms, Austria confirmed the provisions of Campo-Formio (*see above*, p. 156), agreed to the loss of Tuscany as a Habsburg principality, recognized France's satellite republics as sovereign powers and accepted the *Talweg* of the Rhine, that is its central trough or channel, as the boundary between France and the Empire, thus guaranteeing the former a full share of all navigational rights on the great river.

The internal effects of all this within the Holy Roman Empire took two more years to reveal themselves, but in the meantime, Bonaparte was pushing ahead with his 'pacification of Europe' in many other negotiations. In March 1801 the king of Naples came to terms, promising to close his ports to British ships and to maintain 15,000 French troops in several southern Italian towns until peace was fully restored. At the same time, Bonaparte revived the Ligurian Republic in Genoa and created a new Kingdom of Etruria out of Tuscany and Parma for the benefit of the latter's duke, a puppet of France. That summer, it will be remembered, also witnessed the signing of the new Concordat between Paris and the Papacy. Within the space of a year, the first consul had to all intents and purposes reconquered Italy, though he almost contemptuously let Austria keep Venetia. As for Spain, its nervous monarchy was about to launch a war against Britain's ally, Portugal, on Napoleon's behalf, despite his having forced the Spaniards to sell him Louisiana in America for a pittance the preceding year.

4. Europe after the Treaty of Lunéville (1801)

OM OF SWEDEN

St. Petersburg

Stockholm

BALTIC SEA

French Republic with subsidiary
republics and occupied territories.

RUSSIA

OF PRUSSIA
PORTION OUTSIDE EMP (IRE)

Warsaw

ue

Cracow

HABSBURG
DOMAINS
(PORTION
OUTSIDE EMPIRE)

MOLDAVIA

Budapest

WALLACHIA

BLACK SEA

SERBIA

BULGARIA

OTTOMAN

RUMELIA

EMPIRE

ALBANIA

Ionian Islands

GREECE

MEDITERRANEAN SEA

Britain and the War

The great question mark hung over Great Britain, the only power still at war with France. Eager for the title of triumphant peacemaker, but determined not to trade away any of the Republic's trophies of war, Bonaparte opened cautious negotiations with London in March 1801. England's willingness to make terms agreeable to the first consul obviously depended on a complex of factors, domestic as well as foreign. On the latter plane, the British had some liabilities which might well induce them to cease hostilities. Lunéville in February had deprived them of their last major ally on the Continent, Austria. The treaty signed at Florence between France and the Neapolitan monarchy closed them out of southern Italy. By the end of the summer, Portugal would accept the treaty of Madrid, repudiating all ties with England.

Despite these reverses, His Majesty's government could claim certain assets which, as the months of haggling wore on, seriously complicated Bonaparte's diplomatic offensive. Trinidad in the West Indies, Ceylon in the Indian Ocean, the Cape of Good Hope at the southern tip of Africa, all had been seized from their former rulers, Spanish in the first instance, Dutch in the other two. In September 1800 the French on Malta had capitulated, with no chance to hand the island over to Tsar Paul. A year later, in Egypt, the last of Napoleon's expeditionary army of 1798 laid down its arms, on the promise of being shipped home as exchanged prisoners.

Even in the Baltic, where England's position had seemed so dangerous in 1800, the events of 1801 were running in London's favour. The new League of Armed Neutrality (Russia, Sweden, Denmark, Prussia) lost its chief sponsor on the night of 23–4 March 1801, when Paul I was murdered by court conspirators. His son and heir, young Alexander I, soon showed himself much less anti-British than his father; but even before he had a chance to express his views, the Royal Navy struck a shrewd, if ruthless, blow at the northern allies. On 31 March, just a week after the assassination in St Petersburg, an English squadron under Nelson sailed through the Sound into the Baltic. On 2 April, still with no declaration of war, it battered the Danish fleet to pieces in the harbour of Copenhagen. Thereafter, Nelson was ordered scrupulously to avoid hostilities, while Tsar Alexander, as a conciliatory gesture of his own, gave up the Grand Mastership of the Knights of Malta and hence all claim, on Russia's behalf, to that key island. By June, with the Danish navy eliminated for the foreseeable future and with Russia no longer a potential belligerent, the League of Armed Neutrality collapsed. Behind her reasserted naval might, Britain appeared secure.

Yet there remained powerful motives for seeking peace with France. The war-weariness of Englishmen found clear expression at the highest level of government, where Pitt had left office virtually on the eve of the treaty negotiations. Ironically, it was not policy towards France but disagreement with George III over the treatment of Ireland which had brought down the prime minister. Since 1798, when the Irish rebellion failed and Wolfe Tone killed himself, the affairs of the troubled island had continued to plague Britain's war leadership. A separate, subjugated Ireland posed a continuing threat to England's security, both as a scene of recurrent uprisings and as an inviting target for French military intervention. But what was to be done? Pitt's answer had been the dual policy of Union and Catholic emancipation, that is, a series of projects by which the Irish Parliament would be abolished, Irish members elected to an enlarged British House of Commons and Irish Catholics allowed to serve there as they had been serving in Dublin since 1795. To the Catholics, he pointed out that they must support the Union, since only under its terms would Protestant opinion accept granting them the vote as Britons. To Anglo-Irish Protestants, he pointed out the commercial and political advantages of amalgamation, adding that Catholic representation in Parliament would lose all its terrors, inasmuch as Catholic voters, though 75 per cent of the Irish electorate, would be only a minority in Great Britain as a whole. Without this concession to the Catholic population, he argued, union with England would only plunge the Irish countryside into a new and terrible civil war. When someone asked the son of Lord Cornwallis who he supposed would follow his father as viceroy and commander-in-chief at Dublin if Catholic emancipation were rejected, the young man, who clearly agreed with Pitt, replied: 'Bonaparte.'

Unfortunately for the prime minister (and for Britain), only half his policy was adopted. In the spring of 1800 the Irish Parliament voted itself out of existence. That August the Act of Union was passed at Westminster, where Ireland would henceforth be represented as part of the United Kingdom. Pitt, however, found himself unable to keep his promise of Catholic emancipation. Many Protestant leaders, English and Irish alike, continued to oppose it. Still more serious, the king himself considered the proposed appearance of Catholics in the Commons a deadly threat to the Anglican Church, a violation of his own coronation oath, in short, as he called it in January 1801: 'the most Jacobinical thing I ever heard of!'

Faced with George III's intransigence, Pitt resigned in February 1801, after nearly seventeen years as prime minister—in the very week the treaty of Lunéville was signed. Though the fallen giant of British politics continued to advise and to support his friend, Henry Addington, the former speaker of the House who formed a ministry in March, both the prestige and the truculence of the war government had undeniably waned. The new prime minister was not the insignificant quantity suggested by the contemporary jingle: 'Pitt is to Addington as London to Paddington'; but he was a cautious, at times a timid man. From Napoleon's great victories over the Austrians and the spectacle of Britain's own economic problems (serious food shortages, a national debt risen to £500 million and an annual budget which had tripled in eight years), he felt unable to draw any other conclusion than that peace was essential. Increasingly, Pitt's own voice supported him in this view.

Europe after Amiens

The discussions which finally produced the Franco-British settlement lasted for a full year, until March 1802, when the formal treaty was signed at Amiens in northern France. During that year, as we have seen, England had important successes in the Baltic and Egypt; but Bonaparte's trump cards proved more impressive still. Furthermore, the first consul and his foreign minister, Talleyrand, played those cards with great ability. The result was a treaty whose terms filled most British subjects with disgust, however fervently they welcomed peace as such. Egypt, though lost by the French, was handed back to Turkey. Malta was promised once more to the Knights of St John. All Britain's conquests in the Mediterranean and even Capetown in Africa had to be returned to their former owners, leaving only Trinidad and Ceylon as lasting acquisitions. France, on the other hand, merely evacuated the Papal States and the Kingdom of Naples, at the same time recognizing the new Republic of the Ionian Islands under joint Russo-Turkish protection. Otherwise, not a single conquest of the Republic or the Consulate was surrendered. As seen from Paris, the treaty expressed full acceptance of French primacy on the Continent by the power which had so long and so stubbornly rejected it. As seen from London, the settlement offered no more than a respite for financial and perhaps diplomatic recovery. There seems to have been little confidence in England that the peace would endure, but a great willingness to make the most of it while it lasted.

Whatever Addington's weaknesses as a political leader, he was a tidy and by no means unintelligent administrator. He moved swiftly to cut armament costs, released 70,000 of the navy's 130,000 wartime personnel, sharply reduced the regular army (though he kept 95,000 men in uniform, twice as many as had been serving in 1784), abolished Pitt's 10 per cent income tax of 1799 and resorted to a new loan, simultaneously establishing a sinking fund designed to pay off the government's debts over a period of forty-five years. Thus far, his reforms appeared essentially conservative, and as such they were greeted enthusiastically by the landed and commercial classes. In addition, however, the prime minister took other measures which showed how strongly the example of revolutionary-consular France was beginning to influence even its most irreconcilable enemies. Without regard to political principles, whether egalitarian or dictatorial, it was clear that the terrible Republic had developed administrative mechanisms for harnessing national power which no rival could afford to ignore. Thus, Addington instituted an annual budgetary study of public accounts, induced Parliament to take over direct responsibility for official salaries, including many previously paid by the king, and pushed further the cabinet's control over pensions and other charges on the Civil List. Most striking of all, as soon as war broke out again in May 1803, he restored the income tax, this time with an unprecedented provision for collection at the source and with such sharply improved methods of assessment that though the basic rate was only 5 per cent, half that of Pitt's earlier tax, the net yield to the Treasury was four-fifths the old amount.

While Great Britain was striving to put its house in order, other European states reacted in various ways to the unaccustomed lull in international conflict. France's satellite republics, as well as the no less thoroughly subordinated Etrurian Kingdom in Italy, quickly discovered how little attention Bonaparte would pay to his solemn assurance, given at Lunéville, that they would be fully independent. In September 1801, for example, the first consul announced a new constitution for the Batavian Republic, vesting power in an executive council, with only a limited role reserved to a thirty-five man consultative chamber. In the ensuing plebiscite fewer than 17,000 Dutchmen voted in favour of the constitution, while over 52,000 opposed it: but Napoleon blandly announced that the nearly 340,000 eligible votes who had abstained from casting any ballot at all should be recorded as supporters of his authoritarian reforms! In Italy, meanwhile, where the Ligurian Republic was being converted into what amounted to a cluster of French departments around Genoa, the Cisalpine or, as it was now entitled, the Italian Republic was being reorganized under the presidency of Napoleon Bonaparte himself. The satellite system, whatever the treaty of Lunéville might say, was in fact becoming an ever more cynical façade for direct French control. Its conversion into an openly imperial constellation awaited only the first consul's pleasure.

Among the other continental states, the most docile ally of France was the kingdom of Spain, victorious over Portugal in 1801, but exhausted by the six years of war against Britain which ended at Amiens. The weak, ageing Charles IV and Prince Godoy, with his interesting dual position vis-à-vis the king and the queen, clung to their policy of repression at home and deference to the now gratifyingly anti-Jacobin French régime in Paris. Knowing Bonaparte only through his suave, cordial messages, they could assure themselves that a mixture of prudence and Anglophobia would suffice indefinitely to shield the monarchy from outside interference.

Prussia, despite its ill-concealed desire for the British ruler's German domain, Hanover, joined most other states after Lunéville and Amiens in a noncommittal watchfulness. Neither the Prussian nor the Austrian nor any other continental government yet showed much interest in administrative reforms on the French model—here they lagged behind England for the time being, though some would eventually go much further. Leaving aside for the moment the special case of the Holy Roman Empire, it must be said that only one great power on the mainland underwent a major political change during the era of Bonaparte's consulship. This was Russia, where Tsar Paul I had moved from his violently anti-French sentiments of 1799, through furious resentment of his Austrian and British allies in the Second Coalition, to a literally wild enthusiasm for Bonaparte after learning of Marengo in 1800. We have already seen how the tsar's assassination spared the British the threat of a Baltic maritime league directed against them; but we should here identify the domestic causes behind his murder in St Petersburg's Mikhailovsky Palace on that March night in 1801. The important point is that this was no democratic uprising, nor even a revolt by aristocratic liberals. Rather, it was a cabal of powerful officials, Count Panin, General Bennigsen, Count Pahlen (commandant in the capital) and several others. They strangled their ruler out of desperation over his insane outbursts, his capricious changes of policy and his atrocious behaviour towards subordinates, including the military hero, Suvorov, which led all men to fear for their own futures. Having killed the father, they installed his momentarily bewildered son as Tsar Alexander I.

With this single Russian exception, the leading powers remained essentially static. Not so the smaller members of the Holy Roman Empire. The treaty of Lunéville had stipulated that German princes deprived of territories on the left bank of the Rhine, through cession to France, should be compensated on the right bank, primarily through the secularization of church lands. Theoretically, it was the Empire's own Diet, at Regensburg, which was to work out these indemnities. In fact, however, that body became hopelessly divided, the ecclesiastical delegations and those of most of the free cities violently opposing all juggling of boundaries, which the secular princes of course favoured. It was Napoleon himself, with frequent expressions of solicitude for Russian views, who virtually dictated the final settlement.

The first consul's German policy had several different aims. He wished to isolate Habsburg Austria, keep Prussia friendly—though without letting it become a giant power—reduce the number of west and south German states while increasing their size enough to make alliances with them more meaningful, yet keep this buffer zone of principalities clearly dependent on France. On 5 February 1803 the imperial commission on territorial adjustments presented to the Diet a comprehensive resolution, or 'Recess', endorsed by Napoleon and by Tsar Alexander, rapturous in his role as mediator. This document was the *Reichsdeputationshauptschluss*, whose very title has numbed generations of history students. Pushed through the Diet by the secular princes, it satisfied the French dictator's requirements. It also destroyed whatever substance the Holy Roman Empire had retained through the eighteenth century.

The losers within Germany were the prelates and the imperial free cities. Of the latter, forty-two out of forty-eight were abolished— absorbed into territorial states—leaving only the three old Hanseatic ports of Bremen, Hamburg and Lübeck, plus Frankfurt-on-the-Main, Nuremberg and Augsburg. Two of the three electoral archbishoprics, Trier and Cologne, simply disappeared, though the archbishop of Mainz, while he lost his episcopal city itself, survived as a territorial ruler by virtue of translation to lands on the right bank of the Rhine. Most of the other ecclesiastical microcosms were gobbled up by neighbouring secular principalities, of which Bavaria and the new electorships of

Württemberg, Baden and Hesse Cassel were the most lavishly rewarded. Prussia had already received a number of bishoprics and abbeys under a special treaty with France in 1802; but Bonaparte still denied it the dearest prize of all, Hanover, on the convenient grounds that he was currently at peace with the King of England. No matter, the first consul had little to fear from resentment in a Germany whose non-Austrian princes were now his henchmen, bought and paid for. Already the ruler, in one way or another of France, Belgium, Holland, Germany west of the Rhine, Switzerland and much of Italy, as well as patron of Spain, he had now shown that he could even, as one stunned diplomat expressed it, 'redraw the map of the Holy Roman Empire and send it to Regensburg to be stamped "official" '.

The War Resumed: 1803 to the Treaty of Tilsit (1807)

While Bonaparte was thus proceeding with his reorganization of Germany, the brief interval of general peace was already expiring. Just as England had been the last power to come to terms with France, in the spring of 1802, so it was the first to resume hostilities, in the spring of 1803. Napoleon had shown, almost from the day the treaty of Amiens was signed, that he did not propose to be hampered by its terms and that he still considered Great Britain at best a temporarily nonbelligerent opponent. His actions in the Holy Roman Empire, his annexation of Piedmont and his purposeful tightening of controls in the Dutch, Swiss and Italian tributary states showed London that no lasting stability or balance had been achieved on the Continent. Furthermore, rejecting the advice of certain of his councillors, who favoured reviving Anglo-French trade, he first excluded British exports from the Republic, then, in December 1802, proclaimed the ports of Holland and Italy likewise closed to England's merchants. At the same time, he let it be known that the French battle fleet was to be increased by over 50 per cent, to a strength of sixty-six ships of the line.

Faced with a combination of threats, particularly in the Mediterranean, Addington's government kept postponing the evacuation of Malta. Napoleon pounced upon the delay in fulfilling this clause of the Amiens settlement as clear proof of London's bad faith in all respects. His treatment of the British ambassador during the winter of 1802–3 became so abusive as to suggest that he considered a virtual state of war to exist once more. There can be no doubt that British refusal to return Malta to its Knights was a violation of a treaty commitment; but it was a violation to be judged in the light of the first consul's own contempt for countless other promises made and hopes encouraged at Amiens or Lunéville. On occasion Napoleon spoke as though tiny Malta were the hinge of Europe, while dismissing complaints about his own behaviour with the impatient remark: 'Piedmont, Switzerland, Holland are trifles'.

It has never been clear whether or not Bonaparte sincerely hoped to remain at peace with Great Britain, assuming he could move freely in his own vast sphere and bluster with impunity at all who angered him. What does seem clear is that his policies, which drove even the mild and cautious Addington back to formal hostilities, were scarcely those of a man attempting to relax tension. On 17 May 1803, determined to mobilize its own resources before France achieved prohibitive advantages, England abruptly declared war. Two months earlier, at a reception in the Tuileries, Napoleon had snarled at Lord Whitworth: 'You will be the first to draw the sword; I shall be the last to sheath it!' Half of his prophecy had now come true.

War did not at once extend to the Continent, save for the swift French occupation of Hanover in Germany. The Royal Navy, of course, resumed operations at sea, while Bonaparte in turn began to assemble a huge invasion force on the channel around Boulogne. For fully two years, however, other powers hung back, unwilling to commit themselves to a new alliance against the formidable power of France. During this interval, Britain turned once more to Pitt for leadership. Addington's personal hold on the Commons was never very secure, and as a war minister he was thoroughly uninspiring. After months of hesitation, during which King George III complicated matters by suffering another of his recurrent fits of madness, Pitt finally agreed in May 1804 to form a new government. It was a ministry of national defence in which he would have included even his old opponent, Charles James Fox, had the king not objected violently. The French 'army of England' was building all that year; and in December Spain obediently declared war on Britain, bringing an ominous increment of fighting ships to Bonaparte's growing naval strength. As seen from London, the sky was darkening.

If the first consul hoped to keep England isolated by ingratiating other nations, however, he did not show it in 1804. Apprised of a new internal conspiracy against himself in February, he executed several highly placed suspects. General Moreau, the hero of Hohenlinden, barely escaped to America. So far, of course, only French internal affairs were involved. In March, however, Bonaparte ordered the arrest of the young duke of Enghien, an émigré prince of the Bourbon-Condé line, who was living quietly in German Baden, across the Rhine from France. This arrest was effected by sending French cavalry into the territory of the Holy Roman Empire, an arrogant affront to Vienna. More serious, Enghien was summarily executed at Vincennes, after a court martial had convicted him, without real proof, of being an English agent. A thrill of disbelief and horror ran through every princely court in Europe. Indifferent to the shock created by the Enghien affair, the first consul in May had himself proclaimed Napoleon I, emperor of the French, by the Senate and the Tribunate. A national plebiscite approved this action by the remarkable margin of 3,572,329 to 2,569; and on 2 December the coronation, with Pope Pius VII in attendance, though scarcely officiating, took place at Notre Dame in Paris. Small wonder that foreign statesmen who knew their Shakespeare were asking, 'On what meat doth this our Caesar feed?'

The last hesitations of Austria and Russia began to crumble in March 1805, when Napoleon announced that the Italian Republic would henceforth be the kingdom of Italy and that he would himself accept the crown, as in fact he did at Milan in May. The following month the Ligurian Republic was formally incorporated into the French Empire. Meanwhile, on 11 April Russia and England had signed the treaty of St Petersburg, pledging a joint effort to restore the European balance. On 9 August Austria joined this Third Coalition, promising, albeit unrealistically, a total of 315,000 troops. Though Sweden also adhered, Prussia hung back, in the hope that the French would turn over Hanover as a reward for Berlin's neutrality. By the autumn, however, the lines were drawn for the supreme struggle of Napoleon's 'middle years' in power.

The first beneficiary of the vastly expanded conflict was England. To meet the new forces arrayed against him Napoleon wheeled the invasion army back from Boulogne and sent it east towards Germany under forced march. The naval tension remained, however, with control of the Mediterranean at stake. Horatio Lord Nelson, now forty-seven, had arrived off Cadiz, Spain, in late September 1805 and had taken command of a British squadron consisting of twenty-seven ships, including his own flagship, *Victory*. On 20 October the French-Spanish fleet of thirty-three units under Admiral Villeneuve came out of Cadiz; and on the following day, at Cape Trafalgar, Nelson wrecked it so completely in the 'pell-mell battle' he had yearned for that eighteen enemy vessels were sunk on the spot and the other fifteen never saw action again. The price of Trafalgar was the life of England's greatest naval hero, killed on his own quarterdeck by a sniper's bullet. The reward was to be almost a century of unchallenged naval supremacy. When the exhausted Pitt died three months later, in January 1806, that much he could hand on to the 'Ministry of All the Talents' which succeeded him.

Elsewhere, however, the enemies of Napoleon were involved in a two-year nightmare. At the very time Nelson closed in on Trafalgar, the French struck their first blow against the coalition on land, surrounding and forcing the surrender of General Mack and some 50,000 Austrians at Ulm in south-western Germany. Driving straight down the now weakly defended Danube, Napoleon entered Vienna in November and on 2 December, the anniversary of his coronation, confronted the main Austrian–Russian forces near the Moravian town of Austerlitz, seventy-five miles north of the Habsburgs' fallen capital. When the terrible battle was over, 25,000 Allied casualties and 7,000 French lay on the field. Before the end of the month, Austria abjectly signed the treaty of Pressburg, surrendering Venetia and the Dalmatian coast of the Adriatic to Napoleon's kingdom of Italy, as well as various Habsburg lands in Germany to Bavaria, Württemberg and Baden, the former two now elevated to the rank of kingdoms. Before the next year was over, on 6 August 1806, the Holy Roman Empire itself expired, Francis II renouncing its crown in favour of the hereditary title, 'Francis I, emperor of Austria'. Meanwhile, in December 1805, French victories in Italy having vitiated the meaning of Trafalgar in that quarter, Napoleon proclaimed from Vienna the dethronement of the Bourbons of Naples and the accession of his brother Joseph as the new king.

Russia, of course, was still at war, but for the moment it was Prussia whose role suddenly loomed as crucial. The vacillating government of Frederick William III, ruler since his father's death in 1797, had come near to joining the Third Coalition before Austerlitz. After the great battle, however, Berlin had scrambled to make terms with the victor, giving up further west German lands to France and the Hohenzollerns' Neuchâtel in Switzerland to the Helvetian Republic. In return, with Napoleon's permission, Prussia occupied Hanover in the first weeks of 1806 and formally annexed it, an act destined to poison relations with England long after the Prussians had themselves become enemies of France.

Ironically, the suspicion that Napoleon planned to return Hanover to the British king, as part of a possible peace settlement, was one of Prussia's two main reasons for turning against him that summer. The other was fear of his aggressive German policy, especially the founding, on 12 July 1806, of the French-sponsored Confederation of the Rhine, comprising Bavaria, Württemberg, Baden, Hesse-Darmstadt, Nassau and a cluster of smaller states. The emperor's troops now held garrison rights in over half of Germany. By September the Prussian monarchy, more nervous and exasperated than coolly determined, was mobilizing to back up its demand that the French withdraw west of the Rhine. The expiration of this ultimatum, instead of signalling a Prussian advance, found Napoleon with 160,000 men in northern Bavaria, poised to drive north into Thuringia where his newest enemy was concentrated with its Saxon allies. On 14 October he routed one Prussian army at Jena while Davout crushed another at nearby Auerstädt. Never before had even Bonaparte knocked out a major opponent so quickly. On 17 October he entered Berlin while fortresses capitulated on all sides and Frederick William III fell back into East Prussia with the remnants of his forces. Within two months, Saxony, its duke rewarded with the title of king, made a separate peace and joined the Confederation of the Rhine.

Russian support postponed, though it could not prevent, Prussia's humiliation. The French, having cleared Silesia and taken Breslau, turned north against the coalition partners, who fought their pursuers to a bloody statemate at Eylau in early February 1807. After several months for rest and regrouping, Napoleon's army resumed the offensive, took Danzig on the Baltic in May and finally caught the Russian–Prussian forces in a murderous battle of attrition at Friedland in mid-June. Having occupied historic Königsberg and all East Prussia within the next few days, the emperor stood at the tsar's own frontier. Stubbornly though the Russian troops had fought, their field commander, Bennigsen, now felt that he had no choice but to beg his ruler to make peace. On 25 June, Napoleon and Alexander held their famous meeting on a raft in the Niemen River.

The treaties signed there at Tilsit, 7–9 July, purported to settle all differences between France on the one side, and both Prussia and Russia on the other. Out of deference to the tsar, Napoleon left Frederick William III about two-thirds of his kingdom, but limited his army to 42,000 men. The treaty also sheared away all Polish lands taken by Prussia since 1772, in order to form a Grand Duchy of Warsaw under French protection, with the king of Saxony on the throne. The

Prussians further agreed to close their ports to British trade and acknowledged France's right to dispose, as its emperor saw fit, of all German territory on the Rhine's right bank as far eastward as the Elbe. Finally, Frederick William recognized Napoleon's brothers, Joseph, Louis and Jerome as kings, respectively, of Naples, Holland and 'Westphalia', a synthetic Hessian-Hanoverian German state formed that summer as part of the Confederation of the Rhine. The former system of satellite republics was rapidly giving way to a dynastic complex.

Russia at Tilsit likewise recognized the three Bonapartes in Naples, Amsterdam and Cassel (Westphalia's new capital), together with the Saxon grand duke of Warsaw. In return, the tsar received the Bialystok region of what had been Prussian Poland. On the surface, Napoleon's mediation was welcomed to help end the year-old Russo-Turkish war, while Alexander graciously volunteered to supply the same good offices as between France and England. Actually, the French emperor gave a secret promise that he would desert the sultan (whom he had himself induced to attack the Russians) and would not object to the Rumanian principalities' permanent separation from the Ottoman realm. The tsar also secretly agreed to declare war on England if the latter did not, as it surely would not, accept French peace terms within two months.

Napoleon had already instituted the 'Continental System', a general embargo on British goods, the previous November by the Berlin Decree. The programme was to be made more sweeping and more explicit by the Milan Decree of 17 December 1807. Before that happened, Foreign Secretary Canning in London had guessed, correctly, that Denmark was under heavy pressure to join the hostile alliance and would soon either close the Baltic to all English shipping or see its navy taken over by the French for the same purpose. In the first days of September, therefore, a British squadron again, as in 1801, descended on Copenhagen, this time putting ashore landing parties which commandeered no fewer than thirty-three ships, including the entire Danish battle line. All were sailed off to England. This stroke, not surprisingly, brought neutral Denmark into the war on Napoleon's side. Tsar Alexander too declared war, as promised; but during the next five years of technical hostility, the Russians gave Napoleon no more actual help against Britain than he gave them against Turkey—which is to say, none at all. For the moment, the only serious reverse, from London's point of view, was the occupation of its ally, Portugal, by a French army striking through Spain in November 1807.

Napoleonic Europe: Fighting in Iberia and Austria

The 'pacification of Tilsit', so stately in appearance, so superficial in fact, opened a five-year period during which the Napoleonic Empire continued to fight on many fronts, but without having to face any simultaneous array of forces comparable to the Third Coalition of 1805–7. It was also a period which saw the Empire, as such, expand immensely, at the cost of numerous states treated heretofore as at least semi-independent vassals. Finally, it was a period of varied responses, on the part of Bonaparte's enemies, to the French administrative and military techniques which had to be accorded much of the credit for the emperor's victories.

What some historians have considered Napoleon's most fateful decision, one which set his course away from the peaceful consolidation of past gains and towards seemingly endless expansion, he reached in the first weeks of 1808. The docile Spanish monarchy which had ceded him Louisiana (resold by the French to the United States in 1803), had suffered at Trafalgar and elsewhere for its naval alliance and most recently had let Junot's army cross its territory to invade Portugal in 1807. Even such abject pliancy proved not enough for the emperor. For one thing, he seems to have brooded over the incongruity of collaboration with Spain's King Charles IV of the house of Bourbon, a dynasty long since driven from France itself and in 1805, by Napoleon's own action, dethroned at Naples. It may also be that the emperor rightly distrusted a government led by a weak and ageing monarch, whose queen was the mistress of his minister, Godoy, and whose son, Ferdinand, was at once hostile towards his mother and critical of the king himself. It is also important never to lose sight of Napoleon's virtually limitless family pride, expressed this time as determination to place his brother, Joseph, on the Spanish throne.

The manoeuvres employed to achieve this end were as simple as they were brutal, though their complex aftermath mocked the foresight of the man who set them in motion. During the late winter and early spring of 1808, more and more French regiments, ostensibly en route to Portugal, tarried in Spanish bivouacs by order of their supreme warlord, until the northern half of the country was effectively under foreign occupation. In March a political crisis erupted, when a series of popular revolts against Charles IV, the queen and her lover led the king to announce his abdication in favour of the *Infante*, Ferdinand. Temporizing in order to keep a grip on all parties, Napoleon first refused to recognize this change of rulers, then in late April induced the king, the queen and their rebellious son to meet with him at Bayonne, on the French coast of the Bay of Biscay, there 'to compose their differences'. Instead, in an uncommonly degrading scene, the *Infante* yielded to French threats of death (supposedly justified by the queen's statement that Charles IV was not his real father) and abandoned his claim to the throne of Spain. The befuddled Charles thereupon gratefully passed the crown to Napoleon, who bestowed it on Joseph, recently arrived from Naples. A hand-picked *junta* or council of cowed Spanish notables, brought to Bayonne expressly for this purpose, ratified the dynastic overturn.

The Spanish people, proud, devout, suspicious of outsiders and fiercely loyal to their legitimate ruling family, proved to be less accommodating than the Bayonne junta. On 2 May 1808 the populace of Madrid launched a bloody uprising which French troops put down with a savagery calculated to terrify all would-be resistants in the future. What the shooting of hostages produced, however, was a surge of Spanish hatred against the invader, expressed in the warcry 'Dos Mayo!' and in Goya's great series of sketches, 'The Horrors of War'. The situation in Spain was obviously deteriorating into a serious civil conflict, the more ominous from Napoleon's point of view because British armed forces had entered the Iberian arena in their first serious land commitment since the Dutch fiasco of 1799. Arriving in Portugal with some 10,000 troops Sir Arthur Wellesley marched towards Lisbon and at Vimeiro on 21 August 1808, savagely mauled the French forces under Junot. Only a foolish set of changes in the British command, the result of personal rivalries and the thirty-nine-year-old Wellesley's lack of seniority, saved the French from a disastrous pursuit. Even so, while the convention of Cintra (30 August) allowed Junot to retire in good order, Portugal had become a base from which Napoleon would be attacked almost without respite until his final defeat. That autumn a British army under Sir John Moore pushed forward into Spain. By January 1809 it had been driven back to Corunna, where it was picked up by the fleet. The heroic Moore died in action, but this early offensive had served notice that the Spanish rebels could fight on in the expectation of growing foreign assistance.

The spring of 1809 brought new defiance against Napoleon in central Europe. Austria, heartened by French troubles, its army reorganized by Archduke Charles and its government incited by Count Stadion, the foreign minister, to resume hostilities, declared war and launched an

5. *Europe in 1812*

April offensive into Bavaria. Events quickly proved, however, that Napoleon's claws had not as yet been blunted by his recent difficulties. Racing from Spain to the Danube, as he had raced from Boulogne on the channel in 1805, the emperor, at first relying heavily on the German troops of the Confederation of the Rhine, by the end of the month had driven the Austrians back over their own borders. On 13 May he entered Vienna, and pursuing Archduke Charles across the Danube towards Bohemia, he crushed the main Habsburg forces in a series of engagements which culminated at Wagram on 5–6 July. By the treaty of Schönbrunn, signed that October, Vienna bowed once more in humiliation, ceding Salzburg and surrounding territory to Napoleon's Bavarian puppet, western Galicia to the grand duchy of Warsaw, part of eastern Galicia to Russia and further segments of the Dalmatian coast to the French Empire itself. In April 1810, having divorced the childless Josephine, Napoleon married Francis I's daughter, the Archduchess Marie Louise, in solemn rites at St Cloud. When their son, the king of Rome, was born in March 1811, Europe beheld a prince half-Habsburg and half-Bonaparte.

This dynastic triumph was in a sense the culmination of a process of imperial aggrandizement which had advanced by stages ever since the coronation at Notre Dame in 1804. We have already seen how by the date of Tilsit in 1807, the Batavian Republic had become the kingdom of Holland under Louis Bonaparte; the earlier Parthenopean Republic, the kingdom of Naples under Joseph; and portions of Hanover, Hesse-Cassel and other German territories, the kingdom of Westphalia under Jerome. Since 1808, of course, Joseph was king of Spain, while his and the emperor's brother-in-law, General Murat, had replaced him in Naples as King Joachim. The kingdom of Italy and the grand duchy of Warsaw were other principalities controlled from Paris.

Still more striking than this substitution of monarchical for republican satellites, however, had been the growth of the French Empire by direct, formal annexations: Piedmont in 1802, Genoa and the rest of the Ligurian Republic in 1805, Tuscany and Parma in 1807, the Illyrian provinces across the Adriatic from Italy in 1809 and the Papal States that same year. When in July 1810 King Louis abdicated rather than impose on Dutch commerce the ruinous embargo demanded by his brother's Continental System, the kingdom of Holland was abolished through incorporation into the Empire, an action followed that December by the annexation of northern Germany's coastal plain, including the Hanseatic cities, which brought the swelling total of *départements* to over 130. Finally, in 1812, Catalonia in north-eastern Spain was absorbed. The dominions of the *Grande Nation* now stretched all the way from south of the Pyrenees to the Baltic Sea at Lübeck, from the Hook of Holland to Ragusa (Dubrovnik) in what today is Yugoslavia. In addition to Rome, officially styled its second city, this empire of almost 43 million subjects contained Barcelona and Amsterdam, Hamburg, Turin and Florence, to mention only a few of its non-French centres. Not since Roman times had so much of Europe been subject to a single régime.

Napoleonic Europe: the Nations' Internal Affairs

Outside the Napoleonic domains other nations struggled against the spread of French power or remained uneasily neutral, while shoring up their domestic structures as best they could. In England the death of Pitt in 1806 had ushered in the Ministry of All the Talents, with Lord Grenville as first lord of the Treasury (i.e. prime minister), Charles Grey as first lord of the Admiralty and Charles James Fox as foreign secretary. Fox too, however, was near the end of a life which had carried him from the youthful adventures of a Georgian rake through eloquent enthusiasm for the French Revolution at its beginning to bitter enmity towards the authoritarian France of Bonaparte. He died in September 1806 at the age of fifty-seven, the last of the great eighteenth-century parliamentarians. Two other men were meanwhile moving into the centre of British public affairs. One was George Canning, the able and aggressive young foreign secretary in the duke of Portland's ministry, 1807–9, and the author of the surprise attack on Copenhagen during his first months in office. The other man, for the time being still more influential, was Spencer Perceval, chancellor of the Exchequer under Portland and himself prime minister from 1809 to 1812. A politician of no dramatic gifts but very considerable courage, Perceval clung stubbornly to the policy of war against Napoleon, while steering a difficult course between the king, now sinking into his last, long mental illness, and George III's profligate heir, the prince of Wales, who became regent in 1810, but assumed full powers only two years later. By that time Perceval's career was approaching its tragic and unexpected end. On 11 May 1812, while walking through the Commons' lobby, he was shot down by a vengeance-crazed businessman, ruined by the war. It was a senseless murder, history's only case of assassination of a British prime minister.

Through years of fiscal strain and dragging military operations the British political system had ample occasion to demonstrate its unique resiliency and ability to provide a broad consensus in wartime, even among jealously antagonistic factions. There was no giant on the scene, no Pitt the Elder or the Younger, no Lloyd George, no Churchill. There were, however, merchants and bankers who, as we shall see in Chapter x, had evolved some effective techniques of economic warfare— and of economic survival while at war. There were also soldiers and civil administrators who pushed towards a reorganization of the British Army along lines which gave it new hope against the French. Finally, there were politicians including Grenville and Grey and the 'Saints' around the Yorkshire M.P., William Wilberforce, who among them in 1807 steered through Parliament the Act abolishing the slave trade everywhere British rule extended. It was a fitting memorial to Fox, who had long fought the battle of persecuted groups. It was also a demonstration that Napoleon was not truly the champion of freedom against the antique tyranny of all his foes.

In Russia, at the other extreme of Europe, the fact of war was no less central than in England. Even after Tilsit, the armies of Alexander I continued to struggle against the Turks, with growing success, until May 1812, when the spectre of French invasion forced the tsar to make peace. Meanwhile, in 1808-9, Russia had wrested Finland from Sweden, with results for the latter country which will be noted shortly. Amid these military exertions, complicated by the increasingly ominous clashes between Russian interests and those of France, the government of the tsar managed to display considerable interest in domestic reforms and innovation. Innovation, it should be emphasized, did not extend to any real liberalization of the political system. For example, the much-discussed plan for enacting a bill of rights for all subjects never got beyond discussions within Alexander I's entourage, where men like Novosiltsev and Prince Czartoryski (veteran of Poland's Four-year Diet), Counts Stroganov and Kochubei sought without much effect to filter primarily English liberal ideals through a screen of Russian traditionalism. In the field of administrative reorganization, however, western influences were clearly apparent. As early as 1802, eight specialized ministries of a familiar 'European' kind were substituted for the unwieldly old system of collegiate government boards.

After Tilsit in 1807 open emulation of Napoleonic France was the order of the day, as witness the tsar's appointment of the able, though ruthless, Arakchev to the post of war minister, with sweeping powers.

Still more important, in 1808 the gifted young political philosopher and executive, Michael Speransky, a student of French governmental practices, became Alexander's chief personal adviser. Some of Speransky's projects, including his draft constitution of 1809, patterned after Bonaparte's of 1799 and designed to provide both local and national elective bodies, remained dead letters. However, his creation of a Council of State, composed of the country's highest administrators, went into effect in 1810 as another major step on the course set eight years before when the ministries had been established. It would be a mistake to exaggerate either the strength or the consistency of the tsar's own commitment to reform; but at the very least, before turning his attention primarily to foreign affairs from 1812 onward, Alexander presided over these and other examples of that defensive modernization into which the French onslaught drove some of Europe's most conservative societies and the influence of which will concern us in discussing the post-1815 period.

In Sweden one of the most dramatic political episodes of the era produced some surprising results. The Russians' seizure of Finland and their invasion of the Åland Islands, threatening Stockholm itself, produced a violent crisis within the Swedish government. On 29 March 1809 King Gustavus IV, still demanding greater military exertions against Russia and Denmark than his country could support, was arrested by his own army commanders and forced to abdicate. The nobility within the Estates as a whole reasserted the rights it had lost in Gustavus III's coups of 1772 and 1789 (see above, pp. 35 and 96). As king the insurgent aristocrats chose the uncle of Gustavus IV, an elderly gentleman who was crowned as Charles XIII and who promptly made peace with the Russian-Danish alliance, surrendering Finland to the tsar and accepting Napoleon's demand that Sweden join the Continental System, excluding the British from its ports.

Since Charles XIII had no son, the Estates first designated a Danish-German prince, Christian of Augustenburg, as his heir. In May 1810, however, Christian suddenly died, leaving the Swedes confronted by Denmark-Norway's king as a possible claimant to their throne as well. To prevent that unpopular solution, the Estates and King Charles decided to install one of Napoleon's marshals, as yet unnamed, in the position of heir apparent. Their choice, announced in August 1810, fell on Jean-Baptiste-Jules Bernadotte, prince of Ponte Corvo, a tall, dignified Gascon who was a veteran of both fighting and diplomacy in Germany. Napoleon, who incidentally disliked this particular marshal of France, was both surprised and disconcerted. The emperor was no great friend of Sweden, as he had shown not only by urging the Russians to invade Finland after Tilsit but also by 'inviting' them to take Stockholm as well. On the other hand, the invitation was flattering to French pride, and there were possible advantages in having one of his former subordinates in line for the Swedish throne. The imperial permission, which Bernadotte had made a condition of his own acceptance, was somewhat grudgingly given, accompanied by a demand that the new prince royal promise never to take up arms against his French homeland. Bernadotte quite properly refused to bind himself for the future and, also properly, renounced his old title and pension as a prince of the Empire. Though destined not to become king until Charles XIII's death in 1818, Prince Charles John, as he was now styled, immediately took over control of Swedish diplomacy and military affairs. In a sense, Napoleon had given Europe yet another king, though not one who was to prove very satisfactory from the emperor's point of view.

No region of the Continent, not even France itself, underwent greater or more lasting changes during the Napoleonic era than did the German lands. The successive treaties of Lunéville, Pressburg, Tilsit and Schönbrunn, like the deliberations of the *Reichsdeputation* from 1801 to 1803, revolutionized the map of what had been the Holy Roman Empire. The number of German states was greatly reduced, through the absorption by secular principalities of countless bishoprics, free cities and imperial fiefs. However, the states that remained, generally enlarged, in several instances raised to the status of kingdoms and in several others made grand duchies, were even more jealous of one another than the units of the old *Reich* had been.

French influence appeared in several different forms. From 1807 onward, the kingdom of Westphalia, ruled by Napoleon's brother, Jerome, and possessed of a constitution 'made in France', was at once a member of the German state system and a show window for Bonapartist principles of rule. Certain of Napoleon's south German allies, notably Württemberg under King Frederick I and Bavaria and Baden under their energetic ministers, Montgelas and Reitzenstein, introduced reforms aimed at rationalizing bureaucratic control, making church officials essentially civil servants, reducing caste privileges in law and taxation. Even Austria, once Stadion became in 1805 not only its foreign minister but its leader in domestic affairs as well, did honour to hated France by borrowing some of its institutional forms. The creation of a *Landwehr* or militia in 1808, with all adult males made liable to call, showed the belated impact of the *levée en masse* upon Austrian thinking. Ironically, it was the false confidence inspired by this *Landwehr* that led to the disastrous war against Napoleon in 1809, a war which forced Stadion to retire in favour of the former ambassador in Paris, Count Clemens von Metternich. Hence Austria's reform period was cut short before the fallen minister's other projects, administrative, judicial and fiscal, could have much effect. Yet new pressures for change had been created and had to be acknowledged, not least in Hungary where Napoleon had striven, if for the moment without success, to stir up an anti-Habsburg revolt.

It was Prussia, however, which witnessed the most general effort to reorganize a state battered into temporary submission by the French Empire. The name commonly associated with this programme of re-generation after the military disaster of Jena and the diplomatic humi-liation of Tilsit is that of Karl, Baron vom und zum Stein, born an imperial knight near the Rhine in Nassau but already a veteran of the Prussian civil service when he was appointed minister of home affairs in October 1807. Other figures, however, played major roles in Prussia's Reform Era: War Minister Boyen, Generals Scharnhorst, Grolmann and Gneisenau, the philosopher and educator Wilhelm von Humboldt and a man who was both Stein's colleague and his successor in office, Karl August von Hardenberg. Stein himself was driven into exile by Napoleon's wrath in September 1808, after the interception of a letter in which the minister had praised the Spanish rebels and prophesied a new war between Austria and France. Nevertheless, his own activities during that year in office, plus the subsequent efforts of the men who followed him, made the period after Jena and Tilsit one of the most significant in Prussian history.

The reforms enacted by Stein himself included the liquidation of serfdom, as a legal status, throughout the kingdom, effective as of 1810, and its *immediate* abolition on the royal domains in October 1807. This Edict of Emancipation also put an end to the old prohibition against individuals' moving among noble, burgher and peasant occupations. Finally, it obliterated the former distinction between noble and non-noble lands and permitted free sale to any buyer, without reference to his legal order. In 1808 Stein promulgated the important Municipal Ordinance, which gave town governments a new dignity and autonomy in fiscal administration, authorizing the election both of aldermen and of the executive councillors who would henceforth share with the crown the right to choose mayors.

Meanwhile, the Prussian military reformers were introducing a Great General Staff to co-ordinate operations, founding the War Academy for advanced study, opening careers as officers to non-noblemen of proven ability and planning a system of universal reserve service which, like its Austrian counterpart, reflected the dread inspired by France's *levée en masse*. Prussia, they argued, must have highly trained officers and cadres of regular troops; but in addition, it must have masses of patriotic citizen-soldiers, prepared to fight for a cause which commanded popular allegiance. In another area of reform, that of education, the drive to create a more open, more practical and at the same time more competitive system of public schooling reached its culmination with the founding of the University of Berlin under Humboldt's leadership in 1810 and the University of Breslau in Silesia the following year.

There has long been dispute over the primary source of inspiration for these programmes. Was Stein, the country gentleman from the Rhineland, guided by his admiration for England's local and national institutions, which he had observed at first hand during his travels? Or was his ministry dominated by the wish to imitate post-1789 French models? Actually, it would appear that English, French and indigenous German themes are so thoroughly intertwined in the record of Prussian reform as to defy all efforts to disentangle them. One dominant impulse, however, does merit special notice, for it alone lends unity to an otherwise disparate array of administrative, socio-economic, military and educational measures. This was the desire to train and then to mobilize the energies of a new kind of Prussian citizenry, committed by sympathy and enlightened self-interest to a patriotic struggle against the foreign oppressor and, by the same token, against old injustices at home. In this respect, Stein and his collaborators were responding, at the level of public policy, to the same challenge which called forth the philosopher Fichte's impassioned *Addresses to the German Nation* (delivered at Berlin in the winter of 1807-8), the anti-French poetry of the Rhinelander Arndt, the patriotic vehemence of the Moral and Scientific Union, or *Tugendbund*, founded at Königsberg in 1808, and the efforts, gallant but doomed, of Major Schill and others to launch Prussian revolts against Napoleon in 1809.

The reform programme, as such, was by no means triumphant over all obstacles confronting it, including the resistance of countless Prussian aristocrats. Most of the freed serfs, for example, instead of becoming the class of independent farmers Stein had dreamed of, lost out in the scramble to acquire property in land and tended to sink to the status of hired hands on large *Junker* estates. There is no question, however, that local administration, public education and military organization all benefited from the impulse to reform. Prussia emerged with certain assets it was to exploit throughout the nineteenth century and far into the twentieth—long after its leaders had abandoned the reformers' highest ideals of fraternity and justice.

From the Invasion of Russia to Waterloo

We must now return to the great international struggle of Napoleon's era, as it entered its final phase. Earlier, we observed that after Lunéville and Amiens in 1801–2 and again after Tilsit in 1807, there seemed to be some chance of a peace devoted to consolidation within the various power blocs. Both times the hope faded, in the first case because of British reactions to renewed commercial and naval pressure on the side of France, in the second because the emperor turned to an extension of the policy of force, this time directed against Spain. By 1810–11, however, while the Spanish battle lines continued to sway as Wellesley duelled with Masséna and Soult, there again appeared to be a possibility that by concentrating his immense military resources on the Iberian peninsula and by capitalizing on Britain's economic difficulties, Napoleon could obtain a favourable, general settlement. His marriage to a Habsburg heiress, the accommodating attitude of Metternich in Vienna, the impotence of Prussia, the fawning solicitude of most German princes, the quiescence of Italy, Switzerland and the Low Countries, all suggested that Europe was ready to accept the Empire on existing terms. It was in defiance of such prospects that in June 1812 the Grand Army of some 430,000 French veterans and allied troops crossed the Niemen River, launching the invasion of Russia.

Just when Napoleon reached the decision to attack the empire of the Romanovs is not clear. Immediately after Tilsit, it is true, he had begun to send secret encouragement to the Turks in their struggle with the Russians, meanwhile complaining bitterly of Tsar Alexander's failure to take any effective military steps against England or even to enforce the Continental System against British ships entering Russian ports. The gala Erfurt Congress in September 1808, which was supposed to seal the friendship between the two rulers in the presence of nearly forty German kings and princes, in fact produced the first serious indications of reciprocal mistrust. At St Petersburg, with émigrés such as Stein on hand to feed the tsar's suspicions, French plans for Poland

and Napoleon's noncommittal reaction to Alexander's demand for Constantinople were viewed with special hostility. It was Bonaparte, however, and not the Russian ruler, who by the summer of 1811 was actively preparing for the great assault which he believed would knock out his only serious rival on the Continent.

Russia, on its side, hastened to assure itself of freedom to meet the attack with its full forces. In May 1812 peace was concluded with Turkey, and a few days later with Great Britain as well. Sweden was already an ally; for Bernadotte had decided that spring to defy his former emperor, to end the Swedes' costly war against England and to support the tsar in the coming struggle, in return for a Russian promise that Norway should become a Swedish possession. The British were distracted by the opening stages of a two-and-a-half-year conflict with the United States, the 'War of 1812', a long-delayed but probably inevitable result of various frontier disputes, compounded by the Royal Navy's actions in restraint of neutral commerce. Nevertheless, English attacks on French shipping and on French armies in Spain offered the Russians some hope in a long struggle. One of the great questions in 1812, of course, was: how long *would* the war last?

The army of French, Austrian, Prussian, Saxon, west German, Italian and other satellite troops which swept eastward during July and August was the most powerful military force the world had ever seen in action, or would see again until 1914. It took Smolensk on 18 August. On 7 September, at Borodino, the emperor destroyed a third of Kutusov's opposing army, at a cost of one-fourth of his own. On 16 September he was in Moscow, largely deserted save for the small groups of civilians and disguised soldiers who that night began burning the city around its conquerors' ears. For well over a month, technically triumphant but actually frustrated and seemingly confused, Napoleon remained in the outskirts of the ruined city, vainly hoping that the tsar would come to terms. Finally, on 19 October, amid the first warnings of the terrible Russian winter, the Grand Army was ordered to fall back across the scorched countryside towards friendlier territory.

Thus began the long torment of the retreat from Moscow. It has been estimated that of the troops which had crossed the Niemen in June 1812, only 50,000 got back to it. Of the 380,000 casualties, almost half died of freezing, hunger and disease on the desperate winter march.[1] Early in December, leaving what remained of the army under Murat's command, Napoleon hurried back to Paris to crush the most recent of

[1] G. Bodart, *Losses of Life in Modern Wars* (Oxford, 1916), pp. 120 ff.

several conspiracies against him. He also extracted from the Senate a pledge of 350,000 more troops to be raised and equipped—just how was not clear—without delay. These troops were urgently needed, for the Russians, now openly supported by Bernadotte's Swedes, were pushing into Germany. Furthermore, while the Austrians withdrew into watchful neutrality, Prussia, having made peace with Russia in December, declared war on France and its allies in March 1813. Before the end of that month, Prussian troops entered Dresden, driving Napoleon's Saxon henchmen before them.

Meanwhile, with Soult and his forces transferred from Spain to Germany, the marquess of Wellington, as Wellesley had become (he was made a duke in 1814), pushed north-east until on 21 June he caught and smashed the army of Marshal Jourdan at Vittoria. During this same period, English subsidies were being hurriedly granted to a dozen central European allies, to increase the pressure on Napoleon. In August cautious Austria at last declared war on France, joining Russia and Prussia in a formal alliance at Teplitz in September. Even Bavaria left the Confederation of the Rhine to enter the coalition against the French. Finally, in four days of violent fighting around Leipzig, 16–19 October, the allies defeated Bonaparte in what was soon christened the Battle of the Nations. The king of Saxony, the emperor's last major German ally, was taken prisoner; King Jerome fled from his Westphalian realm: and the other west German states hurried to leave the sinking ship. As Napoleon dropped back from the Rhine in November, Wellington crossed the French frontier at the western end of the Pyrenees and stormed into Bayonne. From Holland came news of a general revolt and the expulsion of imperial officers, both military and civil. Everywhere the great structure, built on victory, was sagging in defeat.

Napoleon's chief hope of salvation lay in the endemic jealousy and suspicion among the powers attacking him. In addition, there was some chance that he might capitalize on their monarchs' uneasiness in the face of patriotic demands for mass risings against the French Empire, demands which might threaten other kinds of authority as well. Austria, in particular, had reason to stop short of a total victory which seemed likely to benefit its old rivals, Prussia and Russia, while releasing national passions among the various groups of Francis I's subjects. In 1813 Metternich could still perceive advantages in maintaining Bonaparte, linked as he was to the Habsburgs by marriage, on the throne of a France reduced to manageable size and made less belligerent by adversity. Early in November, therefore, the Austrian foreign minister stole a march on his allies by making a peace overture which guaranteed France the natural frontiers, that is, the Rhine, Alps and Pyrenees as boundaries. This would have acknowledged the erstwhile Republic's conquests through 1796, leaving Belgium, the German left bank and Nice-Savoy under French rule. The emperor refused the offer. On 21 December the armies of the coalition crossed the Rhine and began driving into northern France.

Local victories in February 1814 so exhilarated Napoleon that he again brushed aside peace offers, this time stated in terms of the boundaries of 1792. As a result, the British foreign minister, Castlereagh, was able to secure an Allied agreement, signed 9 March at Chaumont in Champagne, that the war should be fought out, in concert, to a clear decision. For the next three weeks, the French fell back, losing one encounter after another. On 31 March their enemies entered Paris. Simultaneously, in the south, Wellington was finishing the long struggle which had carried him from Portugal to Bordeaux on 12 March and the culminating victory over Soult at Toulouse on 10 April. A week earlier Napoleon had abdicated. On 11 April he accepted the treaty of Fontainebleau, which gave him sovereignty over the tiny island of Elba, off the Italian Mediterranean coast near Piombino, an annual pension of 2 million francs from the restored Bourbon monarchy and the right to keep the title of emperor.

The fears and criticisms of some observers who found this treatment excessively mild were justified by events within a year. Napoleon reached Elba on 4 May 1814; on 1 March 1815 he landed on the southern coast of France once more, determined to rally his former subjects against the foreign powers and King Louis XVIII, one of Louis XVI's younger brothers, whom those powers had placed on the French throne. Thus began the Hundred Days, the oft-told story of which need not be repeated here in detail. As he proceeded north towards Paris, collecting troops en route, Napoleon had several assets still working in his favour. His name and his military reputation had not lost their magic. The Bourbon restoration had been accompanied in many parts of France by a White Terror or persecution of anti-monarchists, who now turned in anger and disgust to welcome the emperor back from exile. Ex-officers, in particular, found themselves intoxicated by resurgent memories of past glory. Marshal Ney, who had promised Louis XVIII that he would bring back the outlawed Bonaparte in an iron cage, met the culprit at Auxerre—and threw himself into his old commander's arms. The Allies, for their part, reacted with a predictable lack of coordination. Not until 25 March, five days after the returned exile had entered Paris, did the Austrian, Prussian, Russian and British governments agree to contribute 180,000 troops apiece to a coalition army under Wellington's command.

Yet the odds against Napoleon's gamble remained prohibitive. At no point in this final campaign did he control more than 150,000 troops, in the face of all Europe rearming against him. Allied forces immediately available totalled almost three-quarters of a million men, some 225,000 of whom were poised in Belgium. The only considerable force supporting the emperor outside France was Murat's Neapolitan army, which invaded the Papal States and pushed north through Italy, only to be routed by the Austrians in the first days of May. The emperor now had no hope save in a smashing victory which would split his enemies and rally all Frenchmen behind him. On 12 June he hurried north from Paris to join his army for a showdown in Belgium. On the 16th, at Ligny, he won a tactical decision over the Prussian forces of Blücher. Two days later, however, on the misty ridge of Waterloo, a few miles south of Brussels, the steadiness of Wellington's forces and the timely arrival of Prussian reserves destroyed over half the French army—and with it the last possibility that Napoleon might reverse the outcome of nearly a quarter-century of warfare. Abdicating for a second time on 22 June, he surrendered on 15 July to the commander of the English warship *Bellerophon* in the Breton port of Rochefort, just in time to escape almost certain execution by the pursuing Prussians. In October the British took him to his final captivity, comfortable but escape-proof, on the remote South Atlantic island of St Helena. There, six years after his Empire's collapse, he died in 1821 before his fifty-second birthday.

The Nature of the Napoleonic Empire

Thus laconically must the writer of a general history turn from a career which has inspired countless multi-volume works. So too must end the chronicle of international events which swirled about the figure of the Corsican cadet who became an emperor. In the next two chapters we shall examine more closely the military aspects of the era and then the diplomatic resolution which came at its close. The story of Europe and Napoleon, however, as it concerns the shifting alliances with and coalitions against him, as well as the political changes occurring in countries outside France during the long struggle, we can here pursue no further.

There remains to be briefly considered only the question posed at the start of the present chapter. What was 'hegemony' as visualized by Napoleon and as resisted by his enemies? A galaxy of French historians have insisted that all their country has ever sought, even under the imperial eagle, was security within its 'natural frontiers', the Rhine, the Alps and the Pyrenees. All the other annexations, whether in Italy or Spanish Catalonia, Germany or Holland or the Dalmatian coast of the Adriatic, were required, so the argument goes, to protect this vital core, the *Grande Nation* itself. And all the battle lines, from Egypt to Portugal to the freezing plains before Moscow, had to be stretched so far because other powers, England above all, would not accept Greater France.

Proceeding from their own assumptions and sentiments, apologists claim that Napoleon could not call a halt to his rampaging armies so long as the British remained at once hostile and out of reach. The Continental System and the coercion required to consolidate it are justified by the thesis that, confronted by England's sea power, the emperor had no choice but to organize all Europe in pursuit of victory. Even his betrayal of Spain in 1808 appears in some treatments as a necessary effort to 'free the Iberian shoulder' for the final struggle against Great Britain.

However, presented with this moving image of an organizer of France who yearned for peace and stability, yet was compelled by defensive considerations to undertake ever more ambitious struggles, the thoughtful student is apt to feel misgivings. *Did* Napoleon in fact see all his wars as part of a master plan to bring England to its senses? We have no evidence that he did. The Spanish venture, for example, he seems to have embraced out of a mixture of dynastic pride and rather petulant distrust of his Bourbon allies in Madrid. Still more difficult to explain away is the aggressive, unbridled tone which the emperor adopted towards Russia in 1812. True, he accused Alexander of failing to support the common front against Britain; but still more vehemently, he denounced Russian ambitions in the Near and Middle East, thereby revealing his own. Furthermore, this allegedly wistful defender of French frontiers proposed, whatever the tsar might feel, to reorganize Slavic Europe around his expanding grand duchy of Warsaw. Even if the British Isles had not existed, it seems unlikely that Napoleon could have long endured Alexander I as a co-arbiter and rival in continental affairs.

Hegemony in Europe has meant many different things to different men at different times. French hegemony, as Napoleon conceived it, was perhaps a less repellent vision than the German hegemony, at once pitiless and vulgar, envisaged by Adolf Hitler. It was also, however, something more ambitious than the kind of paramount power or leadership among a constellation of weaker, but nonetheless comparable states which would satisfy Bismarck, as for that matter it had satisfied Louis XIV in all his pompous pride. Year by year Napoleon seemed to lose the capacity for dealing with other governments or even tolerating their independent existence. Not surprisingly, he ended with virtually all such governments leagued against him. Even in 1813 he was not prepared to accept the natural frontiers so dear to French nationalist historians. As the final tides of defeat washed in, when the Allies offered precisely those frontiers, the emperor refused what he considered an insolent and insulting proposition. By now, it was all or nothing. Or almost nothing—St Helena covers forty-seven square miles.

X

The Changing Face of War

The study of an age of conflict calls for several different kinds of analysis. One has to do with causes, another with results, a third with the narrative of events. Still another must address itself to the contemporary effects of conflict upon society and culture, upon the texture of human life. While we either have given or shall give some consideration to all these problems, we ought now to consider the most obvious aspect of all: the ways in which the struggles themselves were fought.

BIBLIOGRAPHY. Major surveys relating military history to other developments include Nef, *War and Human Progress*, and Vagts, *A History of Militarism* (for both, *see* Bibliography, p. 49), as well as R. A. Preston, S. F. Wise and H. O. Werner, *Men in Arms* (New York, 1956). The standard work on the revolutionary forces remains R. W. Phipps's five volumes, *The Armies of the First French Republic* (London, 1926–39), supplemented by specialized monographs such as M. Lauerma, *L'artillerie de campagne française pendant les guerres de la Révolution* (Helsinki, 1956). For Great Britain, consult C. Oman, *Wellington's Army, 1809–1814* (London, 1912); the more favourable G. Davies, *Wellington and His Army* (Oxford, 1954); A. H. Burne, *The Noble Duke of York* (London, 1949); and *The Letters of Private Wheeler, 1809–28*, ed. B. F. Liddell Hart (London, 1951). The important case of Prussia's army has been studied by W. O. Shanahan, *Prussian Military Reforms, 1786–1813* (New York, 1945), and more recently by G. Ritter, *Staatskunst und Kriegshandwerk*, vol. I (rev. edn., Munich, 1959). An uncommonly interesting sidelight is supplied by J. A. Lukacs, 'Russian armies in western Europe: 1799, 1814, 1917', *American Slavic and East European Review*, vol. XIII (1954). For a lucid account of a single battle, J. Naylor, *Waterloo* (London, 1960), is recommended, while more general theoretical aspects receive attention in the appropriate chapters of *Makers of Modern Strategy*, ed. E. M. Earle (Princeton, N. J., 1945). Naval history can be initially approached through A. T. Mahan, *The Influence of Sea Power upon the French Revolution and Empire*, 2 vols. (the edition quoted in this chapter is the 11th, Boston, 1902), and by the same author, *The Life of Nelson* (rev. edn., Boston, 1918), though the standard account of the era's greatest maritime encounter is now D. Pope, *England Expects* (London, 1959), published in the United States as *Decision at Trafalgar*. Two useful works on amphibious warfare are A. Vagts, *Landing Operations* (Washington, 1946), and E. H. S. Jones,

It is important to ask what changes took place in the nature of warfare in Europe from the end of the *ancien régime* and the revolutionary onslaught to the thunderous climax at Waterloo. In a more general context, it is no less important to ask what those decades represent in a long view of man's history of reliance on organized force. Where in that grim chronicle should we place the revolutionary-Napoleonic chapter?

A distinguished philosopher-historian has seen the era as opening the modern world's experience of total war, fought by mass armies, with tools supplied by mass industry, in pursuit of aims defined by the masses' will to survive and to conquer.[1] According to this view, the marriage of war and industry dates from at least as early as the fifteenth century, but until about the middle of the eighteenth Christian restraints, the traditional caution of princes and the relatively *undeveloped* economic potential for mass warfare prevented the full realization of threatened horrors. Increasingly, so runs the argument, the late 1700s brought into view the motives, the techniques and the implements of modern carnage. It then remained only for the French Revolution to unleash the requisite passions to make such carnage a reality. Whether or not one agrees with this vision of the era with which we are concerned, there can be no doubt about the military significance of the almost quarter-century-long struggle which began in 1792. It witnessed not only the involvement, on an unprecedented scale, of armies and navies but also the marshalling of economic and psychological weapons in the service of vast projects.

Size and Equipment of Armies

Most armies in the eighteenth century, as we saw in Chapter IV, had been small by later standards (*see above*, pp. 61–2). Prior to the 1790s, a major strategic plan or military treaty might call for no more than 18,000 or 24,000 troops—the familiar reckoning in units of 6,000,

---

An Invasion That Failed: The French Expedition to Ireland, 1796 (Oxford, 1950). For the central economic struggle, see W. F. Galpin, *The Grain Supply of England during the Napoleonic Period* (Philadelphia, 1925), and F. Crouzet's extremely important study, *L'économie britannique et le blocus continental, 1806–1813* (Paris, 1958). Finally, 'fiscal warfare' is examined by J. M. Sherwig, *Guineas & Gunpowder: British Foreign Aid in the Wars with France, 1793–1815* (Cambridge, Mass., 1969).

---

[1] This is a central theme of Nef (see Bibliography, p. 49).

traditionally associated with the size of a Roman legion, hung on until the end of the Old Régime. It is true that when Frederick the Great died in 1786, the Prussian army claimed a mobilizable strength of some 200,000 men, as compared with 90,000 at his accession in 1740; yet even in Frederick's bitterest wars, on only two or three occasions did he commit more than 50,000 men to a single engagement. The French monarchy had been known to entrust as many as 100,000 soldiers to a single marshal. Russia had raised still greater hordes for action on its sprawling Turkish, Polish and Baltic fronts. These exceptional cases, however, did not alter the general reliance prior to the Revolution on small, highly trained armies of long-term regulars.

The general expansion of military manpower began with the French levies of 1792, theoretically composed of volunteers but actually fixed by quotas assigned to all the territorial *départements* and filled by lot wherever necessary. The results were *not* immediate. In the first campaign, leading to Valmy, some 70,000 Prussians and Austrians faced at most 52,000 French defenders, of whom only the 16,000 men of Kellermann's *Armée du Centre* appeared ready for battle. By January 1793, however, the combined armies of the Republic on the northern front alone numbered about 122,000.[1] In the course of that year, a far more dramatic increase in French forces stemmed from the *levée en masse* (*see above*, p. 123–148), the general conscription which raised an estimated 450,000 recruits during Carnot's four years as, in effect, war minister.

Armies differed considerably in size on various occasions during the Napoleonic era—Bonaparte's 30,000 in the first Italian campaign, Moreau's 120,000 at Hohenlinden, the 430,000 with which the Grand Army entered Russia in 1812, the 150,000 for the emperor's last, Belgian, campaign. It is thus difficult to generalize about the 'normal' size of Napoleon's field armies at the height of his power. He had perhaps 65,000 men under him at Austerlitz, 85,000 or more at Jena, 165,000 at Wagram, 135,000 at Borodino, 190,000 at Leipzig. At first glance, these figures may not suggest any radical increase over those of pre-revolutionary armies, but note that they refer only to *specific engagements*. In 1808, on the eve of the campaign against Austria which would end at Wagram, the emperor of the French disposed of some 300,000 troops in Spain, 100,000 in France, 200,000 in the Rhineland, and 60,000 in Italy.[2] Heavy conscription at home and in occupied (especially

[1] Phipps, vol. I, p. 152 (*see* Bibliography, p. 226).
[2] *Cambridge Modern History*, vol. IX, p. 345.

German) lands had by that date produced armed masses which dwarfed any known in the past. One expert has calculated that between 1800 and 1815, the number of Frenchmen alone who were called to the colours reached 2 million, with deaths in service totalling 400,000.[1]

Though the enemies of Napoleon, taken together, were obviously capable of matching the military manpower of his Empire, a general lack of either enthusiasm or co-ordination prevented their actually doing so until the final campaigns of 1813–15. In 1812 even the Russians were outnumbered in several key battles, and that same year Wellington in Spain never controlled more than 80,000 troops at any one time, while Soult's imperial legions there, albeit dispersed, still totalled over 200,000. Only after Napoleon's defeat in Russia signalled the beginning of the War of Liberation were truly overpowering Allied forces assembled in central and eastern Europe. By the time of the Hundred Days, the Allies were able quickly to remobilize three-quarters of a million men, 225,000 of them converging on Waterloo alone.

No such numbers could have been achieved without an extension of conscription sufficient to match the tremendous French levies. Russia had long raised its regiments by the drawing of lots in villages, the young peasants thus selected being enrolled for terms of twenty-five or even thirty years. In the Slavic and Hungarian regions of the Habsburg empire, similar methods were used, though the terms of service were generally shorter and the reliance on conscription was somewhat less heavy. The Hungarians in particular enlisted with dependable gusto. Austria, under Archduke Charles's leadership, and Prussia, under that of the post-Jena military reformers, led the German states in the formulation of orderly rules covering recruitment, active duty and service in the reserves. As for Britain, while the government never imposed conscription for active service, it continued to replenish local militia units by the drawing of ballots; and the War Office sought with considerable success to induce militiamen thus enrolled to transfer into regiments of the line bound for Spain, the colonies or, later, Flanders.

During this period, certain interesting and by no means irrelevant changes took place in military uniforms. Perhaps the most important was the marked increase in the degree of uniformity itself within a particular army. In the eighteenth century, real uniformity had still been found only in individual regiments, and then only in the crack regiments of selected regulars. Nevertheless, we can identify certain general features of European military costume on the eve of the Revolution.

[1] A. Meynier, cited in Bruun, p. 72 (*see* Bibliographical Note, p. 392).

Head-dress ranged from the turned-up tricorn and other forms of cocked hat through close-fitting leather helmets and the Russian private's cylinder of soft wool to the high, stiff 'grenadier's cap' suggestive of a bishop's mitre. Some form of swallow-tailed coat was most common, usually adorned with elaborate flaps, facings, epaulets, buttons and frogs. Since the creation of the Black Watch in 1739, Highland infantry had been authorized to wear kilts while serving His Britannic Majesty, but most European soldiers wore short breeches and either long boots or, more often, tightly buttoned gaiters of knee or even thigh length.

As a result less of the revolutionists' aversion to old-fashioned costumes than of the need to attire large new armies more simply and less expensively, military dress by about 1800 had in many countries changed much of its earlier character. Hard campaigning had led to the abandonment of unessential ornamentation. Comfortably loose trousers over shoes, low boots or short gaiters were becoming far more popular than the old breeches. The tall grenadier's 'mitre' had by this time virtually disappeared, though the cocked hat and the snug helmet of leather or metal both retained favour with most armies.

In the ensuing years, Napoleon's forces and the principal armies arrayed against him showed a somewhat puzzling tendency to move back to more highly adorned, even pretentious uniforms. Perhaps this development is to be explained by a combination of imperial pomp in France and the long period of militarization of European life in general. In any event, by 1815 there had evolved a characteristic set of costumes destined to remain in general use for a half-century or more: trousers or long, tight breeches, low boots, high-collared jackets with crossing shoulder belts and stiff, visored hats (*shakos*). There were many exceptions, of course: the plumed helmets and breastplates of cuirassiers, the towering fur headgear of Napoleon's Imperial Guard, the loose tunics and round leather or sheepskin caps of Russia's Cossacks. An entire family of special units in numerous armies sprang from romantic enthusiasm for the dashing cavalrymen of eastern Europe, whose reputation had been legendary throughout the eighteenth century. These *uhlans* and *hussars*, whatever their actual nationality, affected the ornate boots, the richly braided jackets, the capes and the fur hats identified with Hungary and Poland—and their swagger bespoke the élitist arrogance which often accompanies the exotic. The general uniformity achieved by 1815 was nonetheless remarkable.

Weapons underwent relatively few modifications between 1792 and

1815. This fact at first glance seems surprising. It becomes less so if one recalls the very considerable changes in the tools of war which had immediately *preceded* the Revolution and which now received full application. The dreaded artillery of Napoleon, for example, was essentially the artillery created by Gribeauval (*see above*, p. 62) beginning in 1776: standardized field pieces for four-, eight- and twelve-pound balls; the six-inch light howitzer for close bombardment; prefabricated cloth bags containing powder charge, ball and wadding; four- and six-horse teams paired in spans; carriages and limbers made both stronger and lighter by increased use of thin iron supports. By the 1790s all these developments were available to any army wishing to copy them, as was the growing reliance on interchangeable parts (wheels, pins, bolts) and the cannister of round antipersonnel shot recently invented by the Englishman, Lieutenant Shrapnel.[1]

Similarly with hand firearms, the standard weapons were already well established when the general fighting began. Smoothbore flintlock muskets, firing heavy lead bullets from two-thirds to four-fifths of an inch in diameter, albeit with no claim to accuracy beyond a hundred-yard range, had been generally adopted by major armies early in the eighteenth century. Longer muskets with spiral grooves (rifling) in the barrel were by the mid-1700s already prized for their greater range and accuracy. Rifles were especially popular for hunting in the German and Scandinavian lands, and during the American Revolution the British had found them dangerous implements in the hands of snipers from the Ohio Valley and other parts of the colonies. At the same time, these hunting pieces were both fragile and unwieldy in bayonet encounters, while requiring more careful loading and priming than did service muskets. Not until 1800 did the British Army create a full brigade equipped with Baker rifles, and continental commanders were more cautious still. Official conservatism also greeted the Scotsman Forsyth's percussion charge, a small quantity of potassium chlorate, which replaced the flint-sparked ignition of the musket's powder.

[1] One new form of artillery, the explosive rockets developed by Colonel William Congreve in imitation of weapons used against British troops in India during the late eighteenth century, made its appearance in Europe during the Napoleonic period. Some 25,000 of these projectiles are supposed to have been fired upon Copenhagen during the British attack of 1807, and some use was made of them by the Allies at Leipzig in 1813. Napoleon had no interest in this development, however, and even his enemies seem to have made only sparing, occasional use of 'Congreve's rockets', best known to Americans through their national anthem.

Though the inventor produced a percussion lock in 1805, it was to be another ten years before a separate, self-contained percussion *cap* appeared.

Supporting Services

What would today be called 'service forces', responsible for military supplies, construction, medical care, communications and intelligence, were in Napoleon's time still at an early stage of development in relation to the combat arms. Quartermaster functions, for example, were in most armies relegated to the status of part-time duty for soldiers temporarily detailed to forage and to guard requisitioned supplies pending distribution. The French revolutionary armies, noted for their willingness to live off the country in which they were operating, had only contempt for the ponderous supply trains of the eighteenth century; and Napoleon himself, despite his alleged remark that an army travels on its stomach, paid little attention to organized services of supply. In relatively prosperous territory, such as northern Italy, the Rhineland or the Low Countries, military forces could indeed support themselves by foraging and were the more mobile for doing so. In the emperor's later campaigns, however, especially in the barren reaches of Spain and Russia, part of the French armies' difficulties stemmed from the exhaustion of local resources.

British military leadership, far more than that of any continental state, seemed intent on maintaining the operational freedom they associated with having necessary supplies roll with an army. In 1794 was established the corps of Royal Wagoners, resplendent in red jackets, yellow cuffs, blue breeches and leather caps. This body was reorganized in 1799 to form the famous Royal Wagon Train. Wellington, at once meticulous and conservative in this as in other regards, insisted that supply columns, equipped with light, high-wheeled carts, accompany his forces on their long marches through Spain. In the event, this form of mobility, less obvious but more secure than that of the rampaging French legions, helped to bring final victory in the Peninsular War.

With respect to military engineering, on the other hand, France under both the Republic and the Empire could justly claim to lead all Europe. The proud *Génie*, of course, had held a secure place in the French army under the monarchy as well. However, until the Revolution produced the Central School of Public Works (renamed in 1795 the *École Polytechnique*), no nation had ever accorded so high a priority to training in fortification, demolition, bridge construction and related skills. Only by learning from the enemy did Napoleon's adversaries bring their own engineering services up to the competing level they had attained by the Waterloo campaign.

Medical care for troops in action remained, in all armies, dependent on the good offices of the wounded's own comrades and the possible, though largely fortuitous presence of one of the pitifully scarce field surgeons. A major injury was almost certain to result in, at worst, death and, at best, amputation or some other crippling aftermath. Field hospitals were seldom more than sheds or cellars commandeered for this purpose. Despite rudimentary improvements in sanitation and control of epidemics, the loss of life caused by disease during the long Prussian retreat from Jena in 1806–7, for example, or Napoleon's Russian campaign in 1812 is terrible to contemplate. The filth, neglect and inefficiency reported by Florence Nightingale from the Crimea as late as the 1850s had been part of the standard picture of military life prior to that time.

In the related areas of communications and intelligence gathering, the revolutionary-Napoleonic period witnessed certain technical advances, but surprisingly few of major significance. The British system of naval flags denoting letters and numbers had been developing for some time, but it was both expanded and refined by Sir Home Popham in the 1790s. Armies and navies alike relied heavily on hand semaphore signals. However, French experiments with a mechanical semaphore telegraph—signal towers strung across the countryside from hilltop to hilltop—failed to produce any revolution in military communications. Napoleon, never a friend of technological innovation, apparently dismissed the system as expensive, cumbersome and subject to easy interception by hostile observers. The most important such chain actually proved to be one operated by his enemies, the British, between Portsmouth and the Admiralty in London.

It was doubtless this same distrust of gadgetry which led Napoleon to quash another experiment, namely, the use of ground-anchored balloons for purposes of reconnaissance. This had been begun with great excitement in 1794 but was abandoned by French forces after Bonaparte became first consul. The collection of intelligence remained thereafter, as it had been before, dependent upon countless spies, reconnoitring cavalry scouts, the interrogation of enemy prisoners and observation through the light, collapsible telescopes which would not be replaced by binocular field glasses until the mid-nineteenth century.

Tactics

As remarked in Chapter IV (*see above*, pp. 62–3), the eighteenth century's long debate over tactics—thin line versus solid phalanx, *ordre mince* versus *ordre profond*—was still in progress when war broke out in the 1790s. It was doubtless inevitable that the first military efforts of the new French Republic should be based on the violent, largely undisciplined onslaught of masses of men; for the armies of the Revolution were hastily recruited and had little time to develop either the precision of movement or the coolness in musketry required by the *ordre mince*. Their counterbalancing asset was the wild *élan*, the enthusiasm of troops who began by defending what was for them a holy cause and who came to believe, after battles like Jemappes and Fleurus, that no force on earth could withstand their bayonets.

In this collision between the armed hordes of French recruits and the well-drilled but generally unenthusiastic regiments of the Allies, both sides started by proclaiming the virtues of their respective tactics. Actually, however, each began almost at once to take steps which betrayed its recognition of the other's capabilities. Robespierre himself sponsored the shortlived School of Mars in 1794, hoping that young Jacobins could be taught sound principles in the proposed fifteen-week course without losing their zeal for the headlong attack. After Thermidor this particular experiment was dropped, but Carnot recognized too clearly the value of operational discipline not to insist on increasingly careful training of the Directory's armies. Conversely, by the end of the 1790s the enemies of France were translating their concern over the revolutionary style of assault into specific tactical adjustments. Unfortunately for the Allies, none among them developed a coherent new system of defence—still less of attack—until the roll of French victories had begun to appear endless.

In certain respects Napoleon's favoured tactics recalled the mixture of precision and temerity, of manoeuvre and impact, which had been Guibert's ideal before 1789. This, however, is only a part of the story. On the one hand, Bonaparte's reliance on swiftness of movement, his willingness to employ thin screens of infantry to conceal the disposition of his main forces, his use of cavalry probes and harassment by teams of snipers did mark him as an heir of the *Ancien Régime*. On the other hand, in his insistence on the crushing, decisive charge, on relentless pursuit and on wholesale carnage as an end in itself, he revealed his debt to the Revolution.

It is a fact worth noting that the armies which finally destroyed the French Empire owed their ultimate success to two sharply opposed principles of action. On the one hand, the Russians had relied heavily on the mass assault long before the French, and nothing about the latter's military record from 1792 onward inclined them to change. Similarly, Prussian military recovery after 1806 was to a considerable degree achieved by abandoning the precise movement of files in favour of a more dashing, if less disciplined 'onrush of patriots'. The battle of Leipzig in 1813 may be seen as the climax of this development; for in that four-day mêlée of savage bayonet charges and confused retreats, central and eastern European forces simply wore out Napoleon's army, finally beating it at its own game.

At the other extreme, the British had by this time transformed the eighteenth-century *ordre mince* into a set of tactics which succeeded in Spain and would soon share much of the credit at Waterloo. Wellington was not a blind traditionalist. He reduced the old three-rank formation to a more efficient double line for swift, alternating fire over a wide front. He employed skirmishers to punish advancing columns before the latter reached his infantry. Above all, he used terrain with a skill rivalling Napoleon's own, in order to shield that infantry until its fire power could have full effect. Basically, however, he remained wedded to the principle that an unshakeable line of well-trained men, often formed into a square, could withstand and eventually disperse the most furious charge. In part, this strategy was determined by the very nature of his forces, which had to make up in precision for what they lacked in sheer weight of numbers. The problems of overseas supply, combined with Parliament's refusal to impose conscription, set stringent limits on British military manpower available on the Continent—even at Waterloo, it amounted to only 25,000 to 30,000. At the same time it must be said that Wellington's system was also the product of his own cold, orderly mind and of his estimate of potential French weaknesses.

Given the scale and complexity of warfare during our period, important developments in command organization were doubtless inevitable. In 1793 Britain revived the office of commander-in-chief, a position which had been merged with the other functions of the king since the mid-eighteenth century but was now entrusted first to the aged Lord Amherst and then, in 1795, to Frederick, duke of York and Albany. Much criticism has been directed at this second son of George III and at his alleged inability to keep his mistress out of matters of army administration, at his unrealistic strategic views, at his personal vacillation in combat. More recent studies, however, have brought a distinct reaction in favour of the duke of York, crediting him with having laboured conscientiously to overhaul his country's military organization.

Under his aegis the adjutant-general's department was expanded, training regulations were modernized, financial accounting was improved, provisioning of troops was brought under more centralized control and the chain of command was somewhat better defined. Not that the diligent duke, from his office at the Horse Guards in London, succeeded in co-ordinating field operations to the liking of everyone. In 1808, for example, he left the gifted General Moore for several months in a subordinate position under the two senior nonentities technically commanding the British forces in Portugal. The increased paper work was galling to many officers including Wellington, who wrote from Spain in 1810 to the under-secretary of state for war: 'My Lord, if I attempted to answer the mass of futile correspondence that surrounds me, I should be debarred from all serious business of campaigning'.[1] Despite Wellington's angry contempt for 'the futile drivelling of mere quill-driving', however, he owed more than he would admit to the duke of York's efforts as commander-in-chief.

Napoleon, as France's chief of state and at the same time her supreme war lord, had distinct advantages in seeking to maintain centralized control over military planning and operations. Even he, of course, encountered periodic frustration because of poor intelligence, slow communications, the vanity of subordinate commanders or some unforeseen change of circumstances. Despite his subsequent complaints about slow or faulty obedience to his orders, however, Napoleon's strategic control in general set a new standard for European armies.

The emperor's continental opponents, be it said, were not strikingly successful in meeting that standard in his own time, despite widespread efforts to strengthen the machinery of command. Austria's best field general, Archduke Charles, was never quite sure what to expect from his brave but mercurial regiments. Tolstoy's brilliant caricature of Napoleon and Kutusov in *War and Peace*—the former convinced that he was directing a great army, the latter aware that he was merely being swept along by one—is misleading in that it underestimates Bonaparte's actual power, but it may well contain a valid comment on the Russians' own experience. In Prussia, though the army reformers unquestionably began to work great changes for the future through their expansion of

[1] E. J. Kingston-McCloughry, *The Direction of War* (London, 1955), p. 38.

the General Staff, Scharnhorst himself had to admit that once operations began, an old warhorse such as Blücher would go where his
experience and his hunches sent him.

Officers and Men

All armies were struggling to find the best strategic unit, large enough
by itself to offer decisive weight in specific engagements, compact
enough to react swiftly to changing threats and opportunities. By the
latter half of the nineteenth century there was to be widespread acceptance of just such a self-contained battle unit: the *division*, its three or
four infantry regiments accompanied by their own supply train, artillery, engineers, signal company, etc., its commanding general entrusted
with considerable discretion in the conduct of local operations. In the
period we are considering, however, variation and lingering confusion
were still the ruling characteristics. The division, to be sure, had been
tried as an experiment in the French army as early as the 1770s, and
Napoleon frequently used such units for specific tasks. The British
'Light Division', which won fame in the Peninsular War, was formed in
1803 out of three regiments superbly trained by Sir John Moore. Last
but not least, the Prussian leaders tried brifly, in 1813, to impose a
standardized divisional structure on their renascent army. Nevertheless the great wars ended with all armies still largely organized on the
basis of regiments, constantly regrouped into shifting patterns of
brigades and corps.

In such circumstances, a major burden inevitably fell on officers
of company and field, i.e. regimental, grade. Just who the colonels and
majors, captains, lieutenants and ensigns of the period were, where in
society they came from, how they were selected and how trained, are
questions which have never to my knowledge elicited broad, comparative inquiry. We do know that the French army suffered serious
decimation of these ranks in the early 1790s, through royalist emigration, that the promotion of noncommissioned officers from the old army
and of promising recruits subsequently built an able, new officers' corps
and that the latter's heavy casualties, especially in the Russian campaign, may have been the most damaging single blow suffered by
Napoleon's Empire.

In most other countries, some commissions were regularly granted
in the field, for valour in action, but many more were conferred upon
landed gentlemen (considered the natural leaders of peasant levies) or

were purchased by aspiring young men of wealth. The duke of York, though critical of Britain's system of venality and favour, never tried seriously to do more than mitigate its worst effects, noting as he did so that at least the old system permitted the rapid promotion of Wellington. In the Habsburg lands, the county rolls of landed titles determined, almost alone, what military rank a young man might initially receive—and in many an instance, how high he could rise. Needless to say, the Russian Empire looked to its nobility for officers.

Prussia's case is the most complex, for the Prussian army of the eighteenth century had been noted for the near monopoly enjoyed by its landed gentry, or *Junkers*, so far as access to commissioned ranks was concerned. After Jena, however, General von Scharnhorst and his colleagues in the Military Reorganization Commission quickly concluded that able young men of middle- or even lower-class origins must be permitted to rise in the service. Training schools for new ensigns were established in three cities; and in order to provide more advanced officers' training, the old Military Academy was revived and shortly renamed the War Academy. By the time it resumed hostilities in 1813 the Prussian army boasted an officers' corps which, for the time being at least, could rival the French in its openness to talent.

Before leaving the subject of land warfare we should ask how the common soldier saw this long period of struggle. A great deal, of course, depended on the army to which he belonged. As for the troops of Napoleon, despite terrible casualties (indeed, perhaps in part because of the rapid promotion which they necessitated), fighting spirit seems to have remained extremely high to the very end. Even the screams and curses of dying men along the emperor's road back from Moscow did not echo so loudly as to drown out the cheers which greeted his return from Elba in 1815 or the defiant shouts of French regiments at Waterloo. Napoleon offered glory, loot, advancement and those ringing exhortations which marked him as one of history's true masters of the technique known in modern jargon as 'opinion control'.

Here again, the Prussian reformers after 1806, bent as they were on mobilizing the patriotic devotion of citizen soldiers, were frankly imitative of the French model. In place of brutal floggings, they insisted that troops be accorded decent treatment under fair discipline. The abolition of corporal punishment for minor offences was in fact one of the handful of unqualified victories scored by Scharnhorst, Gneisenau and their associates against the enemies of change. When Napoleon himself said of the Prussians at Waterloo, 'these animals have learned something', he failed to recognize that they were no longer the 'animals' of Jena nine years before.

Elsewhere, cruelty and contempt on the part of officers with regard to enlisted men remained a depressingly common pattern. Russian soldiers were serfs of the state and were treated accordingly, a rough paternalism being the best they could hope for. Austrian, Italian and Spanish practice was little better; and a Saxon colonel in 1812, even while serving as an ally of the French, regularly spoke of his regiment with ambiguous possessiveness as 'my swine'. British commanders, having no conscripts in their charge and necessarily cognizant of the 'scarcity value' of English and Scottish soldiers, seldom permitted themselves the excesses of brutality displayed by many of their continental opposites. Corporal punishment was still meted out freely in His Majesty's forces, however; and numberless dispatches, notably including those of Wellington, breathe aristocratic scorn for the lowborn rabble in the ranks. It is necessary to call to mind an enlightened trainer of men like General Moore or visualize the genial militia colonel, riding a 'low pony' and hence dubbed 'Punch on a pig' by Private Wheeler and his comrades,[1] in order to understand how the latter could retain as much affection for the service as they apparently did.

Naval Forces

The men who fought at sea tended to be very different, in personal background, in training, even in appearance, from the soldiers on land. The modern enlisted seaman's uniform—short jacket or middy, bell-bottomed trousers, neckerchief and round, flat cap—was popular among the British well before the end of the Napoleonic Wars and was beginning to be copied by most other navies, though the older broad-brimmed hat was still much worn. Naval officers of all nations tended to cling more tenaciously than did their army colleagues to costumes of a traditional, eighteenth-century style, including silk knee breeches, white stockings and cocked hats.

That this formal, conservative look should have been especially characteristic of Britain's Royal Navy was in one sense paradoxical. For to an infinitely greater degree than her army, the island kingdom's navy offered advancement to able men of humble, or at most quite modest, origins. This same contrast held true as between the British

[1] *Letters of Private Wheeler*, pp. 14–16 (*see* Bibliography, p. 226).

and other European navies. Even the French, after a period of decimation of officers during the Terror, quickly fell back on former noblemen, trained under the Old Régime—Villeneuve, for example, Magon de Clos-Doré, and Count de Ganteaume—for many of their highest commands at sea. As for the Spanish and the Russians, their admirals and senior captains were virtually without exception high aristocrats.

All the more striking, therefore, is the roster of British commanders who served under Nelson, himself one of eleven children of a Norfolk country clergyman. Though some of these men were of the gentry—and one of them at Trafalgar was a Scottish lord, the earl of Northesk—many more sprang from families of traders, seamen, farmers or parsons. All, however, had shared a rigorous training, often beginning as midshipmen when only twelve or thirteen years old, and had worked their way up. It may be that the formal attire of these officers and their punctilious etiquette served an important purpose in ironing out differences of social rank, while creating the *esprit de corps* needed for the success of a ship or a flotilla. In any event, the Royal Navy seemed to build its own aristocracy.

Crews were still put together by a combination of enlistment and impressment, the latter amounting to kidnapping potential sailors ashore, having them turned over by civilian jail officials or even taking them from merchant ships at sea. The work of the press gangs went on continuously, in France no less than elsewhere, for the patriotic zeal that filled land regiments seems not to have extended to ships. Once a naval vessel sailed, with a crew at least half of whose members were likely to have been impressed, it might remain at sea for several years, bringing supplies aboard by boat. When it finally docked, there were sure to be desertions, in spite of the dangers facing penniless seamen in a strange port. Discipline was brutal under the lash and the cat-o'-nine-tails, a wicked little many-stranded whip; quarters were cramped; the work was hard and dangerous; medical care was primitive; the food comprised a mixture of weevil-infested biscuits, maggoty gruel and dried meat of almost rocklike consistency.

A modern observer is inevitably puzzled to find that common seamen thus recruited, living under such conditions and led by haughty, sometimes tyrannical officers, could bring themselves to fight as bravely as most did in countless engagements of the period. Why, one is tempted to ask, were the British naval mutinies at Spithead and the Nore in 1797 not frequently repeated instead of remaining, as was in fact the case, quite isolated events? In seeking an answer, we should recall that for many of these men—unskilled labourers, vagrants, jailbirds—life on land had been even harder than life at sea. If the meals aboard ship were bad, they were at least regular. Naval justice was ordinarily no more savage and was generally less capricious than that of criminal courts ashore. Existence among the crowded hammocks below decks was preferable to shivering in city hovels or prison cells; there might be material windfalls in the form of prize money, and the crews themselves often developed a rough camaraderie of danger, a share in the pride which the sea has always imparted to its own.

One more category of naval manpower should be identified: the marine infantry or 'marines'. Most eighteenth-century navies had assigned units of soldiers to duty aboard warships, the British and Dutch having actually begun to do so as early as the 1660s. The period which concerns us, however, witnessed some expansion and still more regularization of this practice. By the end of the long struggle, all naval powers had companies of marines, attired in distinctive uniforms of army cut and attached for long terms to specific vessels. After 1802 Britain alone had some sixty companies, operating out of four major ports. Marines were used to pour musket fire on enemy ships from decks and rigging, to carry out occasional landings (usually small ones) and, significantly, to enforce discipline upon their own ships' crewmen.

The sailing vessels which fought the battles of this tumultuous age were essentially those of the eighteenth century: sailing ships of the line, plus the smaller, faster frigates and gun sloops. These fleet units did not change significantly in size or fire power between 1792 and 1815. Nelson's flagship, H.M.S. *Victory*, for example, with its displacement of 3,500 tons, an overall length of 186 feet and a crew of 660, was considered a powerful instrument of war. Possessed of 102 cannon capable of firing 12-, 24- and 32-pound balls with reasonable accuracy up to one mile, plus a pair of the deadly short-barrelled carronades for sweeping enemy decks at close range with 68 pounds of grape shot apiece, a powerful instrument it certainly was. At Trafalgar only two of the other twenty-six British ships involved were its equals in armament or manpower. Most of the remainder carried seventy to eighty-four guns. Even Spain's huge *Santissima Trinidad*, with its 130 guns and its crew of over 1,000, and the Russians' ponderous 110-gun *Rostislav*, left over from Catherine the Great's formidable navy, could not have been considered better than even matches for the *Victory*. Yet the latter had been launched in 1765.

There were, to be sure, certain novel projects advanced during the long wars. Napoleon's army of England, poised on the channel coast from 1803 to 1805, was supposedly to be equipped with hundreds of long, flat galleys, in which the French invasion troops would row themselves across to Kent and Sussex during a calm when the Royal Navy lay helpless under empty sails. A few such galleys were actually built, but only a few—the emperor had too much else on his mind.

Far more dramatic, as well as more prophetic, were the American Robert Fulton's offers, first to the Directory and then to Napoleon, of both steam-propelled barges and underwater warships. In July 1800 Fulton's submarine, the *Nautilus*, was launched at Rouen; and the next year it successfully exploded an underwater mine which it had affixed to an abandoned hulk in the port of Brest, both impressing and horrifying the French officers for whom the demonstration was staged. Napoleon having remained, as usual, unconvinced by mechanical ingenuity, the impartial inventor set off for Britain with his plans in 1805. The Admiralty apparently recognized the danger to conventional vessels which submarine attack might constitute; but it saw no reason whatever why a navy with the world's greatest surface force should help to develop this form of warfare. So Fulton went home to more peaceful achievements on the Hudson River, while in Europe the great, square-rigged ships of the line sailed on unchallenged—for the time being.

Tactics at Sea

As with the units employed, so with strategy and tactics, the naval wars of the revolutionary-Napoleonic age witnessed little outward change. Those powers which had overseas colonies continued to detach warships from home squadrons in order to accompany or (depending on its nationality) to seize shipping en route, to protect distant outposts and to attack enemy settlements, as the British did in 1802 when they wrested Capetown from Napoleon's Dutch Allies.

The distances covered by some of these forays were prodigious in view of the technical problems involved, not least the weeks of waiting for each set of orders or intelligence reports carried by a messenger sloop. In 1805, for example, Lord Nelson took the British Mediterranean fleet from near Toulon, France, to Egypt (February), thence to Malta and back to the waters off Toulon (March), to Sicily (April) and then Gibraltar, across the Atlantic to the West Indies (11 May to 4 June), back to Gibraltar (July) and finally to England, arriving in mid-August for what turned out to be less than a month of home leave.

During all that time, while the Admiralty in London waited anxiously for news, Nelson never sighted the French-Spanish squadrons he was pursuing. Only in October, after those squadrons had assembled at Cadiz and sailed forth as the Combined Fleets in a dash for Gibraltar, was he to get his 'pell-mell battle' at Trafalgar.

Such a battle, once joined, might begin as a duel of lines, with each admiral able to exercise some tactical control through the use of signal flags. Inevitably, however, the developing action became a mélée of individual ships, each seeking to deliver its broadsides to best advantage. The effect of such fire could be ghastly, for the broadside might be released only a few yards away from the undefended stern of an enemy vessel, sending a hail of cannon balls, grape shot and deadly flying splinters the length of the hull below decks.

Trafalgar, history's last major battle between fleets under sail, deserves a moment's special attention. For, as several commentators have pointed out, it was a puzzling victory. The Combined Fleets of France and Spain lost twenty-three of their thirty-three ships, sunk or captured, with casualties amounting to some 4,400 dead and 2,500 wounded. The British lost their great admiral, 448 others dead and 1,214 wounded—but not one of their twenty-seven vessels. What Nelson had done was to sail into the strung-out enemy line with two parallel columns of ships, his own division and Admiral Collingwood's, breaking the line at two points as planned. Until those penetrations were achieved, however, the oncoming British, gliding forward slowly before a light wind, had to take head-on a long series of French and Spanish broadsides directed at their own bows. Even with all three lines scattered after contact, with individual ships trading broadsides and boarding attempts, it is not immediately clear why the toll should have been so one-sided. The Combined Fleets had some of the world's best-designed ships, handled by crews which fought stubbornly under a number of brave and able officers.

It seems likely that at Trafalgar, as in numerous other engagements of the period, the British advantage lay partly in superior equipment, especially cannon, but still more in experience. While their enemies spent months at a time penned up in various ports, ships of the Royal Navy were constantly at sea in large numbers. Hence, at Trafalgar and elsewhere, they were better handled in the scramble for position, their rate of fire was higher, and their gunnery was more accurate. What Nelson brought to naval warfare—at Cape St Vincent, the Nile, Copenhagen, Trafalgar—was not an elaborate set of new theories, but rather a clear awareness of British assets and a personal ferocity, an almost frantic eagerness to get at and to smash the enemy. He conceived every battle as one of annihilation. In his demonic intensity, supported by the experienced skill of his forces, he was to the war at sea what Napoleon was to the war on land. Together, these two commanders embodied the real changes in warfare, beneath the surface of apparent continuity in weapons and tactics.

Amphibious Warfare

Setting aside for the moment the matter of blockades, we have still to consider one more topic here: amphibious operations. The transporting, debarking and, where necessary, re-embarking of bodies of troops can have crucial strategic importance, as the Second World War emphatically revealed. They are actions, however, which need especially elaborate preparation, the most carefully timed execution and adequate provision for a subsequent flow of supplies to the forces on shore. Judged by such requirements, the landing attempts of the revolutionary-Napoleonic wars were generally speaking unimpressive enterprises.

For one thing, marines were not yet conceived of as a service specially trained and equipped for sustained sea-to-land action. As we have already observed, marine companies were parcelled out to individual ships of the line, primarily to perform shipboard duties. Hence, the amphibious forces, such as they were, tended to be unprepared and often recalcitrant infantry regiments, marched aboard crowded transports for movement to some ill-prepared assault. That picture holds true for British landings on the French west coast in 1795, to support the Chouan rebels; at Ostend in 1798; with the Russians against Holland in 1799; against Cadiz in 1800; on Walcheren Island in 1809; and for countless less significant actions. It holds equally true for French efforts to launch effective operations in Ireland and in Wales during the 1790s. Napoleon's initially successful invasion of Egypt in 1798 can fairly be called a triumph of impudence and luck over existing conditions— and the luck ran out very quickly. As for the joint Russian-Turkish conquest of the Ionian Islands in 1798-9, the virtual absence of resistance by the small French land forces made the campaign militarily insignificant.

Apart from the Peninsular War, a vast land campaign partially supported from the sea, there were only two actions during the entire period which to modern eyes appear genuine amphibious victories.

One was the disembarkation of some 5,500 British troops under Abercrombie and Moore at Aboukir Bay, near Alexandria, in March 1801. Here, the generals had made reasonably careful plans, covering among other things the initial post-landing movements of the troops once ashore. Their reward was a victory, over sharp opposition, and the first step towards the eventual defeat of Napoleon's abandoned army in Egypt. The other successful landing was the hit-and-run British assault on Copenhagen in 1807. In general, however, interservice rivalry in the field—stiff-necked navy officers' prejudices in the British case, matched by the contempt of army men for admirals in the French, Spanish and Russian—completed the work of lethargy and inexperience at home.

The era's greatest amphibious operation, of course, was never attempted. From 1803 through the summer of 1805, Napoleon's first Grand Army crouched along the channel coast, with its chief concentration at Boulogne. Intricate plans for the invasion of England were prepared, revised, discarded, replaced by others. French cities and army regiments gave funds for men-o'-war and landing barges to be named in their honour. The emperor repeatedly ordered ships of the battle line to assemble off Brest and to wrench control of the channel away from the British long enough for his legions to 'jump the ditch'. At other times he seemed to be counting on oared galleys. In England, alarm beacons were prepared, militia were drilled, small forts of heavy brickwork (martello towers) were constructed along the south-east coast, and the Admiralty watched nervously for any threat of a French or French-Spanish naval concentration.

But no invasion came. Weeks before Trafalgar ended the danger that Britain might lose, if only briefly, her naval supremacy, the Grand Army had left Boulogne, marching towards the Danube to smash the continental partners in the Third Coalition. It may never be known whether or not Napoleon was serious about his invasion plans. He insisted that he was; but he also framed the requirements for a successful landing in England in such a way that he could easily avoid the showdown, yet place the blame on his admirals' incompetence or timidity, or both. Perhaps, as some have argued, he merely used the camp of Boulogne to train a huge army for operations elsewhere, welding it into a force wholly committed to himself in his new guise as emperor. However that may be, the French 'army of England' never set sail. Instead, it marched out of the naval sphere altogether, to become the army of Austerlitz and Jena.

Economic Warfare

Far from being a separate aspect of the revolutionary-Napoleonic wars, the economic struggle, in which belligerents sought to cripple their enemies' trade, financial strength and supply of life's necessities, was closely bound up with the course of military events in general. No sooner had war broken out in 1792–3 than the money power of Great Britain in particular emerged as an important weapon. Promises of financial subsidies from London bought allies against the Revolution and sometimes kept them in action even after punishing setbacks.

It cannot be maintained that such allies offered much hope of completely defeating France—that had to await the later outbursts of popular patriotism in Spain, Russia and central Europe. Nevertheless, financial grants kept the fight going year after year, without Britain's having to raise and maintain large permanent forces of its own. If it is true that British subsidies between 1793 and 1815 amounted to approximately £52 million, expenditures under this heading amounted to less than 6·5 per cent of the kingdom's total war disbursements—some £830 million.[1] Not the least remarkable feature of the long series of wars is the fact that when they finally ended, Great Britain's public debt was almost twelve times that of France—the latter having been helped by repeated confiscations and indemnities from conquered lands. Yet King George III's credit, as even French bankers had to admit, was infinitely stronger than the Emperor Napoleon's. The answer lay in trade.

The commercial warfare of the 1790s saw hundreds of British ships taken as prizes by French privateers. Nevertheless, the average loss to Britain's merchant marine, including the big East Indiamen plodding home from the orient, remained quite steady at around 2·5 per cent per year from 1793 to 1800, certainly no crushing toll. Contrast this result with the systematic sweeping away of French ocean commerce. By 1799, the Directory admitted officially that 'not a single merchant ship is on the sea carrying the French flag'.[2] Small French coastal vessels naturally continued to slip from port to port, but for exports from overseas the Republic had come to rely on American and other neutral ships.

A good indication of the part commercial warfare played in Europe's general conflict is the dramatic increase in its importance during and

[1] Vagts, *Militarism*, pp. 144–5 (*see* Bibliography, p. 49).
[2] Mahan, *Influence of Sea Power upon the French Revolution*, vol. II, pp. 223–4 and 219 (*see* Bibliography, p. 226).

after the crucial years 1805-7. For it was those years which saw Trafalgar clinch Britain's naval supremacy, but which also witnessed Napoleon's defeat of the Third Coalition and his diplomatic triumph in the Tilsit settlement. Now, as Admiral Mahan was later to explain, the struggle entered a new phase:

> The battle between the sea and the land was to be fought out on Commerce. England had no army wherewith to meet Napoleon; Napoleon had no navy to cope with that of his enemy. As in the case of an impregnable fortress, the only alternative for either of these contestants was to reduce the other by starvation. On the common frontier, the coast line, they met in a deadly strife in which no weapon was drawn. The imperial soldiers were turned into coastguardsmen to shut out Great Britain from her markets; the British ships became revenue cutters to prohibit the trade of France. The neutral carrier, pocketing his pride, offered his services to either for pay, and the other then regarded him as taking part in hostilities.[1]

It is all too easy, when studying Napoleon's Berlin and Milan Decrees of 1806-7, on the one hand, and Britain's Orders in Council of 1807-9, on the other, to develop a misleadingly neat picture of the struggle thus joined. *On paper*, the emperor's Continental System closed every European port controlled by France or one of its allies to all British ships and all other ships which had touched the British Isles. Furthermore, such ships were defined as outlaws, fair prizes for any French privateer. The aim was theoretically unlimited—to starve England into surrender—though few French officials seem to have considered that a real possibility, preferring to rely instead on general economic depression to exhaust their enemy's will to fight.

As for retaliation from London, beginning with the famous Order in Council of 11 November 1807, it amounted to a formal blockade of all continental ports not open to British ships. Neutral vessels might still visit French-controlled ports in Europe, providing they stopped in England both going and returning, to submit to inspection, reload and pay the prescribed duties. Otherwise, they were subject to confiscation as blockade runners. All this represented a particularly heavy blow to the American carrying trade, and was so intended. For while American shipments to Europe from the West Indies and elsewhere had been a supplementary resource for England, they had been far more valuable to France.

[1] *Ibid.*, II, p. 289.

What of the realities behind this haughty exchange of threats and prohibitions? First, note that both sides had declared blockades so vast as to be unenforceable (and hence, under recurrent interpretations of international law, not legal at all). Every month innumerable ships defied the prohibitions of the emperor and His Britannic Majesty alike. American and other blockade runners were almost always to be found at anchor in Brest, Nantes and Amsterdam. At the same time, Napoleon's régime proved incapable of preventing the British themselves from smuggling goods into Europe on a massive scale. The islands of Malta in the Mediterranean and Heligoland in the North Sea became bustling depots for this contraband trade. Anxious to maintain the supply of precious timber from Sweden and Russia, the Royal Navy for several years offered a regular convoy service of warships in the Baltic, to escort 'neutral' merchantmen (often British vessels carrying false registration papers) past the hostile Danish coast en route to ports in England.

A bizarre aspect of the trade war was the major adversaries' purposeful circumvention of their own regulations. Great Britain often permitted neutral cargoes to evade its 'stop and reload' requirements— for a price or for political advantage in Holland, Russia or other nations. Napoleon, on his side, was prepared to relieve temporary surpluses at home and to accumulate gold by permitting specially licensed exports to England. Following the harvest of 1809, which was plentiful on the Continent but disastrous in England, the imperial government licensed the shipment across the channel of over 1,300,000 quarters of wheat, almost exactly five-sixths of Great Britain's total wheat imports for 1810.[1] In certain other years, notably 1808, 1811 and 1813, to be sure, the emperor applied his restrictions rigorously, hoarding foodstuffs for his armies. But the picture is scarcely one of a sustained, coherent effort to starve a foe.

Is the proper conclusion, then, that the economic war was a farce, winked at in all knowledgeable circles? Most certainly not. Most of the concessions and exceptions were made not out of indifference to advantages they might bring the enemy, but out of the recognition that the home economy, be it French or British, sometimes urgently required the stimulation or relief which only a partial easing of restrictions could provide. Blockades and embargoes, after all, are notorious for cutting both ways. The basic determination to break the other side remained until the end as constant as it was savage.

[1] Galpin, p. 196 (see Bibliography, p. 227).

It must also be kept in mind that certain very real effects did flow from the economic struggle. In Britain's case, if the threat of starvation was never deadly, given the increase in home production and the guaranteed volume of imports, the temporary fear which followed a crop failure such as that of 1809 was a serious political factor. Still more significant was the financial strain of the seemingly endless war, a strain which literally wore out many men responsible for public credit and tax income during financial crises such as those of 1808 and 1810–1811. As for British exports, Napoleon's tightening of the Continental System dropped them from a high of £66 million in 1809 to £44 million in 1812, despite the ingenuity of London's businessmen in finding new markets, especially in Latin America.[1] It is worth adding that the costly distraction of the war with the United States in 1812–14 was a direct outgrowth of the European commercial struggle as a whole. In many respects, that struggle ended none too soon for England.

In the French Empire, the danger of starvation was even more remote than in Britain; for Europe is a productive continent and the supply of staple foods remained quite secure. The officially sponsored exploitation of the sugar beet (the properties of which had been known since the mid-eighteenth century) was a good example of an intelligent, but not essential, response to the reduction of imports from overseas, in this case West Indian cane sugar. The issue was quite literally one of frosting for the Frenchman's cake.

Several other results of the economic conflict were particularly serious for the Republic and the Empire. That conflict began as early as 1793, and never ceased, to undercut the fiscal credit of a system denied the recuperative promise which goes with large-scale foreign trade. It brought depression to industrial centres such as Lyon and to great seaports from Genoa and Marseille to Hamburg and Amsterdam. As for political complications, those which it imposed upon Britain, in America and elsewhere, paled by comparison with the troubles it stirred up for Napoleon. In order to maintain his Continental System he outraged wealthy groups in France itself, in the Germanies, in Switzerland, in Italy. To plug serious leaks in the System, he deposed his own brother, the defiant King Louis of Holland, then annexed the Dutch and north German coastal strip, stretching his Empire all the way to the Baltic. Whether or not the tsar's refusal to bar British-sponsored neutral shipping from Russian ports was a principal cause or only a pretext for the invasion of 1812, it was unquestionably the issue which signalled

[1] Crouzet, *passim* (*see* Bibliography, p. 227).

the final rupture between the erstwhile allies. One may argue that Napoleon could have treated all these problems differently, but there is no denying that they were both real and perplexing.

Perhaps the best balance is struck by saying that commercial and fiscal warfare was basically Britain's rather than France's game. Napoleon could at least partially deny his island enemy the European market, but he could not deny such a sea power the markets of the wider world. And since one inevitable result of blockades and embargoes was a reduction in neutral shipping, the chief loser was sure to be the party more dependent for commercial stimulation and foreign markets on the carrying services of neutrals. That party was France and its landbound Empire.

Patriotic Propaganda

As was to be expected in the midst of fierce collisions both between rival political systems and among competing patriotisms, the revolutionary-Napoleonic era gave birth to propaganda in abundance. Books, leaflets, cartoons, broadsides, orders of the day, speeches, poems, songs all were employed to whip up the enthusiasm of contending masses, while attempting to undermine the confidence of enemies. Unfortunately, we have no way of gauging the independent effects, whether positive or negative, of such propaganda; but certain characteristics of the warfare of ideas nevertheless merit at least passing reference.

It should come as no surprise to any student of this epoch that the appeals of the 1790s were more general, more systematic, more broadly ideological than were those of the Napoleonic years, when loyalty to this or that national state seemed the dominant public emotion. In this respect, clearly, there was an important shift in the arguments used to justify or to motivate group action. The anti-revolutionary powers of 1792 and 1793 regularly announced that 'the crowned heads of Europe', supported by 'all humanity', had no choice but to condemn and to punish the men responsible for the 'horrors unfolding in France'. The 'good, old law' was invoked against these men, who in turn claimed to represent the rights and interests of mankind against 'reactionary tyrants'. In contrast, by 1805 Nelson's signal flags at Trafalgar read: '*England* (not God or Humanity or Great Britain or even the king) expects every man will do his duty'. The next year, seeking to rally the Prussian forces and to continue resistance after the disaster of Jena,

Gneisenau insisted that 'our country deserves no less than sacrificial loyalty'.

Despite changing values, a number of propagandistic techniques showed a high degree of consistency throughout the period. Indeed, allowance made for the evolution of media, certain devices have been characteristic of struggles going back at least to the religious wars of early modern times, and in some cases to medieval conflicts. The often shrill insistence, for example, that God was with one's own legions and against the enemy's rang from British pulpits throughout the tense years of waiting for a French invasion, just as it was heard in the Protestant, Catholic and Orthodox churches of Prussia, Austria and Russia when the War of Liberation began. It was no less prominent in Napoleon's Imperial Catechism of 1806 (*see above*, p. 178).

On a more distinctly human plane, each contending party tried to make sure that its enemies received all the discouraging news which could be reported or, if necessary, fabricated. A colourful English cartoon of the winter following Trafalgar and Austerlitz shows a rotund John Bull on the Dover Cliffs, facing a particularly disreputable looking Corsican on the heights above Boulogne. Through the air across the channel are seen flying two streams of bulletins, those from England carrying announcements of naval victories (and conveniently labelled 'Truth'), those from the Continent (just as succinctly tagged 'Falsehoods') listing Allied defeats in central Europe. In this case both sets of claims happened to be true, but exaggeration and distortion mark countless news sheets and leaflets which survive in various collections.

Along with motives of patriotic pride and hatred for the national foe, appeals to fear played an important part in domestic and foreign propaganda alike. Napoleon believed as firmly as had the Jacobins in terror's paralyzing effect on an enemy. He made not the slightest effort, for example, to suppress reports of the mass executions carried out by his troops in Madrid after the 1808 uprising. At the same time, French propaganda at home spared no detail in portraying either the starvation which awaited Europe unless England were defeated or the orgy of murder and rape which presumably would accompany an invasion of *la patrie* by any of her continental enemies. Similarly explicit were British cartoons showing what life in London would be like under a French occupation.

One significant form of propagandistic appeal, by no means novel but advanced to an especially high level of vehemence in this period, was addressed to actually or potentially disaffected groups under enemy rule. The British fed a steady stream of verbal encouragement, sporadically accompanied by physical aid, first to the Chouans and other French rebel elements, then later to dissident Dutchmen, Germans, Swiss, Italians and Spaniards. The French in turn welcomed visits from leaders of Irish, Polish and other insurgent movements, sending back with them effusive words of sympathy. Napoleon's own proclamation to the Hungarian gentry, dated May 1809 and published in Magyar, German and French, failed to win them to his service, but it was a masterful attempt to capitalize on old resentments against the Habsburgs.

In all these respects, the era we are considering represented merely a segment, albeit an important one, of the long development of psychological warfare. In one other regard, however, it appears in retrospect to have been unique.

The great conflicts of history have characteristically seen emotional antagonism, receptivity to crude propaganda, the willingness to view all enemies as essentially inhuman, increase steadily for as long as the fighting continued. To that general pattern the revolutionary-Napoleonic wars offer an exception. It seems clear that, terrible though the battles from the turn of the century to Waterloo unquestionably were, they were fought by men for whom the enemy seemed *less* a creature of another species than he had in the 1790s. The great collision of ideologies, of systems, of quasi-religious zealots was over by the time Napoleon became first consul. Thereafter, contending nations 'smote and shuddered and smote again'; but their armies (Spain's after 1808 offering the principal exception) tended to look, to act and even, leaving aside specific allegiances, to think more alike than had those in action at Valmy or Jemappes. In this, the soldiers presumably reflected attitudes widely shared by civilian populations. For the propagandist, it was almost certainly more difficult in 1810 or 1814 than it had been in 1793 or 1794 to convince most Europeans that the Devil really *was* on the other side, whichever side that might be. The carnage continued. Indeed it mounted. But it was no longer supported by any emotion grander than national egoism and the determination to dictate the eventual terms of peace.

It is well to acknowledge certain limitations which have been intentionally imposed upon this excursion into the conditions and techniques of war in a warlike era. That countless qualifications and interesting details have had to be omitted from so compressed an essay need scarcely be pointed out. More general questions of range and emphasis, however, have necessarily been dealt with according to the author's best judgment.

Nothing has been said of the development of general military *theory*, despite the important intellectual efforts of such commentators as the Prussian, Clausewitz, and the Swiss, Jomini. This omission might be explained by limitation upon space, but the real justification lies in the fact that these theoretical reflections were not so much a part of the age itself as a part of its legacy to subsequent generations. Napoleon certainly applied calculation of a high order to his operational plans, organizational arrangements and decisions in the field. So did Carnot, Scharnhorst, Wellington and, if I read the record correctly, Suvorov. There is a great difference, however, between the hard, experienced pragmatism of such men and the elaborate intellectual structures created by even the most brilliant observers. For the years we have been examining only the former had reality and meaning.

There has also, throughout most of this chapter, been a deliberate concentration on the principal contenders. This has not sprung from any indifference to the armies of Turkey or Spain or Bavaria, the Danish or the Portuguese navy, the place of Holland or Sweden in the mercantile struggle. It is essential, nevertheless, to recognize the *progressive concentration of power in certain major states* as one of the period's most significant characteristics. In the cold-blooded reckoning of force, the only armies which ultimately made much difference were the French, the Russian, the Prussian, the Austrian and, for reasons unrelated to numerical size, the British. Similarly, naval interest must be focused primarily on England and France, secondarily on Spain and, to a still lesser degree, on Russia. Economic warfare, in turn, involved all of Europe, but at the centre of the struggle were France, Great Britain and, increasingly in the later years, Russia. If those three powers are the only ones demanding attention under all these headings, that is no illusory result. For they were the giants whose struggles finally did most to determine the outcome of the broader drama.

One last question of emphasis concerns the placing of the period 1792–1815 in Europe's long chronicle of warfare, an issue raised at the outset of this chapter. It has been argued here that the amount of specific, technical innovation was distinctly limited, remarkably so given the duration and the intensity of conflict. A long series of novelties were advocated by individuals or small factions; but either, as was true of steamships, submarines and military balloons, they were not adopted at all, or they received only the grudging, partial reception accorded rockets and the semaphore telegraph. As for battle tactics, it should be observed that the two climactic battles, Trafalgar at sea and Waterloo on land, were old-style victories, won by eighteenth-century methods.

Yet there is something more to be acknowledged, something which transcends tactical and material innovation, or its absence, and makes the epoch one of towering significance to anyone pondering war and human history. It involves the central, brutal aspects of mass and intensity. As noted earlier, the wars here considered brought into conflict hundreds of thousands instead of tens of thousands; and these hosts were armed with the products of existing technology, developed in the eighteenth century but never before produced and put to work on such a scale. Whole peoples went forth to kill and be killed, under commanders whose conception of victory or annihilation outsoared the bounds of earlier imagination.

XI

The European State System after Napoleon

Earlier, in Chapter IV, we surveyed the political map of pre-revolutionary Europe and identified its most important features. Having since observed the international drama of the ensuing quarter-century, especially the shocks administered to the old state system by the French Republic and Empire, we should now consider what followed upon the latter's collapse. In doing so, we must distinguish between those characteristics of the period 1815–30 which had survived from the eighteenth-century pattern (or were restored) and those which were undeniably novel.

A certain mixture of old and new is at once encountered in the very conditions influencing the conduct of diplomacy. As in the eighteenth century so in the nineteenth, Europe's diplomats were an aristocratic

BIBLIOGRAPHY. In addition to numerous national histories already mentioned, or to be noted in later connections, there are several works dealing with international affairs during the post-Napoleonic period which deserve mention here. The best short study of its subject remains H. Nicolson, *The Congress of Vienna* (London, 1946), while readers in search of entertaining, if gossipy, detail, may refer to A. de La Garde-Chambonas, *Anecdotal Recollections of the Congress of Vienna* (London, 1902), anonymously translated from the French. During the past half-century, four scholars have directed close attention to major diplomats of the 'congress era', each author devoting himself to a statesman of his own nationality: H. von Srbik, *Metternich: Der Staatsmann und der Mensch*, 2 vols. (Munich, 1925); G. Lacour-Gayet, *Talleyrand* (Paris, 1928–34), especially vol. II; C. J. Bartlett, *Castlereagh* (London, 1966); H. Temperley, *The Foreign Policy of Canning, 1822–1827* (London, 1925). Srbik also deals at length with the German complexities in his *Deutsche Einheit*, vol. I (Munich, 1935). On Alexander I, see especially W. Naef's excellent monograph, *Zur Geschichte der Heiligen Allianz* (Bern, 1928). Among recent books of a more essayistic nature are H. G. Schenk, *The Aftermath of the Napoleonic Wars* (London, 1947); L. C. B. Seaman, *From Vienna to Versailles* (London, 1955); and H. A. Kissinger, *A World Restored: Metternich, Castlereagh and the problems of peace, 1812–22* (Boston, 1957). Finally, the best general treatment of the crucial events in Greece is C. M. Woodhouse, *The Greek War of Independence: its historical setting* (London, 1952).

corps of urbane practitioners, accustomed to conversing (usually in French) over dynastic interests, boundary changes offset by 'compensations' and a long list of equally familiar issues. Even during the prolonged turmoil, save for a brief period in the 1790s, and then only in France, neither the personnel nor the procedures of diplomacy had really been revolutionized. Napoleon's own *methods* had been far more traditional than his increasingly ambitious *aims*. With his defeat, old assumptions and old techniques appeared certain to dominate the work of re-establishing the disrupted network of relations among an array of independent states.

Actuality, however, differed from appearance. The polite language of negotiation might still refer to kings and princes, but it would never again be possible to avoid speaking of peoples as well. Diplomacy remained hidden, in its detailed manoeuvres; but in most countries its results had now to be explained to many more citizens than would have felt either competent or interested before the Revolution. Europe was still generations away from sustained, widespread debates over foreign policy; but the mobilization of whole nations, first France and then her enemies, had by 1814–15 produced, so to speak, a larger and more critical audience—parliamentary deputies, journalists, businessmen, students—whom the cool professionals of diplomacy could ill afford to ignore.

Prolonged warfare had wrought another significant change: a hardening of awareness that certain states disposed of preponderant force, and with it the rights and responsibilities of great powers. The latter phrase, be it noted, first came into general use during the conferences at the close of the Napoleonic era. We have seen that, even before 1789, England, France, Prussia, Austria and Russia had in fact constituted such a group of powers. Nevertheless, the etiquette and the formal language of the Old Régime had taken for granted the sovereign equality of countless lesser polities. Nothing destroys polite fictions so effectively as does the test of head-on conflict, and in the gigantic struggle extending all the way from 1792 to 1815 precisely this kind of destruction occurred. However ingratiating might be the tone adopted by the great powers towards weaker states, men would not thereafter confuse protocol with the realities of unequal might.

The Two Treaties of Paris

The necessary precondition for a general reordering of Europe was the dissolution of the superstate created by French arms and French diplomacy in the two decades preceding Napoleon's invasion of Russia. Once the conqueror was defeated, the victorious Allies found themselves beset by the difficulties which inevitably overtake a broad coalition as soon as it has achieved its initial, essentially negative, aim of victory over a common foe. In the spring of 1814, with the armies of the Grand Alliance occupying Paris and with Bonaparte shipped off to his island realm of Elba, the would-be peacemakers faced some hard decisions.

There were sharp differences of opinion over the degree of punitive harshness with which the French nation deserved to be treated. The Prussians, remembering their abject humiliation in 1806, were especially bitter. The British and Austrian foreign ministers, Viscount Castlereagh and Prince Metternich, on the other hand, favoured generous terms as offering the best hope for Europe's pacification. Closely tied to this question, of course, was the problem of giving France a government to replace the Empire. There was no instant unanimity supporting the return of the Bourbons, in the person of the executed king's brother, Louis XVIII.[1] The mercurial Tsar Alexander I, who now saw himself as both the liberator and the arbiter of Europe, skipped lightly from one alternative to another. One moment his solution was a new French Republic for which he would supply a constitution, the next it was Sweden's Bernadotte as king of France, and so on through several other possibilities. However, Castlereagh and Metternich, once the latter gave up hope of a Bonapartist succession, insisted on a Bourbon restoration, while the supple Prince Talleyrand, having abandoned Napoleon with characteristically shrewd timing, worked effectively to convince the other victors that only the old dynasty could make France a reliable member of the family of nations.

The treaty of Paris, which emerged from these and countless smaller debates, was signed on 30 May 1814. It incorporated the restoration of the Bourbon monarchy and granted the lenient peace terms which seemed necessary to make Louis XVIII secure upon his throne. The French were accorded the boundaries of 1792, including such early conquests as Avignon and certain small areas on the Flemish and Savoyard frontiers. They were charged no war indemnity and were allowed to retain the art treasures which Napoleon in particular had shipped home in abundance. In return, France recognized the independence of formerly occupied states—Dutch, Belgian, German, Swiss and Italian—

[1] The former *dauphin*, son of Louis XVI, had been styled 'Louis XVII' by monarchists prior to his death in a Parisian jail cell in 1795.

at the same time ceding to England the islands of Santa Lucia and Tobago in the West Indies, Mauritius in the Indian Ocean and Malta in the Mediterranean. Save for the return to Spain of its old share of San Domingo, no other colonial concessions were imposed upon a France which had emerged from the long holocaust remarkably undiminished.

The other, more general European questions broached at Paris were referred to the great congress which it was agreed should convene forthwith in Vienna. Before that body completed its work, however, Napoleon's return from Elba and the renewed bitterness of the Hundred Days overturned the mild settlement just outlined. Some five months after Waterloo, on 20 November 1815, was signed a second treaty of Paris, an agreement animated by a far more severe attitude on the part of the Allies than had prevailed the previous year. The French now surrendered the slices of Savoy and Flanders they had retained in the first treaty, as well as the Alsatian fortress of Landau (to the German Confederation) and all territory north of the Lauter River (to the kingdom of Bavaria's Palatinate). Countless art objects had to be returned to European palaces and museums. A cash indemnity of 700 million francs was imposed, while France was also committed to bear the cost of a 150,000-man Allied army of occupation for a period of up to five years.

Still not reduced beyond its pre-revolutionary boundaries, save on the northern edge of Alsace, the erstwhile *Grande Nation* had nevertheless felt the impact of foreign vengeance. Whether or not that nation could soon resume a major role in European affairs thus loomed as one of the immediate future's weightiest questions. The answer, however, would depend on developments in many places other than Paris and on negotiations the subjects of which often seemed remote from the 'French question' proper.

The Congress of Vienna

While the last hectic scenes of Napoleon's adventures were still being played out, far broader issues were decided by the general diplomatic assembly which had been agreed upon in the first treaty of Paris. Never before in history had so many rulers and principal ministers met to hammer out a comprehensive peace settlement. The Congress of Vienna was charged with nothing less than the task of putting Europe together once more and of seeking to establish conditions which would give this work of reconstruction a reasonable chance to survive.

The Austrian capital, into which came pouring the august delegations that September of 1814, was a city of about 250,000 inhabitants. Above its picturesque medieval centre rose the Stephanskirche, Vienna's treasured cathedral, surrounded by a profusion of shops and cafés in the narrow, twisting streets. Scattered through the old city were great town houses of the Kaunitz, Thurm und Taxis, Esterházy and other princely families. Some of these ornate mansions were rented to visiting diplomats—Talleyrand, for instance, moved directly into the Kaunitz Palace—while in others the Austrian owners themselves presided over a whirl of receptions, banquets and balls. The most lavish social centre of all, however, was the Habsburgs' palace, the sprawling Hofburg, where Emperor Francis I entertained his fellow monarchs day after day, at crushing expense. Through all the soirées, dinners, sleigh rides and hunting parties ran the twitter of gossip about the tsar's, Prince Metternich's and other famous men's love affairs. Only slightly more consequential was the whispering of diplomatic secrets, real or alleged, a traffic which kept large numbers of people busy without producing much effect on the actual course of deliberations.

The cast of players was certainly one of the most remarkable ever brought together under such auspices. Never far from the centre of attention was the unstable tsar, one moment generous, the next petulantly self-regarding, consistent only in his unpredictability. With him he had brought three Russian diplomats: Counts Nesselrode (the foreign minister), Razumovski and Stackelberg. More important, however, in influencing Alexander I's views on a wide range of specific issues were his foreign advisers: the German Stein, the Polish Prince Czartoryski, the Swiss tutor La Harpe, the Alsatian Baron Anstett, the Greek Capo d'Istria from Corfu and another island-born politician, the Corsican Pozzo di Borgo. Small wonder that Russian policy so often proved difficult to foretell or even to follow. Greedy for spoils in the Balkans, determined to write his own prescription for a restored Polish kingdom, loftily claiming a dominant voice in western European affairs as well, the tsar both puzzled and exasperated other national spokesmen.

Among the latter, none seemed at the outset more likely to wield decisive influence than did Austria's foreign minister of five years' standing, Clemens von Metternich. A Rhinelander, like Stein, this enigmatic man was in other respects almost the perfect opposite of that sincere but impetuous reformer. Handsome, witty, voluptuous, oblique in manoeuvre, but tenacious in defence of his central preoccupations—peace, stability and continued aristocratic leadership for Europe as a whole and for the patchwork Austrian Empire in particular—he was, as he himself shrewdly observed, 'bad at skirmishes . . . but good at campaigns'. By his side, to assist in the composition of papers both public and private, hovered the German author (and translator of Burke), Friedrich von Gentz.

Two other figures deserve our immediate attention. One was Robert Stewart, Viscount Castlereagh, the British foreign secretary, who reached Vienna in mid-September and took a modest house in which he lived quietly with his wife throughout the months of deliberations. No less handsome than Metternich, this Anglo-Irish aristocrat was quite different in personality: correct in his personal life, coldly polite to strangers, sometimes effective in debate but always strangely clumsy in written expression. Like Metternich, however, he clung stubbornly to a ruling conception of the need to stabilize Europe, in his case not so much by ensuring social and political 'legitimacy' as by creating a durable balance among sovereign powers. 'Balance of power' has attracted so much criticism, including blame for starting wars, that it is important to recall the by no means unintelligent calculations which led Castlereagh and the younger Pitt before him to adopt the position they did. That position, in brief, rested on the belief that genuine national interests, clearly recognized, could create in Europe an equilibrium of forces which would make war unfeasible for any one power, or even for a coalition unless directed against a single aggressor.

The remaining major protagonist was the French foreign minister, whose right to speak at all had yet to be established when the Congress of Vienna began. A secret article inserted in the first treaty of Paris the previous May had reserved to the great powers of the Quadruple Alliance—Russia, Austria, Britain and Prussia—the determination of Europe's future ordering. France, the other great power but also the recently defeated enemy of the Allies, was promised no voice in that determination. Nevertheless, the French representative at the Congress was not one to accept a role of silent impotence, for himself or for his country. The sixty-year-old Prince Talleyrand-Périgord, though physically crippled since childhood, stands out in history for his truly phenomenal ability to land, figuratively, on his feet after each political somersault. A bishop of the Catholic Church under the Old Régime, revolutionary deputy to the Estates General of 1789, exile in America during the Terror, then foreign minister under the Directory and supporter of Bonaparte's seizure of power, he had headed Napoleon's foreign ministry until 1807. Thereafter he had gradually detached himself from the emperor, whose abdication he helped to engineer in 1814. Now once more France's leading diplomat, this time for Louis XVIII, he arrived on the Viennese scene with his uncanny sense of timing, the resiliency won through hard experience and the sharp logic of an unsentimental mind.

Other delegates, as personalities, counted for rather less, though the Prussians, led by their uninspiring King Frederick William III, clearly had to be taken into account. The head of their working diplomats was Prince Hardenberg, Stein's old collaborator but never a social, as distinct from administrative, reformer. Accompanying him, and badly needed because of Hardenberg's deafness, was the educator and philosopher, Baron Wilhelm von Humboldt, as well as a bevy of military and technical advisers. For the rest, neither the Swedish spokesmen nor the Vatican's emissary, Cardinal Consalvi, nor Spain's pompous ambassador, Don Pedro Labrador, could do more than clamour to be heard. The sultan of Turkey, rival Italian factions, over thirty German princelings, even the Jews of Frankfurt were also among the myriad interests represented, but their agents were in fact little more than observers.

Representatives of the great powers met repeatedly with one another and, depending on the issue at hand, with those of other parties. Meanwhile, a total of ten special committees concentrated on designated questions ranging from the reorganization of Germany and Switzerland to such topics as population statistics, diplomatic precedence and the slave trade. The Congress of Vienna was actually a combination of such committee hearings and of informal talks among leading delegates, extending over a period of some eight months. There was no plenary session of all participants until the signing of the comprehensive treaty or, as it was called, the Final Act.

Going back to the opening of the Congress and to the host of problems which confronted Europe's assembled diplomats, it is important to recognize that from the outset a difficult mingling of restoration and innovation had to be attempted. There was no possibility of simply reimposing the pre-revolutionary map—too much had happened in the quarter-century which was ending in 1814. In Germany, for example, the former 300 states had been reduced by the *Reichsdeputationshauptschluss* of 1803 (*see above*, pp. 201–2) and by subsequent settlements to only thirty-nine political units. Newly consolidated kingdoms and grand duchies, all counting themselves among the final victors' would brook no discussion of a revived Holy Roman Empire's welter of political microcosms. A special question involved the future status of Saxony, whose king had remained an ally of Napoleon until the battle of Leipzig and now was treated as a defeated enemy of the Allies, his entire realm demanded by neighbouring Prussia.

Tsar Alexander's project for a Polish kingdom, with himself as king, impinged sharply on the German problem. The Russian monarch hoped to recover for Poland all of Prussia's share in the partitions of 1793 and 1795, in return supporting Frederick William III's wish to annex the whole of Saxony. Similarly, if Alexander had his way, Austria would return Cracow and Polish Galicia, against compensations in Italy and Dalmatia. The situation in Italy, be it said, was thoroughly confused, for there were conflicting claims to virtually every square mile of that sundered peninsula. Even the Bourbons of Naples could not be sure of recovering their patrimony from King Joachim (Murat), who was loud in his protestations of devotion to the Allies and whose Queen Caroline, though a sister of Napoleon, was also one of Metternich's former mistresses. Meanwhile, Switzerland awaited a new constitution, the future of the Low Countries remained obscure, and the Scandinavian settlement agreed upon between Sweden and Denmark at Kiel in January of 1814 would be in jeopardy unless it were ratified by the great powers.

Of all these knotty problems, the two which proved to be crucial were those involving Poland and Saxony. By the last days of 1814, in fact, disagreement among the great powers had become so intense that a complete breakdown of relations between Russia and Prussia on the one side and Austria and England on the other loomed as a distinct possibility. A westward projection of Russian power into the large Polish state envisaged by Alexander and the creation of a new north German giant if Prussia were permitted to gobble up all of Saxony were prospects which neither London nor Vienna would accept. Pitt's old dream, pursued by Castlereagh, the dream of a Prussian-Austrian-British alliance to restrain both France and Russia, had already foundered on the mutual hostility of the two German powers and on Prussia's effort to win great rewards by collaborating with the tsar.

It was at this point that Talleyrand intervened. His achievement was a brilliant *tour de force*, and it was decisive. Having already made himself the spokesman for all the nations excluded from the deliberations of the 'Big Four', he now convinced Castlereagh and Metternich that what they needed above all was active French collaboration. (Once he had done so, by the way, he at once stopped complaining about 'great-power dominance'.) On 3 January 1815 the representatives of Austria, Great Britain and France signed a secret agreement to resist the most extreme demands of Russia and Prussia by force of arms if necessary. The Big Four had in this sense become the Big Five. Even during the Hundred Days, though the old Allies once again took the field against Napoleonic France, the *Bourbon* France for which Talleyrand spoke remained an active partner in a quite different coalition.

No one can say with absolute assurance whether or not the Anglo-French-Austrian agreement to threaten the Russians and Prussians with military action was merely a bluff. Perhaps it was no more than that, for while the French nation proved willing that spring to rally behind Napoleon's final effort, it might well have refused to join with unfamiliar allies in a war over central European boundaries. There can be no doubt that Castlereagh, for his part, would have been hard put to secure support in Parliament for such a war. If the threat was a bluff, however, it succeeded against what proved to be no very stern resolve on the part of Alexander I and Frederick William III. These monarchs, both of whom received almost immediate reports of the secret treaty, promptly began to moderate their demands. Within six weeks, the Polish and Saxon questions had been resolved by compromise. Thereafter, the other issues before the Congress were settled with relative ease and with a dispatch which had seemed beyond the realm of possibility during the dangerous stalemate of mid-winter.

The Final Act was signed on 9 June 1815, pending Napoleon's final defeat. As already indicated, the Polish arrangement represented a compromise. A kingdom of Poland—Congress Poland as the nineteenth century would know it—was resurrected under Alexander I and ostensibly guaranteed a constitutional régime far more liberal than that of the tsar's Russian patrimony. To help form this new entity, Prussia disgorged the Warsaw region, though not Posen, while Austria gave up western Galicia, allowed Cracow to become a free city, but retained all Polish lands previously annexed by the Habsburgs south and east of the Vistula. In return, the Prussian monarch obtained the northern 40 per cent of Saxony, the last remaining strip of Swedish Pomerania on the Baltic, all of the Hohenzollerns' past holdings in Westphalia, plus a solid, heavily populated tract on the left bank of the Rhine from south of the Moselle to the Dutch frontier. Francis I of Austria, for his part, was accorded Venetia and Lombardy in Italy as a satellite kingdom, Illyria and Dalmatia on the east coast of the Adriatic, the Bavarian Tyrol and the former archepiscopal principality of Salzburg. If Russia had moved west, through its extension of control across Poland, so had Prussia and Austria as a result of these compensations.

Despite a storm of criticism from liberal and nationalist groups, a loose confederation was the only superstructure accepted by Germany's thirty-five essentially unreformed principalities and four surviving free cities (Frankfurt, Hamburg, Bremen and Lübeck). The political problems facing the new German Diet, established at Frankfurt under permanent Austrian chairmanship, will be discussed in Chapter XII. Meanwhile, the work of political regrouping also went forward in the Low Countries, Switzerland and Scandinavia. The old United Provinces and Austria's former Belgian domain were joined to form a 'kingdom of the Netherlands' under the Dutch stadtholder, now styled King William I and at the same time grand duke of Luxemburg, in which capacity he was counted as a member prince of the German Confederation. The Swiss Confederation was revived and indeed expanded, for its twenty-two cantons would henceforth include the erstwhile republic of Geneva and the principality of Neuchâtel, once again a fief of the Prussian king, Finally, Sweden's Crown Prince Bernadotte obtained confirmation of the cession of Norway by Denmark the previous year, though the Norwegians received a separate constitution purporting to guarantee their traditional rights.

Elsewhere, régimes of the past were declared legitimately reinstalled: in Spain, in Sardinia (which acquired Genoa), in the Italian Papal States (though not in Avignon and its territory, which were left to France), in Tuscany and in Modena. Despite Spanish protests, the north Italian duchy of Parma-Piacenza was awarded to Marie-Louise, Napoleon's empress and the daughter of the Austrian emperor, to hold for her lifetime but not to transmit to her son. After Joachim Murat blundered by supporting Napoleon in the Hundred Days, the Bourbon King Ferdinand I was returned to Naples, there to rule what was now termed the Kingdom of the Two Sicilies.

Of all the major powers, England apparently had least to show for its military and diplomatic efforts. It had annexed nothing on the Continent, had returned scores of overseas points occupied during the long years of warfare and had failed to secure any effective agreement to abolish the slave trade, a matter of both moral and economic interest in London. On this last point, the Final Act of the Congress included a resolution condemning in principle the traffic in slaves but leaving to future negotiations the question of how its actual suppression was to be achieved. Nevertheless, Great Britain emerged with some very considerable advantages. First, there were the islands already ceded by France. In addition, the Dutch flag did not go up again in place of the Union Jack over either Ceylon or the Cape of Good Hope, nor did that of Denmark over Heligoland in the North Sea, while strategic Malta became a British possession. At Ghent, in December 1814, England's potentially dangerous war with the United States had ended with a return to the *status quo*.

Most important of all, when in late February 1815 he turned over to Wellington responsibility for British interests at Vienna and started home to London, Castlereagh took with him the assurance of a restored European balance. It was not precisely the one he had gone to the Congress hoping to achieve. It involved more reliance on France, and less on Prussia, than he had originally preferred. But it offered the promise that his country would not soon again have to face, alone, a giant hegemonical power on the Continent.

Congress Europe

To Metternich, to Castlereagh, to Alexander I, to Talleyrand and to many others who had joined in the Vienna settlement, that settlement was more than a single act of diplomacy. Each hoped, for reasons of his own, that it would signal the creation of a permanent system of consultation, a genuine 'concert of Europe'. During the next seven years, the powers did in fact assemble for four additional congresses. The system as such, however, proved incapable of perpetuating itself. In order to judge its brief record and to understand its collapse, we must first identify the several bases upon which different parties believed it should rest.

The earliest, and most obvious, support for collaboration lay in the military partnership which had beaten Napoleon. Castlereagh's anxious efforts to give definite form to the alliance of Britain, Austria, Russia and Prussia had produced the pledge of solidarity against French aggression signed at Chaumont in March 1814. Disrupted by the diplomatic crisis over Poland and Saxony the following winter in Vienna, this agreement recovered full life and vigour during the Hundred Days. Finally, on 20 November 1815, the day they signed the second treaty of Paris, the four major victors solemnly renewed the Quadruple Alliance, each committing itself for twenty years to contribute 60,000

6. *Europe in 1815 (after the Congress of Vienna)*

men if there were any further attempt by France to overturn the peace settlement.

Castlereagh never abandoned the view that the Quadruple Alliance was the bedrock upon which must rest all other arrangements designed to ensure a balance of power. He welcomed the return of France to peaceful ways, and he had already shown himself willing, at Vienna, to enter into special agreements with Talleyrand. But French energy and French resentment, he believed, would constitute a potential threat to Europe for a long time to come. Thus, whatever efforts were made to restrain other nations, the wartime allies should be sure to keep a cautious eye on their formidable enemy of the preceding quarter-century.

Not surprisingly, the tsar of All the Russias conceived of stability as based on principles quite different from those of England's foreign secretary—and on a quite different sort of treaty. Having taken no direct part in Napoleon's second defeat, Alexander in 1815 was something less than the conquering hero, the focus of rapt attention, he had been a year earlier. While Wellington and Blücher finished the military business in Belgium and northern France, he sojourned first in the Rhineland and then in Paris, with Baroness von Krüdener at his side. This Latvian-born German woman, an unsuccessful novelist, a veteran of love affairs, but at fifty-one scarcely more than a self-hypnotized religious mystic, helped Alexander to immerse himself in vague, ostentatious piety. One day in September 1815, for example, he arrayed the entire Russian expeditionary force in France before eight open-air altars, to which the baroness addressed herself in turn, performing before each what apparently was meant to be an inspirational dance.

Despite this curious feminine influence, the tsar could justly claim as his own the concept of a personal agreement among monarchs, founded on religious sentiments; for he had been discussing such a possibility for more than a decade. The Holy Alliance which he signed with Emperor Francis I and King Frederick William III on 26 September 1815 seems innocuous enough at first reading. The Russian, Austrian and Prussian rulers promised to treat one another in accordance with 'the sublime truths which the Holy Religion of Our Saviour teaches' and to watch over their respective peoples 'as fathers of families'. There was no reference to suppressing progressive movements and no effort to limit the pact to the three eastern autocracies which initially concluded it. On the contrary, all other European rulers were invited to subscribe to its terms. Eventually, all did so save three: the sultan, who was not that devoted to the religion in question; the pope, who would not join with Orthodox and Protestant monarchs; and the prince regent of Great Britain, who explained that his country's constitution forbade him to enter into such a personal agreement.

Bland and unobjectionable as the tsar's project may appear—and doubtless *did* appear to many of its signers—the Holy Alliance began at once to disrupt the hoped-for concert of Europe. It was, as liberal critics pointed out in speech and in print, a compact among rulers, not among nations or peoples. Furthermore, the grounds for the British prince regent's non-participation suggested an incipient division within the *Quadruple* Alliance itself, as between absolute and constitutional monarchies. But most serious of all, the tsar's brainchild threatened to make the defence of 'decent Christian order' an excuse for repression, aimed at even the most respectable opponents of established régimes. In fairness to Alexander I, it must be said that the use of the Holy Alliance for this purpose was less his work than that of a man who scoffed at pious mysticism, Prince Metternich.

The Austrian minister seemed to many observers at the time, as he has to many since, the evil genius of tyranny and reaction, who believed that even if history could not be reversed in all details, it should at least come to what his adviser, Gentz, referred to as 'a full stop'. On the other hand, he has been praised by numerous admirers for having recognized that what Europe needed most was rest and recuperation, for having resisted the divisive, potentially violent force of nationalism and for having sought to keep international affairs in the hands of cultured, cosmopolitan aristocrats. Whichever view one favours, it seems clear that Metternich's definition of 'legitimacy' provided an uncommonly consistent principle underlying both his foreign and his domestic policies as Austria's chief minister during nearly forty years. The empire he served, if it were to survive at all, required peace without and a respite, within, from the nationalist agitation of Germans, Italians, Hungarians and Slavs. A man committed to two such aims was not apt to be disturbed by charges of repression.

The combination of the tsar's religiosity and Metternich's increasingly negative conception of legitimacy presented the British government with an unwelcome set of problems. Castlereagh clung to the hope that a stable European balance could be arrived at among nations whose internal political systems, within broad limits, remained their own business. Parliament, he felt sure, would never support a policy of recurrent intervention in the domestic affairs of various states. It seemed just as unlikely, however, that the other great powers would agree to refrain

from intervening wherever there was a threat of revived 'Jacobinism'—
and Jacobinism was fast becoming a smear word for the most moderate
constitutional liberalism. In the years immediately after 1815, London
was left with no choice but to pursue a course of reserved participation
in international conferences, hoping for the best.

The first such meeting, the Congress of Aix-la-Chapelle in the
autumn of 1818, actually seemed to augur well for the future of consultation among the great powers. Present for Great Britain were the
foreign secretary and Wellington; for Austria, Francis I and Metternich; for Russia, the tsar, Nesselrode and Capo d'Istria; for Prussia,
Frederick William III and Hardenberg; for France, the Duc de
Richelieu (Talleyrand having resigned as foreign minister after the
Congress of Vienna to become Louis XVIII's chamberlain). Richelieu
was not admitted to all the discussions, but Aix-la-Chapelle nevertheless
marked the end of the postwar treatment of France as a defeated enemy.
Though the Quadruple Alliance was reaffirmed, another, Quintuple
Alliance was formed, with French participation, 'to protect the arts
of peace' and to increase general prosperity. The last details concerning
payment of the indemnity of 1815 were settled, after which it was
agreed that all occupation forces should leave French soil. In addition,
some further progress was made towards a more generous definition of
Jewish rights, towards abolition of the slave trade and towards an improvement in Sweden's and Denmark's embittered relations.

Yet the meeting at Aix-la-Chapelle, encouraging as it seemed in
many respects, provided the first unblinkable evidence that the congress
system itself was endangered by fundamental disagreements among the
nations involved. The tsar kept talking of 'sacred principles of order'
and the need to create an international army to protect those principles
everywhere. At the same time, he urged all monarchs to grant constitutions for the wellbeing and tranquillity of their peoples. That in itself
was enough to make Metternich oppose the creation of an international
police force to defend such ill-defined aims. Far more blunt was
Castlereagh's warning that his government condemned all efforts 'to
provide the transparent soul of the Holy Alliance with a body'.[1] Even
a new revolt in France, he said, would justify intervention only if
prudent calculation were to indicate that the disorders threatened the
peace of Europe.

Against this background it is not difficult to see why the next two
congresses witnessed a growing alienation between England and the

[1] Quoted in Artz, p. 161 (*see* Bibliographical Note, p. 392).

continental powers, especially since both meetings dealt with the issue of intervention. The first of them, at Troppau, Silesia, in October 1820, considered the revolutions then in progress against the disreputable Bourbon monarchs of the Two Sicilies and of Spain. Castlereagh did not attend, but he sent a British delegation instructed to oppose any project for sending foreign troops into either the Italian or the Iberian peninsula. The English effort to block such action proved unavailing. The Spanish question was temporarily left in abeyance, but the other powers at the congress voted to authorize military action by Austrian forces in Italy and to ask that a Russian army of 90,000 men also stand ready to march from Poland if needed.

Before these military operations actually began, still another congress assembled, this one in January 1821 at the Austrian town of Laibach in Carniola. Once more the powers of the Holy Alliance affirmed their determination to intervene wherever a legitimate régime was in danger of being overthrown. Once more the British spokesman declared that no treaty in existence justified such intervention unless a direct threat to international tranquillity could be demonstrated. This time there was no real effort on either side to reach a compromise. As Sir Harold Nicolson has written: 'The Great Coalition was thus finally dissolved; the Concert of Europe had disintegrated; the Holy Alliance had succeeded in destroying the Quadruple Alliance; the Conference System had failed'.[1]

Within only a matter of weeks after the Congress of Laibach, combinations of Austrian and local royalist troops crushed both the revolution in Naples and a shortlived uprising which broke out among Piedmontese subjects of the king of Sardinia in March 1821. The Spanish insurgents, however, still held the upper hand in their struggle with Ferdinand VII. Hence, on 20 October 1822, the five great powers came together at Verona for what proved to be the last of the era's conferences involving them all.

In many respects, the Congress of Verona was scarcely more than a funeral service for earlier hopes of cooperation between Great Britain and the Continent. Castlereagh, after a long physical and nervous decline, had killed himself that August at his country home. His place as foreign secretary had been taken by George Canning, a man quite untouched by any lingering desire to get along with the autocratic régimes which ruled in Vienna, in St Petersburg, in Berlin and—since the return of the *Ultras* in 1820—in Paris. Under Metternich's prodding

[1] Nicolson, *Congress of Vienna*, p. 268 (*see* Bibliography, p. 255).

the diplomats at Verona moved towards intervention in Spain. This decision, needless to say, was taken against the advice of Britain's delegate, Wellington. The latter, on Canning's orders, served notice that 'come what may' his government would have no part in such a venture. Nevertheless, the other powers were committed to action. Having managed to ward off an insistent Russian offer of troops, they commissioned France to send an army across the Pyrenees. The victory of French forces over the Spanish rebels in the summer of 1823 brought a sigh of relief to most continental ministers, though it enraged their liberal critics. It also put an end to any lingering hope that Great Britain might still move back into the European system which Castlereagh had worked so hard to help create.

Mention of Castlereagh and of his strivings suggests the need to guard against the danger of oversimplification. Because he was a Tory and his eloquent successor was a liberal independent, because the two men were personal rivals, because Castlereagh shared in the fashioning of the Vienna settlement while Canning denounced it, an earlier historical tradition saw the one as Metternich's henchman and the other, as Metternich's enemy. In actual fact, the signal change in British policy occurred during Castlereagh's ministry. It began as early as the Congress of Aix-la-Chapelle in 1818 and was accentuated by those of Troppau and Laibach in 1820–21. The line of increasing withdrawal from continental involvements, which Canning pursued relentlessly from 1822 onward, was no doubt for him far less a cause of sadness than it had been for his predecessor, but it was none the less a line which Castlereagh had clearly traced.

As for the other powers, Austria would seem to have come nearest to getting what it wanted from the successive congresses: the snuffing out of potentially contagious revolts in Italy and Spain without a massive Russian re-entry into central and western European affairs. By the same token, Tsar Alexander had been compelled to moderate his more extreme ambitions as self-designated arbiter of Christendom. For the time being, Prussia remained what it had been at Vienna in 1814–15, a weak third among the eastern powers. From certain points of view, France might appear to have made good use of the congresses to recover her international standing. So she had, but her involvement in Spain following the decisions taken at Verona proved expensive, unpopular at home and embarassing for her ostensibly constitutional government. The other states of Europe could only look on, with varying degrees of official approval, as their more potent continental neighbours sought to impose tranquillity not by experimenting with reform but by stifling it.

Diplomacy after Vienna: Italy, Spain and Portugal

It can be argued that the congress system need not be thought of as defunct, merely because consultation in large and highly publicized colloquies had broken down. Groups of diplomats of various nationalities went on meeting in one or another capital to discuss current issues, and later decades would witness several congresses not unlike those of Vienna and Aix-la-Chapelle—at Paris in 1856, for example, and at Berlin in 1878. To confuse the continuation of traditional diplomatic procedures with the survival of the experiment begun in 1814–15, however, would be to miss the latter's most important feature. For the central question had been whether or not *all* the great powers, definitely including Great Britain, could agree on the conditions for international stability, and then regularly deliberate in common over the maintenance of those conditions. Conceived thus, the 'concert of Europe' was moribund by 1820 and dead by 1822. What followed was a frank resumption of power-political manoeuvring—complex, multilateral and, be it granted, successful for almost a century in preventing a general war—but not truly *conciliar*. After Verona, now one and then another major state took the initiative, employing means and encountering responses most of which would have been familiar to eighteenth-century statesmen.

At the risk of obscuring such critical problems as Russian-Polish tensions and the troubles in the kingdom of the Netherlands, to be discussed in Chapter XII, it is both possible and useful to examine international relations during the 1820s in terms of three major sources of disagreement. One was the effort of the conservative powers to sustain oppressive, and in several cases grossly incompetent, régimes in the Italian and Iberian peninsulas. The second involved the degree of European political influence which could be imposed on colonial settlements overseas. The third centred on the 'eastern question', as it developed during the Greek War of Independence against Turkey.

The first of these issues, despite British opposition, appeared to have been settled by Austrian intervention against Neapolitan and Piedmontese rebels in 1821 and by the French invasion of Spain, to rescue Ferdinand VII, in 1823. The Italian cauldron, however, continued to simmer and occasionally broke into a boil, at one instant in

Parma, the next in Modena, the next in the Papal States. None of the sporadic riots and assassinations overturned an established régime, thanks largely to the busy Austrian regiments; but Metternich complained that no other power fully shared his determination to uphold legitimacy. Neither Paris nor Berlin had any material stake in Italy comparable to Vienna's, while Russia, after the death of Alexander I in 1825, showed signs of increasing preoccupation with its own Polish and Balkan interests.

As for the two Iberian kingdoms, each in its own way was proving just as troublesome as was Italy for statesmen committed to order as an absolute value. No sooner had the Duc d'Angoulême's expeditionary force defeated the Spanish rebels, in August-September 1823, than King Ferdinand launched a savage reign of terror. Hundreds of liberals were executed in gruesome fashion. Thousands more were imprisoned or driven into exile. Like his relative in Naples two years before, the unbalanced ruler of Spain was encouraged in these measures by the Austrian and Prussian emissaries to his restored court. Angoulême, on the other hand, was horrified at the sadistic excesses of revenge; and from Paris Louis XVIII, indecisive but not inhumane, denounced the aftermath of his army's victory as a betrayal of the honour of French soldiers. In the circumstances, there was little cause for surprise when in October Canning curtly refused even to have England represented at a proposed congress to discuss the future of Spain. For the remaining ten years of his life, however, undisturbed by foreign criticism, Ferdinand VII would practise his own version of that fatherly care espoused by the Holy Alliance.

Developments centring on Portugal followed a different but scarcely a calmer course. Given the proximity of British naval power and the absence, at first, of sustained fighting among the Portuguese themselves, even Metternich found himself unable to plead for intervention on the Italian-Spanish model. The conservative courts, therefore, looked on nervously as King John VI returned from Brazil in 1821 to accept a liberal constitution, applauded when he repudiated it the following year, only to shudder once more at his announcement that some form of parliamentary rule was still his goal. When John died in 1826 the same governments noted with approbation the reactionary plans of the new regent, Dom Miguel. This time, however, it was Britain which intervened by sending a military force to support the Portuguese constitutional party. (Castlereagh's old prescriptions against meddling in the domestic affairs of other countries were, in Canning's view, to be applied selectively!) The English, prematurely reassured by Dom Miguel's suave promises, withdrew in 1827 after sixteen months in Lisbon; and as we shall see in Chapter XII, the regent's almost immediate resumption of attacks on the liberals touched off open civil warfare. Here it need only be emphasized that in this maritime kingdom the Holy Alliance failed to make its weight felt in any decisive manner.

The Americas and the Monroe Doctrine

Directly related to the troubles in Spain and Portugal was the second dominant issue of the post-congress era. This was the question of the continental powers' right or, more to the point, their ability to reverse the outcome of colonial rebellions across the Atlantic. Here the position of Britain was naturally crucial, and Canning's personal influence proved decisive. In 1825, without waiting for any statement by another European government, he suddenly announced that His Majesty recognized the independence of several republics—initially Argentina, Colombia and Mexico—which had been born, over the course of the preceding decade, out of revolts within the former American empire of Spain. The same year, Canning likewise extended formal recognition to Brazil under its constitutional emperor, Pedro I, eldest son of John VI of Portugal.

The flamboyant foreign secretary did not rely exclusively on British naval power in calling 'the New World into existence to redress the balance of the Old', as he expressed it to the House of Commons. Needless to say, the chief obstacle to any effort by continental powers to reimpose Spanish and Portuguese rule upon Latin America was the Royal Navy, warmly supported in this task by Britain's merchant class. Canning, however, was eager to dramatize both the morality and the political soundness of playing the friend to constitutional liberalism and the self-determination of peoples. It was for this reason that he welcomed messages of thanks from liberators such as Bolívar and San Martín. Ironically, it was no less for this reason that he helped to make an American charter of isolationism an important document of European history.

In Washington, D.C., on 2 December 1823, President Monroe sent to Congress his annual message on the State of the Union. Contained therein was a lengthy passage based especially on the views of the secretary of state, John Quincy Adams, and devoted to the territorial interests of the United States in the Western Hemisphere. The Monroe

Doctrine, as this section came to be known, comprised two distinct assertions. The first, inspired by Russian settlements pushing down the Pacific Coast from Alaska to what is now the San Francisco region, was that 'the American continents . . . are henceforth not to be considered as subject to future colonization by any European power'. The second had to do less with fresh colonization than with intervention in already established settlements. Referring to the possibility that the powers of the Holy Alliance might act against Brazil and the new Spanish American republics, the message read: 'We owe it . . . to candor, and to the amicable relations existing between the United States and those powers, to declare that we should consider any attempt on their part to extend their political system to any portion of this hemisphere as dangerous to our peace and security'.[1]

It would be quite wrong to assume that Canning welcomed Monroe's and Adams's sweeping pronouncements as support, pure and simple, for his own opposition to the Holy Alliance. The non-colonization clause was distasteful to Britain at a time when the westward extension of the U.S.-Canadian border had yet to be determined. Furthermore, the Americans, after temporizing, had in effect ignored Britain's offer of a joint declaration forbidding European attempts to restore the lost Portuguese and Spanish colonies. Last but not least, Canning was personally anything but an admirer of the bumptious young nation which had fought two wars against his own country in the preceding fifty years and had now seized as its own a policy which he would have developed rather differently.

Nevertheless, the Monroe Doctrine did in a broader sense fit into the foreign secretary's scheme of things. British commercial interests—as Canning, who sat in the Commons for Liverpool, was quite aware—welcomed the opening of trade with Spanish America, unhampered by the restrictions so long imposed by Madrid. (An independent Brazil, given England's influence at Lisbon, seemed less necessary, but not in itself unattractive.) Liberals, in France and England alike, generally hailed the United States' initiative as supplying a programmatic basis for quarantining the New World against the devices of European autocrats. More immediately, it helped to justify British refusal to participate during 1824 in a proposed new congress of powers to discuss Latin America. Finally, though he still sought for a time to reconcile

[1] D. Perkins, *A History of the Monroe Doctrine* (rev. edn., Boston, 1955), p. 28. The same author's *The Monroe Doctrine, 1823–1826* (Cambridge, Mass., 1932), is a more detailed analysis of origins and initial effects.

Portugal and Brazil, Canning was quite prepared to play upon the danger that the United States might itself establish control over the new Spanish republics as a reason for Madrid to accept their full independence as the lesser of two evils.

It is not necessary to adopt the foreign secretary's very generous self-evaluation in concluding that his five years in office were momentous ones for what we have come to call the Atlantic community. Before an early death ended his career in 1827, he had laid the groundwork for that use of British naval power which would continue until the end of the nineteenth century—as a force which militarily (save in the 1860s) separated the United States and Europe from one another, and South America from them both. However limited, even parochial, Canning's motives may have been, the implications of his policy were tremendous.

Greek Independence

The third and last great issue to be noted here broke into the open on 2 April 1821 when the Orthodox Archbishop Germanos officially repudiated Turkish rule and thereby converted Greek unrest into an avowed war for independence. Not only in Greece but in Serbia as well, Ottoman control of south-east Europe had been under increasingly sharp attack since the turn of the century. Certain political ideals of the Enlightenment, the example of the French Revolution, the dawning awareness of distinct cultures and potential nationhood, all had helped to inspire resistance against the existing order in the Balkans. It was the Greeks' outright demand for freedom, however, which first lifted such resistance to the status of a public question for Europe in general.

The struggle thus begun unfolded on several different levels. The military chronicle as such was at once complicated and terrible, for both Christians and Muslims slaughtered their enemies with a ferocity which sickened men who had walked on the bloodiest of Napoleonic battlefields. The spring of 1821 saw the Morea (the ancient Pelopponesus) wrested from Turkish control with remarkable speed and apparent ease. The sultan's forces, still dominated by the corrupt and indolent Janissaries, were no match for the furiously attacking rebels. In the first two years of fighting, not only the south but Attica as well passed into the hands of the insurgents, though the Turks exacted a ghastly vengeance by massacring or enslaving some 30,000 island inhabitants of Chios in the Aegean.

Then a mixture of internal and external difficulties overtook the Greeks. Their commanders in the field often refused to consult one another about strategy or to abide by such battle plans as were from time to time agreed upon. Peasants of the interior showed increasing resentment towards the more sophisticated maritime Greeks, the merchants who dominated the provisional government. By 1824 these two elements were in open armed conflict.

While these developments were in progress Sultan Mahmud II finally resigned himself to paying the price of military aid from his virtually sovereign tributary, Egypt's Muhammad Ali. The latter demanded Crete for himself and the Morea as a principality for his son, Ibrahim Pasha; but in return he provided the first well-organized Muslim army to appear in Greece since the outbreak of hostilities. First seizing Crete, the Egyptian forces under Ibrahim crossed to the mainland and began the systematic reduction of rebel strongholds, among them Navarino in 1825, Missolonghi in 1826, Athens in 1827. The brutality of this campaign, combined with indications that Ibrahim meant literally to depopulate the Morea for the benefit of future Egyptian settlers, forced the warring Greek factions back together. In April 1827 they elected the late tsar's old Corfiote adviser, Capo d'Istria, president of Greece for a seven-year term. By that time, however, the chance that anything which could be termed 'Greece' would survive the Ottoman-Egyptian onslaught seemed exceedingly slight.

The turning of the tide and the ultimate failure of the sultan's and Ibrahim Pasha's offensive resulted from a number of simultaneous developments, many of them occurring outside the Balkans and far from the deep blue waters of the eastern Mediterranean. Involved were at least two quite distinct forms of action. One was popular and extended over most of the Christian world: an epoch-making surge of sympathy for the Greek cause. 'Love for the Greeks', or 'Philhellenism' as it was called, had its roots in religion (the Cross was at war with the Crescent), in classical education (were the descendants of Herodotus and Thucydides, Plato and Aristotle not fighting for their lives?) and—reflecting the domestic political tensions besetting many nations—in liberal sympathy for the heirs of Pericles as they struggled against an alien despotism. Writers as different in other respects as the Vicomte Chateaubriand, Ludwig Uhland and Percy Bysshe Shelley lent their literary gifts to the task of convincing literate Europeans that this was a war for civilization. Lord Byron actually gave his life for the cause, succumbing to disease at Missolonghi in 1824, after he had contributed thousands of pounds to the Greeks' effort and had organized an auxiliary military contingent at his own expense. Support in the form of money, supplies and volunteers came from America—where countless town names in upper New York State, the Ohio Valley and elsewhere recall the Philhellene enthusiasm—from the French royal government, from Swiss societies, from German princes. The king of Bavaria even sent an army brigade.

It was in the midst of this public clamour that important events occurred on the other level, that of governmental decision-making by the great powers. Russia, almost by reflex hostile to the Turks, had at first encouraged the Greek rebels. In 1821 Alexander I permitted General Ypsilanti, of Greek Phanariot stock (*see above*, p. 40) but a tsarist army officer, to launch an invasion of Moldavia-Wallachia aimed at freeing both Rumanian and Greek Christians from their Ottoman overlords. Ypsilanti, however, failed miserably, not least because the Rumanian gentry almost without exception hated Greeks more bitterly than they did Turks. Simultaneously, Metternich began a successful campaign to convince the tsar that the radicals of Greece were as bad as those of Naples and Spain, and that they should be left to their fate. England's Castlereagh, and for a time Canning after him, took the view that since a Turkish defeat would only add to Russian power, intervention on the rebels' behalf would be foolish. With France and Prussia both inclined to vacillate, Metternich had no great difficulty in blocking concerted action for Greek independence throughout the first five years of the war.

By 1826, however, popular indignation, sharply increased by the Egyptians' cruelty, was subjecting this policy of aloofness to very considerable pressure for change. Perhaps even more important, the views of several leading European figures were hardening in opposition to those of the cool aristocrat in Vienna. King Charles X of France, certainly no friend of liberal-constitutional movements in general, had nevertheless caught the Philhellene fever (primarily for religious reasons) and become critical of Metternich. At St Petersburg, 1825 had brought the death of Tsar Alexander I and the accession of his brother, Nicholas I, a ruler who felt no personal obligation to act in concert with Austria and who was determined to exploit every advantage over the Turks which fate might place before him. Finally, the British official attitude, as personified by Canning, had grown increasingly pro-Greek —an evolution reflecting not only the demands of public opinion but also the foreign secretary's dawning awareness that blank refusal to act would leave the field clear for a unilateral Russian triumph over Turkey.

In April 1826 at St Petersburg, therefore, the duke of Wellington signed a protocol which committed the Russians and the British jointly to impose their mediation upon the belligerents, the solution envisaged being an autonomous Greece under the nominal suzerainty of the sultan. As we have already seen, however, the war ground on amid mounting indications that the Turks and their Egyptian allies would win a total victory. It was to prevent such an outcome that on 6 July 1827, France joined the co-signers of the previous spring in a three-power agreement, the treaty of London, which provided that if either side in the conflict continued to spurn mediation, all three powers would lend naval support to the other.

A British-French-Russian squadron hovered about the Morea that summer and autumn, its English commander, Admiral Codrington, being under a quite remarkable set of orders to block all Turkish and Egyptian supplies, without letting the operation 'degenerate into hostilities'. Ibrahim Pasha was in fact prevailed upon to halt operations for several weeks, pending further discussions; but on 20 October 1827 Codrington received news at sea that the Muslim armies had resumed full hostilities on shore. For a veteran of Trafalgar, one of Nelson's most devoted disciples, the next move was virtually automatic. The admiral sailed his flotilla into the harbour of Navarino. Firing began, in circumstances of some confusion, and within the space of just three hours the close-packed Egyptian-Turkish fleet was virtually annihilated. Before the end of the year all three intervening powers, though still technically at peace with the sultan, had recalled their ambassadors from Turkey.

It was Tsar Nicholas who ended this ambiguous state of affairs and initiated the climactic chain of events. Late in April 1828, against the wishes of Wellington's newly formed ministry in London but with French approval, the Russian imperial government declared war on the Sublime Porte. During the next few months, it still appeared that diplomacy might achieve more than arms; for while the Russians were meeting unexpectedly stiff Turkish resistance in the Rumanian provinces, British and French representatives negotiated the final evacuation of the Greek mainland by the Egyptian army. The next year, however, told a very different story. Early in June the Russian general, Diebitsch, won a great victory at Kulevcha, just north of the Danube's mouth, and immediately thrust his army southward across the Balkan

Mountains into Thrace. On 20 August 1829 he took Edirna (Adrianople).

Never before had Russian troops stood so close to Istanbul, but they were seriously weakened by disease and exhausted from the long forced marches. On the advice of General Diebitsch, therefore, the tsar decided to negotiate with the Turks on relatively generous terms. By the treaty of Adrianople, concluded on 14 September, Russia secured the entire Danube delta on the Black Sea, the promise of a large cash indemnity and sweeping pledges of Christian religious supremacy in the Rumanian principalities. For the rest, the Russian armies evacuated their other recent conquests.

The same treaty, and the same autumn, brought the triumphant end of the Greeks' battle for independence. At Adrianople the sultan promised to accept the London Protocol, that is, to permit Greece autonomous status under his nominal suzerainty. Before the final terms were signed on 30 November 1829, however, the British, Russian and French representatives had increased their demands to include absolute independence for Greece (minus Crete, which was left to the Egyptians). The Porte was thus compelled to let Europe's diplomats write the conclusion to this chapter in the history of the 'eastern question'. There were many further chapters still to come, but here, looking ahead to later developments, we should perhaps simply emphasize the suspicion between London and St Petersburg which underlay even the momentary collaboration of the two governments.

The ultimate success of the Greeks and their supporters in many lands had another important aspect. It constituted a more serious defeat for Metternich than had any other occurrence of the 1820s, even including the isolation of the New World from action by the Holy Alliance. Austria was virtually excluded from the great-power negotiations during the last years of the war in Greece, unwilling to endorse the decisions reached, unable to prevent their being taken. But the defeat was not simply a matter of reduced diplomatic influence for Vienna. Its still more ominous portent, from Metternich's point of view, lay in the emergence of an international public opinion endorsing the national and constitutional goals of the Greek rebels. Liberals and nationalists from Hungary to Belgium and from Poland through the Germanies to France took heart at this triumph of their chosen heroes over an avowed autocracy. By his own lights, Metternich was quite justified in looking upon the Greek revolt as a threat not just to the Turks but to his own domestic and international system as well. At this point, however, we begin to encroach upon the subject matter of the chapter to follow.

The European Powers in 1830

Before turning from the story of international relations to that of domestic politics within individual states, we should perhaps ask to what extent, and in what respects, the European state system of 1830 had come to differ from that of 1780. For, as always in the study of history, mere narrative might obscure important elements of both continuity and change, unless we essay one final look across the half-century with which this volume deals.

Up to a point, it is fair to say that the last fifteen years of that half-century witnessed a genuine restoration of earlier relationships. The pattern of roles in the 1820s was more akin to that of the 1780s than to the sprawling chaos of the revolutionary-Napoleonic era. England, for example, had resumed a posture of aloofness from any coalition on the Continent, though it was by no means so dangerously isolated as it had been at the end of Lord North's ministry. Russia, however assertive it remained with respect to the Balkans, had largely abandoned Alexander I's bid for influence in western and central Europe. Austria, under Metternich as under Emperor Joseph II before him, wielded great influence in many areas but was ineffectual in the south-east. Prussia was again the junior partner in the German dualism, not the standard bearer of reform and national revival it had seemed at the end of Napoleon's reign. The situation of France under Louis XVIII and Charles X was similarly reminiscent of the 1780s, when the monarchy's desire to influence the course of foreign affairs had far exceeded its actual ability to do so. Even the fact that there were still five great powers—the same five—may strike us as proof that the old order had survived the tempest intact.

Nevertheless, in at least two respects, Europe's state system was far different at the end of our period than it had been at the beginning. One change was geographical, and perfectly visible: there were many fewer political entities showing on the map. During these decades the consolidation of large and medium-sized states, already in progress for several centuries, had taken another giant step forward. The kingdom of Sweden and the kingdom of the Netherlands constituted the largest indigenous political entities yet to appear in Scandinavia and the Low Countries, respectively. Spain and Portugal appeared unchanged on a solid-colour map; but France and Prussia had been allowed to absorb a number of small principalities, free cities and ecclesiastical holdings, while Austria's sway had been extended around the northern and eastern shores of the Adriatic Sea. In Italy, the former republic of Genoa had at last fallen to the House of Savoy's Sardinian kingdom. Even Switzerland had been increased by its incorporation of Geneva.

To be sure, certain minuscule states survived, entitled to manage at least their own internal affairs: Andorra in the Pyrenees, for example, and Monaco on the Mediterranean Riviera. The fully sovereign republic of San Marino existed in the heart of the Italian Papal States. In general, however, the progress of consolidation during the half-century ending in 1830 had been impressive. This was true even of divided Germany. Four free cities and such tiny principalities as Anhalt, the two Lippes and the Landgraviate of Hesse-Homburg still figured among the thirty-nine members of the Confederation as it emerged from the Congress of Vienna. But aside from Austria and Prussia, the new German political scheme gave special prominence to four other kingdoms (Bavaria, Württemberg, Saxony, Hanover) and a number of sizeable grand duchies (Baden, Hesse-Darmstadt, Hesse-Cassel, Oldenburg, Holstein, Mecklenburg-Schwerin). Thus, a dozen states controlled about 90 per cent of the Confederation's total area.

Elsewhere, the picture was more confusing and the drift of developments less easy to characterize. In the case of Poland, for example, the kingdom erected in 1815—Congress Poland—gave the illusion that the work of the late eighteenth-century partitions had been at least partially undone. To a realistic observer, however, the appearance of this Russian puppet, with the tsar as its king, could not hide the fact that one of the larger European nations of 1780 was no more. On the other hand, the birth of an independent Greece at the very end of our period constituted an extremely significant change in the map, one pregnant with meaning for the future of the crumbling Ottoman Empire.

If the reduction in the number of states was one critical change separating the European scene as we now leave it from that with which we began, a second was the altered conception of states themselves, as diplomatic protagonists. Earlier, as we saw in Chapter IV, what a sovereign power essentially *was*, in relation to other powers, had been little more than its monarch or chief magistrate, its restricted aristocracy and its entrenched bureaucracy, military as well as civil. The French Revolution, both in its spread and in the conditions which resistance to it called into being, had banished that older, simpler situation beyond recall. Henceforth, as was briefly suggested at the beginning of this chapter, not merely *states* but also *nations* would have to be taken into account.

Needless to say, the reality of the 'people's voice' differed radically as between Russia, for example, and Great Britain or France. Even in the latter kingdoms, public opinion on foreign affairs was still no more than a slowly emerging and only grudgingly recognized force. Nevertheless, almost everywhere in Europe, the age of the Restoration was filled with that peculiar tension which is produced when deeply entrenched habits of thought and action are in conflict with permanently altered circumstances. The tendency of diplomats trained in the old school to behave as though the revolutionary-Napoleonic drama had been an isolated episode, an aberration, ran squarely into the sentiments of other men for whom it had been an unforgettable experience. How could anyone who recalled the *levée en masse* in France, the rising of the Spanish *pueblo* against Bonaparte, the ferment of the War of Liberation in Germany ever again accept cold dynastic calculation as the sole determinant of foreign policy? By traditional standards, Metternich, Castlereagh and Talleyrand were unquestionably masters of diplomacy; but it was Canning, with his histrionic gifts, his awareness of popular emotions and his solicitude for the interests of not at all aristocratic merchants, who most clearly represented the dawn of a new age.

XII

Restoration Politics

The title of this chapter, if narrowly construed, would be misleading. For the domestic affairs of European states between 1815 and 1830 were much too complex to fit any simple notion of 'a world restored'. Nevertheless, behind virtually every post-1815 political debate lay memories of the revolutionary-Napoleonic experience and the conflicting lessons different men believed it had to teach, depending on whether they saw it as a sickness, now happily cured, or as a season

BIBLIOGRAPHY. Politics cannot, obviously, be well studied in narrowly political terms. Economic analyses to be singled out include D. S. Landes, 'Technological change and industrial development in western Europe, 1750–1914', Chapter 5 of vol. VI, *Cambridge Economic History of Europe* (rev. edn., Cambridge, 1965); W. O. Henderson, *The Industrial Revolution on the Continent* (London, 1961), together with the *The Zollverein*, by the same author (2nd edn., London, 1959), and his *Britain and Industrial Europe, 1750–1870* (Liverpool, 1954); J. H. Clapham, *The Economic Development of France and Germany, 1815–1914* (4th edn., Cambridge, 1955); and H. R. C. Wright, *Free Trade and Protection in the Netherlands, 1816–1830* (Cambridge, 1955). For the religious background, one can consult J. N. Moody *et al.*, *Church and Society: Catholic Social and Political Thought and Movement, 1789–1950* (New York, 1953), and K. S. Latourette, *Christianity in a Revolutionary Age* (New York, 1958–59), vols. I–II. Of the individual countries, Great Britain has attracted an especially large number of important treatments of political developments *per se*. Even the most select list of these monographs must include E. Halévy, *England in 1815*, and its sequel, *The Liberal Awakening 1815–30* (both rev. edns., London, 1949); K. G. Feiling, *The Second Tory Party, 1714–1832* (London, 1938); A. S. Turberville, *The House of Lords in the Age of Reform* (London, 1958); and D. Read, *Peterloo: The Massacre and Its Background* (Manchester, 1958). An excellent supplement to the above is J. A. Reynolds, *The Catholic Emancipation Crisis in Ireland, 1823–1829* (New Haven, 1954). Concerning France, the classic work is now G. de Bertier de Sauvigny, *La Restauration* (Paris, 1955), though F. B. Artz, *France under the Bourbon Restoration* (Cambridge, Mass., 1931) retains its value. The crucial Belgian situation is perhaps best approached by turning first to H. Pirenne, *Histoire de Belgique*, vol. III (new edn., Brussels, 1950), then to C. Bronne, *L'Amalgame: La Belgique de 1814 à 1830* (Brussels, of hope, now temporarily frustrated. The drama so recently ended obviously did not offer answers to all new questions, but it had left behind a set of powerful associations and sentiments which were bound to affect the way in which such questions were posed.

Take the matter of language itself. It is useless to argue that a fact is the same fact regardless of the words used to express it, or that a human event has the same historical meaning whatever its participants are called at the time or however their motives are labelled. The truth is that terminology has power in its own right. In presentday politics, for example, it makes a very great difference to all concerned whether a given proposal is identified as liberal, progressive, socialistic or 'Red'. Still greater is the impact of such terms as 'Bolshevik', 'Fascist', 'neo-Nazi'. The period which concerns us echoed to many comparable epithets.

At the head of the list unquestionably stood 'Jacobin'. There remained, to be sure, some avowed Jacobins in Europe after 1794, and even after 1815, but far fewer than the lavish use of the name would suggest. As early as 1801, it will be recalled, George III rather mysteriously concluded that Catholic Emancipation was 'Jacobinical'— and rejected it in horror. Time after time, men who favoured even the most limited constitutional or social reforms were singled out by their opponents as Jacobins, by implication nostalgic for the Terror and eager

---

1948), and H. Haag, *Les origines du catholicisme libéral en Belgique, 1789–1839* (Louvain, 1950). The best synthesis dealing with Germany is F. Schnabel, *Deutsche Geschichte im neunzehnten Jahrhundert*, vol. II: *Monarchie und Volkssouveränität* (Freiburg, 1949), but an important addition is W. M. Simon, *The Failure of the Prussian Reform Movement* (Ithaca, 1955). On Austria, see A. J. P. Taylor, *The Habsburg Monarchy, 1809–1918* (London, 1948). A recent collection of contemporary readings, *Metternich's Europe 1813–1848*, Mack Walker, ed. (New York-London, 1968), contains a number of interesting selections bearing not only on Austria but on the other major powers as well. Southern Europe may be studied with the help of R. Gambra Ciudad, *La primera guerra civil de España, 1821–23* (Madrid, 1950); G. T. Romani, *The Neapolitan Revolution of 1820–21* (Evanston, 1950); M. Petrocchi, *La restaurazione romana, 1815–1823* (Florence, 1943); and several portions of C. and B. Jelavich, eds., *The Balkans in Transition* (Berkeley, 1963). Much more than just Poland's eventual uprising is examined in R. F. Leslie, *Polish Politics and the Revolution of November 1830* (London, 1956). Of the many studies devoted to Russian affairs, M. Zetlin, *The Decembrists*, trans. G. Panin (New York, 1958), has not entirely superseded A. G. Mazour, *The First Russian Revolution, 1825* (Berkeley, 1937), while a welcome biography is M. Raeff, *Michael Speransky: Statesman of Imperial Russia* (The Hague, 1957).

to erect new guillotines. On the other hand, the mildest conservative could become in hostile eyes a selfish reactionary, an 'aristocrat' in the usage of 1789. Other evocative words and phrases—Old Boney, *Dos Mayo*, The German Rhine, Rights of Man, Throne and Altar—inflamed emotions without in most cases doing much to clarify thought.

Another legacy of the recent past lay in several social groups that had counted for little in political life before 1789, but subsequently had come into prominence. Journalists were one such element. Despite elaborate efforts at governmental censorship, the Fourth Estate had arrived to stay. University students too, especially active in Germany prior to 1815, would henceforth be found at the barricades when rebellion flared almost anywhere on the Continent. The very mention of barricades reminds us that the urban crowd itself, that mixture of shopkeepers, workers, drifters and idealistic men of some wealth and education so characteristic of Paris during the Revolution, would from time to time throughout the ensuing decades take to the streets of many another European city.

Perhaps the most significant new political element, however, was 'the military'. Most army officers of the Old Régime had been either professionals, largely indifferent to high policy, or courtiers playing soldier. For better or for worse, Napoleon, his commanders and the commanders who fought against him had given the military almost everywhere in Europe the combination of prestige and self-consciousness needed to make it a genuine force in civil affairs. It was a force at times progressive, at other times reactionary, but seldom quiescent. We shall observe the results in Spain, in Italy and in Russia, to mention only a few instances.

Still another characteristic carried over from the stormy age just ended was the role of radical societies, heirs of the French revolutionary clubs and of anti-Bonapartist fraternities (*Philadelphes* in France, the *Tugendbund* or 'League of Virtue' in Germany, etc.). These emerged briefly into full view in 1815, only to become secretive once more as various governments' security police (itself a notable feature of the period) forced all proscribed agitation underground. Freemasons in Poland, Switzerland, Austria and elsewhere, *Carbonari* and *Adelfi* in Italy, members of the student *Burschenschaften* in Germany, United Slavs and related groups in Russia, brethren of the *Philiké Hetaeraea* in Greece and the Greek exile communities, all represented expressions of defiance to established régimes.

In a man such as Filippo Michele Buonarroti (1761–1837) we encounter a striking embodiment of these societies, their methods and their inter-relationships. Born in Pisa of noble Tuscan parentage, educated as a lawyer and early attracted to Freemasonry, he was forced to leave Florence in 1789 after having written too enthusiastically about the French Revolution. By 1793 he was in Paris, an honorary French citizen, avowed Jacobin and admirer of Robespierre. Upon the latter's fall, Buonarroti continued to dabble in Dutch and Italian affairs, then joined actively in Babeuf's 'conspiracy of equals' against the Directory. Arrested when that plot collapsed, he was finally freed in 1806 and moved to Geneva, where he stayed for some fifteen years, attending meetings of both Freemasons and Jacobins while plotting with the *Philadelphes* in France to overthrow Napoleon.

After the emperor's fall, this tireless pamphleteer, letter-writer and organizer of rebellion continued his international struggle for egalitarian ideals, now directed against all 'restored tyrants'. No one else can have been in touch with so many conspiracies between 1815 and 1830. Buonarroti's writings were passed around the France of Charles X. He spent a good deal of time in Brussels during the 1820s, and disciples of his took leading parts in the eventual Belgian rising against Dutch rule. He quarrelled with Mazzini over the future shape of a free Italy, but agreed that a free Italy there must be. His own secret organization encouraged and advised dissidents all the way from Warsaw to Madrid. In truth, he deserved to be called, as a recent biographer has called him, 'the first professional revolutionist'.[1]

No single career should dominate our view of a period. Buonarroti's, however, is significant for what it reveals of the general situation; it would have been impossible for even the most tireless revolutionary to find ingredients of revolt in a pool of calm self-satisfaction. Clearly, Europe after 1815 was no such pool. Official repression struggled virtually without respite against a number of challenges to the *status quo*. Because the repressive side of the contest is so often emphasized at the expense of other factors, we should do well to look first at certain problems which either reflected or appeared to call for changes in the established order.

Economic Changes

Many of the disputes which concern us here were quite narrowly political, in that they turned on questions of national independence,

[1] E. L. Eisenstein, *The First Professional Revolutionist: Filippo Michele Buonarroti, 1761–1837* (Cambridge, Mass., 1959).

constitutional guarantees, voting rights, and so on. In the immediate background, however, were a number of other issues—economic, social, religious and administrative.

Perhaps the most obvious, though certainly not the most fundamental, economic concern after 1815 involved public finances. We know that by the end of the Napoleonic Wars both France and Great Britain were thought by many experts to be close to national bankruptcy. Such was the resiliency of the two economies that both escaped this fate, but they did so only after hard trials. The recovery of the French monarchy was particularly impressive. Under Louis XVIII, two ministers, Baron J.-D. Louis and Count Luigi Corvetto, so effectively overhauled the system of tax collection and official accounting that by 1818 the indemnity of 700 million francs had already been paid to the Allies, the principle of honouring the debts of the Empire firmly established and the credit of the Crown assured. Needless to say, this had not been achieved without bitter outcries from all the interests pinched by fiscal rigour and reform.

In England, the rapid abandonment of war taxes, in the initial euphoria of peace and victory, at first only sharpened the crisis confronting the earl of Liverpool's government. The British national budget for 1815, more than £83 million,[1] had been the largest ever known in any country. Now, with drastically reduced income, and at least momentarily reduced foreign trade, the greatest money power of the age seemed threatened with collapse. Once again, however, the resources and resourcefulness which had made possible the long resistance to Napoleon combined with some good luck to avert disaster. Exports both to the Continent and to the wider world began to climb once more, and industry joined commerce in the revival of Great Britain's prosperity. It would be wrong to envisage that revival as immediate. By the early 1820s, however, the most acute fears of public bankruptcy had been dispelled. Even the speculation in Latin America, resulting in the new crisis of 1825, only shook the Bank of England, it did not topple it.

Other states gripped by fiscal troubles could show little to compare with the French and British recoveries. The Prussia of King Frederick William III in 1815 had an unprecedented public debt of 217 million *Thalers*. Administrative reforms and grim economy could do no more than stabilize a parlous situation. To correct it, a major increase in the kingdom's productivity would be required, and that still lay several decades in the future. In Russia, the tsar could maintain a court, with

[1] E. Halévy, *England in 1815*, p. 381 (*see* Bibliography, p. 285).

the income of his own immense properties, and an army, through conscription and requisitioning. However, the plundering of treasury and people alike by provincial governors, who pocketed a huge share of the farmed-out *vodka* revenues, for example, scarcely permits us to speak of national finances. Austria at long last founded a national bank in 1816; but Metternich characteristically refused to offend the privileged aristocracy by reforming the tax system, preferring instead to borrow large sums from private bankers, notably the brothers Rothschild.

The various Italian states, with the partial exception of Sardinia-Savoy, generally seemed oblivious to standards of financial responsibility. They maintained their theoretical solvency only by borrowing and by the use of police power. The kingdom of the Netherlands, its combined deficit more than doubled in 1815 by the Waterloo campaign alone, cast about desperately for income, settled on a combination of taxes on grain and meat—and as a result, made its Belgian subjects more embittered than ever. King Ferdinand's war-ravaged Spain was running an annual deficit of £5 million in December 1816, when Don Martin de Garay was named secretary of the treasury. Garay made a valiant effort at reform. He consolidated personal taxes into a single levy, negotiated increased fiscal support for the clergy and from town merchants, and drafted plans to reduce the national debt over a period of years; but his projects made so many enemies that in 1818 he was forced to resign, and the Spanish treasury sank back into day-to-day juggling of its books.

Régimes with such unstable finances might well have pondered the role which the threat of national bankruptcy had played in the French crisis of the 1780s. On the other hand, as noted earlier, each state had its police mechanism for use against critics. Problems of public finance *alone*, it should also be noted, are unlikely to bring down a régime unless accompanied by misfortunes in war or more immediate, tangible kinds of popular grievance. Food, clothing, shelter—these are the wants that can become politically decisive. But why should such wants have been felt after 1815, during years of peace, by a basically rich continent then experiencing increases in both its agricultural and its industrial productivity?

One very important part of the answer lies in the continuation, indeed the acceleration, of population growth. That growth, from about 140 million in 1750 to 187 million in 1800, was to go surging on towards an estimated total for all Europe (including Russia west of the Urals) of some 266 million by 1850.[1] Great Britain's roughly 12·4 million inhabitants as of 1810 had risen to 14·3 million by 1820 and ten years later, at the end of our period, stood at 16·5 million. Ireland by that time (1830) contained 7·8 million souls, almost three times its population of just sixty years earlier. Between 1800 and about 1850, the tsar's subjects in European Russia increased from 37·5 million to almost 62 million, while Italy's growth in the same years was from 18 million to 23 million and the German Confederation's, 23·5 million to 34·5 million. France was rather more stable in its numbers, going from something over 27·3 million in 1801 (for the area of 1831) to about 31·9 million by the latter date. The population of Paris, however, doubled in size during the first half of the century, passing the million mark before 1850.

This last statistic deserves to be stressed. Taking Europe as a whole, in the early nineteenth century the rise in population continued to be greater in rural than in urban areas. The dramatic growth of the French capital, however, serves to highlight a portentous development, the rush to particular cities: to Brussels (70,000 in 1815, 251,000 in 1850), to Milan (170,000 in 1800, 242,000 in 1850), to Vienna (247,000 in 1800, 444,000 in 1850), to Berlin (172,000 in 1800, 419,000 in 1850). And it was the 1820s which witnessed an especially sharp jump in urban population figures. During that decade alone, the six largest cities of the English midlands grew in the aggregate by over 40 per cent. The misery of overcrowded cities had particularly ominous implications for political life.

Though several explanations have been advanced to account for this general upsurge in Europe's numbers, some of them will scarcely bear close analysis. It cannot any longer be seriously argued, for example, that the death rate declined sufficiently to provide the answer, especially in view of the persistence of appallingly high infant mortality. Epidemic disease had receded somewhat since the early eighteenth century; but smallpox, typhoid and, periodically, cholera still inflicted heavy losses of life. Sanitation and preventive medicine had not yet begun the remarkable progress they would make in the later 1800s. A recent essay directs attention to two factors which seem more significant in the causal pattern: (1) a substantial decline in the average age of marriage during the late eighteenth and early nineteenth centuries, while the rate of illegitimate births still remained very high, and (2) the rapid spread of the humble potato, nourishing, easily grown on small plots and

[1] Population figures are from Köllmann, *Raum und Bevölkerung*, pp. 143 ff. (*see* Bibliography, p. 20).

admirably resistant to either drought or frost.[1] So far as political effects are concerned, this change in the diet of needy Europeans and its contribution to population growth present us with a notable case of historical irony. For the rise in number of living persons, especially in cities, only heightened the incipient panic which greeted any threat to the food supply, be it a bad harvest or artificial restraints on edible imports.

Among the most unsettling factors must also be included the effects of early industrialism: the swift making and losing of private fortunes, the *relative* decline of small manufacturing in towns, the gradual reduction of the 'putting out' system in village and farm, and the inevitable resistance to the new machines on the part of craftsmen still tied to older ways. Included too were bewildering shifts in supply and demand, as one innovation after another brought sudden increases in this or that category of saleable goods, accompanied by equally sudden shortages of currently needed raw materials. Included, above all, was the imperious presence of the factory. Here was a new entity, social as well as economic, in which workers of narrowly limited skills serviced the tireless machine, a despot which demanded constant attention yet was capable, if superseded by a better machine elsewhere, of suddenly abandoning its own servants to idleness and destitution.

England, as we have seen, had already shown the way in factory growth before the French Revolution. By the mid-1700s, certain British manufactures, cotton in particular, were already displaying that combination of reliance on machinery, concentration of labour under supervision and rational planning with respect to both the raw material and the finished goods markets which we associate with modern industrialism. The special role played by cotton is not hard to explain. It was, and is, a tough, uniform fibre, admirably suited to mechanical processing and infinitely more plentiful, given the Indian and American sources of supply, than its elegant rival, linen. In addition, the cotton industry was comparatively young and hence could expand without having to overcome all the traditional restrictions still hedging the older crafts. Finally, cotton answered the immense demand of a new market in part created by its own low cost, a market for cool, comfortable summer garments and for underclothing, which most Europeans began to be able to afford only in the late eighteenth century. Where cottonmaking led—towards increased scale and concentration of production—other industries, such as wool, brewing, soapmaking and metal stamping and casting, rapidly followed.

[1] W. L. Langer, 'Europe's initial population explosion', *American Historical Review*, vol. LXIX (1963).

As for Great Britain's early lead in industrial development, it is not quite so simply accounted for. Many contributory explanations have been put forward, among them the long accumulation of manufacturing skills in an island kingdom untouched by land warfare and recurrently the haven for continental refugees; comparatively good roads and especially water transport; the unique merging of different forms of capital, making income from landed wealth far more readily available for business investment than it was across the channel; a well-developed banking and credit system; an active home market, swelled by a rising population which nevertheless felt reasonably safe in spending money on comforts and utensils; a still more active foreign market served by a large merchant marine and guarded by a powerful navy.[1] Doubtless all these and still other reasons must be borne in mind if we are to understand why, with respect to industry, Britain in 1815 was the tutor of Europe.

For the ensuing period, a few observations and statistics will show the growth of manufacturing and suggest its political significance, both in Great Britain and on the Continent. On the British side, for instance, whereas some 2,400 power looms had been weaving cotton in 1813, there were 14,150 in 1820 and no fewer than 55,500 in 1829, while the production of pig iron, only 258,206 long tons in 1806, by 1830 stood at 678,417.[2]

On the Continent, emulation of British techniques, the appearance of further inventions, the gradual improvement of transportation, the expansion of credit and governmental encouragement to meet a growing domestic market brought the first modest evidences of a new industrialism. French cotton production, to take an important example, climbed substantially, as the industry moved out of Paris to Lille in Flanders, Rouen in Normandy, Mulhouse in Alsace. In the last-named town there were 426 power looms in 1827, but 2,123 just four year later.[3] Prussia, whose Institute of Trades (*Gewerbe Institut*) was founded in 1821, also saw a rise in textile production. By 1831 an industrial census of the kingdom revealed 252,000 linen looms in operation, chiefly concentrated in Silesia, where putting out to private homes persisted.[4] During

---

[1] D. S. Landes in *Cambridge Economic History of Europe*, especially pp. 274–318 (*see* Bibliography, p. 285).

[2] *Ibid.*, pp. 316 and 325.

[3] *Ibid.*, p. 389.

[4] J. H. Clapham, *The Economic Development of France and Germany*, p. 92 (*see* Bibliography, p. 285).

the short lifetime of the United Netherlands, King William I offered generous subsidies, especially favourable to Belgian industry. He brought the English engineer, John Cockerill, to start the manufacturing of machinery at Seraing in 1817, sent Roentgen to Britain to study metallurgy in 1821, consulted Omalius d'Alloy on the latter's methods of blending metals, and pushed ahead with vast canal projects. What all this meant to Belgian cities is suggested by the fact that in 1830 Ghent alone was estimated to have eighty textile mills of various kinds, employing 30,000 men, women and children.[1]

Admittedly, most of the rest of Europe lagged behind the French-Prussian-Belgian pace. For the Continent as a whole, the period from 1815 to 1830, in fact, might best be thought of as one of education and 'tooling up'. Even for the relatively favoured areas just mentioned, with the exception of Belgium, the real spurt to overtake Great Britain still lay in the future, around mid-century. Nevertheless, the first decades after 1815 witnessed the emergence of the political problems, the clamour, the dislocations accompanying industrial growth and competition in their early, ill-understood stages.

Commerce too constituted an economic concern of immediate significance to public life. The kingdom of the Netherlands, for example, had a major stake in commercial activity, both the carrying trade long practised by its Dutch subjects and the exportation of finished goods produced by its Belgian ones. For a time, the coal of Belgium, mined in quantities far exceeding the total French production, seemed likely to remain a major export; but the demands of the Belgian iron industry itself rose so rapidly that by 1830 the country was actually beginning to import coal from Great Britain. Note, however, that the European coal trade, whichever way it was moving—including the route from west German mines to French blast furnaces—was a critical factor in national economic growth.

Throughout our period, European states kept their tariff barriers high, with one great exception. That exception was the United Kingdom, which in the mid-1820s began to move towards freer trade in most manufactures (*see below*, pp. 317–18), because its lead in industrial development made it an aggressive exporter. When it came to the protection of agricultural interests, however, England's own policy was at least as exclusive as those of most continental countries. British landowners, encouraged to extend their plantings of grain during the long Napoleonic siege, faced a drastic fall in prices when peace came. To save them (and

[1] H. Pirenne, *Histoire de Belgique*, vol. III, p. 469 (*see* Bibliography, p. 285).

ostensibly to maintain food production against future war needs), the government adopted the Corn Law of 1815, prohibiting all imports of foreign grains unless a domestic shortage pushed the price in Britain above 80 shillings a quarter, i.e., eight bushels. Basically Great Britain remained protectionist with respect to foodstuffs, to the chagrin of both the earners and the payers of industrial wages. Despite mounting agitation, repeal of the Corn Law and its successors would not come until 1846.

An example of other countries' trade policies reveals France in 1822 pushing its duty on British iron (50 per cent *ad valorem* in 1814) to an unprecedented 120 per cent, and the French tariff of 1826 set new records for customs charges on textiles. As for grain, the Bourbon monarchy had as late as 1817 been compelled to import needed wheat and rye; but the growing spectre of Russian competition led French producers to insist on the high protective barriers finally enacted amid bitter debate in 1819. Elsewhere on the Continent, in the Netherlands, in the German, Italian and Scandinavian states, in Spain and Portugal, public policy followed this French model so closely as to require no special comment.

A separate issue arose in Prussia. For while its external duties remained high, the Hohenzollern kingdom embarked soon after the liberation on a sweeping consolidation of its own internal market, and then began negotiations designed to expand the newly created free trade area. Frederick William III's tariff decree of 1818 simply abolished all customs barriers dividing the provinces and other historic subdivisions of his realm. The following year, tiny Schwarzburg-Sondershausen in Thuringia signed a treaty which brought it into the Prussian tariff system. Thus was born the famous customs union (*Zollverein*), which by 1834 would include the bulk of non-Austrian Germany and a generation after that would play its part in Bismarck's fashioning of a German Empire ruled from Berlin. In 1819, however, a contemporary could scarcely have been expected to perceive any deep economic or political significance in the adherence of Schwarzburg-Sondershausen, whose population was 45,000!

Religion

Turning from the economic to the religious background of public events, we at once see evidence that Catholicism was recovering from the losses and humiliations of the revolutionary-Napoleonic crisis. Indeed, this recovery reversed even some features of the pre-1789 situation. In 1814 the Society of Jesus, outlawed in 1773 by the Vatican because of pressure from numerous secular rulers, was reinstated by Pius VII. The Jesuits thus resumed in the open their mission of education and conversion. As we shall see in the next chapter, Catholic thinkers as diverse as the Savoyard de Maistre, the Frenchmen Bonald and Chateaubriand, the German Gentz and the Swiss Haller (the last two converts from Protestantism) led the intellectual counterattack against the heritage of the 'Godless Revolution'. At the same time, there was a visible increase in church attendance and sacramental observance, not uncommon in the aftermath of great secular convulsions.

It was doubtless inevitable, under the circumstances, that both the Holy See, under Pius VII and his successor, Leo XII (1823–9), and the prelates in wholly or partially Catholic countries should speak on various subjects with a new confidence. This restored tone of authority, in turn, produced its own reaction from the side of more liberal Catholic leaders, for the most part younger laymen. Both in Belgium and in France, we shall encounter 'modern Catholics' denouncing the hierarchy's support of political reactionaries, support which these critics believed would alienate the Church from the mass of its own followers. In Italy too, their counterparts pleaded with ecclesiastical leaders to repudiate local tyrants.

At the same time, clashes between Catholics and non-Catholics went on embittering European politics. In Ireland religious hatreds had grown worse since the Act of Union in 1800. And England itself after 1815 saw the mounting demand of Catholics for full legal equality join that of Protestants outside the Church of England for repeal of the hoary Test Act (see below, pp. 317–18). Needless to say, the hostility and fear separating Dutch Calvinists from Belgian Catholics contributed nothing to the unity of the 'United' Netherlands. As for France, the Huguenots as well as the Jews seemed more secure and less resentful than under the Old Régime, especially in view of Louis XVIII's confirmation of freedom of worship in his 1814 Charter. Even here, however, the murder of numerous Protestants by royalist mobs during the White Terror of 1815 was a reminder, mercifully brief, that old wounds could still bleed. Despite the small size of its Protestant minority, Italy offered an interesting and significant extension of religion into politics. Resentful of the Catholic hierarchy's political role, exposed to the legacy of the Reformation while exiles in Great Britain or Switzerland, many of the future leaders of the Italian national rising, the men of the *Risorgimento*, embraced Protestantism under the Restoration.[1]

Europe's Protestants had issues of their own to divide them. The seemingly abrupt, though in fact long-matured, decision of Frederick William III of Prussia in 1817 to decree the union of his Lutheran and Reformed (Calvinist) subjects, was promptly denounced by numerous 'Old Lutherans', some of whom eventually emigrated. The mere fact that most Prussian Calvinists and 'modern' Lutherans accepted the Church of the New Prussian Union only increased Old Lutheran suspicions. Similar unions were carried out in several other German states, notably Hesse-Cassel, Nassau and Baden, with broader popular support; but everywhere civil and ecclesiastical authorities were obliged to make allowances for continuing variety among liturgies and forms of parish organization.

Disagreement among Protestants over questions of public policy was also clearly in evidence. In Germany, it is true, the most significant development, an espousal of deep social conservatism by Lutheran leaders, was not to appear until the middle years of the century; but even before 1830 the lack of religious progressivism was apparent in the home of the Reformation. Far different was the case of England, where the Dissenters' political demands on their own behalf merged with their humanitarian attacks on slavery and on the Anglican divines' alleged lack of social conscience. It is not easy to identify the specifically religious content of such reformist zeal, as distinguished from the politics of middle-class Englishmen in general, but it is nonetheless important to note that the Dissenters, 'Evangelicals' as well as Methodists, continued to clothe their statements in the sonorous language of faith.

Almost everywhere in Europe, as a matter of fact, religious conflict entered and influenced public life. In Russian-occupied Poland, the Catholicism of the people clashed with the rulers' Eastern Orthodox beliefs. In Russia itself the westernizing quasi-Protestant views of Alexander I and advisers such as Golitsin and Kiselev drove conservative religious leaders into a mounting frenzy. In the Balkans, where Christian subjects could expect nothing better than contemptuous toleration from their Turkish sovereign (himself beset by Muslim fanatics), the Greek Orthodox clergy distinguished itself by its vociferous hatred of all other faiths.

[1] G. Spini, *Risorgimento e protestanti* (Naples, 1956).

Conservative Administrative Reforms

Let us pass to one more sign of the times, having little to do with questions of piety. This was administrative reorganization, imposed from above. Between 1815 and 1830 the reforms decreed by established régimes seldom if ever carried the sweeping, potentially revolutionary implications of Napoleon's or Stein's. Instead, they were selective, limited and explicitly conservative efforts to shore up the structure of authority, with a minimum of threat to existing privileges. Yet despite their authors' motives, these administrative changes inevitably trod on various toes, excited complaints and thus exacerbated the resentment expressed over larger questions of the day. The legacy of the Revolution, like the defensive reflexes it had called forth, continued to agitate a system barely re-established on shaken foundations.

Some of these technical reforms have already been mentioned in other connections—the tightening of French treasury procedures by Louis and Corvetto, for example, and Garay's revision of Spanish taxes, as well as the new Prussian tariff system of 1818. In the polyglot Austrian Empire Francis I rejected Metternich's proposal of 1817 to clarify the governmental structure by setting up a supreme chancellor, with subordinate chancelleries for Austria, Hungary, Bohemia, Transylvania, Illyria-Dalmatia and the Habsburg holdings in Italy. Even in Vienna, however, the establishment at long last of a Ministry of Finance in 1816 showed that the impulse to match French administrative innovations of the preceding period had not wholly spent itself.

The relative importance of this phenomenon, of course, varied widely from country to country. In England, specifically administrative reform played only a minor part in these turbulent years. By 1815 there was no doubt that the cabinet was an entity to which only the occupants of key offices belonged, but the period which concerns us ended without the emergence either of a clearly defined principle of solidarity around the prime minister or of ministerial responsibility to the House of Commons. Treasury practice, like Admiralty and War Office procedures, remained essentially as the younger Pitt had left them. When Englishmen argued over reform, as we shall see, they meant something quite different.

At the other extreme was Russia, where *only* administrative projects constituted any meaningful expression of reformist thinking. One project, the military colonies which by 1816 comprised 750,000 people, was finally suppressed by the tsar in 1831, but not before it had stirred up deep resentment and lent fuel to the smouldering resistance. Alexander's minister, Arakchev, had insisted that this elaborately organized system would produce a stronger army and at the same time bring better food, housing and medical care to masses of Russian subjects. To most of the peasant-soldiers, however, such benefits were not worth the increased work and discipline.[1] On the other hand, in 1822 the governmental and economic reforms enacted in Siberia by Speransky effectively replaced archaic modes of local administration and opened a new land of economic promise.

A final example takes us once more to the newly created kingdom of the Netherlands. There all efforts at administrative rationalization automatically became political questions. This was so because such efforts were aimed, among other things, at furthering the 'amalgamation' of Dutchmen and Belgians. In appearance, William I's reign opened with a return to old forms. The Napoleonic *départements* were named provinces once more, and prefects gave way to restored governors. In fact, neither the areas nor the offices were basically changed. The French model was repudiated in words, but it was retained in practice. Similarly, the metric system of weights and measures was carried over from the Empire, though the *names* of units were changed to Dutch. The important point is that the king alone decreed all these provisions for his mixed kingdom. Dutchmen who cherished local autonomy thus had cause to grumble, as did Belgians who recalled their struggles with another energetic monarch, Emperor Joseph II.

Patterns of Restoration Politics: Central and Northern Europe

Yet despite the importance of economic and social issues—public finances, demographic shifts, industrial concentration, trade incentives or restraints—of religious tensions, of administrative changes, our attention should not be too long diverted from the explicitly political debates of the restoration years. For politics could not then, and cannot now, be dismissed as mere window-dressing for other interests. Political *parties*, as distinct from homogeneous sects, cliques or court factions, were no longer strange or new. We saw them at work in the French revolutionary assemblies and in many countries divided over the question of how to react to the Revolution. Even earlier, during the 1780s in Holland, Poland and elsewhere, we identified groupings of men

[1] R. E. Pipes, 'The Russian military colonies, 1810–1831', *Journal of Modern History*, vol. XXII (1950).

of diverse socio-economic backgrounds who nevertheless shared certain opinions regarding the conduct of government. Finally, for anxious Europeans after 1815, the history of English parliamentary struggles combined with the arresting example of the American Revolution to suggest lines of argument and forms of action.

For many of these men, the burning question was how to make the *nation* a focus for men's highest loyalty, in pursuit of both domestic peace and external power. For others, the central issues involved the legal rights of individuals, rights to be defined and protected by written *constitutions*. For still others, battle was joined over the participation of more citizens in public affairs, especially through the extension of freedom of expression and of *voting* rights. Before the end of our period, be it added, social and economic discontent was beginning to produce what we can identify as *socialistic* demands for greater sharing of wealth and comforts. For the time being, however, the political stage resounded primarily to the claims of nationalism, constitutionalism and democratic reformism, sometimes in conflict among themselves, but more often merging into a broad attack upon traditional forms.

Allowance made for national variations in tone and timing, one may sketch a general pattern of domestic politics within European states during the first years following Napoleon's defeat. At the outset, on all sides were heard optimistic calls for reform, some of them carried over directly from the resistance to Bonaparte, others born of the conditions of the Restoration itself. Conservative régimes, by contrast, braced themselves to defend the old order, using military resources assembled during years of war. Few rulers or ministers were prepared to attack the problems which spawned unrest. Instead, state power was typically applied to the task of repression, of crushing the opposition, in short, of attacking symptoms rather than causes.

To understand this swing towards repression we must look briefly at the motives and the forms of reaction, as well as the forces against which it was directed, state by state. In the Austrian Empire, for example, patriotism itself, at least the newer, French variety of patriotism, seemed a patent threat to the established order. It is worth remarking that not even Prince Metternich paid such close, continuous and apprehensive attention to that threat as did Emperor Francis I himself, who gave as his motto: 'Rule, and change nothing'. For who could have felt more acutely than a Habsburg, heir to a dynastic complex of various nationalities, the disruptive force of the hunger for national self-determination? His response was to play off Germans against Hungarians, both against

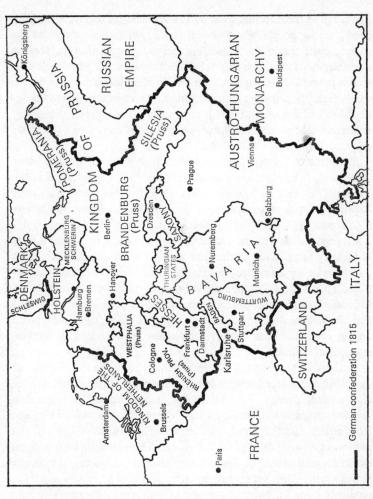

7. *The German Confedera-
tion in 1815*

Slavs, and all three against Italians. The stationing of regiments far from home, among people whose speech and customs were foreign to the troops, made it feasible to use Austrian army units to crush popular demonstrations of a type they might actually have joined in their own native provinces. At the same time other doctrines than nationalism were anathema to the government. Austria's secret police hunted down liberal constitutionalists, tax objectors, violators of religious censorship and many others just as diligently as it did spokesmen for the subject peoples.

Metternich's personal influence was most apparent in that other Austrian-led complex: the German Confederation. It is true that the Federal Diet met in Frankfurt, not in Vienna. However, the chief Austrian delegate was president of the assembly *ex officio*, and Metternich regularly got his way by dint of parliamentary manoeuvres, diplomatic negotiations with individual German states and occasional threats of military force. Weak as the Diet was, it proved useful in providing an umbrella for concerted, 'legitimate' resistance to demands for reform. That it did so, despite the survival of quite considerable constitutional groups in the governments of several principalities—Bavaria and Württemberg among them—was evidence of the fear which spread among even moderate conservatives when confronted with demonstrations of violence.

In October 1817, at the Wartburg, the Thuringian castle that had once sheltered Luther, several hundred members of liberal and nationalist student groups (*Burschenschaften*) assembled to hear speeches and sing songs. Ostensibly called to celebrate the tercentenary of the Reformation and the fourth anniversary of the battle of Leipzig, the rally was primarily devoted to demands for German unification under a national constitution. In the evening, after the customary torchlight parade, many *Burschen* stayed together, built a large bonfire and proceeded to burn a number of symbols of authority: a corporal's cane, a pigtailed military wig, a cavalryman's leather corset and some slips of paper bearing the titles of books by accused reactionaries.

This adolescent display, disquieting though it was to solemn folk, would scarcely have warranted sweeping countermeasures, had it not been followed by a shocking crime, emotionally if not logically related to the Wartburg Festival. On 23 March 1819 the poet and pamphleteer, August von Kotzebue, who was known to have been a paid agent of the tsar and whose works had been among those symbolically burned by the Wartburg demonstrators, was stabbed to death in his home at

Mannheim. The assassin was Karl Ludwig Sand, a theology student from the University of Jena and a disciple of the fanatical nationalist, Karl Follen. Sand was beheaded for his crime, but its repercussions continued to influence German politics for years.

To exert pressure on the Federal Diet, Prince Metternich first met with the king of Prussia at Teplitz in July 1819. A month later, at another Bohemian town, Carlsbad, he assembled the chief ministers of the nine largest German states. In addition to creating a federal commission to investigate seditious agitation all over Germany, this group presented the Diet with a series of laws which the deputies in Frankfurt meekly passed that September. The new legislation, commonly referred to as the Carlsbad Decrees, outlawed both the *Burschenschaften* and *Turnvater* Jahn's gymnastic clubs for patriots, imposed a stringent press censorship and placed university faculties under close police surveillance. The official course of the German Confederation was set: demands for reform were not even to be countenanced, let alone satisfied—they were to be crushed as treason.

Prussia's role in all this was scarcely less important than Austria's. Ever since 1807 the eyes of German liberals had been turned hopefully to Berlin, where the ideals of Stein and of the Reform Era were assumed to have survived among many high officials. But Frederick William III, fearful and petulant, was no reforming monarch. The Kotzebue murder, following the Wartburg festival, confirmed his darkest suspicions. As a result, he warmly endorsed the Carlsbad Decrees. When the great army reformer, Boyen, and the University of Berlin's founder, Humboldt, tendered their resignations in protest, their offer was curtly accepted. Patriots such as Jahn were imprisoned. Others, including Arndt, were ousted from academic positions. Still others chose exile, which in the case of Görres meant asylum in once-hated France. Stein's colleague and successor as minister president (i.e., Prussian prime minister), K. A. von Hardenberg, though an administrative reformer, had never shared all of the reform movement's social impulses; but even his willingness to compromise in 1819 could not save him from the political eclipse in which he lived out the last three years of his life.

Other European governments adopted measures quite consistent with the Austrian-Prussian solution for Germany. In Denmark, the opposition—nationalists stunned by the loss of Norway, constitutionalists embittered by King Frederick VI's disregard for past promises, particularists in the border provinces of Schleswig and Holstein—could only bow before their stern ruler. Charles XIV, as Bernadotte became upon

ascending the Swedish-Norse throne in 1818, policed the separate
assemblies of estates for Sweden and Norway with barely veiled hostility. In the United Netherlands, William I's Dutch subjects found the
constitution of 1815 less liberal in its application that it had appeared on
paper and viewed the compromises with Belgian economic interests as
objectionable acts of a royal autocrat. Still more serious was the discontent of the Catholic Belgians, numerically under-represented in the
combined States General and resentful of the Dutch Calvinist officials
who administered the kingdom's affairs.

The Mediterranean Lands

In fairness to these northern monarchs, however, it must be said that
neither political resistance nor governmental harshness reached its
peak in the lands washed by the North Sea and the Baltic. Instead, for
the Restoration's bloodiest chapters we must look to the Latin kingdoms
in the south. Spain's re-established Ferdinand VII simply ignored his
former pledges of respect for the constitution drawn up by the national
assembly or *Cortes* at Cadiz in 1812. Resentment against his capricious
cruelty, against the selfish courtiers and churchmen around him, and
against the crown's inept response to the colonial revolts in America
finally burst forth in January 1820. The uprising began, appropriately,
at Cadiz, where two regiments of troops revolted under Colonel Rafael
Riego and proclaimed the constitution of 1812. Matched by other rebellions in northern and eastern Spain, the Cadiz movement quickly
swept Riego to power in Madrid, and on 9 March the king, a virtual
captive, swore an oath to the constitution.

The Spanish revolutionists, though split between the radical majority
(*Exaltados*) in the Cortes and the more conservative *Moderados*, clung to
power for over three years against the denunciations of aristocrats and
bishops alike. In April 1823, however, the French army of the Duc
d'Angoulême crossed the frontier to enforce the decisions of the Congress of Verona (*see above*, pp. 271–2). Assaulted thus by disciplined
foreign troops, the insurrectionary régime collapsed in a matter of
months, its last stronghold, the Trocadero fortress by the Bay of Cadiz,
surrendering on 31 August. Riego was publicly hanged and sections of
his dismembered body were displayed in various cities. Hundreds of his
supporters, though supposedly protected by Ferdinand's earlier promise
of amnesty, were tortured and killed by royal command. For the next
ten years Spain would live under a crowned sadist.

In Portugal, where the Spanish uprising evoked an inevitable response, revolt erupted in the summer of 1820. By 1822 King John VI felt compelled to accept the liberals' demands and return to Lisbon as a constitutional monarch, leaving his son Pedro behind in Brazil as the ruler of an autonomous kingdom. Within a year, John felt secure enough to reduce the constitution's liberal features, but that was not enough for the reactionaries at court. The latter, who made the ruler's second son, Miguel, their standard-bearer, continued to press for an end to all constitutional guarantees. When John died in 1826, Dom Miguel assumed real power, as regent for Queen Maria II, the daughter of Brazil's King Pedro. Two years later, Miguel was ready to cap his policy of suppressing all opposition by taking over full royal power. In May 1828 he declared Maria unfit to rule and formally abolished the constitution; and that summer, the young queen having fled to England, he proclaimed himself king of Portugal, in theory as absolute as Spain's Ferdinand was in fact.

Closely related to the Iberian troubles were those of splintered Italy. In the Two Sicilies another Bourbon, Ferdinand I, uncle of his Spanish namesake, also had to face a constitution of 1812, this one originally drafted on the island of Sicily with British help. Apart from the executioner, whom one of Ferdinand's ministers called 'the crown's first servant', the chief props to Neapolitan tyranny were a corrupt court, a bigoted higher clergy and masses of desperately poor, superstitious subjects. Its principal opponents were to be found in the liberal professions, the small, insecure middle class and certain groups of disgusted army men.

Next to the Two Sicilies, the Italian territory which suffered most from dishonesty and ignorance in government, despite the efforts of certain enlightened churchmen, was the Papal States. At Rome, amid the splendour of monuments to political and spiritual greatness, the reactionary Catholic party (*Zelanti*) proved capable of blocking every proposed reform, whether of education, justice or economic conditions. By comparison, the grand duchy of Tuscany, under its Habsburg archduke, Ferdinand III, seemed almost free and prosperous; but here too the swarms of secret police could never be forgotten. In the other grand duchies of the north, Modena, Lucca and Parma (the last ruled by Napoleon's former empress, Maria Louisa), autocracy and extortion were twin principles of government. Far richer, and somewhat better administered, was the Austrian conqueror's own Lombard-Venetian kingdom. There, education, communications and commerce all benefited from Habsburg rule. This remained, however, the rule of foreigners. Whereas Metternich's policies predominated in the Two Sicilies and the four grand duchies by virtue of family alliances and military dependence, in Milan and Venice Austrian control was direct.

At the northern extreme of Italy, in mountainous Piedmont and Savoy, the Sardinian monarchy of Victor Emmanuel I also deserved to be contrasted favourably with the Two Sicilies or the Papal States. Though traditionally suspicious of foreign ideas and fearful of change, the government at Turin could at least point to reasonable honesty in administration and to a tax load kept comparatively light through the help of commercial duties from the newly acquired seaport of Genoa. Nevertheless, as time would show, the fact that this regimented, lacklustre polity could be praised by a visitor from Naples or Rome did not mean that it was free from smouldering discontent.

Against this general Italian background, the events of 1820–1 assume their full significance. Early in July of the former year, the garrison at Nola, a few miles east of Naples, broke into open revolt. Specifically, the mutineers were protesting against Austrian influence in the Kingdom of the Two Sicilies, especially in its military affairs; but their demands extended to general reform as well. The leader of the spreading rebellion was General Guglielmo Pepe, a disaffected officer who succeeded for the time being in uniting army dissidents with the politically more doctrinaire *Carbonari*. The latter had early that summer begun to emerge from their secret clubrooms for sporadic demonstrations. Somewhat surprisingly, the oath which these insurgents extracted from their momentarily cowed King Ferdinand was not to the Sicilian constitution of 1812 but to *Spain's* hallowed charter of that same year.

As in the Spanish case so too in the Neapolitan, a determined revolt seemed at first to have triumphed with almost incredible ease. However, on the island of Sicily a further rebellion broke out, this one directed against the revolutionary government—in Sicilian eyes just another expression of the mainland's authority. Meanwhile, in January 1821, blandly stating that he wished to secure international approval for the new constitution, Ferdinand I went off to Laibach with a personal appeal for Metternich's aid. As we already know (*see above*, p. 271), the result of that conference was prompt intervention by Austrian troops, the military defeat of the rebels at Rieti on 7 March, and the restoration of a vengeful king, now relieved of all constitutional limitations. General Pepe made good his escape to England by way of

Spain, then still controlled by his fellow revolutionary, General Riego; but most of the other Neapolitan rebels were far less fortunate.

8. *Italy in 1815*

Revolutionary outbreaks flared briefly in the Papal States and in the grand duchies, but none was sufficiently widespread or coordinated to avoid being crushed at once by police action. Not so in Piedmont. There, a junta of army officers and professional men, joined by a few liberal nobles, revolted in March 1821. Undaunted by the depressing news already arriving from Naples, these insurgents demanded war

307

against hated Austria and a constitutional monarchy under their some-what embarrassed hero, Prince Charles Albert, nephew of the king. Victor Emmanuel, however, though he abdicated the throne and named Charles Albert as temporary regent, designated as the new mon-arch his own brother, Charles Felix, then residing in Modena. The young regent hesitantly declared for a constitution, but only pending the approval of Charles Felix. The latter repaid this deference, upon arriving in Turin, by exiling his nephew to Tuscany and immediately calling for Austrian military aid. On 8 April, 1821, at Novara on the route from Milan to Turin, the rebels were defeated by a combined royalist-Austrian force. With that decision the Piedmontese revolution, like so many others in Italian history, became one more lesson in frus-tration, concluded amid executions, imprisonments and sentences of exile.

The Balkans and Eastern Europe

In the two great eastern empires, the Russian and the Turkish, his-toric patterns of rule had suffered no such interruption as the power and the example of France had brought to the rest of Europe. Even the lands of the tsar and the sultan, however, had felt the repercussions of the revolutionary-Napoleonic upheaval and, in the years after peace returned, the stirrings of political unrest.

In 1815, for example, only two years after the first Serbian revolt, that of Kara George, had finally been stamped out by the Turks, a second rising occurred. This time the leader of the Serbs was Milosh Obrenovich, half patriot and half dynast. When Kara George returned from his Austrian refuge in 1817, he was assassinated by command of the jealous Obrenovich. By the end of that year, the Turks decided to recognize Milosh as prince of Serbia—in effect the area around Belgrade —and to leave him considerable independence in his role as vassal of the sultan. For the time being, the cruel vendetta between the houses of Obrenovich and Karageorgevich was forced into the background, to await its bloody renewal a few years later. Meanwhile, in his own inter-est, Prince Milosh imposed upon his fellow-countrymen an oppressive régime of 'order' which actually exceeded the harshness of direct Ottoman rule.

We have already traced the far more decisive course of the Greek rebellion in the 1820s (*see above*, pp. 277–82), because of its significance for diplomatic history in general. Other Balkan risings, such as that of

1821 in Wallachia, proved abortive. Montenegro, under Prince-Bishop Peter I, was a petty tyranny recognized as independent by the Turks since 1799. Bulgarians, on the other hand, had to await the second half of the nineteenth century for any loosening of the Ottoman grip. So had the Rumanians south of the Danube, while those in the principalities of Moldavia and Wallachia still obeyed their *hospodars*, the local rulers who owed allegiance to the sultan but in fact relied heavily on Russian protection. As for Albania, it was still an integral part of European Turkey.

Nevertheless, for the Turkish as for the Spanish monarchy, the crumbling of imperial power created serious problems at home. Sultan Mahmud II (1808–39), seeking to rebuild the power of his dynasty over the Balkans and the Middle East, found two of the worst obstacles to his effort in Istanbul itself. One was a reactionary Muslim sect of dervishes, the *Bektashi*, who joined large landowners in opposing every project for administrative reform as being foreign-inspired, i.e., 'un-Turkish'. The other was the proud military corps of Janissaries, once crack troops recruited in the Balkans and granted sweeping privileges, but now a corrupt order which would neither fight for the sultan against his enemies nor countenance any basic reorganization of the army. While the Bektashi and the Janissaries retained their standing, Mahmud's régime could only be that sorriest of political spectacles, an ineffectual despotism.

In Russia too, as we have observed (*see above*, p. 297), the monarch had to contend with religious reactionaries, the Old Believers. At the same time, Alexander I was caught between the demands of his Finnish and Polish subjects on the one hand and, on the other, the resentment of Russian aristocrats against any concession to these 'conquered peoples'. In Finland, the tsar did permit a comparatively high degree of autonomy, leaving the Lutheran Church untroubled, sanctioning the continued use of Swedish as the official language and entrusting the administration to native officials. While the genuine liberalism of this policy could easily be exaggerated, Finnish self-government stood as an object of envy for many other nationality groups in eastern Europe.

Unfortunately for all concerned, Alexander's Polish experiment suffered a disillusioning fate. Under the constitution drafted by Prince Czartoryski for 'Congress Poland', Warsaw was to be as clearly the capital of a self-governing state as was Finland's Helsingfors (Helsinki). In 1815 the Poles were guaranteed their own army, their own bureaucracy and their own Diet, comprising a royally appointed

Senate and an elective Chamber of Deputies. As matters turned out, however, the Russians kept a suspicious eye and a firm grip on Polish affairs, forbidding the Diet to discuss finances, retaining command of the army under Alexander's brother, Constantine, and dominating the administration through the agency of the tsar's commissioner, Novo-siltsev. It is true that as late as 1818 promises of further liberalization came from St Petersburg; but the very next year sharply increased censorship was decreed for Poland, and shortly thereafter, Alexander warned the Diet not to formulate further complaints.

In Poland, as in so many other countries, restrictions excited resist-ance, which in turn elicited further oppression. By the early 1820s several clandestine organizations had been uncovered in Warsaw, and the leader of one of them, Major Valezy Lukasinski of the National Patriotic Society, was packed off to prison with his principal associates. Debate in the Diet was muzzled so effectively as to render farcical the now infrequent sessions of that body. At universities such as Warsaw and Vilna, liberal-nationalist professors, not to mention student leaders, were arrested and consigned to Siberian prison camps. Within a decade after 1815, the dreams of Alexander and of Czartoryski, dreams of a contented Polish kingdom under Russian protection, had vanished before the harsh reality of authoritarianism and the hatred it pro-duced.

Within Russia proper the tsar's last years were marked by increasing reliance on a single, ruthless minister, Arakchev, and a fanatical adviser, the monk Photius. Every expression of modernism, whether religious, political, economic, or intellectual, was proscribed. Inevitably some of Alexander's subjects, including a number of army officers who had served in western Europe, began first to grumble, then to plot. A secret society, the Union of Salvation, was formed under Colonel Paul Pestel in 1816, at a time when the tsar was still indulgent towards ostensibly progressive movements. By 1820, now clearly illegal (given the change in Alexander's views), the organization had become the 'Southern Society' and had embraced a republican programme, as well as a plan for liquidating large estates. Another group, composed of intellectuals and westernized aristocrats around Prince Sergius Tru-betskoi and named the Northern Society, also espoused freeing the serfs, in emulation of Stein's Prussian reforms, but favoured instead of a republic a liberal monarchy under the Romanovs. There were still other secret coteries, including the United Slavs, who longed to develop a solid front with Poles, Czechs and the Russians' other ethnic brethren.

Finally, numerous Freemasonic lodges indulged in forbidden political debates. Yet despite this ferment among scattered groups of officers and intelligentsia, the empire of Alexander, on the eve of his death in 1825, offered a picture of oppression to reassure the most apprehensive enemy of change.

France and Britain: Authority versus Liberty

France and the British Isles have been intentionally placed at the end of this brief survey of immediate post-1815 conditions. In both cases, reactionary policies typical of the age clashed with western European notions of political freedom and constitutional safeguards which to much of the rest of Europe still seemed novel or academic, or both. Somewhat ironically, therefore, the two great antagonists of the late struggle now shared the distinction of posing in its most compelling and most difficult form this question: how far could authoritarian rule be pushed, in the face of libertarian principles expressed in parliamentary forums?

France's White Terror, which followed the initial defeat of Napoleon in 1814 and was revived with increased ferocity after the Hundred Days, was not, let us remember, an expression of royal policy. Louis XVIII, whom the vicissitudes of long exile had lent a degree of restraint and common sense rarely encountered in a modern Bourbon, openly deplored the mob attacks upon accused republicans and Bonapartists. Nevertheless, while the government did not condone the riots in Orléans or in Languedoc, the lynchings in the Vendée or in Alsace nor the murder of Marshal Brune at Avignon, pressure from the Ultras (extreme monarchists) did compel the king and his ministers to take certain steps against the loudly denounced enemies of 'throne and altar'. Thus, press censorship was tightened, commissions were set up to expose seditious acts or even ideas and numerous officers were brought to trial for having remained loyal to Napoleon. Among these last was the dashing and courageous Marshal Ney, executed by a firing squad at Paris in December 1815.

Yet Louis XVIII tried, on the whole successfully, to stand by the constitutional charter he had promulgated upon his return to France. After the first frenzy of vindictive rancour subsided, his subjects enjoyed more legal protection for their rights than did most other Europeans of the time. The king maintained his attitude of firmness and moderation despite the opposition of his own brother, the Comte d'Artois, despite the existence of a clamorous Ultra majority in the Chamber of Deputies elected in 1815, despite the humiliating presence of 150,000 Allied troops in the country and despite the near panic engendered by the miserable harvest of 1816. By September 1816 Louis actually found it necessary to dissolve the Chamber before its Rightist majority could launch an open rebellion. Though he had scarcely hoped for so much, the new elections turned back the tide of extremism which had threatened to engulf both the king and his charter. The Chamber they produced still contained representatives of both the right (Ultras) and the left (Liberals), but a large centre bloc permitted business to go forward under the moderate ministries of the Duc de Richelieu, Dessolles (1818–19) and Decazes (1819–20). During those years the government stabilized the food supply, reorganized finances, paid off the war indemnity (thus freeing the country of occupation troops), liberalized the electoral law, eased censorship and broke the reactionaries' grip on the army high command. When one considers that all this corresponded in time to the Carlsbad Decrees, Arakchev's harsh expedients in Russia and Ferdinand VII's despotism in Spain, the course followed by Louis XVIII's régime appears strikingly atypical.

Yet reaction came to France as well. It came, like similar developments in many other places, in the wake of a senseless atrocity. On 13 February 1820, as he was walking out of the Paris Opera, the Duc de Berri, nephew of the king, was stabbed to death by a demented veteran of Napoleon's armies, one Louvel, who believed he had a mission to exterminate the royal family. Though clearly the act of an individual lunatic, the murder was immediately seized upon by the Ultras as proof of the Liberal menace and of the government's criminal weakness. Decazes was forced to resign in favour of a second Richelieu ministry, this one committed to stern measures. Censorship was sharply increased, a new electoral law benefiting large landowners was passed, and numerous officials distasteful to the right were pushed into retirement.

In response to these measures, the familiar undergrowth of secret societies, including French Carbonari, began at once to appear. For a year or two, plots against the government showed up in various localities, especially garrison towns; but every overt display of resistance was smashed, and before long the disorganized Liberal resistance lapsed into despondent inactivity. Only their bitterness and the memory of their martyrs to police terror remained. As for the royal government, it could only drift, or be driven, farther and farther off Louis XVIII's desired course. Surrounded by the ruins of his conciliatory hopes, the old king died in 1824, to be succeeded by the Ultras' darling, the Comte d'Artois, as Charles X. Now indeed the Revolution seemed a fleeting memory, as though history after thirty-five years had come full circle. For on the throne sat the most anachronistic of the French Bourbons, the prince royal who had wanted bayonets turned on the National Assembly at Versailles in 1789 and who seemed to epitomize the charge against his family that 'they had learned nothing and forgotten nothing'.

Finally, what of the United Kingdom? So far as Ireland was concerned, the government of the prince regent carried on where that of George III had ended. With no Catholic representation at Westminster and no parliament left at Dublin, the Irish masses toiled in sullen voicelessness. Their quiescence under English officials and absentee landlords was destined to end shortly, but in the first years after Waterloo, a curious air of stagnation seemed to hover over the land.

In England, Scotland and Wales, on the other hand, there was no lack of excitement from 1815 on. The Whig opposition in Parliament, to be sure, was still demoralized by years of wartime Tory rule and virtually immobilized by its own fear of revolution. Many of the older Whigs frankly embraced the views of such government leaders as the lord chancellor, Eldon, and the home secretary, Viscount Sidmouth (Henry Addington), who saw danger in even the slightest suggestion of change. Other men, however—Anglican Evangelicals, Methodist Dissenters, Philosophical Radicals of the Utilitarian school—attacked the outdated and unfair distribution of seats in the Commons, the overpricing of poor men's bread under the Corn Law, the corruption and insensitivity of royal officials, the selfish exclusiveness of town oligarchies. Some of these critics worked through organizations, for example Major John Cartwright's Hampden Clubs. Others, including that most vehement of journalists, William Cobbett, trumpeted their reformist views through inexpensive newspapers and pamphlets. Still others shared Henry Hunt's reliance on oratory before mass audiences.

As in many other countries, so too in Britain, a brief interval of governmental hesitancy and relative freedom for dissenters came to an end amid conservative charges that public order itself was in peril. In December 1816, excited by the speeches they had heard at an open air meeting near London, some rioters broke into a gun shop, stole a number of weapons and accidentally shot a bystander. Two months later, while the House of Commons was still discussing this outrage, an unidentified projectile shattered the window of a coach in which the prince regent was riding. Jolted into action by fear, the squires and merchants in Parliament voted to outlaw public meetings, to close all unlicensed clubs and to suspend for one year the right of Habeas Corpus, which guaranteed anyone under arrest a prompt trial on specified charges. Agitation did not cease at once; for while Cobbett sailed to America, many other would-be reformers continued to publish. Nevertheless, official pressure was mounting rapidly, as shown by the number of publishers and journalists brought to trial for sedition or even treason.

Such was the troubled atmosphere in August 1819, when a vague report reached London of 'cavalry action against a mob' in Manchester. Lords Liverpool and Sidmouth rushed off congratulations to the officials of that Midland city, though when more news came in, the prime minister and the home secretary had reason to qualify their initial enthusiasm. A huge assemblage of people at a protest rally in St Peter's Fields, near Manchester, had been waiting quietly to hear 'Orator' Hunt when a nervous officer abruptly ordered a cavalry squadron, which was standing by, to advance on the platform. The crowd at first gave way slowly before the mounted troops, then, apparently seized by the idea that an attack was beginning, broke into panicky flight, trampling several persons to death and injuring many more. This was the Manchester Massacre, or, as it was sardonically called, the Battle of Peterloo.

Despite widespread criticism of the Manchester fiasco and the contempt expressed by recalling Wellington's real victory over real enemies, the Portland ministry used the shock of violence to secure additional police powers. That November (1819) Parliament passed the Six Acts, which made the enactments of two years before seem mild in retrospect. Under the new laws, unauthorized parades and other paramilitary demonstrations were forbidden. So were private meetings called to hear political or religious protests. House searches for arms were authorized, as was the seizure of allegedly seditious works by direction of any magistrate. The rights of the defendant in a criminal action were reduced, though certainly not abolished, by the tightening of trial procedures. Finally, newspapers and small journals were subjected to a heavy tax, in order to restrict their sale among the poor. These provisions were enacted over a slowly emerging body of Whig opposition in the Commons, but enacted they were.

One culminating incident, more clearcut than Peterloo, was also, in its way, more shocking than even the murders of Kotzebue in Germany and the Duc de Berri in France. In February 1820, only a few weeks after death had at last freed George III from his lonely world of madness, a plot to murder the entire cabinet was uncovered. Its leader was a well-known radical orator, Arthur Thistlewood, whose rage over the Six Acts and despair at the accession of the prince regent as George IV had driven him to homicidal frenzy. The plan which he and his fellow-conspirators hatched at their secret meeting place in London's Cato Street involved the assassination of the Tory ministers at a banquet, seizure of the Bank of England and the establishment of a revolutionary government. One of the plotters, however, was a police spy (who incidentally pressed for wilder and wilder additions to the scheme), and at his prearranged signal the constabulary burst in upon the assembled conspirators. Five of them, including Thistlewood, were hanged on 1 May, after a trial which had called forth lurid comparisons with Guy Fawkes and the Gunpowder Plot of two centuries before.

Thus Great Britain, its people at once nervous and cowed, entered the new reign under a government which abroad rejected Metternich's vision of an international conservative alliance, but at home embraced an authoritarianism to match that of many continental states. With Louis XVIII's search for moderation abandoned in France, with Austria and Prussia agreed that historical change was an evil in itself, with Russia's tsar divorced from his erstwhile liberalism, with cruelty and superstition enthroned in Madrid, Naples and the Romagna, with British political wisdom for the time being encased in the Six Acts, a reform-minded European could scarcely view the future with much hope. On the other hand, to a conservative—and a man might be such not from selfishness or ignorance but from simple fear of disorder— that same future offered a reassuring vision of stability. The Revolution, that awesome engine of movement, seemed at last to have spent its force. Repression, whether one hated or welcomed it, appeared triumphant in the mid-1820s. Yet nothing was to be more characteristic of Europe's dynamism, its literally *restless* history, than the disintegration of that triumph even before 1830, where our narrative ends.

Reform in Britain and the Irish Problem

Any scheme of historical periodization, as we have previously remarked, is useful only if it is recognised to be an imperfect approximation. Thus, in the present case, the Greek War of Independence, so important for its stimulating effect on liberal idealism in countless lands, actually broke out *before* oppression reached its extreme in Spain under Ferdinand VII, or France under Charles X or Portugal under Dom Miguel. Conversely, authoritarian rule remained outwardly secure in some European countries long *after* signs of movement had thrust themselves to the surface in others. Nevertheless, the fact that new forces did not assert themselves everywhere at once in the middle and later 1820s should not blind us to the changes that did occur, nor to the remarkable brevity of the 'full stop' which seemed to have been imposed during the first years of that decade.

With respect to Britain, it is customary to date such stirrings from as early as the summer of 1822, when George Canning came to the Foreign Office after Castlereagh's suicide. In fact, however, it was not so much the unorthodox foreign secretary as several of his Tory colleagues who revived the cause of domestic reform. One of them, Robert Peel, had entered the government as home secretary several months before the advent of Canning. It would be difficult to imagine a sharper contrast in personalities than that between Sidmouth, the tense, sincere conservative, and this energetic, self-confident young administrator, the son of an industrialist, a commoner surrounded by fellow ministers most of whom were peers of the realm. Peel was not the calm, consistent statesman his later admirers sought to portray; but even at the start of his brilliant public career there was arresting evidence of a quick, inventive intelligence and, most of the time, a winning generosity of spirit. Another vigorous recruit from the world of business and finance was William Huskisson, who in October 1823 became president of the Board of Trade, the first holder of that office to be given cabinet rank. A minister of the more familiar aristocratic stamp, but also a proponent of liberal economic theories, was F. J. Robinson (the future Viscount Goderich), who became chancellor of the exchequer in 1823.

The very fact that such men as Peel, Huskisson and Robinson could win positions of power so soon after the apparent victory of reaction suggests that Lord Liverpool, prime minister until 1827, had never looked upon the Six Acts as a permanent answer to all challenges. It also proves that George IV, whatever the scandals of his private life (his reign opened with an attempt to divorce Queen Caroline amid sordid recriminations), was no tyrant. It is true, of course, that the Whigs, in Henry Brougham, Earl Charles Grey and Lord John Russell, possessed leaders who applied increasingly effective pressure on the government. Nor can we safely ignore writings of the socialist and philanthropist,

Robert Owen (*see below*, p. 343), of William Cobbett, home from America since 1819, and of numerous Benthamite Radicals. Nevertheless, the responsible officials who after 1822 spoke for reform were members of the very party which until then had seemed incapable of rising above the fears of an Eldon or a Sidmouth.

What were some of the new steps? One of the most important came in the field of commercial policy and was the work of Huskisson. His first budget, setting a course which was to be followed with growing confidence from 1823 onward, lowered import duties on textiles, iron, sugar, beverages and a number of other foreign products. Needless to say, the poorest Englishman felt no immediate improvement in his standard of living as a result of the progressive freeing of imports. Yet the process now begun under George IV was destined one day to give Victoria's England a level of comfort superior, in its breadth of distribution, to any the past had known.

Peel, in the meantime, was pushing through legal reforms of similarly modest appearance—and similarly prophetic significance. He revised the criminal code, cutting in half the number of capital crimes (which had stood at over 200) and reducing the penalties attached to a number of lesser offences. His motives, be it noted, were not purely humanitarian; for as home secretary he was concerned over, and hoped to decrease, the number of acquittals traceable not to the defendants' probable innocence but to juries' refusal to endorse senselessly harsh punishment. With Huskisson's support, he also sponsored the repeal of the Combination Acts, thus permitting labourers to organize legally. This measure, long fought for by the articulate Benthamite, Francis Place, was passed by the Commons in 1824. The ensuing wave of strikes led to a new law the following year, denying trade unions the right to order work stoppage; but their right to combine for purposes of bargaining over hours, pay and working conditions was henceforth secure in theory.

Down to January 1828 (Liverpool had resigned in April 1827, to be followed by Canning and then, on the latter's death in August, by Goderich), the pattern in the Tory government had for several years been quite clear. A handful of young middle-class reformers in the cabinet had faced the aristocratic wing, more numerous but less vigorous, with successive prime ministers mediating the struggle as best they could. When Goderich was replaced by the stiff-necked duke of Wellington, however, a major shift seemed inevitable. For now the prime minister himself was the very personification of the conservative peerage, an opponent of Corn Law reform, an outspoken believer in the Combination Acts and a supporter of harsh criminal justice.

Yet a recurrent chapter in British history was about to unfold once more. To the surprise of Wellington's anxious opponents, and the rage of his former henchmen, the political clock did not stop. Its hands kept moving. The new prime minister, who had only a year earlier successfully opposed Canning's proposal to lower duties on grain, now found himself obliged by the critical food shortage to steer through parliament (in June 1828) the first substantial reduction in the Corn Law schedule. This modification in the thirteen-year-old legislation was only a short step toward its final repeal in 1846, but the process of erosion had begun. Indicative of Wellington's unacknowledged conversion is the fact that there was no general defection on the part of would-be reformers within his government. For while Huskisson did resign in May 1828, Peel had already returned to the Home Office by that date (having been omitted from Canning's and Goderich's cabinets), and many less prominent men were encouraged by his example.

The final events of the decade in the United Kingdom were in part shaped by political developments in Ireland. In order to understand how that island returned to the central arena of British affairs, it is necessary to recall the situation left behind by Pitt's inability to achieve Catholic Emancipation following the Act of Union in 1800. What Pitt had failed to do was to make Catholics eligible for *election* to Parliament (or appointment to various other offices). Catholics, including those in Ireland since 1793, could nevertheless still *vote* for MP's. During the first quarter of a century following the Union, to be sure, this right to vote seemed to mean little in itself, since it could not be used to send one of their own faith to Westminster. Furthermore, an election day generally found the uninformed, unorganized Irish tenant farmers, and even many small freeholders, being herded to the nearest county seat by agents of the local landlord, there to vote, without secrecy, in accordance with his stated wishes.

Then, in the mid-1820s, two new currents came together to form a powerful stream of agitation for change. One stemmed from the adoption by England's own liberal Whigs and Radicals of religious emancipation as a necessary step towards a more popular form of government. In 1825 one of the leaders of the opposition in the Commons, Sir Francis Burdett, with the support of the most powerful 'new Whig' of all, Lord John Russell, introduced a bill calling for the abolition of religious tests as a limitation on eligibility to hold office. The bill survived its first reading, but it could not be passed at the time. For one thing, it faced the potent opposition of Robert Peel, whose experience as a youthful official in Dublin had left him uncharacteristically negative towards any reform affecting Ireland. Still more important, the Lords gave an unequivocal warning that their hostility was such as to make pointless any further discussion of the pending measure. The problem, however, could not be permanently shelved.

Meanwhile, in Ireland itself, a new political organization had appeared: the Catholic Association. Founded in 1823, this body soon had a chapter in nearly every parish of the south and west. It also possessed an unprecedented resource, a campaign fund of its own. This was the Catholic Rent which was created early in 1824 and was dependent on personal contributions solicited—in some cases virtually extorted—with the help of the clergy. It proved so productive that by the end of its first year in existence its regular weekly yield was about £700.[1] Finally, the Association had found a leader, Daniel O'Connell, who was at once a shrewd lawyer (as witness his movement's success in skirting the perils of illegality) and an effective, if crude, public orator.

The Association, begun as an organ to express Catholic needs and grievances in the most limited, material sense, quickly broke loose from such modest aims and became a major political force. It instructed formerly bewildered peasants concerning their interests and their rights; and without recourse to the landlords, it turned out farm tenants to vote in hordes, under discipline which offered the police no excuse to complain of mob violence. In 1826, with O'Connell leading the campaign, the tenants of the marquis of Waterford defied his choice of his own brother for Parliament and instead elected another candidate, a Protestant of course, but one endorsed by the Association. Similar upsets occurred in Louth, Armagh and several other counties. When angry landlords sought to retaliate by evicting their disobedient tenants, the latter were given relief from the Catholic Rent. Then, early in 1828, O'Connell took the last, long step. A Catholic, and as such excluded from a seat in the House of Commons, he nonetheless

---

[1] The value of the 'Catholic Rent' is not easily translated into present-day monetary terms. However, some idea of the huge amount represented by £700 a week may be gained by noting some sample wages in England in the mid-1820s: 14s. per week for woolcombers and 10–12s. for weavers (both in Yorkshire), as little as 4s. 6d. for agricultural workers in the southern counties. Rates of income in Ireland, though not available in detail, were surely even lower. *See* J. L. and B. Hammond, *The Skilled Labourer, 1760–1832* (London, 1927), p. 201, and *The Village Labourer, 1760–1832* (London, 1932), p. 159.

accepted nomination for a by-election in County Clare. Again the farmers trooped in, voted quietly, and quietly went home. O'Connell's victory was so overwhelming that his principal opponent actually withdrew before the final day's voting.

Now the decision moved back to Westminster. For the British government, the issue was clear. Would it defy the Catholic voters of County Clare and refuse to seat O'Connell? For a time Peel insisted that such was the only course open under the law and that any concession would be disastrous. Against his view stood not only the Whig opposition leadership but also a number of Tories, including some Protestant Irish landowners, fearful of the burning and looting which might erupt if the Association's thus far exemplary self-control went unrewarded. Although the final choice was made by the duke of Wellington, with his great prestige and his unquestioned conservatism, it was Peel, convinced at last, who framed and presented the necessary legislation. In May 1828, after 155 years in force, the Test Act was repealed by both Houses. Henceforth, no man could be excluded from office simply for refusal to take the sacrament of the Church of England, though he could still be so excluded for being a Roman Catholic.

Some months later, in April 1829, the far more explicit and positive Catholic Emancipation Bill became law. Under its terms, communicants of the Roman Church were declared eligible to sit in Parliament and to hold other public charges save for those specified in a short list: lord chancellor, lord lieutenant of Ireland and a few more. The government's surrender was far from total. Catholic foundations were still denied either legal standing or financial support from public taxes. Catholic office-holders were required to swear a special oath to uphold the monarchy's Protestant succession. Almost 200,000 subjects in Ireland lost their right to vote under a hurriedly established property qualification. Nevertheless, in spite of the dogged survival of religious hostility, the cutting line now was property, not creed. Another of the ancient limits upon political action had begun to yield to calculations more typical of a frankly materialistic society.

In view of the initiatives of Canning and Huskisson and Peel, the grudging flexibility of Wellington and the acquiescence, however reluctant, of the king at each critical point, one may well ask why the Tories fell from power in 1830. Part of the explanation must be sought in the death of George IV that June and the threat which some men saw in the accession of his deeply conservative brother, William IV. In the elections required by law after a monarch's death, the Whigs made good use of this fear, increasing their strength in the Commons by some fifty seats.

Another factor, however, was the attitude of Wellington and his cabinet colleagues. They had moved, or in some cases been pushed, as far as they were prepared to go. Tariff reforms, legal and judicial reforms, politico-religious reforms, all these the Tory ministers had accepted piecemeal. In so doing, no doubt, they had helped to create the very expectations of further change which swept them from office in November 1830. For what they could not accept was the fundamental reform of Parliament itself, to which Earl Grey and the Whigs were now committed. Huskisson alone had believed in that, and Huskisson was gone—out of the cabinet in 1828, killed in 1830 under the wheels of a steam locomotive at the opening of the Liverpool and Manchester Railway. The steel gods of a new age, it seemed, took sacrifices even among their own prophets.

The Restoration Challenged in France and the Low Countries

It would be idle to suggest that the British ferment of economic expansion and political reform was at this early date fully matched by any nation on the Continent. In western Europe, however, other pressures, often characterized by variants upon the Catholic-liberal fusion we have observed in Great Britain, began to cast doubt on the permanence of the Restoration's supposedly final accommodation of throne and altar. The latter alliance, be it said at once, still had powerful blows to strike. In France, for example, the Villèle ministry in 1825 won passage of an Indemnity Law on behalf of aristocrats previously deprived of their lands by the Revolution. This was followed the next year by a Law of Sacrilege against defamers of the established Catholic hierarchy. Finally, in 1827, the government struck at its critics in the middle class by ordering the dissolution of their most prized institution, the *Garde Nationale*, leaving the professional army unchecked by any citizens' militia. But progressive Catholics such as Lamennais and Montalembert were now joining their eloquent voices to those of secular liberals, among them Benjamin Constant, with his esteem for the British constitution, Victor Cousin, who recalled the anti-authoritarian side of Montesquieu's early teachings, and the acerb publicist and historian, Adolphe Thiers.

The first serious warning to the royalist-clerical party in France was the Liberal victory at the polls in November 1827, this despite a sharply limited franchise. It began to be clear that a property qualification for voting would not protect a conservative régime if well-to-do business-men decided they must oppose landed and Church interests. For the next two years Charles X temporised, seeking to lean on the compromise ministry of Martignac but in fact winning little praise from either the Right or the Left. By August 1829, the king had worked himself up to one of his characteristic displays of blind exasperation. He dropped Martignac abruptly and announced that the Prince de Polignac, nick-named 'the Ultra of Ultras', would head the government, without re-gard for any ministerial responsibility to the Chamber of Deputies.

Censured by the Liberals' parliamentary majority, Charles dissolved the Chamber in the spring of 1830, only to be rebuffed once more by a new Liberal victory in the May elections. His response—the July Ordinances which dissolved the Chamber yet again, imposed further censorship and provided for rewriting the electoral law—touched off the final crisis. Its story belongs to the succeeding volume in this series. Here, however, as a concluding tribute to the political sagacity of Charles X and Polignac, we should remark that two days after the ordinances were promulgated on 26 July, the street barricades were up in Paris. On the 27th, the capital was under rebel control; and just nine days later, the Chamber's Liberals proclaimed a new king of France, Louis Philippe of the house of Bourbon-Orléans. An entire conception of monarchy, that of the *ci-devant* Comte d'Artois, had come crashing down, to be replaced by another more to the liking of his old bourgeois enemies.

The other striking instance of the Restoration's collapse in western Europe occurred in Belgium. There, in 1827, the king of the United Netherlands, groping for ways to control the Liberal and the Clerical opposition parties, attempted to strike at both almost simultaneously. By suddenly increasing the censorship, he proposed at last to muzzle 'Jacobins and separatists'. By concluding a Concordat with the Vatican, which promised him the right of veto in all episcopal elections, he sought to bring Belgium's Catholic hierarchy to heel. The latter action turned out to be especially impolitic; for the Belgian prelates included many conservatives who had previously resisted demands from the younger and more impatient members of their flocks, such as the parlia-mentary deputy Baron de Gerlache, for collaboration with the Liberals. After the promulgation of the Concordat, enraged against the crowned Calvinist in the Hague, these bishops muted their former prohibitions against the alliance. Nothing more active on their part was required.

In July 1828, the two parties' leaders announced agreement on joint demands for a responsible ministry, a free press, independence for all schools and the cessation of government interference in religious affairs.

Thus began the sundering of the United Netherlands, which nevertheless survived two more years of agitation, the rise of lower-class resentment over economic troubles, and a series of ineffectual attempts at suppression on the part of the royal government. Perhaps only the new French uprising of 1830 could have brought matters to a head at Brussels. In any event, within a month after the Parisians' July Revolution the first unqualified demands for Belgian independence of the House of Orange appeared in print. On 4 October, amid threats of intervention by Russia and Prussia and counter-warnings from Great Britain to the eastern powers, a provisional government in Brussels declared its formal separation from the Dutch. A nine-year struggle was under way, but it would end as the rebels of 1830 insisted it must: with independence for Belgium.

Autocracy Refurbished: Turkey and Russia

In northern and in most of central Europe, there was nothing comparable to the alarums and excursions of Britain, France and Belgium. The later 1820s witnessed no significant political developments within the Scandinavian kingdoms. The same must be said of Germany, though the accession of the Philhellene and putatively liberal Ludwig I as king of Bavaria in 1825 raised some shortlived hopes that the reform tradition of Montegelas might be revived. With respect to Prussia, we should observe the impressive growth of her tariff union: Hesse-Darmstadt joined the Zollverein in 1828 and the following year the two large south German kingdoms, Bavaria and Württemberg, did likewise. These tariff treaties, however, were of immediate significance solely for their commercial, not for their political, implications.

The only notable political developments in all of *Mitteleuropa* during these years occurred in Switzerland and, in very different form, Hungary. For the Swiss, 1828 and 1829 saw the beginnings of constitutional advance, the 'Era of Regeneration'. Under the pressure of growing popular demands for broader suffrage and legal guarantees of individual rights, including freedom of expression, the ruling oligarchies in more than half of the twenty-two cantons began to make limited concessions. In its evocation of democratic themes, this movement was at once nostalgic, looking back towards the French Revolution, and precocious, foreshadowing the more general agitation in other lands during the 1830s and 1840s. The actual changes in cantonal constitutions prior to 1830, however, were only modest hints of the future.

The same must be said of Hungary's major event of the decade, the revival of the Diet in 1825 following Francis I's unsuccessful twelve-year effort to rule without it. At first glance, the Hungarian Diet's structure and role seemed to mock liberal aspirations, for the Table (or House) of Magnates was exclusively composed of the highest aristocrats, prelates and officials, while the Table of Deputies spoke only for the country's gentry and for a scattering of towns. Yet the Hungarian nobility of the 1820s, like the French of the 1780s, by insisting on its right to assemble, with a few commoners in attendance, had restored the institutional cadre for opposition to the Habsburg monarchy and Austrian dominance. From 1825 on the moderate liberal, Count Stephen Széchenyi, had a place in which to be heard; and close after him in time would come the far more radical nationalist and constitutionalist, Louis Kossuth, admired by many of the lower nobles.

In southern Europe, by contrast, the torpor which had followed the revolts of the early 1820s hung on for the remainder of the decade. Italian resentment, which would soon lend strength to Giuseppe Mazzini's Young Italy movement, slumbered sullenly beneath the blanket of authoritarian repression. Similarly in Spain, it was hard to conceive of any basis for liberal resurgence. Only Portugal, where Dom Miguel had deposed his niece in 1828, still resounded to the catchwords of constitutionalism. And even there, where the civil war would end in 1834 with Miguel banished and Maria II restored to the throne, the only meaningful victory was a purely dynastic one.

As for the Balkans, we have already watched Greece struggling towards national independence through a welter of international complications and internecine disputes. Elsewhere, as earlier remarked of Bulgaria and the Danubian Principalities, there was no significant change. The gains in religious autonomy which accrued to Serbia under the treaty of Adrianople in 1829 and the subsequent Turkish concessions to Milosh, including the title of Hereditary Prince in 1830, belong to the record of Ottoman decline and Obrenovich aggrandizement, rather than to any chronicle of growing freedom.

Oddly enough, considering the generally turbulent history of the 'Lesser Slavs' and the coming Polish Revolution of 1830, it was neither in the Balkan lands under Turkish rule nor in Warsaw that the most explosive events occurred as our period approached its end. Instead, the

Ottoman and Romanov capital cities themselves witnessed a pair of crises, isolated no doubt but highly significant for the future. Let us look first towards Istanbul.

We have seen how a combination of reactionary Bektashi dervishes and haughty, albeit indolent, members of the Janissary corps had saddled Sultan Mahmud II with a bigoted religious policy and a corrupt, ineffectual military establishment. Humiliated by his impotence in the Greek crisis, whether in seeking to resist Russian and British diplomatic pressure or in dealing with his imperious Egyptian ally, Mahmud devoted the spring of 1826 to planning what can only be called a royal uprising. He began by convincing his religious entourage that only a complete military reform, involving the very structure of the army, would make possible their longed-for holy war against the infidels. Thereafter, he abruptly announced the formation of new military units and notified the Janissaries that they could either enter the reorganized forces or leave his service.

On 15 June, as the Sultan had expected, the corps revolted, defying the Sublime Porte itself from the apparent security of the palatial Janissary barracks. In a bizarre scene, which coupled reminders of the Bastille with the suppression of any army mutiny, Mahmud's own troops, surrounded and supported by a mob whipped up by dervishes, assaulted the fortified barracks. Once artillery had breached the walls, the horde of attackers swept into the luxurious compound, burning its contents and slaughtering its defenders. When the smoke cleared after two days of fighting, several thousand Janissaries were dead (the precise number is unknown), and the power of the corps, indeed the corps itself, was obliterated. Ottoman despotism seemed more secure than ever; but an example had been set, an example of military opposition, with popular support, directed against a privileged caste. Many years later, the Young Turks would prove themselves, in an interesting way, the twentieth-century heirs of a sultan.

Only a few months before the Janissaries were massacred, a very different kind of example had been set in Russia. There the death of Alexander I in December 1825 triggered a peculiar succession crisis—and offered the Northern and Southern Societies, the United Slavs and other dissidents an unexpected opportunity to rebel. The presumptive heir was Alexander's brother, Constantine, the military commander in Warsaw. However, in view of the latter's stated disinclination to rule, his younger brother, Nicholas, had been designated by agreement among the late tsar and the two grand dukes themselves. This seemed clear enough. However, when word came that their elder brother was dead of a fever in Taganrog, Nicholas and Constantine fell into a bewildering disagreement over procedure. The former insisted that he would not accept the crown until Constantine renounced it publicly, while the latter refused to undertake the responsibility of issuing such a proclamation. Nicholas was in due course persuaded to announce his own accession, but not before the so-called Decembrist Revolt had taken place.

The initial rising occurred in St Petersburg, where members of the Northern Society spread charges among the garrison troops that Nicholas was an illegal pretender and that Constantine, a sincere constitutional reformer (which he was not), was being ruthlessly destituted of his rightful throne. On 14 December elements of the Moscow Regiment and several other Guard units, answering the call of Prince Troubetskoi and his fellow conspirators, announced their allegiance to Constantine (legend has it that many of the soldiers thought 'Constitution' was his wife) and marched into the Senate Square. There they stood numbly in the bitter cold for several hours, while the Northern Society's leaders alternately made speeches and argued over what to do next. At dusk a cavalry brigade called up by government commanders charged the mutineers. When this effort failed, artillery was wheeled into the square and fired point blank at the half-frozen rebels, who finally broke into flight, leaving the pavement cluttered with their dead and wounded.

The rebellion was over in the capital, but in the far-off Ukraine the Southern Society, with some help from United Slav leaders, persisted in trying to mount effective resistance. Late in December an insurgent army marched against Kiev, only to be routed in its first encounter with forces loyal to Nicholas. All the main figures in both Societies were captured, and five of them, including Colonel Pestel and the poet, Ryleev, were hanged. Prince Troubetskoi, in view of his exalted birth, escaped with exile; but over 100 other accused conspirators were sent to Siberia by a special court. This body, it may be noted, included the veteran reformer, Speransky, now thoroughly intimidated by his autocratic new tsar. The Decembrist revolt, like the destruction of the Janissaries at Istanbul and the revival of the Hungarian National Diet, failed to change a basically authoritarian régime. Still, it shared with these other developments in the East a symbolic importance which transcended its immediate effects. Far from reflecting any concessions to his critics, Nicholas I's thirty-year reign was in fact to be one of the most oppressive in all the long history of the Romanovs. In that sense, the Decembrists can be charged with having brought on their fellow-subjects only grim reaction. Yet it is not too much to say that a particular Russian revolutionary tradition—at once romantic and libertarian, intellectual and aristocratic—first found expression in the chaotic events of 1825.

Restoration and New Themes Reviewed

If in the early 1820s a European might have been excused for thinking that he was living through a complete and permanent return to the Old Régime, by 1830 he could have decided that, on the contrary, the Revolution had been resumed and that the Restoration had been only an interlude, a brief interruption in the vast changes begun almost a half-century earlier. Indeed, if formulated carefully enough, the latter proposition would even now be difficult to refute. Our European of 1830, however, would have been wrong to conclude that some features of the contemporary situation—Parisians in revolt, Belgians rising against a foreign monarch, Britons deep in constitutional debates, Hungarians denouncing Austrian rule, Poles girding to resist Russians —represented literal *repetitions* of scenes from the 1780s. For the late eighteenth century's revolutions were not being re-enacted in 1830, any more than the Old Régime had been reincarnated in all its details a decade-and-a-half before. Instead, the period between the Congress of Vienna and the July Revolution offers abundant proof that, while history plays many recurrent themes, it never repeats them without variations.

Let us first recognize that, whatever their intentions, the statesmen of Metternich's time, with their Congress System, their suspicion of change, their reliance on a conservative alliance of throne and altar, actually created something discernibly different from the Old Régime. For example, eighteenth-century governments had in general displayed a notable lack of solicitude for their respective church hierarchies. The legitimists of the Restoration were actual innovators, therefore, when they committed rulers, courtiers and bureaucrats alike to a solemn repudiation of Enlightenment scepticism.

To take another example, again admittedly one of degree, conservative monarchs after 1815 tended to count more heavily than had their predecessors before 1789 on organized military action against dissidents, both within and across national borders. It is true, as we saw in

Chapter v, that the 1780s had seen Prussian troops used in Holland, Austrian in Belgium and French in Geneva. Such scattered expeditions, however, could scarcely be compared with the almost ceaseless activity of regiments, from Peterloo to St Petersburg, from Spain's Trocadero to Italy's Novara, from Naples to Istanbul, in the period we have been examining. This change must be explained, no doubt, partly by the fact that great wars tend to bequeath increased armies, together with the habit of using them, and partly too by the frequency, noted earlier in this chapter, with which other military formations turned up on the insurgents' side in post-1815 crises.

Finally, with respect to governmental practices under the Restoration, it should be observed that police espionage and systematic censorship assumed a prominence they had never known in the eighteenth century. Here again, the altered nature of the opposition—organized parties, secret societies, press attacks, military cabals—must be cited. If the Old Régime had deployed fewer *agents provocateurs* and left censorship largely to venal incompetents, the explanation must surely be that it had felt less threatened by the kinds of resistance to which it was accustomed. The fact remains that the French revolutionary experience had supplied established governments with increased motivation, as it also had suggested to them new possibilities, for coercive action against internal enemies.

Since the existing order in 1830 was basically different from that which succumbed in 1789, it should be no surprise to find that there were also major differences between the two revolutionary crises. The fact that many slogans, carried over from the earlier drama, were brought out and used again must not mislead us. The prominence of memories, legends and historical references inspired by the 'Great Revolution' was itself one of the elements which in 1830 distinguished the new crisis—not only in France, but in England and Belgium and Italy as well—from the old. A revolutionary *tradition*, inspiring to some, terrifying to others, has been a factor in every revolution experienced by Europe in the nineteenth and twentieth centuries, as it could not be in 1789.

What made the revolutions of 1830 non-repetitive in a much broader sense, however, was the set of ideas and of groups involved. Constitutional theories, nationalist sentiments, democratic credos, economic doctrines, some of them in existence but none of them fully developed in the eighteenth century, had by now come vigorously into play. At the same time, political parties, classes and social groups, far removed from earlier conceptions of nobles, guildsmen or peasants, had emerged as the units of action in this new world of national passions, of broad confrontations between conservatives and liberals, and of bewildering economic change. By 1830, in other words, we are farther from 1780 than a span of fifty years might ordinarily suggest. Just how far can be appreciated even more fully when we turn, as we now shall, to the realm of systematic thought.

XIII

Intellectual Ferment in a Revolutionary Age

One way to place the period 1780–1830 in Europe's intellectual history would be to show it as a confused and relatively formless interval of transition between two much more clearly defined phases. The great crisis of dissolution and restoration did indeed seem to sweep away the world of the Enlightenment, while the world to which, and of which, most of the great systematizers of the mid-nineteenth century— Comte, Mill, Marx, Darwin—would speak did not emerge fully formed

BIBLIOGRAPHY. Among the literally countless works on intellectual history, it is impossible to select more than a handful as having been especially helpful to the author, at the same time citing the excellent chapters on this subject in *The New Cambridge Modern History*, vols. VIII and IX (*see* Bibliographical Note). As for political, social and ethical thought, often inextricably intertwined, the following should be noted: G. Sabine, *A History of Political Theory* (3rd edn., New York, 1961); J. P. Mayer, *Political Thought in France from the Revolution to the Fourth Republic* (3rd edn., London, 1961); F. Manuel, *The Prophets of Paris* (Cambridge, Mass., 1962), and the same author's *The New World of Henri Saint-Simon* (Cambridge, Mass., 1956); E. Halévy, *The Growth of Philosophical Radicalism* (rev. edn., London, 1949); C. Brinton, *Political Ideas of the English Romanticists* (London, 1926); R. Aris, *History of Political Thought in Germany from 1789 to 1815* (London, 1936); L. Krieger, *The German Idea of Freedom* (Boston, 1957); K. W. Epstein, *The Genesis of German Conservatism* (Princeton, 1966); and C. Schmitt, *Politische Romantik* (2nd edn., Munich, 1925). A deservedly influential study of the general shift from eighteenth-century cosmopolitan values to nineteenth-century nationalistic ones in Germany is Friedrich Meinecke, *Weltbürgertum und Nationalstaat* (7th edn., Munich-Berlin, 1928). Though 'popular' by professional standards, the collection of long essays by the distinguished German scholar, K. Jaspers, *The Great Philosophers*, tr. R. Manheim (New York, 1962), contains one of the best available analyses of Immanuel Kant's thought. Of the growing volume of studies dealing with the history of science, and its offspring, I should single out two works by C. Gillispie, *Genesis and Geology* (Cambridge, Mass., 1951), and *The Edge of Objectivity* (Princeton, 1960); together with A. and N. Clow, *The Chemical Revolution* (London, 1952); E. Mayr, *Animal Species and Evolution* (Cambridge, Mass., 1963); H. E. Sigerist's collected essays, *On the History of Medicine* (New on the morrow of that crisis. One trouble with drawing so simple a picture is that it does not do justice to the ways in which many of the Enlightenment's favourite themes continued to influence men's thinking, even as thrones toppled, old states disappeared and new social forces thrust themselves into prominence. Another difficulty is that to visualize any period as essentially a hiatus, a gap, is to obscure the very meaning of *transition* itself. Just as on the one hand the sovereign ideas of the eighteenth century went on claiming followers after 1789, so on the other the quest for more comprehensive, overarching systems of explanation and prediction began well before 1830. Instead of cutting our period loose from what preceded and followed it, we must recognize within its thought the intermingling of legacies from the past and anticipations of the future, as well as some major contributions of its own.

A characteristic of the revolutionary-Napoleonic era and its immediate sequel was, inevitably, the direct, intense relationship between abstract theorizing and bewildering events. The confrontation of ideas by occurrences, continued as it was amid tension and tumult for over a quarter of a century, shook many cherished doctrines for the simple reason that they did not explain what was happening. The same confrontation inspired thinkers to search history and philosophy and observable human behaviour for theories that *would* explain and, where possible, serve as guides to action. The pressure of great problems and the urgent need for answers, in a setting from which many familiar signposts have been swept away, may suggest certain affinities between that epoch and our own.

Political Speculation: Enlightenment and Revolution

Considering the narrative of the period, we are not surprised to find political issues, questions of man and the state, looming large among

---

York, 1960); and F. Klemm, *A History of Western Technology* (New York, 1959). There are, of course, many manuals of historiography; but doubtless the most important single interpretation of the period here dealt with is, for all its curious overemphasis on Goethe, F. Meinecke, *Die Entstehung des Historismus* (Munich-Berlin, 1936). I confess to a special liking for R. G. Collingwood's highly personal *The Idea of History* (Oxford, 1946), on which I have based many of my remarks about the German school. An anthology edited by F. Stern, *The Varieties of History* (New York, 1956), contains good selections perceptively introduced, while B. Mazlish, *The Riddle of History: The Great Speculators from Vico to Freud* (New York, 1966), is an interesting guided tour through metahistory.

objects of intellectual fascination. Here, it seems to me, one should be especially careful not to misinterpret the legacy of the eighteenth century. The Enlightenment, as such, had *not* been rich in political theory. Montesquieu, to be sure, had espoused the separation of powers, not only among the executive, legislative and judicial branches of government, but also among different orders of men. Note, however, that his doctrine could survive only in the barest, most narrowly institutional terms in a society which saw the importance of 'orders' waning, as that of classes and parties waxed. Rousseau had applied the theoretical notion of the social contract to an assertion of popular sovereignty, had evoked the almost mystical concept of the General Will and had written brilliantly on the ethical challenge of reconciling external law with individual integrity; but he had said nothing about the actual bases and forms of modern government which could guide his admirers in action.

Voltaire had, of course, been interested in governmental power, for what it could do to further his chosen causes, such as the suppression of privilege and the destruction of organized religion; but to the structure of government he remained largely indifferent. In pursuit of his aims, he would gladly have used the monarchy in France, Parliament in England, bourgeois voters in Geneva. As for other, non-French figures such as Hume, Lessing and Beccaria, not one had transmitted any political doctrine, strictly defined. The case of Immanuel Kant is more complex, and we shall have to examine him a bit later in connection with one of the major lines of political thought that developed in our period. Yet for Kant, as for Rousseau, questions of society and the state were essentially subordinate to a central concern with personal ethics.

Perhaps the best way to test the Enlightenment's contribution to political thought, once the Revolution came, is to consider the work of a man who formed a personal link between the two epochs: Marie Jean Antoine Nicholas de Caritat, marquis de Condorcet. In 1789, at the age of forty-six, Condorcet was already established as a famous philosopher and scientist. He welcomed the national uprising and became an active politician, serving in the National Convention after Louis XVI's deposition; but he opposed the execution of the king, espoused the cause of the Girondins (*see above*, p. 126) and died in prison during the spring of 1794, almost certainly cheating the Jacobins' guillotine of another victim. While hiding in Paris prior to his final arrest, he composed the *Sketch for a Historic Picture of the Progress of the Human Mind*, a document often referred to since as 'the testament of the eighteenth-century Enlightenment'.

The question now before us is how much of that testament was political. The answer is: very little. This is not to deny the significance or the poignancy of the optimism with which this proscribed and hunted nobleman viewed his own time in history and, even more, what he confidently described as 'the future improvement of the human race'. For Condorcet, the history of mankind arranged itself into ten epochs, from the first ('Men United into Hordes') on through the eighth ('From the Invention of Printing, to the Period When the Sciences and Philosophy Threw off the Yoke of Authority') and the ninth ('From the Times of Descartes, to the Formation of the French Republic'), to the glorious tenth, about to dawn. In this culminating epoch, the author foresaw 'the destruction of inequality between different nations; the progress of equality in one and the same nation; and lastly, the real improvement of man'.

It is a mistake to portray Condorcet, as is sometimes done, lingering over dreams of moral improvement and the miraculous perfection of human nature. A visionary he undoubtedly was, in the sweep and the irrepressible confidence of his views; but it is interesting to note his insistence on the need to advance *physical* wellbeing, in the belief that the resulting sense of security would breed benevolence and, at last, genuinely decent relations among mortals. The fact remains, however, that he was not a political theorist but a moralist and a scientist, cast in the prophetic mould.

If the Enlightenment had so little governmental theory to hand over, did the ideals, at once critical and reformist, of the eighteenth century have anything at all to offer a thoughtful man of the ensuing period? They did, but their contribution lay primarily in posing practical aims and demonstrating practical methods for the pursuit of those aims. The Revolution itself, in its efforts to increase administrative efficiency, minimize unjust discrimination in legal and fiscal matters and make the welfare of a nation's whole people the measure of its government's success, exemplified the highest values of the early modern reformer.

So obvious is the point just made that we sometimes overlook the more paternalistic and hence non-revolutionary side of the tradition, including the record of the more generous among the 'enlightened despots'. I am thinking here not of cynical rulers such as Frederick II of Prussia or Catherine II of Russia, who exploited their much-publicized concern for Enlightenment in the interest of selfish autocracy, but rather of certain other figures of the second half of the eighteenth century who were genuinely, if not always prudently, swayed by the most humane currents of contemporary thought. These included Emperor Joseph II, his brother Leopold (grand duke of Tuscany for forty-five years and Holy Roman emperor from 1790 to 1792) and Charles III of Spain (died 1788). Without such monarchs to look back on, it seems doubtful whether monarchy itself could have survived the revolutionary crisis as successively as it did.

Not just the enlightened despots, of course, but also a number of enlightened ministers represented to the new era an ideal of benign authoritarianism, which Napoleon and after him the crowned heads of the Restoration evoked as an actual theory of government. In Austria, for example, where 'Josephinism' became a rallying cry within months of the reforming emperor's death in 1790, no man embodied that heritage more explicitly than did Baron Joseph von Sonnenfels. Born in 1732, in 1746 converted from Judaism to Catholicism with his recently ennobled father, Sonnenfels had a distinguished record as a public servant under the Habsburgs. To the very end of his life, in 1817, he represented the highest standards of honesty, efficiency and concern for the public good. As a Josephinist, he remained throughout an anti-clerical enemy of his own adopted Church, with respect to issues of privilege and political influence; but his principal efforts in the intellectual sphere were directed towards rationalizing and humanizing the Austrian legal system. Appointed commissioner for the codification of laws in 1791, he laboured for two full decades on the project, which produced the Criminal Code of 1803 and the Civil Code of 1811, both of them more liberal, in several important respects, than the corresponding portions of the Code Napoleon.

Other Enlightenment reformers in office included Prussia's Baron vom und zum Stein, whose efforts we sketched in an earlier chapter (*see above*, pp. 217–19). For Stein, no less than for Sonnenfels, the value of benign and orderly administration was beyond question, from the points of view of ruler and ruled alike. Not least among those state officials whose training and interests still identified them with the eighteenth century, well after 1789 announced the end of the Old Régime, were the Spaniards, Floridablanca and Aranda. Even under Charles IV and despite their hostility towards the Revolution, both respected the aspirations to improve Spain through rational planning which had inspired Campomanes and Jovellanos under Charles III. Finally, it is not hard to identify echoes of Enlightenment legalism and reformism, delivered from above, in political figures as widely separated as Maximilian von Montgelas (Bavaria's chief minister from 1799 to

1817), Count Stadion in Vienna and, in the England of the 1820s, Huskisson and Peel.

Yet when all has been acknowledged with regard to the Enlightenment's influence, it must be recognized that many conservatives were no more charmed by it after 1789 than they had been before. Equally important, and the more startling because of more recent appearance, were the assaults on the eighteenth century, both its evils and its proposed remedies, by men who insisted that nothing short of a clean and total break with old forms of government would suffice. The Revolution was an event, or better, a cascading flood of events; but it was also the expression of new and radical views concerning the state, the individual and the claims of both. These views characteristically went far beyond those of the Enlightened philosophers, demanding for the individual the right to participate in, not just benefit from, decisions of public policy, but at the same time giving the state sweeping powers to reshape society and to pour the nation's manhood into war.

A good representative of the revolutionary position, in part because his career spanned the American and French revolts, is Thomas Paine, born an English Quaker in 1737. Having emigrated to the New World in 1774, Paine within two years made himself famous by publishing a pamphlet, *Common Sense*, which succinctly and energetically set forth the colonists' case for rebellion. To the extent that the American Revolution succeeded in breaking an old political tie and creating a new nation, it gratified Paine. To the extent that a war of independence fell short of immediately creating a powerful, centralized government, it disappointed him. Back in Europe on the eve of the French crisis, he found himself surveying revolutionary possibilities more to his liking.

By 1791, when he published the first section of his book, *The Rights of Man* (the second appeared in 1792), his assault on authority and privilege was ready to be launched. His conclusion was uncompromising:

Whatever the form or constitution of Government may be, it ought to have no other object than the *general* happiness. When instead of this it operates to create an increased wretchedness, in any of the parts of society, it is on a wrong system and reformation is necessary.

He denounced the 'gentlemen' who dismissed the rights of man as a faddish novelty, as though newness were itself a fault; and he offered in reply a metaphor in which the challenge of the future was expressed in the miracle of springtime:

. . . Though the vegetable sleep will continue longer on some trees and plants than on others, and though some of them may not *blossom* for two or three years, all will be in leaf in the summer, except those which are *rotten*. What pace the political summer may keep with the natural, no human foresight can determine. It is, however, not difficult to perceive the spring has begun.

The buoyant revolutionary optimism of a Thomas Paine, like the careful language of the National Assembly's great declaration, from which he had taken his book's title, seems a far cry from the harsh, suspicious preaching of Maximilien Robespierre before the National Convention, as it moved deeper and deeper into the Terror. Yet in fairness it must be conceded that the two revolutionaries' situations were scarcely comparable. Paine, the renegade Englishman, ran certain risks as a member of the Convention; but he did not have great personal responsibility for translating precepts of political change—of the people's seizure of power in the state—into actual policies affecting public order, national finances and the prosecution of war.

Robespierre did have such responsibility. The least engaging, in his humourless self-righteousness, of all the Revolution's leaders, he was also the most consistent. The Terror itself he saw as a necessary work of purification, not as an end in itself, though he never had time to develop in any detail his vision of what France might be once the great purge was over. What saves him, for those who consider him saved, from the role of a bloodthirsty fanatic is the suggestion that beneath his heavy rhetoric lay an awareness of what a real revolution had to cost. That is, he drew pitiless but, in his view, inescapable conclusions about the destruction of privilege and the creation of popular sovereignty, conclusions which involved an ever-widening assault on laggards and compromisers, all in the name of human progress.

Any attempt to reduce the democratic wave of the Revolution to a coherent theory of the state encounters several obstacles. First is the variety of meanings, different men, avowed 'revolutionaries' all, gave the Revolution itself. In this regard, it is instructive to contrast the incipient anarchism of Buonarroti (*see above*, pp. 287–8) with Babeuf's socialistic appeal to make the state a powerful agent for the material betterment of the population (*see above*, pp. 130–1). Second, certain vehement enemies of the Revolution, such as William Cobbett in England (1775–1835), appropriated parts of its platform, including the denunciation of corruption screened by pomp and favouritism, and thereby confused still further the definition of popular revolt.

Third, and most important, modern democratic doctrine had quickly revealed some serious internal contradictions and difficulties. It demanded participation by all citizens in the work of government; but in a large state, no such direct, continuing participation is in fact possible, and the practical effect of this demand is easily reduced to sheeplike assent by plebiscite. The doctrine called for liberty to be guaranteed by equality; but the craze for equality, in so far as it went beyond equal opportunity and legal rights, proved in many cases to threaten individuals' freedom to develop their differing abilities. It also became clear that an old régime is not toppled and replaced by a weaker one, that a sort of upward spiral of state power is implicit in successive shocks of revolution and that the new nation, conceived as a 'people', made demands on all its citizens that could only be administered by a strong, potentially oppressive government. Such observations do not suggest that we should discount the immense significance of democratic aspirations for the development of modern Europe; but they warn us not to oversimplify the practical effect of such aspirations.

The Proliferation of Political Theories

Reactions against the Revolution, both as event and as theory, were of course intense—and as varied as its claims. The earliest and one of the most telling counter-revolutionary statements was Edmund Burke's *Reflections* of 1790 (*see above*, p. 141). As we have already seen, Burke's chief insight, blurred but not negated by his imperfect knowledge of previous and existing conditions in France, lay in his distinction between the metaphor of the state as an organism, the product of long, complex growth, and that of the state as a machine, which could from time to time be dismantled, cleaned and reassembled like a watch or a power loom. The mechanical image, along with much incidental brutality and injustice, he identified with the Revolution; and he considered it a tragic error.

One reason Burke has so often been referred to as the founder of the modern conservative tradition is that many other positions adopted in opposition to revolutionary aims and methods now appear too dated to claim relevance to present issues. In 1811, for example, the Russian historian, Karamzin, urged Alexander I by means of a famous memorandum drafted for the tsar's sister, Grand Duchess Catherine, to abandon Speransky's reform projects and return to the autocratic principles of Catherine the Great—not readily exportable as a conservative philosophy. At the other extreme, a Moritz Arndt lamenting Germany's humiliation in his patriotic poetry or a Samuel Taylor Coleridge apologizing to the Swiss, in his 'France: An Ode' (1798), for ever having 'cherished one thought that . . . blessed your cruel foes'[1] were simply reacting emotionally to specific current events, not framing general principles of government.

Nevertheless, it cannot be said that Burke's answer to the Revolution was the only influential response at the time or that his temperate, relativistic form of conservatism was the period's sole legacy to the modern Right. A quite different, flatly reactionary position was taken by Count Joseph de Maistre, the Savoyard nobleman driven from his homeland by the French invasion of 1792 and thereafter the aristocratic émigrés' most impassioned spokesman. In some respects, de Maistre appears as isolated from changing reality as was Karamzin. In fact, however, he linked religious with political order in a way which was to appeal far more strongly to men of the Restoration than the Russian's proposed return to enlightened despotism possibly could.

In his *Considerations on France* (1796) and a flood of subsequent writings, de Maistre equated impiety with rebellion, loyalty to the Roman Catholic Church with social stability, the Protestants of the past with the Jacobins of the present. At least once he suggested that the Inquisition, had it been maintained in full vigour, might have prevented the French Revolution. All this sounds slightly mad until one recognizes that on the Continent conservatives who lacked England's deep-rooted but flexible political tradition were desperately groping for a principle of order. In de Maistre they read that if governing aristocracies would only be devout, revolution stood condemned as sacrilege. The slogan 'Throne and Altar' summarized his message nicely after 1815.

For the French Viscount Louis de Bonald, more restrained than de Maistre in expression but no less reactionary at heart, there could be no compromise with notions of civil equality and popular representation. In his eyes, even the modest constitutional concessions of Louis XVIII at the restoration of the Bourbon monarchy were at once craven and foolhardy. The model, he insisted, should have been the glorious monarchy of Louis XIV, dead just 100 years. Using very similar arguments,

[1] A. Cobban, ed., *The Debate on the French Revolution*, 2nd edn. (London, 1963), p. 379.

338

the Swiss patrician, Ludwig von Haller, in his *Restoration of Political Science* (1816), hailed the return to power of kings, nobles and oligarchs after the despicable interlude of disrespect for established religion and legitimate rule. The corporatist's repudiation of democracy was nowhere more baldly stated.

Still another line of counter-revolutionary argument took a form which also was historical but more explicitly legalistic. When the earl of Eldon, England's lord chancellor (with one short interruption) from 1801 to 1827, boasted of the judicial campaign against individuals and newspapers charged with sedition, he did so in the stated belief that existing law was both a sacrosanct expression of established relationships and an instrument for the suppression of change. None of the provisions for orderly evolution defended by Locke in the seventeenth century and cautiously acknowledged by Burke in the eighteenth survived in Lord Eldon's theory. The law was there; let it be enforced. The legislation of the French revolutionary assemblies was not, in his view, law at all, being instead the destructive expression of levelling greed and envy. To the natural question just when, in the past, new legislation *had* been legal—and it must have been, to create the existing corpus of law—no clear answer was forthcoming from the lord chancellor. Eldon was himself willing to suspend parts of the constitution when necessary in the interests of repression, as witness the Six Acts of 1819; but to reformers he conceded no such right.

A somewhat more sophisticated version of conservative legalism appeared in the work of F. K. von Savigny, the Prussian jurist and one of the new University of Berlin's first professors in 1810. Savigny shared Lord Eldon's distaste for statutory change, but he devoted himself more seriously to finding the roots, and thus glorifying the ageless wisdom, of existing law. Thus, with the help of the great student of folklore and Germanic customs, Jakob Grimm, he established himself as a major legal historian. His one frankly political treatise, *On the Vocation of Our Age for Legislation and Jurisprudence*, published in 1814, represented the most considerable effort by a student of law to refute the Revolution's central premise, namely, that civic institutions may rightfully be judged and, if found wanting, abolished on grounds either of rationality or utility, or both. One of Savigny's disciples, Friedrich Stahl, published in 1827 a book, *The Philosophy of Law from an Historical Viewpoint*, thus beginning a career destined to carry his master's views forward into the nineteenth century.

It was doubtless inevitable that Germany, the land of Savigny and

Stahl, of Fichte and Arndt and Gentz, should have been at the very centre of the reaction against the French Revolution. In this disorganized and humiliated country, whose institutional foundations had been cracked by the great storm, the quest for order took on an agonized urgency, while the contagious fever of nationalism was particularly intense. Yet the picture is not a simple one. For admiration of Burke, imitation of de Maistre, concurrence with Eldon, loathing of Jacobins and French imperialists by no means exhausted the full range of German intellectual response. Still another line of argument, which was not a simple extension of the eighteenth-century Enlightenment, not an adaptation of revolutionary theses and not just another appeal to established authority, is encountered in Immanuel Kant, at the beginning of our period, and in Georg W. F. Hegel, near its end. In a summary chapter it is impossible to do justice to these giants of modern German philosophy. We should, nevertheless, at least try here to understand their efforts—differing but related, since Hegel built on Kant—to absorb the experiences of their times into theoretical systems not themselves specifically political in emphasis.

Kant, like many other intellectuals, was at first exhilarated by tidings of the French Revolution that reached him in the quiet East Prussian university town of Koenigsberg. It did not offend him to see human institutions subjected to the test of rational criticism. The issues involved belonged to the world of *phenomena*, amenable to understanding and ethical action, in short, to what he termed 'practical reason'. The limits of 'pure reason', which he had examined in his famous *Critique* of 1781, did not apply to political arguments. Kant was, after all, a figure of the Enlightenment, one who admired Rousseau, believed in the pursuit of happiness (albeit subject to his very special definition thereof) and called for an end to the human mind's state of 'tutelage'. Furthermore, in his *Eternal Peace* (1795) he favoured *republics*, though by this term he seems to have meant responsible governments combining freedom, power and law, which could include monarchies or aristocratic oligarchies as well as democracies. Above all, Kant's moral philosophy contained an absolute standard by which an act's rightness depended not on its results but on the doer's motive. Hence, as the modern philosopher, Karl Jaspers, has observed, he 'supported [the French Revolution] not because of the immediate practical consequences, not because of its "deeds bad and good", but because of the state of mind manifested in its origins'.[1]

[1] K. Jaspers, *The Great Philosophers* (*see* Bibliography, p. 330), p. 355.

Why then did Kant, before his breakdown in 1798, come to oppose imitation of the Revolution in Germany and to repudiate the original in France? The answer must be sought in his view of human nature, which was more pessimistic than Rousseau's, and in his view of political change, which was distinctly evolutionary. The possibility that man's good will, his 'will to good', could ever be perfected to a point where he would be entirely happy obeying laws shaped by his own and others' wills, seemed to Kant slight, but also irrelevant. The *idea* of legality, the perfect meshing of personal morality and public order, was at the same time a vision of perfect freedom, a goal that gave direction to history even if it might never be attained. While the slow striving went on within human nature, sudden attempts to leap forward were hopeless, distracting and potentially retrogressive. Thus, Kant could both admire and deplore the Revolution as a well-motivated, doomed effort by imperfect mortals.

What had been in Kant a view of politics and history derived from ethical premises became in Hegel, the south German schoolteacher, a view of history under which ethical judgments respecting politics became relative, rightness or wrongness being determined by the given stage of dialectical progress toward fulfilment of the Idea. The Idea is freedom, not in the sense of inalienable, natural rights but rather, as in Kant, in the sense of man's inner will and the state's outer compulsion reconciled. The emphasis, however, on freedom in Kant's definition of individual happiness, rooted in perfect morality and hence legality, has slipped towards discipline as a good in itself. Its ultimate expression now appears to be a highly authoritarian state, not unnaturally associated by many of Hegel's readers with a sort of idealized, much strengthened Prussian monarchy. In 1802, be it added, he had published a book, *The Constitution of Germany*, in which he urged his fellow-countrymen to drop their false, anarchic ideas of freedom and study the great geniuses of state power, Machiavelli and Richelieu in particular.

Yet Hegel would never have called himself a conservative. Indeed he was not one. His entire theory of the dialectic, as it emerges for instance from *The Philosophy of Right* and his *Natural Law and Political Science* (both published in 1821), is one of change, of progress towards the realization of freedom, his 'Objective Will', achieved by challenges to and reversals of successive historical situations. Thus the dialectic explains progress by collision. The trouble with Hegel's mighty system of historical explanation is greatest for one seeking a basis on which to judge any given political régime. Since progress depends on opposition and the destruction of the *status quo*, the French Revolution as seen from the 1820s had been 'right'. Yet Napoleon's Empire too had been 'right' in reversing some aspects of the Revolution—that is, it had fulfilled its historical role—and the Restoration appeared just as 'right', in that it had emerged from the defeat of Napoleon and was a valid next stage of the dialectic. It thus both enjoyed a claim to men's loyalties at the time and faced the certainty of reversal, in its turn, when the next stage was ready to emerge. It is ironic but understandable that Hegel, for whom terms such as revolutionary and reactionary were literally meaningless as applied to himself, left behind him at his death in 1830 a corpus of thought to which monarchists and anti-monarchists in 1848, Communists and Fascists down to our own day could all turn for support of their several definitions of the state in relation to the individual. Karl Marx (born in 1818) owed him more than that: a theoretical framework for history as a whole.

Social Thought

This era of understandably sharp political debate, much of it launched from differing standpoints regarding history, also witnessed impressive growth in what we now call the social sciences, especially in economics and sociology. Not that all theories of society propounded between 1780 and 1830 were truly scientific. Much that was visionary, even poetic, survived amid the mounting appeal to objectivity, quantification and rigour in analysing evidence. For the scientific and the impressionistic alike, however, decades of terrible warfare and the misery inherent in early industrialism posed—especially in the two great western powers, Great Britain and France—a challenge to explore the human relationships underlying formal issues of law and government.

Even before the Revolution, the Enlightenment had produced, in Morelly and the Abbé Mably for example, adumbrations of modern socialism's characteristic emphasis on poverty as the central problem of mankind and on collective action, necessarily at the expense of liberalism's individualistic values, as the only answer. As we have seen, Gracchus Babeuf was unsuccessful in his attempt to push France towards a socialistic revolution in the Thermidorean period after 1794. It should also be noted that in the revolutionary decade, the pure liberal position had strong defenders among the opponents of 'big government' and its levelling propensities. One such was the Count de Mirabeau, warning against the *fureur de gouverner* in his *Discourse on National Education*

342

and numerous speeches. Another was the Prussian aristocrat and individualist, Wilhelm von Humboldt, author in 1792 of *Ideas for an Attempt to Fix the Limits of the State's Activity*. Nevertheless, as year after year the spectacle of social dislocation, economic exploitation and mass suffering appeared to grow worse, there emerged a definite body of thought later identified condescendingly by the Marxists as 'utopian socialism'.

Some of the latter's exponents were less theoretical than practical in the contributions they sought to make. Thus Robert Owen, the wealthy textile manufacturer, put his faith in demonstrating, at his mill town of New Lanark, Scotland, what a clean, orderly, well-fed, well-housed and well-schooled industrial community could be. Owen, be it noted, was in no sense a *state* socialist; he called for leadership from enlightened businessmen and distrusted governmental intervention as strongly as had Mirabeau or Humboldt. Though he published several treatises, notably *A New View of Society* in 1813 and *The Book of the New Moral World* in 1820, he was seldom abstract and preferred to buttress his appeal by descriptions of New Lanark. Certain English Radicals of the 1820s, Thomas Hodgkin, Charles Hall and others, would dwell on the labour theory of value and the social implications of unearned income, especially rent, in their indictments of capitalism. But it was Owen's prestige, his pragmatism and his evidence drawn from experience which really launched modern British socialism.

To understand the other great stream of socio-economic reform, it is helpful to consider the succession of what an American scholar has called the 'prophets of Paris'—Turgot and Condorcet in the eighteenth century, Henri de Saint-Simon, François Marie Charles Fourier and August Comte in the nineteenth.[1] Obviously, a great distance separates the royal minister under Louis XVI from the apostle of Positivism living under the July Monarchy of Louis Philippe. Yet there is much to be gained from recognizing, beneath personal and doctrinal differences, a persistent confidence in man's ability to find and correct the causes of social ills, an acceptance of the obligation to prescribe remedies, that were indeed prophetic both in tone and in content.

For present purposes, the two most important French social theorists were the Count de Saint-Simon (1760–1825) and his slightly younger contemporary, Fourier (1772–1837). (Comte too wrote random pieces during our period and actually served for a time as Saint-Simon's

[1] F. Manuel, *The Prophets of Paris* (*see* Bibliography, p. 330).

secretary, but his own influence began to be strongly felt only after 1830.) As for Saint-Simon himself, it would be hard to imagine a more bizarre figure. Born into a poor but prestigious noble family, he began his career as an army officer, fighting in the American Revolution and thereafter serving on special missions as a military engineer in Mexico and Spain, and as a diplomatic agent in Holland. He made a fortune in land speculation during the French Revolution, was imprisoned for almost a year at the height of the Terror and then, on his release, launched himself upon a course of unsuccessful business deals and prolonged frustration as a writer. In 1812–13, literally maddened by his failure to win influential support for his views, he spent several months in a Parisian mental hospital. Thereafter, however, he recovered his sanity and began to attract the circle of younger men who constituted nothing less than a cult by the time of his death.

Saint-Simon's ideas were diffuse, his knowledge uneven and his prose style turgid; but he clung doggedly, and in the long run effectively, to a central insight, namely, that industrialism was forging a wholly new world. His treatise, *Of the Industrial System* (1821), argued that the old order, grounded on feudalism and Christianity, was in the process of being replaced by something altogether different. The utopian element lay in the vision of a non-exploitive, increasingly productive society in which the workers would grow affluent under the wise guidance of scientists and business leaders. More to the point, however, was the engineer Saint-Simon's recognition that industrial society was creating a new élite, a scientific-managerial bureaucracy, in short a technocracy. He looked to a future in which rational direction by this élite would ensure the betterment of all mankind (note the echo of Condorcet).

Fourier, whose *New Industrial World* was written in 1827, might have taken his title directly from Saint-Simon, but he was far less willing than the now deceased seer to accept depersonalization under a vast socialistic structure. Instead, many of the works of this former commercial agent from Besançon are more concerned with the psychological and sexual aspects of individual personality than with society as a whole. If there was much of Condorcet in Saint-Simon, in Fourier there was at least as much of Rousseau. Nevertheless, like Robert Owen, Fourier was attempting to define a basis, at once progressive and practical, for improving life in a changing Europe. His solution was not, as Saint-Simon's and Owen's were not, the abolition of private property but rather, in Fourier's case, an elaborate system of sharing the wealth. Small industrial communities, or 'phalansteries', were to be formed and their members to divide the net income: three-twelfths to management, four-twelfths to the providers of capital and five-twelfths to labour. With characteristic use of psychology, Fourier sought to engage the worker's self-interest in the task of production, as well as in the common life of the industrial unit as a social organism.

These early socialists had to face several forms of resistance, two of which may be singled out for special attention. One was romantic nostalgia for an older, explicitly medieval set of values and relationships. In its political expression, we have already encountered this motif in de Maistre, Bonald and Haller (see above, pp. 338-9). In its application to social forms, it appeared particularly as the glorification of the middle ages by a wide variety of European writers. A good example of this tendency was the French novelist and politician, Viscount F. R. de Chateaubriand, who in 1802, long before the Restoration brought him to high office, published The Genius of Christianity, a wistful evocation of the ages of faith and order. Or consider the novels of Sir Walter Scott, with their generous knights, sturdy yeomen and faithful servants. Scott's world of the middle ages had its villains, evil individuals of all ranks, but its hierarchical social structure was shown as healthy and comforting. Whether it seemed so to medieval people may be debated; but there can be no question, judging from Scott's immense popularity, that he was giving a large segment of the early nineteenth-century reading public the kind of escape it wanted.

More solemn than Chateaubriand and more concerned with religion than Scott was the medievalism of the first generation of German Romantics, writing just before and after the turn of the century. In some cases their idealization of a golden past is ludicrous, as in the poet Wackenroder's title for a book submerged in bathos: Heart-outpourings of a Song-loving Cloister Brother. One of the several ardent converts to Catholicism who led this movement in Germany, and no doubt the ablest writer it produced, was the aristocratic Prussian, Friedrich von Hardenberg, who wrote under the pen name 'Novalis' and whose essay, Christianity or Europe (1799), was a sort of manifesto published just two years before its author's death. Here are some illustrative sentences: 'Those were bright, glorious times, when Europe formed but one Christian land; when one Christianity dwelt throughout the civilized part of the world, and a great mutual interest bound together the most remote provinces of this wide spiritual empire. . . . A filial confidence

345

closely united men to their instructions. . . . How contentedly could each one fulfil his daily work. . . .'[1]

If Romantic corporatism accepted some organizing role for society, powerfully seconded by the Church, but rejected the egalitarian side of nascent socialism, the other antisocialist attitude, that of 'classical' economics, rested on the opposite pair of theses. That is, it had no use for corps or orders of men, but neither would it accept any extensive planning or control by the state or by any other representative of 'society' in general. Born of generous efforts by eighteenth-century philosophers, notably Adam Smith and the French Physiocrats, to break down artificial, irrational barriers to commercial development and to discover the true springs of productivity, it was in our period moving rapidly to become what its critics would call 'the dismal science'.

No single writer did more to buttress the forbidding side of this doctrine of economics ruled by egoism and the free play of forces than did the Englishman Thomas Malthus. In 1798, disgusted by what he considered the vaporizing of men such as Condorcet and William Godwin, author of the utopian *Social Justice* five years before, Malthus published an *Essay on Population*. This has continued ever since to influence not only economic thought but also the apologetics of imperialism and biological theories of environment and natural selection. For Malthus, the rationale of population growth, and hence of possible improvement in the masses' standard of living, was as clear as it was discouraging. Given man's capacity for propagation to the absolute limit of numbers supportable by any given level of food supply, the author saw no hope of lifting the race by increasing subsistence. Indeed, he argued, since food production could at the very best increase, generation by generation, in no more than an arithmetic progression—1, 2, 3, 4, 5—while population, left to follow its natural tendency, would follow a geometric progression—1, 2, 4, 8, 16—the 'improvement of mankind' was an illusion beckoning disaster. The only reason the worst does not happen, he explained, is that natural checks, including famine, pestilence, war and 'vice' (abortion and infanticide) prevent the possible rise in population from being fully realized.

Malthus did not seek to spell out any theory of wages or profits. Rather, he thought of himself as a scientific student of demography and, when he urged self-restraint in regard to procreation, as a moralist. The implications of his theory for a ruthless young capitalism were

[1] J. Hexter, ed., *The Traditions of the Western World* (Chicago, 1967), pp. 542–3.

none the less apparent. If anything more than subsistence only breeds misery for the mass of mankind, then bare subsistence should determine wages, all excess value produced by technical progress and increasing scale of manufacturing being reserved to the entrepreneur and such stockholders as have put up capital in his support. In the event, the 'possessing classes' showed themselves disposed, out of a mixture of pious altruism and enlightened self-interest, to deal back a fraction of the profits, in the form of largesse to schools, hospitals, orphanages and so on. Yet consider the distance separating Fourier's proposal to make the workers actual shareholders in his industrial communities from the spirit which informs Hannah More's 'Charge to the Women of the Shipham Club' (1801). The italics are Mrs More's:

> Let me remind you that probably that very scarcity has been permitted by an all-wise and gracious Providence to *unite* all ranks of people *together*, to shew the *poor* how immediately they are dependent on the *rich*, and to shew the *rich* and *poor* that they are all dependent on *Himself*.... *You* are *not* the *only* sufferers ... it has fallen in some degree on all ranks.... We trust the poor in general, especially those that are well instructed, have received what has been done for them as a matter of *favour*, not of *right*.[1]

The subtlest and least harsh of the early classical economists was David Ricardo. A successful London businessman, descended from Sephardic Jewish immigrants from Spain by way of Holland, Ricardo saw himself as the disciple and continuator of Adam Smith. However, in his *Principles of Political Economy and Taxation* (1817) he went far beyond Smith's explanation of a healthy division of labour and exhange of products in a stable, though competitive, market. Ricardo, confronting a dynamic scene of rapid and often brutal expansion, pushed on to inquire 'into the laws which determine the division of the produce of industry amongst the classes who concur in its formation'. Gone is Smith's optimistic prospect of general enrichment of the whole society, now replaced by the frank recognition that the classes —industrial capitalists, landed proprietors, labourers—are in direct conflict over their respective shares in the growing wealth.

By singling out the tension between landed and capitalist interests, including the former's interest in high grain prices and the latter's in inexpensive bread (as a factor influencing minimum wages), Ricardo provided some of the earliest weapons for the long battle against the

[1] A. Cobban, *The Debate*, p. 415.

Corn Law (*see above*, pp. 294–5 and 318). But still more important, by accepting labour as the essential variable determining a product's real cost, from which a classical economist would argue that wages, above all, must be limited if profits are to be high and capital is to accumulate, he riveted the attention of capitalist and socialist alike on a crucial issue. It was characteristic of Ricardo's balanced, dispassionate presentation of that issue that it suggested other responses than the classical economist's. Only two years after the *Principles of Political Economy and Taxation* appeared, the Swiss historian and social critic, Simonde de Sismondi, brusquely reversed the coin in his *New Principles of Political Economy* (1819): 'The earnings of the entrepreneur sometimes represent nothing but the spoliation of the workers.'[1]

Outside the range of socialistic, Romantic and classical-economic writings, of course, many less sweeping but more concrete proposals for the betterment of society appeared in our half-century. In Switzerland J. H. Pestalozzi began during the 1790s to show the importance of a flexible, interesting school environment in bringing out the best in any child; and his widely translated *How Gertrude Teaches Her Children* spread Pestalozzian gospel of free, secular, humane education from East Prussia to Robert Owen's model school at New Lanark. Meanwhile, British Evangelical reformers, many of them Tories in politics, pressed for various moral reforms, including the abolition of slavery throughout the world and the advancement of religious education at home and abroad. Their most articulate spokesmen, the so-called Clapham Sect around Bishop Wilberforce and Zachary Macaulay, failed to attack social and economic ills in England with sufficient zeal to win the respect of a Radical such as Francis Place; but they deserved better than the savage criticism directed at the 'Saints' by Cobbett.

Jeremy Bentham and his followers, the Philosophical Radicals, are not easy to place in the history of social thought *per se*, though Bentham's Utilitarian ethics and his confident use of the pleasure-pain standard of judgment had obvious legal and political implications. He was highly pragmatic in his view of society, as he had been conservative with respect to government until convinced in the 1820s that only a broadened franchise and parliamentary reform could guarantee needed changes in the law. He rejected any notion of corporate interests, insisting that individuals alone provide the units for the pleasure-pain calculus; and his proposed judicial system was geared to the defence

[1] Quoted in F. Artz, *Reaction and Revolution*, p. 209 (*see* Bibliographical Note, p. 392).

of personal rights, to rationally conceived punishments in criminal cases and, in civil, to both the protection of property and the minimizing of artificial inequalities in wealth. For the Utilitarian, a single good—the greatest happiness (most pleasure, least pain) for the greatest number of subjects—offered a clear and simple guide to the solution of any issue of social policy whatever. In this sense, Bentham's popular, because reassuring, theories of government, society and economics were inextricably bound up with his definition of morality, of which more in a moment.

Ethics: Philanthropy, Utilitarianism, the Categorical Imperative

It can, I think, be said of the period we are considering that with respect to ethics, amid all the individual statements or restatements of personal views on right and wrong, there were three major themes which could claim a degree of philosophical interest. One of them, the ideal of philanthropy (literally, the 'love of mankind') hearkened back to a very old impulse to perform good works, an impulse sanctified by Christian charity but not finally dependent on any formal religious teaching. A second, the Utilitarianism of Bentham's Philosophical Radicals, was firmly rooted in the rationalism and the individualism of the eighteenth-century Enlightenment. A third, the 'categorical imperative' of Immanuel Kant, though its formulator was at once a Christian and a philosophe, rejected the Enlightenment's rational calculus of benefits to individuals as well as the ideal of simple charity as being, both the one and the other, incapable of supplying an independent standard of ethical judgment.

A word must be said about the role of organized religion in all this. There is no denying that in the late eighteenth and early nineteenth centuries, as in all ages, theological premises continued to shape the ideas of many men and women concerning the moral life. For the Evangelical 'Saints' and for the more radical Nonconformists in England, for Catholic converts among the German Romantics, for such strikingly different Catholics by birth as Bonald, Chateaubriand and Constant in France, for inward-looking Old Lutherans in Prussia and Old Believers in Russia, specific versions of the Christian message presumably dictated specific responses to the recurring choices which punctuate each personal life. The same was surely true of the increasingly divergent varieties of Judaism, whether orthodox, conservative or modernist.

Yet the contribution of theology as such to ethical debates during the half-century under discussion was remarkably thin. By that I mean only to point out the extent to which such debates were pursued without any heavy reliance on theological references or proofs. The Catholic revival brought with it, at least for the first couple of decades after 1815, little evidence of new energy at the upper reaches of formal thought and even less concern for doctrinal guidance in personal or social ethics. As for the Protestants, even a giant such as the University of Berlin's F. D. Schleiermacher (died 1834), who addressed himself to a rethinking of God's relationship to His creatures, quite explicitly denied that religion must give practical, ethical guidance to those creatures in their relations with each other. The reforming zeal of the Nonconformist fathers of the early Factory Acts in England, as well as the stirrings of what would become Social Catholicism on the Continent, revealed not so much the direct application of abstract theology to the problems of mankind as the generous, but also very general, impulse of Christian humanism. Church leaders could insist on the continuing relevance of the moral teachings of Christ—or Moses—but they could scarcely have been expected to satisfy the demand of an increasingly critical civilization for standards which need not rely on any particular religious belief.

Of the three themes mentioned at the beginning of this section, philanthropy did, of course, offer a chance for the pious to demonstrate their 'applied religion'. Thus Bishop Wilberforce and other members of the Clapham Sect denounced human slavery as an affront to the equal love of God for all mankind and at the same time pressed to bring the Bible into the lives of the poor as the greatest bounty they could receive. Even the bishop, however, implied on occasion—as did Zachary Macaulay more frequently and more emphatically—that slavery was equally an affront to human reason and goodness of heart. In many other cases, including those of Owen and Fourier, the ideal of philanthropy required no divine sanction at all, a circumstance which won Owen in particular the enmity of the Saints. About the most that can be said of the philanthropic impulse was that it rallied men, some religious and some not, who found in the commandment to do good for others sufficient inspiration to lead them out of the moral desert of naked self-interest.

Far less sentimental, but seemingly more precise, was the Utilitarian assertion that a good act is one that serves to maximize the pleasure and minimize the pain of individual humans, including the doer as one, but only one. If we are anxious to choose the 'right' action among several open to us, we need only ask ourselves which, in the event, is likely to bring the greatest happiness to the greatest number. Critics of the Benthamite creed have pointed out the lack of any logical connection between, on the one hand, a hedonistic (pleasure-oriented) definition of happiness combined with an egoistic (self-centred) notion of motivation and, on the other hand, a faith that social progress must result from the rational, unselfish effort by individuals to promote a quantitative increase in the total supply of human happiness. The Utilitarian usually replies partly by denying that his idea of happiness is limited to animal pleasures and partly by asking: 'Have you a clearer, more measurable criterion to offer?'

Perhaps a more serious charge against the Utilitarian ethic is that it does not seek to evaluate the goodness of men but only of their actions, that it addresses itself not to *motives* but to the predictable *effects* of behaviour. If stated too harshly, this accusation is not altogether fair, at least not to Bentham; for in his *Principles of Morals and Legislation* (privately circulated in 1780, but first published in 1789) he was much interested in human 'dispositions'—good, bad or depraved. He did however, insist on separating the 'tendency' of an act, i.e., its influence on human happiness, from the 'motive which gave birth to it'. This distinction permitted him to call the sale of bread to a hungry man, at the regular price, a good deed which nevertheless offers no basis for judging the baker to be either better or worse than other men. If the price were extortionate, of course, the motive—and hence the baker—would be bad. The *theft* of bread for selfish reasons is bad as regards both tendency and motive; but a theft motivated by the desire only to feed starving children ceases to be mischievously motivated though it remains a lawless and antisocial, hence a bad, act. There is also provision for acts of good tendency *and* generous motivation (pure beneficence), not to mention others of good tendency and 'semisocial' motivation (the love of reputation)—the distribution of free bread to the poor might be of either type. Hence Bentham and his followers, in their eagerness to define and to encourage socially useful reforms, including new legislation, did in fact often seem to examine 'tendencies' of behaviour more eagerly than they sought to evaluate motives. If a given member of Parliament were willing to support a revision of the penal code, for example, it was difficult to keep worrying about the degree of beneficence or self-interest that lay behind his vote.

At just this point the era's other great ethical system collided head-on with Utilitarianism. For Kant, the categorical imperative is binding on man without regard to the results of specific acts. It is an ethic of pure intention—moral evil is entered upon or avoided the moment the individual decides to do something, or not to do it. The will is 'good in itself' if it wills good, whence Kant's own approval of the French Revolution's initial impulse but practical rejection of its results (*see above*, pp. 340–1).

In his *Fundamentals of the Metaphysics of Morals* (1785), the Koenigsberg philosophy professor framed the categorical imperative itself in the following terms: 'In all cases I must act in such a way that I can at the same time will that my maxim should become a universal law.' At first glance this may seem only an unnecessarily complicated version of the Golden Rule; but it is in reality quite different from the invocation, at once benign and practical, to 'do unto others as thou would'st have them do unto you'. For what Kant is saying is that your every act, at whatever cost to yourself or to other people, must express a principle of action that can stand the test of rational appraisal. Specifically, can or cannot that principle be universalized—can it be generalized indefinitely without becoming meaningless? By this test, theft is evil because its 'maxim', to use Kant's term, would if universalized end all private ownership and thus rob theft itself of meaning. Similarly, murder is evil because if universalized the principle of one man's right to kill another by his own decision would obliterate human life—and with it, murder. The same can be said of adultery in relation to marriage.

Certain of Kant's opponents have suggested that in practice Kant's rule appears to support social institutions and the general welfare, that it is really little more than Utilitarianism under a disguise of Idealism. Such a claim, however, ignores the distinguishing characteristic of the Kantian imperative, namely, its passing of moral judgment on the individual will *prior* to any given act and *irrespective of the results*. It is a judgment coloured neither by self-interest nor by considerations of social usefulness. Furthermore, the simple examples given above are not the only ones that can be visualized; there are others in which the happiness of the greatest number may not benefit even incidentally from an individual's obedience to the categorical imperative. Take the case of a man tempted to lie, in order to cover information which a small but heavily armed gang of criminals will surely use to destroy him, his family and a whole village full of his neighbours. Is he morally justified in lying? 'Of course,' Bentham would say, with a shake of the head at such a preposterous question. 'No,' Kant would insist, 'for the principle of untruth, if universalized, would extinguish the very conception of truth and hence of prevarication as well.' There is no evidence that the philosopher actually expected any human being ever to be capable of such Stoic indifference to his own and others' immediate wellbeing. But for Kant this standard of moral purity is what the 'good will' must strive toward, a peculiarly chilly East Prussian image of the Grail.

Natural Science

Although Kant and Condorcet were both, among other things, contributors to scientific inquiry, while such major scientists as Joseph Priestley in England and Antoine-Laurent Lavoisier in France became deeply involved in political action (the latter dying on the guillotine in 1794), the progress of science in our period must be treated as an essentially independent phenomenon. With two exceptions—the great public institutions for research and teaching created by revolutionary-imperial France and the crucially important University of Berlin, founded by a Prussia reacting to defeat by Napoleon—there are no important material links between the achievements of pure science and the chronicle of public events from 1780 to 1830. On the contrary, many of those achievements reflected a high degree of international communication and cooperation which survived the divisive assault of warfare between peoples.

The closing decades of the eighteenth century, irrespective of the watershed of 1789, witnessed the growing institutionalization of learning in general and of science in particular. The establishment in 1780 of the American Academy of Arts and Sciences at Boston, on the fringe of the European world, the appearance of new academies in Dublin and Turin during the ensuing three years, the creation of the Literary and Philosophical Society of Manchester in 1785, like that of the less formal Lunar Society of Birmingham a decade before, all testify to the era's scientific energy. Similarly, according to the tabulation of a modern specialist in this field, of the sixty-nine scientific journals founded in the second half of the century, twenty were launched in the 1780s and twenty-five in the 1790s.[1]

As for revolutionary France, it should be stressed that not the delirious first five years but the far less dramatic period of the Directory

[1] D. McKie in *The New Cambridge Modern History*, vol. VIII, p. 136 (*see* Bibliographical Note, p. 392).

constituted the time of organization (in some cases, reorganization) for the 'scientific establishment'. When the *Institut National* was founded in 1795, as the supreme arbiter of higher learning, science was ensconced as the largest of its three divisions. At nearly the same time, the mighty *École Polytechnique* began its work of bringing rigorously selected students together with the élite of French scientists and engineers. Another creation of the Directory, the *École Normale Supérieure*, was, as we know (*see above*, pp. 179–80), less successful until its thorough reorganization by Napoleon in 1812; but it too was destined to have a major role in the systematic teaching of science. During the first years of the new century the establishment of technological and scientific institutes, or *Technische Hochschulen*, in a half-dozen of the larger German capitals reflected the prestige of the French model. Perhaps the most tangible symbol of that prestige, the metric system, extended its sway over the Continent decade by decade, providing a conveniently standardized language of measurement to the still rising wave of scientific, mathematical and medical journals.

Italian, Swedish and Dutch names appear prominently in the chronicle of the scientific crusade, but the overwhelming majority of its leaders were Frenchmen, Britons and Germans. From their Parisian institutes and schools, the French dominated many fields with lofty self-assurance, though never with indifference to developments taking place elsewhere. In England the twin traditions of individual, often amateur, endeavour and unofficial associations relying on private patronage continued, with many of the most important contributions being made by men of a very practical bent, as opposed to strong theoretical, especially mathematical, grounding. (Scottish scientists, though equally practical, seem to have included in their ranks rather more of the theoretically and mathematically trained, perhaps because Scotland's universities as such were already heavily involved in scientific inquiry even before our period.) But it was the Germans who relied most consciously on the concentration of research in their widely scattered universities. The latter had for the most part escaped the torpor which had gripped their French and English counterparts in the sixteenth, seventeenth and eighteenth centuries and entered the nineteenth with Berlin in particular prepared to supply the organizing and radiating point for a proud system of academic science. These national differences were not absolute—new, French-style technical institutes appeared alongside Germany's universities, and the British Isles had their formal Royal Academy as well as their private Lunar Society—but the general lines of variation are worth identifying for the help they provide in understanding several different styles of attack on the problems of science.[1]

In the space available, it is not possible to do more than suggest the range and briefly illustrate the significance of the late eighteenth and early nineteenth centuries' scientific contributions. In mathematics, for example, the application of differential equations to physics and astronomy by J. L. Lagrange in his *Analytical Mechanics* of 1788 and the precision of Gaspard Monge's *Treatise of Descriptive Geometry* (1799) gave scientists the algebraic and geometric tools they needed to penetrate relationships previously difficult to fathom and often still more difficult to record. The work of these two Frenchmen created powerful echoes in Germany, both in the isolated brilliance of Karl Friedrich Gauss (1777–1855), measuring celestial orbits at the University of Göttingen, and in the mathematical seminar begun in 1825 by Karl Jacobi at the University of Berlin.

The modern scientist's other essential instrument, along with mathematical conceptualization and notation, has of course been observation pursued with ever-increasing ingenuity and exactitude, as well as sophistication in the designing of controlled experiments. Nowhere was the last quality more strikingly demonstrated during our period than in chemistry, suddenly emergent from sluggish centuries of descriptive vagueness and bizarre deductions. As early as the 1770s the English Nonconformist minister, Joseph Priestley, had isolated oxygen and shown its general relationship to both combustion and respiration. Within only a few years Priestley's friend and correspondent, Lavoisier, had demonstrated in his laboratory at Paris that air is not an element, as it had long been assumed to be, but a compound of which only about one-fifth is respirable and combustible. These discoveries, supported by Daniel Rutherford's almost simultaneous achievement in isolating nitrogen or 'noxious air', began a chain of important investigations that by the turn of the century had not only revolutionized the learned world's understanding of gases, liquids and fire (overthrowing the old belief in 'phlogiston' as a 'combustible principle', an actual substance released from all substances when burning) but also opened a challenging field of inquiry into the nature of compounds generally.

Thus in 1808 John Dalton in England announced a system of atomic classification on the basis of differing *weights*, as opposed to shapes. The

[1] C. Gillispie in *The New Cambridge Modern History*, vol. IX, *passim* (*see* Bibliographical Note, p. 392).

next year, in France, J. L. Gay-Lussac published the ratios by which *numbers* of particles combine in various gases. By 1815 an Italian, Americo Avogadro, was ready to argue that the supposed combining unit of compounds, the molecule, might itself be a particular cluster of discrete atoms. Even without reference to Avogadro, the way was now clear for the great Swedish chemist, J. J. Berzelius, to issue in 1818 his pioneering work, a table of elements and compounds, with the former's combining weights and the symbols by which they are still identified. Just as Jacobi had carried French mathematical analysis back to the University of Berlin, so another gifted German, Baron Justus von Liebig, upon his return to the University of Giessen from Paris in 1826, set up a soon-to-be-famous chemical laboratory on the basis of his own studies under Gay-Lussac. It was to be decades before all the implications of theories such as Avogadro's would be recognized; but by 1830 the 'chemical revolution' was already well past its first stage.

Advances in a much older science, astronomy, can best be epitomized by the career of Pierre-Simon Laplace—made Count de Laplace by Napoleon and a marquis by Louis XVIII. His *System of the World* (1796) and its sequel, the multi-volume *Celestial Mechanics* (1799–1825), provided powerful support to the Newtonian explanation of gravitational mechanics. It also spelled out in detail the nebular theory of the solar system's derivation from the cooling of an original formation of flaming gases. His *Analytical Theory of Probabilities* (1812) meshed with the efforts of Gauss at Göttingen to reconcile perfection in celestial movements with the practical difficulties of human observation. The success of Sir William Herschel as far back as 1781 in identifying a previously unknown planet, Uranus, from his Slough observatory had done much to encourage observers; but the profound mathematicians on the Continent still pondered the irreducible margin of error.

Like chemistry—which it was beginning to influence profoundly—physics was moving ahead at an awesome pace. With respect to electricity, for example, it is perhaps enough to point out that many of the basic terms we use for various processes and units of measurement are tributes to scientists of the period under review. 'Galvanizing' (stimulating by use of a current) refers to Luigi Galvani of Bologna (1737–98), demonstrator in 1786 of the effect of electrical impulses on a frog's nerves and muscles; the 'volt' (energy), to Alessandro Volta of Como (1745–1827), inventor of the condenser, the electrometer and, in 1800, of the 'electric pile' or wet cell storage battery; the 'ampere' (current) to A. M. Ampère of Paris (1775–1836), mathematical student of electromagnetism as well as rival of Avogadro as a precursor of atomic research; and the 'ohm' (resistance) to Georg Simon Ohm of Cologne (1787–1854), analyst of the relationship among energy, resistance and current. A crowning achievement, quite literally dynamic, was Michael Faraday's work in London during the 1820s on the production of electrical current from a magnetic field.

Another area of the highest importance to physics was the study of heat. In 1799 an American-born researcher, Sir Benjamin Thompson, who had also been named Count von Rumford by the elector of Bavaria, released the results of experiments proving that heat in itself is weightless and hence immaterial, a necessary basis for investigating its properties as a form of energy. Just twenty-five years later this particular cycle of discoveries reached its culmination in the treatise of a French *polytechnicien*, N. L. Sadi Carnot, constituting nothing less than the manifesto of thermodynamics as a pure science: *Reflections on the Motive Power of Heat*. Here, as in several other areas already noted, the contribution of mathematical abstraction and prediction, specifically Joseph Fourier's *Analytical Theory of Heat* (1822), was very great. If space permitted, a comparable summary of investigations into optics by a succession of English and French scientists would provide the background for Thomas Young's and Augustin Fresnel's quite separate, but mutually reinforcing demands in the first quarter of the nineteenth century for the abandonment of the corpuscular in favour of a wave theory of light. The Englishman's and Frenchman's findings were further buttressed by the electroscopic experiments of a Bavarian optician, Joseph von Fraunhofer (1787–1826).

In two other scientific disciplines, those of geology and biology, great debates raged over the formation of the planet Earth and the origin of its creatures. Dominating the geological argument was the disagreement between the Neptunists, who credited the action of water with the formation of rocks and the shaping of terrain, and the Vulcanists, who emphasized the role of igneous matter, that is, its initial emergence from the cooling of incandescent gases and its subsequent eruptions from the earth's still molten interior. By 1785, however, when James Hutton published his *Theory of the Earth* in Edinburgh, something like the eventual synthesis of both aqueous and igneous explanations was emerging, in that Hutton evoked both water *and* heat as agents in the fashioning of the Earth's surface.

As a matter of fact, Hutton's efforts to resolve one debate was to be overshadowed by his contribution to the starting of another, involving nothing less than the relationship between prehistoric and historic events. For his 'uniformitarian' doctrine insisted that all past changes, however remote in time, must somehow be explainable by the operation of slow cooling, sedimentation, erosion, eruption and other phenomena still observable in his own day. To the shocked rejoinder from biblical literalists, but also from many scientists, that such a scheme posited absolutely preposterous stretches of lapsed time, Baron Christian Leopold von Buch, a Prussian nobleman, replied in 1810 that his analysis of Scandinavian rocks proved previous estimates, whether theological or scientific, with respect to the Earth's age to be wholly inadequate. Others joined Buch in seeking to stretch the geologist's available time span; and in 1830 a Scottish compatriot of Hutton, Charles Lyell, began to publish his magisterial *Principles of Geology*, a fully worked out statement of the uniformitarian position.

Biology was a subject that owed undeniable debts to Lavoisier and Laplace for experiments with respiration in the former's Parisian laboratory during the 1780s, to the Germans Karl von Baer and Friedrich Wöhler for their pioneering discoveries during the late 1820s in embryology and organic chemistry, respectively, to the histologist, Xavier Bichat, and the physiologist, François Magendie—both French giants of the intervening period. However, the most visible and exciting struggle, as seen by contemporaries, was waged over the familiar issue of animal species, their origin and differentiation. It was no accident that this conflict paralleled those of the geologists, for the two sciences had a common interest in palaeontology and especially in the use of fossils as evidence.

The three main protagonists were all Frenchmen working in the great research centres of the Empire and the Restoration monarchy. The Chevalier de Lamarck, author of a *Zoological Philosophy* (1809) and a *Natural History of Invertebrates* (1815–22), in the latter work revealed the skills of an able anatomist, classifying organisms by rigorously observing their structures and functions. Already in the earlier book, however, he showed a more impressionistic, even poetic, side in his insistence on the organism's ability to adapt directly to its environment and then, in reproducing itself, to transmit the characteristics produced by that adaptation. Whatever this view may have contributed to a general interest in some process of evolution, the distance that separated the image of the giraffe, passing on by inheritance the long neck developed by constant stretching for leaves on high branches, from the Darwinian doctrine of natural selection is obvious.

It was actually Lamarck's more conservative colleague, G. L. C. Cuvier, who came nearer to adumbrating that aspect of Darwin's eventual system, as published in 1859. For while he insisted on the fixity of species, each designed by its Maker to function successfully in its particular environment, in his *Animal Kingdom* (1817) he was very close to asking how environmental *changes* might affect a species by favouring some and not others of the individual variants which even his notion of fixity had to recognize. Here, as his direct opponent, Etienne Geoffroy Saint-Hilaire (1772–1842), was to charge, a presupposition not unlike that of some geologists concerning the Earth's age blinded Cuvier to the fact that in rejecting Lamarck's notion of inheritance of acquired characteristics, he need not cling to eternal, because divinely differentiated, species. In 1830, just as our period ended, Geoffroy Saint-Hilaire's assault on behalf of biological metamorphosis against Cuvier's belief in fixity erupted in the august surroundings of the French Academy of Sciences.

Before leaving the history of science, in one of its most exciting periods, we should note the interaction between scientific advances and several other important aspects of European life. The 'scientific method' was increasingly admired and emulated by practitioners in other fields of knowledge. Saint-Simon thought himself a thoroughgoing scientist, whatever the Marxists were to say later—in support of their claim to being *really* scientific. August Comte was already writing in the 1820s of the need for careful observation, exact quantification and dispassionate analysis of society, while coining phrases such as 'social physics' to describe his concerns. History composed in accordance with scientific standards was becoming an explicit ideal at about the same time, as we shall shortly observe in historiography's own context; and economics appeared even more susceptible to the quantifying, if not yet the abstractly mathematical, side of the scientists' techniques.

In the light of this obvious carry-over into other disciplines, it seems ironic that the period we are discussing should have seen the first clear signs of a split in the world of learning, between scientists on the one hand and, on the other, those scholars who clung to the verbal and individualizing preoccupations of what they insisted was the 'humane' thinker. This confusion over the boundaries of the humanities, born of forgetfulness as to the central role of science in the tradition of man-centred knowledge, continues to plague us today. It must be blamed in part on those historians, belletristic authors, classicists and others who have been too lazy or too self-satisfied to recognize in scientific rigour one of the highest qualities of human thought and in scientific progress towards our doubtless never-to-be-complete understanding of the world a cultural achievement having implications for history, literature and the other arts as well.

In part also, however, the schism which was appearing in the early nineteenth century was the fault of the scientists themselves. Even the many who did not, as some did, heap scorn on literature's fascination with the idiosyncratic and on history as uncomprehending narration nevertheless tended increasingly to draw apart in a sort of international fraternity—or to be more accurate, a growing number of distinct fraternities, as special fields proliferated within science itself. The French *École Polytechnique*, the German universities and *Technische Hochschulen* made the scientist a professor, but he was becoming a special kind of professor who concentrated on his seminars for advanced students and often seemed to care more for his correspondence with fellow specialists in other cities and other nations than for conversation with his non-scientific colleagues at home. A more generous conception of humane learning remained available, as it still does, to pull together a culture splintered by the force of expanding knowledge, but no one looking back on the age of Monge and Lagrange and Joseph Fourier, of Berzelius and Gauss and Lyell can fail to appreciate the intensity of that force.

One area of European culture which felt the shock of science with special acuteness was traditional religion. The dispute between Cuvier and Geoffroy Saint-Hilaire over fixity versus metamorphosis of species became, for a conservative theologian, an agonizingly important confrontation in which Cuvier *had* to be right if adoration of God's role as a perfect Creator was to survive. The success of a chemist such as Wöhler in synthesizing an organic substance (urea) carried an implicit challenge to the most sacrosanct assumptions about the nature of life itself. But even biological research had less immediately startling implications for religion than did geological. The geologist was probing the very history of the planet, not as a sudden construction by the God of Genesis but as the work of heat and cold, of water and air that could only be envisaged as having consumed prodigious time spans. If Hutton and Lyell and their fellow uniformitarians were right, if man could understand how the globe on which he lived had assumed its present form simply by observing processes still going on, what was left of the drama of Creation? Modern theology had as yet barely begun to grope towards a conception of God and the world sophisticated enough to co-exist with this ruthless destroyer of old 'truths', the scientist.

If the spiritual side of existence was rocked by the advance of the sciences, the other, material side felt curiously little effect, at least for the time being. That the political history of our period should have been quite separate from the scientific is easy to accept; but most students are surprised to find a comparable lack of connection between science and that other powerful complex of changes, the Industrial Revolution. Yet it is true that technology seemed to have a distinct chronology and a practical, inventive, but not theoretical, life of its own. Like most generalizations, this one is subject to qualification. In the 1780s, for example, the great French chemist, Count Berthollet, applied the experimentally established bleaching properties of chlorine to a textile industry previously burdened with the need to bleach cloth on sunning frames in open fields; and in 1816 Sir Humphry Davy, relying partly on his theoretical knowledge of combustion, invented a miners' safety lamp which would not ignite subterranean gases because of metal gauze screening the oil flame.

Nevertheless, it would be easy to exaggerate the number and significance of such exceptions. Thus, while James Watt knew of Joseph Black's discovery of 'latent heat' in the 1760s, there is no evidence that Watt needed any such theory in order to develop the separate condenser for his improved steam engine—experience with the older Newcomen engine might well have been all he needed. Even such important discoveries as the method for extracting soda from seawater (patented by Nicolas Leblanc at Paris in 1791), or the usefulness of large leaden vessels for the economical production of sulphuric acid, came not from the laboratories of pure science but from empirically based attacks on the felt needs of the chemical industry itself. Needless to say, the findings of scientists with respect to electricity, magnetism, thermodynamics, molecular structure, botany, geology and many other subjects were destined to revolutionize industry, agriculture and mining; but *that* revolution still lay well ahead, beyond 1830 and the end of our particular period.

Historiography

The period we have been studying, important to the historian for its social, ethical and scientific thought, witnessed one other development at once original and portentous: the birth of history itself as both a discipline and a profession. Several different influences and impulses combined to produce this phenomenon. Once achieved, the emergence of history as an object for systematic inquiry and, still more, of 'historicism' as an intellectual stance had sweeping implications for modern thought in general.

Throughout most of the nineteenth century, and well into the twentieth, the *eighteenth* was so regularly dismissed as 'anti-historical' that more recent writing may actually have overcompensated, by underestimating the changes in this field which did come in the late 1700s and especially in the early 1800s. We are regularly reminded today that learned Benedictine monks and others had been assembling documentary collections for decades before Voltaire's *Age of Louis XIV* offered, in 1752, a novel conception of cultural history, that Montesquieu had written some ancient, and Hume some British, history, that Gibbon's *Decline and Fall of the Roman Empire* (1776–88) still stands as a towering, if opinionated, classic. All this is true; it is important not to underrate the Enlightenment's historical reach or grasp. Nevertheless, it is equally necessary to recognize that when dealing with the past most eighteenth-century writers indulged in little genuine empathy, as distinguished from antiquarian curiosity or polemical heat. For some writers, including Rousseau and Condorcet, history was not strictly a field of inquiry at all, but instead a canvas on which to present the vast theoretical designs they used in order to place mankind in its contemporary setting.

No doubt the easiest to identify among several different stimuli to the reconstruction of history for its own sake was the challenge of the revolutionary-Napoleonic epoch itself, the call to interpret the present at least partly in the light of the past. Burke tried his hand at some French history in his *Reflections* of 1790, though this was far from being the strongest feature of his essay. De Maistre, the counter-revolutionary émigré, was by no means unskilful in his use of historical arguments linking the Revolution with the Reformation and other past challenges to authority; and he used history to lecture his fellow-aristocrats on their impiety, sloth and ignorance. On the other side, in defence of the Revolution, French writers such as the journalists, Adolphe Thiers and François Mignet, both of whom began publishing histories in 1823, offered detailed arguments based on the record of their own times. Thus, well before 1830, the great debate over the Revolution, destined to engage Michelet, Tocqueville and many after them, was in full swing.

Certain other influences fed the growth of historical interest, without having specific reference to the events of the age. One of these was the upsurge in archaeology and in fascination with the systematic exploration—as opposed to literary admiration—of classical and pre-classical antiquity. The latter effort received its greatest lift from Napoleon's doomed expedition to Egypt in 1798. The future emperor had with him several French archaeologists, who stayed on in the valley of the lower Nile for several years after General Bonaparte had slipped home to become first consul. It was a squad of soldiers working for them who in 1799 uncovered at Rosetta, near Alexandria, a stone bearing inscriptions in Greek, in hieroglyphic and in 'demotic' (or shorthand) hieroglyphic. Not until 1822 was it made clear by Champollion that the two ancient Egyptian texts were identical in meaning with the Greek (a section of dynastic chronicle from the Ptolemaic period); but once that guess proved correct, the deciphering of Egyptian records suddenly opened a whole world of history. The thrill of excitement which ran through the educated society of Europe was comparable to that inspired in our own day by observations brought back from the dark side of the moon.

It was the classical world of the Greeks and Romans, however, that continued to grip most firmly the modern imagination. The two-volume *History of Rome* published in 1811–12 by the lecturer at the University of Berlin, Barthold Georg Niebuhr, was a major attempt to get beyond both Gibbon's polemics and the long-revered Livy's inaccuracies to a 'scientific' recovery of the vast Roman drama, from the pre-Republican origins to the end of the Empire. Niebuhr was no stylist; but especially in his much expanded second edition of 1827–32, after further research during a seven-year sojourn as Prussia's emissary to the Vatican, he added greatly to the understanding of Roman legal, political and social institutions.

By the time Niebuhr published even his first edition, the other branch of classical history, that dealing with Greece, could boast some major advances of its own. The eighteenth century, like the middle ages and the Renaissance, had of course nourished strong views of ancient Hellas. Rousseau had surprised his fellow-Encyclopedists by praising disciplined, unphilosophical Sparta over Athens; and Goethe's whole biography, from his youthful sense of 'Germanness' in the 1770s through his discovery of Italy (old and new) to the form and values of the second, 'classical' part of *Faust* was in one sense a long pilgrimage back to the civilization of Greek antiquity. In 1805 Goethe published

Winckelmann and His Century, a tribute to the mid-eighteenth-century scholar whose *History of Ancient Art* (1764) had done so much to inspire interest in Egyptian, Etruscan, Roman and, above all, Greek aesthetics In the 1820s, with the Greek War of Independence, that interest soared higher still, as Lord Byron hailed:

> The isles of Greece, the isles of Greece!
> Where burning Sappho loved and sung . . .
> Eternal summer gilds them yet.
>
> *(Don Juan*, Canto III, Stanza 86)

This continued, and indeed intensified, reverence for classical antiquity needs to be stressed, not least because our period might otherwise appear to have been wholly in the thrall of another, more novel historical awakening: the rediscovery of the middle ages. The romantics' fascination with what they took to be a world at once orderly and colourful, that of the medieval church and feudal-manorial society, has already been mentioned in connection with their political and social ideas. But there was more to it than a mere rejection of the Revolution's levelling tendencies, or a revulsion against the ugliness they saw in modern cities, factories and parliaments. Here again the eighteenth century had bequeathed several important themes. Giambattista Vico's regard for the *spirit* of once-scorned ages past, Herder's love of the old 'folk language' enshrined in Alsatian idiom, Justus Möser's exaltation of the annals and the customs of his home town in Lower Saxony (*Osnabrückische Geschichte*, 1768 ff.), all had emphasized the value to be found in Europe's history between the age of Rome and that of the Renaissance.

By the early nineteenth century, older collections of medieval charters, edicts and other 'diplomas' were being supplemented by vast new projects in the field of documentary editing and publications, best typified by the *Monumenta Germaniae Historica* launched in 1823 by the Hanoverian archivist, G. H. Pertz, with the active support of the old Prussian reform minister, Stein. Here, of course, we perceive the force of patriotism as a motive for antiquarian delving. The same motive, combined with a passion for order and symmetry, would soon energize the French scholars of the July Monarchy to catalogue documents of the middle ages and the Old Régime in scores of departmental and municipal archives.

The sharp increase in the volume of archaeological and documentary sources becoming available to historians in the early decades of the nineteenth century has moved some observers to relate this phenomenon to the Industrial Revolution. It may be true that, for better or for worse, some modern historians have been satisfied to take the supply of raw material at hand and to convert it into a finished, marketable product by sifting and smelting, moulding parts and ultimately assembling them in accordance with a preconceived pattern or blueprint. That, however, is far from an adequate description of how most history is written. Much more influential—leaving aside the ambition to make history a true form of literature—have been two other preoccupations, one scientific and the other philosophical, which are still as influential, despite countless mutations, as they became in the early nineteenth century with the mature Hegel and the young Ranke.

The philosophical attempt to define the structure of man's history and to characterize the process it embodies is somewhat, though only slightly, older than the scientific effort to recreate the past according to the canons of a new discipline. In saying this, I must relegate to the sphere of theology such medieval visions of Providence working through history as St Augustine's *City of God*, in which human strivings and errors are only dim reflections of the true drama of redemption from sin and the divine offer of immortality. I must also set aside a few early modern figures, notably Vico at the beginning of the eighteenth century, who, however suggestive of later concerns, were not representative of any major intellectual movements in their own times. Instead, let me suggest that the modern search for a philosophy of history, as process, began only in the late 1700s and was to a remarkable degree centred in Germany.

The German thinkers of this period included some whose chief contribution lay in their insistence on 'understanding' (*Verstehen*) at the highest, or at least most general, level of abstraction. Certain of these men, such as Wilhelm von Humboldt (1767–1835), proceeded from a rationalistic faith and used many of the liberal, individualistic assumptions of the Enlightenment. Others, above all Humboldt's colleague in the University of Berlin, Schleiermacher, clung to a more explicitly theological approach—not Augustinian, but dedicated to explaining God to man by every available means, including the penetration of history's workings. A rather different contribution, less abstract but more substantial in its variegated richness, was that of Herder, in his *Ideas for the Philosophy of Human History* (1784–91).

Once again, however, it was the mind of Immanuel Kant that produced the questions and suggested the answers ensuing generations were to find most stimulating, if at times exasperating. In his essay, *An Idea for a Universal History from the Cosmopolitan Point of View* (1784), Kant examines the natural laws governing human acts, which acts were in his terms 'phenomena'—not the 'noumena' that lie beyond the reach of practical evaluation. Almost inevitably, having adopted such language, he slipped into the highly debatable identification of historical with scientific laws. Equally important, however, he sought to give meaning to history by falling back on two of his favourite general concepts: (1) the idea of freedom as man's ability to shape laws for himself on the basis of reason applied to historical experience, and (2) the possibility of progress through the conflict or collision of egoism, lust and ignorance with the rational responses of a humanity gradually becoming surer of its way. Here, as in so many other connections, Kant's piquancy lies in the coupling of his generally gloomy view of human nature with his positive assertions about the power of reason to educate men in self-discipline. This message he formulated abstractly, but its relevance to the chaotic world of Europe after 1789 is not difficult to see.

The younger generation of German historical thinkers influenced by Kant included Friedrich Schiller, whose inaugural discourse as a professor at Jena in 1789 took the form of a lecture on universal history—what it is and why we study it. The great poet's answers include a genuine historicist's appeal to recapture, through research and through vicarious understanding, all we can learn of past societies, their religious beliefs, artistic values, social structure, as well as their wars and politics. Less future-oriented than Kant, he saw the present, however imperfect, as the final stage of human progress about which a student of history could justifiably offer opinions. That is to say, the future might well hold further promise, but it was not of a kind even the most 'philosophical' historian could pretend to delineate.

In another of these contemplative Germans, F. W. J. Schelling, especially in his *System of Transcendental Idealism* (1800), we encounter in its purest form the idealistic view of history, namely, that it is, along with nature, one of the two expressions of the Absolute—perhaps most simply described as pure Reason at work in the world—and that it is compounded of the intelligible thoughts and actions of intelligent beings. This conception (which, like the rest of its author's systematic Idealism, was to have a particularly strong influence upon the nineteenth-century Russian intelligentsia) dignified both mankind and its history. However, the limitations of such a credo when applied to the

reconstruction of real thoughts and actions, often irrational and sometimes unintelligible, account for Schelling's failure to shape western
historical thought, despite all his insistence that the Absolute could at
last be found everywhere in action.

The towering figure in the early German historical school, of course,
was Hegel; and his published lectures on the *Philosophy of History*
(1822–3) may be taken as that school's most sweeping manifesto. The
Swabian sage, some of whose political views, themselves strongly
shaped by historical tenets, we have already noted in passing, was
indebted to Kant for the importance of 'antinomies', that is, of conflicts
and collisions of ideas in history. However, unlike both Kant and
Schelling, he denied that history and nature are related as to their laws
and structures. Nature, he insisted, knows only the repetition of
phenomena in cycles or in recurrences that may be complex but are
nonetheless predictable if we know all we need to about the conditions
and the variables involved. This was helpful to some of the experimental
chemists of the day, notably to Liebig (*see above*, p. 356), but not to
the pre-Darwinian biologists searching for a dynamic principle of
evolution.

History, on the other hand, was for Hegel neither aimless nor even
cyclical. Instead it was the record of human *thought*, progressing
across the centuries toward greater and greater rationality, which in
turn constitutes true freedom of the will. The process he perceived was
not one of direct advance, but instead a dialectical one of theses or
motivating ideas generating their own antitheses and of the syntheses
produced by such conflicts becoming new theses, each in its turn.

Whereas Hegel owed much to Kant, and presumably to Schelling,
with respect to his historical idealism, he shared with Schiller the belief
that the dialectical process he was describing must be seen as culminating in the present. That process, as was to be pointed out in attacks
on Marx's later adaptation of it, *need* not be seen as ending at any
particular stage or point in time; and both theorists have been justly
criticized for setting their own, by no means self-evident, terms for
ending the game, so to speak. To Marx the end would be the classless
society, the proletarian thesis become final synthesis. To Hegel, quite
unnecessarily from a philosophical point of view, the emerging pattern
of national state power, especially as embodied in the Prussian monarchy, promised the realization of full freedom of the rational will
under understood and accepted discipline. Perhaps if he had shared
Schiller's vision of history as concerned with much besides law or

politics, Hegel might have seen his own times as part of an ongoing experience, more complex than his dialectic perhaps, but also more interesting.

Less as a reaction against philosophical idealism applied to history than as an effort to satisfy history's own demands upon knowledge and objectivity, the other, 'scientific', strand of Germany's very great contribution in this period began to appear in the 1820s. We have already seen how archaeology and the spreading interest in documentary collections had been providing more and more source material for students of the past. On the other hand, the works of Thiers, Mignet and other chroniclers of the Revolution seemed to challenge the very possibility of history's being written without partisan bias.

It would in fact be difficult to imagine an interesting work of history which avoided all acknowledgement of the author's point of view; but in Leopold von Ranke we encounter a man clear about his own convictions, yet determined to reconstruct as fully and fairly as possible the narrative which seemed to him to emerge from the diplomatic and other documents in the great archival centres of Berlin, Vienna, Rome and elsewhere. His often quoted announcement that he would try to write history 'as it really was' appeared in the preface to his first major work, *The History of the Romance and Germanic Peoples from 1494 to 1535*, which began to come out in 1824 and the next year won the young Saxon-born schoolteacher in Frankfurt an der Oder an adjunct professorship at the University of Berlin. The study, as its title indicates, was a fresh appraisal of the Reformation, seen in the context of the European state system and set against the background of differing Latin and Teutonic civilizations. The goal of seeking to re-create objective reality in carefully documented detail (*not* of achieving total recall, which he recognized as impossible) would sustain Ranke through a long lifetime of research and writing and made him the first man ever to build a substantial fortune simply as a professional historian.

As has already been suggested, Ranke was not detached from the times in which he lived. His next major publication after the *Romance and Germanic Peoples* was a timely book on *The Serbian Revolution* (1828); and in the 1830s he became what amounted to a political journalist, albeit an exceedingly scholarly one, as he attacked the revival of French revolutionary influences. The latter he hated above all because history was for him a story about states, powers—despite the rather misleading reference to 'peoples' in the title of his maiden work.

Years later, in 1871, when the Second Empire had been founded in Germany, he would hail the end of the 'revolutionary episode' as though history itself had in some sense been interrupted for eighty-two years. Yet this deeply conservative observer of his age, who is reliably reported to have been called to a chair at Berlin in 1825 by the hated censor of German academic life, Kamptz, to counteract liberal agitation,[1] never abandoned his claim to objective erudition. In fact, even he expressed worry over the Prussian censorship in the 1820s and considered the possible advantage of being published in Saxony. It must be added that his judgment of *individuals* in history, irrespective of nationality or party, was remarkably consistent in its sanity and fairness.

Ranke's colleague at Berlin in 1825 (and for five years thereafter, before moving to Halle) was Heinrich Leo, a former *Burschenschaftler*, an admirer of Hegel, a devoted historian of Italy and of the middle ages, an advocate of ecumenical peace among Christian denominations—and a vehement opponent of Ranke. Scorning 'source criticism' as a method, Leo sought instead a total grasp of cultural history. Before the middle of the nineteenth century, he was to turn, in strictly political terms, more conservative than Ranke; but in the 1820s he opposed his famous rival on grounds both of vaguely defined 'progressivism' and of distaste for what he considered the mechanistic approach of archival specialists.

It is tempting today to applaud Leo for having criticized scientific history, since we are apt to judge the latter by the arrogance of some of Ranke's disciples. But Ranke himself was far from arrogant; and surely his methodological rigour, his energy, his patience, his search for basic themes in political history all combine to justify the attention he receives from students of the nineteenth-century European mind. If we find his ideas dated, this is because they presupposed a structure we can no longer recognize as wholly adequate; but the same would be true of a modern scientist judging, while still respecting, a Laplace or a Cuvier.

[1] M. Lenz, *Geschichte der Königlichen Friedrich-Wilhelms Universität zu Berlin* (Halle, 1910), vol. II, pp. 255–7.

XIV

Society and Culture in 1830

This concluding chapter is somewhat shorter than those preceding it, for two reasons. First, we are essentially looking backward. The present volume is not intended to introduce its readers to mid-nineteenth-century conditions, something that H. Hearder's volume in the *General History of Europe*, covering the years 1830–88 (1966), does very ably. Second, our journey across the decades from 1780 to 1830 had best end with some thought directed to a quite specific question, namely, in

BIBLIOGRAPHY. Valuable background for the social history of selected countries in the later years of our period will be found, for Great Britain, in A. Briggs, *The Age of Improvement* (London, 1959), and D. Thomson, *England in the Nineteenth Century* (London, 1964); for France, in R. Burnand, *La Vie quotidienne en 1830* (Paris, 1957); and for Germany, in G. Bianquis, *La Vie quotidienne en Allemagne à l'époque romantique* (Paris, 1958). With respect to emigration, see M. L. Hansen, *The Atlantic Migration, 1607–1860* (Cambridge, Mass., 1941), and the important monograph on the crucial German case, M. Walker, *Germany and the Emigration, 1816–1885* (Cambridge, Mass., 1964). The roles of food and dress may be approached through E. P. Prentice, *Hunger and History* (New York, 1939); B. Payne, *History of Costume* (New York, 1965); and F. Boucher, *20,000 Years of Fashion* (New York, 1967). The best introduction to the pictorial and plastic arts is still G. Pauli, *Die Kunst des Klassizismus und der Romantik* (Berlin, 1925), vol. XIV of the *Propyläen-Kunstgeschichte*. Available in English, but actually more heavily Germanic than Pauli in its emphasis, is F. Novotny, *Painting and Sculpture in Europe 1780–1880* (London, 1960). Also important, in the light of France's eventually pivotal position, is W. Friedlaender, *David to Delacroix*, translated by R. Goldwater (Cambridge, Mass., 1952). The soundest general manual of musical development probably remains Alfred Einstein, *A Short History of Music*, translated by E. Blom (5th edn., London, 1948); but see also the same author's more specialized *Music in the Romantic Era* (New York, 1947) and J. Barzun, *Berlioz and the Romantic Century* (Boston, 1950). A valuable study of the expansion of the reading public, though at a humbler level of literacy than the people who receive most attention from Q. D. Leavis (*see* Bibliography, pp. 20–1), is R. D. Altick, *The English Common Reader* (Chicago, 1957). Unfortunately, comparable analyses are lacking for the Continent, but one may get some idea of evolving literary taste in Europe what ways and to what extent European society and culture had *changed* between these two dates. Was our selected half-century just an arbitrary slice of time cut from an ongoing chronicle? Or can it also claim to have witnessed a shift in forms and values so crucial as to make the revolutionary-Napoleonic era a true turning point in the history of the peoples of Europe? Several different kinds of analysis can be brought to bear on this problem.

The Growth and Distribution of Population

We have earlier observed (*see above*, pp. 290–2) that the rise in population continued apace from the eighteenth on into the nineteenth century. Obviously, a Europe of some 230 million inhabitants in 1830 was bound to differ radically in many respects from one of perhaps 165–170 million in 1780. This was especially true because by the second quarter of the nineteenth century these added millions were beginning to show up increasingly in the cities, helping to create the urban giants some of which were identified in Chapter XII. At the end of our period, to be sure, even the largest European cities had not wholly lost the character of congeries of small towns only imperfectly absorbed by the 'urban sprawl' of London and Paris, Vienna and Berlin. Yet such cities were well on their way to becoming modern metropolises, vast organisms destined, as Oswald Spengler would remark in the twentieth century, to have more traits in common one with another than any would share with the provincial towns of its own country. Numerous men and women who were children in 1830, would live out their lives within these huge municipalities, in many cases never seeing the countryside at all.

Wealth there was in the city, for those who controlled the factories and for the suppliers of goods needed by the swelling ranks of urban dwellers. But for many more there was only the misery of smoke and filth and disease—and the constant, nerve-wracking dread of unemployment. As Robert Southey wrote in his *Colloquies* of 1829:

---

as a whole from H. E. Hugo, ed., *The Romantic Reader* (New York, 1957). Among the countless national studies, let us here single out just a handful of especially helpful works: R. Jasinski and later collaborators, *Histoire de la littérature française*, *vol.* II (rev. edn., Paris, 1966); P. Moreau, *Le Romantisme* (Paris, 1932); F. Flora, ed., *Storia della letterature italiana*, vol. IV (rev. edn., Milan, 1956); R. Pascal, *The German Novel* (Manchester, 1956); and D. S. Mirsky, *A History of Russian Literature* (New York, 1927).

The new cottages [stand] naked, in a row. How is it, said I, that every thing which is connected with manufactures presents such features of unqualified deformity? . . . Time cannot mellow them; Nature will neither clothe nor conceal them; and they remain always as offensive to the eye as to the mind.[1]

Southey shared this distaste not only with romantic nature-lovers such as Chateaubriand in France and Novalis in Germany, but also with decidedly non-aesthetic social critics and journalists. Robert Owen's real, and Charles Fourier's imaginary, workers' colonies were conceived partly out of a desire to escape the worst features of urban concentration. For William Cobbett, in his *Political Register* of 12 July 1817 it was the contrast between potential natural wealth and actual poverty that was most shocking:

Here are resources! Here is wealth! Here are all the means of national power, and of individual plenty and happiness! And yet, at the end of these ten beautiful miles, covered with all the means of affording luxury in diet and in dress, we entered that city of Coventry, which, out of *twenty thousand inhabitants*, contained at that very moment upwards of *eight thousand miserable paupers*. [Italics his][2]

This quotation from Cobbett suggests a condition which was one of two especially striking features of urban life by 1830, in relation to that of fifty years before. The poor had known disease and idleness in eighteenth-century cities, as the drawings of Hogarth would alone suffice to prove. But previous fluctuations in lower class income—as between just poor wages and actual destitution—had been less abrupt than those produced by the factory system. Thus the extremes of affluence and misery generated with bewildering speed by that system seemed more cruel even than the endemic inequities of an earlier day.

The second contrast between 1780 and 1830 arose from the fact that whatever its failings, and they were many, the Old Régime's complex of guilds and parishes had provided, with the family, a set of crude cushions against absolute hopelessness for most inhabitants. It was the apparent loss of even the most rudimentary sense of social responsibility that shocked critics of the new economic order and

[1] Quoted by R. Williams, *Culture and Society* (*see* Bibliography, p. 4), pp. 23–4.
[2] *Ibid.*, p. 14.

would turn a Marx or an Engels, at least part of the time, as nostalgic as the most romantic admirer of the middle ages. A classical economist, on the other hand, could argue from Malthus (*see above*, pp. 346–7) not only that wages should be low and employment precarious but also that alms themselves represented social folly. This supposedly applied to the agrarian poor, dispossessed by enclosure of common lands, no less than to factory workers.

Considering the background of rising population, rural want and urban problems, one might expect to find a record of massive emigration to other lands throughout the early nineteenth century. Here, however, we must take care; the picture is not that simple. For one thing, poverty does not make emigrants of those unable to find the means to move. Furthermore, the American economic crisis of 1819 and settlers' reports home concerning the harsh, uncertain conditions of life in the young United States, the parallel findings of emigrants sent to Canada under official British auspices and the suffering of Germans in Brazil or along the lower Danube en route to the Russian Caucasus all worked to discourage many who might otherwise have left their homes in Europe. Specific disasters, such as the 'famine summer' of 1822 in Ireland and the winter floods of 1825 in the Rhineland, produced periodic upsurges of emigration; but compared to what was impending, they were brief in duration and limited in scale.

The truth is that in 1830, following a bitter winter for virtually all of Europe and amid equally bitter political and social upheavals in many nations, the great 'Atlantic migration', as one economic historian has called it,[1] was about to enter an unprecedented phase. Through the early 1820s, Tsar Alexander's Polish lands had seemed more attractive to emigrants, especially Germans, than had the United States. So, for shorter periods, had Brazil and Canada and the Caucasus, though no reliable statistics are available. As the decade ended, however, a dramatic change was becoming evident. American industry was beginning to organize itself and to demand a greatly increased labour force, at the same time guaranteeing a warmer welcome than it had previously shown recruits from Europe. The movement beginning about 1830 is best gauged by the fact that the number of westbound transatlantic passengers during the next ten years was *five times* the corresponding figure for the 1820s. By 1900 some 35 million people would have made the crossing to the United States alone. After a complicated history of false starts and disillusionments, the westward rush was on, contrasting

[1] Hansen, *The Atlantic Migration* (*see* Bibliography, p. 370).

sharply with the relatively cautious attitude towards, emigration still typical in 1780.

Some Aspects of Daily Life

Although details of food and dress and manners can sometimes amuse without revealing much that is fundamental to history, the latter would be cold and inhuman if it did not include occasional efforts to recapture some of the most mundane, but also most tangible, features of past life. So at least a short excursion into day-to-day social reconstruction is necessary before we touch upon higher realms of creativity. For changes in what people wear, what they commonly eat and what they say or do in ordinary social intercourse reveal other, often more elusive, features of man's existence—aspirations, tastes, estimates of other men, attitudes toward comfort and security.

The dress of the aristocracy and of upper income groups in general is of course the easiest to study, not only because such clothing was shown in fashion magazines at the time but also because the garments' intrinsic value has led to the survival of many of them in museums and private collections. The changes between 1780 and 1830 in the case of well-to-do women's apparel may best be summarized by contrasting the high, elaborate powdered wigs and sweeping satin gowns of Marie Antoinette and her entourage with the very different silhouette of ladies in 1830. In the intervening period, the 1790s had witnessed, at least in France and French-dominated Europe, some extreme affectations including near-nudity of bosoms and thin, streaming gowns, while the succeeding Empire style, though more chaste in its use of opaque materials and simple sheath skirts, had retained high waists and very low necklines. By the end of our period, however, this classical model had yielded to quite a different one: a lateral emphasis on bare shoulders (for evening) above high straight necklines, pleated and ruffled leg-of-mutton sleeves, wasp waists and wide, flaring skirts, built out over pantaloons and crinoline underskirts of horsehair or stiff cotton. Hair styles of the 1820s had replaced the curls or natural coiffures of the Empire with topknots, often elaborated to form bizarre rolls, wings and horns. These were still to be seen in 1830; but topknots were becoming simpler and were in some cases being wholly replaced by curls or rolls over the ears. Millinery, on the other hand, had reached one of its extremes of variety and fancy, ribbon-bedecked straws and wide-brimmed hats of flowers vying with all manner of lacy caps and bonnets.

The 'high style' for men had also changed markedly. If the excesses of French dandies (*Incroyables*) under the Directory and of Beau Brummel's English imitators under the Regency were no more to be seen, neither were the tricorns, bicorns and other forms of cocked hat, the colourful satin suits with knee breeches (as in Gainsborough's 'Blue Boy') or the expansive, embroidered waistcoats of the 1780s. Instead, the favoured costume for the affluent male now tended to combine a double-breasted tail coat or cutaway of sombre hue, lighter-coloured long trousers, a high collar with cravat or scarf and a top hat, usually with a rolled brim and a wide flaring crown. Powdered wigs had largely disappeared, save for ceremonial use and for regular wear by certain stubborn oldsters. More popular now was free falling hair, long but not queued, for those who fancied themselves romantics, and for most other men, short-cut hair with a curled forelock piled up in front. Relatively few moustaches and fewer beards were to be seen at this time; but sideburns, usually more slender than bushy, were in vogue.

No glance at *haute couture*, of course, would suffice alone to distinguish the earliest from the latest years covered by our survey. In all ages, the dress of peasants and workmen has changed less markedly than has that of people with money and leisure to follow the fashions. Nevertheless, we know from sketches and written accounts that shorter hair and either breeches or long trousers were supplanting the manes or queues and the smocks or aprons of eighteenth-century labourers. Lower-class women naturally wore simple bonnets or caps little influenced by the millinery explosions in Mayfair, the Tuileries or Charlottenburg; but these same women, as compared with their grandmothers, generally wore simpler—and in summer cooler—clothes, with cloaks or short capes when needed. Their plain skirts and aprons lacked the bulk which was rather puzzlingly apparent in even the poorer eighteenth-century costumes.

What of the middle classes? At this point there emerges a significant fact, noted by virtually all historians of dress, namely, that in the period we are reviewing the difference in dress between aristocratic and comfortable, but non-noble, groups in society became less and less striking. To be sure, anyone could still have told, simply by looking at those present, that he was at a dinner in Vienna's Esterházy palace and not in the town house of an Austrian banker, at a garden party given by the duke of Saxe-Weimar and not one given by Herr Krupp of Essen. Yet the contrast was not so nearly total as it would have been, in 1780, between princely and bourgeois gatherings. In part, no doubt, this reflected a decline in acceptance of the high nobility's theoretical *separateness* from the rest of society, as opposed to the *superiority* in degree which was still generally conceded. In part, it presumably revealed the effects of mass production in textiles. Whatever the cause or causes, by 1830 the clothing of Europeans generally drew the distinction between the titled and the non-titled less than that between the well-to-do and the poor. Even in the case of cotton cloth, unquestionably a boon to all but the most depressed levels of society, there remained a great difference between fine muslin or poplin on the one hand and cheap, coarse denim on the other.

Changes in the European diet—or better, diets—are more difficult to characterize in general terms than are those in dress. However, at least three features of the end of our period deserve notice. One was the increase in availability and consumption of starchy and/or sweet foods. The production of cereal grains, for flour and porridge, was rising markedly: rye in the Junker estates of eastern Germany, wheat in Bavaria, northern Italy and southern France, maize in the Danube valley, oats in Scotland. Even before the great influx of Russian and American grain in the second half of the nineteenth century, bread, cakes, noodles and other doughy foods were being produced at a rate which, save for the very worst years, appears to have been gaining on even a rising population.

Meanwhile, the potato was at or near the highest point of importance in its history. Easy to grow in either small or large areas and in poor soil, it resisted many perils that attacked grain crops; but the fact it was so popular and so intensively cultivated suggested certain dangers. These were realized in the Irish famine of 1822; for the potato, like any other inbred organism, could and did develop special diseases of its own; and even this hardy ground dweller was not immune to the most extreme freezes, floods or droughts. Yet the suffering in Ireland had been only a brief and soon forgotten warning. Not until the more protracted potato famines of the 1840s, in Ireland and on the Continent, would the possible tragedy implicit in too heavy reliance on a single food source lead many Europeans to reduce somewhat the role of the potato. If, however, one considers the dependence on potatoes and bread in most of Europe even today, one can get an idea of the even greater importance of carbohydrates a century and a half ago.

Increased availability of starches, combined with the rise in sugar imports from the canefields of the New World and in beet sugar production, suggests that that non-existent figure, the average European, was apt to be hungry *somewhat* less often in 1830 that his grandparents may have been in 1780, but that he was not necessarily any healthier. From a nutritional standpoint, the really significant changes—a substantial rise in the consumption of proteins and the purposeful increase in the serving of fresh fruits and garden vegetables for their own value—awaited greater knowledge about diet, which came to northern and western Europe toward the middle of the nineteenth century, and to the south and east considerably later than that. In 1830 an egg or a 'bit of meat' was still a rarity for a large proportion of the European population, while the tomato, one of today's most popular plant foods, remained suspect as a poisonous weed.

The second feature of dietary history demanding attention, the importance of regional variations, can be only briefly noted here. The *average* Englishman probably had more pudding and a little more meat than did his counterpart in northern France, who in turn could depend on more, and better cooked, fresh vegetables. The Italian had to make up in cereal *pasta* what he lacked in virtually all meats save poultry or veal (on feast days) and sausages padded with flour and garlic. Gruel or porridge was common almost everywhere for the poor; but while the Russian or Bulgarian might add onions or leeks, and the Pole a scrap of pork rind, a Dane was more likely to enjoy on the side a hen's or duck's egg, or a piece of cheese, while the Alsatian or the south-west German would turn to cabbage, especially in the form of sauerkraut. More beer than wine was drunk in most of north and central Europe, more wine than beer in the south and south-west; for, aside from the special case of Great Britain's reliance on imported port, sack and claret, the beer and wine 'trade' was still in its infancy. The vast and recently increased system of canals might have served; but in fact neither brewing nor distilling nor wine-making would emerge as major industries, pitched to national and foreign markets, until the coming of the railroad and the steamship. In 1830, a well-stocked and varied cellar remained one of the surest signs of atypical taste *and* affluence.

The third characteristic of food as a feature of our period's social history is particularly important, for it demonstrates a parallel with the record of costume. It is the distinction between wealth and poverty, as opposed to that between social ranks defined in legal or honorific terms. In Russia, for example, great aristocrats, merchants and government officials seem to have adopted tea-drinking as a regular practice by the end of Alexander I's reign, at the latest; yet the Russian masses would scarcely know this exotic beverage for another half-century or more. Berlin's courtiers, army officers, bankers, merchants and bureaucrats enjoyed Rhenish wines and Dutch cheeses, ate well at dinner, *à la française,* and then consumed jelly-cakes and cream buns with coffee or chocolate late in the evening, while their humbler fellow subjects ate, usually at midday, a collation of gruel or rye bread, potatoes and perhaps some lard or salt pork, washed down with thin beer. In France, where eighteenth-century cookbooks had still carefully distinguished the *cuisine bourgeoise* from the *cuisine des grands* (aristocrats), the well-to-do in cities and chateaux now enjoyed, without regard to rank or calling, a diet whose refinement bore little or no relation to the bread and cider of a Norman farm hand or the fish stew and sour wine of a Marseillais longshoreman.

A society increasingly divided into only a few crudely defined layers—affluence, minimal comfort, destitution—was bound to show, in manners as in food and clothing, fewer distinctions and less exact prescriptions than had that of the Old Régime. Yet in the sphere of decorum, of public social behaviour, some fairly obvious gradations did survive the onslaught of crass differentiation in terms of wealth or poverty. In most countries there were many representatives of old families who clung to a notion of gentility, of *politesse,* regardless of their economic situation. At the other extreme, even among the rich, noble and non-noble alike, there were numerous self-styled Bohemians (in this sense, 'gypsies') who defied social conventions and showed their self-conscious alienation from tradition by turning for company to thieves, drunkards and whores, while jeering at the sharp business practices and furtive adulteries of the 'respectable'. Finally, almost everywhere there were subtle barriers of inflection in speech and ease in manner which made it harder for the man of new wealth to ignore his birth than he might have expected.

It would be all too easy to exaggerate these older variants in behaviour and by the same token to underrate the self-confidence which rich men displayed, or ignore the nagging shame which bore down on poor men, even those with ancient titles. It is nonetheless important to recognize that while wealth, and the education it made possible, increasingly set some Europeans apart from others without regard to traditional nuances, a residue of the latter persisted. There were still the supple, witty, often dissolute, generally nobly born or ennobled creatures of princely courts and aristocratic salons. There were equally comfortable but more heavily self-righteous merchants, bankers and higher government officials, who worshipped the solid bourgeois values, preached honesty (even when they did not practise it) as preferable to polish, and characteristically denounced the lewdness and blasphemy in speech which many aristocrats seemed to share with the lower orders. Lastly, defying classification in strictly economic terms, which would have placed many of them below skilled labourers, there were hordes of impecunious but 'orderly' clerks, small shopkeepers and minor bureaucrats, the Uriah Heeps of a still quite status-conscious society.

Changing Themes in Art and Letters

For a long time historians almost routinely described the period which concerns us as one dominated by the clash of neoclassical and romantic motifs in the plastic and visual arts, in music and in literature. Just how the allegiance to the discipline, symmetry and monumentalism of the Greco-Roman inheritance could co-exist in a single culture with the more emotional, personal and often, by association, medieval preoccupations of the romantics was not always made very clear. Their reciprocal hostility, however, tended to be taken for granted. Increased understanding of the shadings and varieties of both neoclassicism and romanticism has in recent decades helped to illuminate the less tidy but more plausible relationship we now perceive between these powerful schools of taste.

An oversimplified contrast between neoclassical order, on the one hand, and romantic sentimentalism, on the other, obscures the extent to which both schools expressed the fascination of Europeans with the faraway, be it antique Greece and Rome or the Gothic middle ages or the 'mysterious East'. True, the classical ideal had since the Renaissance been the more familiar, apparently the more nearly timeless. It was also somewhat easier than the romantic to combine with representational realism in art. Take, for example, the Grecian scenes and Napoleonic portraits of the painter J. A. D. Ingres (1780–1867), a student of Jacques-Louis David in Paris but also of Italian masters in Florence and Rome. Yet the exotic and the exaggerated also appear in Ingres's work, notably in the lush nudes of his Moorish harem scenes. If the long lifetime of Goethe, down to his death in 1832, was in some of its aspects a journey from pre-romantic enthusiasm to neoclassical restraint, the still longer life of Ingres was a brilliant, sometimes baffling odyssey in the opposite direction. Additional warnings against unduly simple labelling come to us from the passionate but carefully constructed symphonies of Beethoven (1770–1827), admired by the ageing Goethe himself yet claimed by the romantics as well, and from the intermingling of stylistic canons in the paintings of Théodore Géricault (1791–1824) and Eugène Delacroix (1798–1863). Note especially Delacroix's 'Liberty', a half-naked Grecian goddess, rallying the top-hatted insurgents of Paris at the barricades in 1830.

Yet the neoclassical and the romantic, however intertwined, can still be usefully distinguished by anyone seeking to visualize the European scene in the early nineteenth century. On every side, it seemed, loomed great Greco-Roman structures, some begun before the Revolution but many more produced during the generation after Napoleon I made himself a new Caesar. The most abbreviated list of examples will serve to remind us of what neoclassicism meant for the architecture of the period: in Paris, Chalgrin's *Arc de Triomphe* (1806–37), the *Bourse* or stock exchange (1808–26), the Church of Saint Madeleine (started under the old monarchy, but redesigned and recommenced in 1807); in Milan, Cagnola's Arch of the Peace (1806 ff.); in London, John Nash's great, curving Regent Street (1813 ff.); in Berlin, Schinkel's State Theatre (1818–21) and his Old Museum (1822–8); in Bavaria, Leo von Klenze's Glyptothek or museum of sculpture (1816–30) at Munich and the same designer's Parthenon-like 'Valhalla' near Regensburg (begun in 1830).

Spurred by archaeological discoveries, by Philhellene rapture during the Greek War of Independence and by the impulse to commemorate military heroics and dynastic triumphs, architects not unnaturally looked for inspiration to the glories and the grandeur of Athens and Rome. So too did sculptors such as Antonio Canova (1757–1822) in Italy, Gottfried Schadow (1764–1822) and Christian Rauch (1777–1857) in Prussia, Ludwig Schwanthaler (1802–48) in Bavaria and Bertel Thorwaldsen (1770–1844) in Denmark. Finally, among the painters, after J.-L. David and J.-B. Regnault (1754–1829) came the generation of François Gérard (1770–1837) and P. N. Guérin (1774–1833), Frenchmen who glorified their powerful nation by using allegories from classical antiquity.

Even the quieter style called 'Biedermeier' in Germany—a domesticated, bourgeois adaptation of 'Empire'—can only be fully understood in terms of more imposing models of neoclassical dignity and balance. The term *Biedermeier* (or *Biedermaier*) did not actually appear until 1850, in the title of a book by Ludwig Eichrodt entitled *Poems of the Swabian Schoolteacher, Gottlieb Biedermaier*; and by then it was already a somewhat wistful evocation of the prudence, docility and limited horizons of German middle-class existence from 1815 through the 1830s. In house construction, it connoted simple, boxlike rooms with large windows—no rococo swirls or domes. In home furnishings, it stood for curved chairs and settees, commonly of cherry wood or mahogany veneer instead of gilt or ivory-painted surfaces. In dress, it dictated sober colours and modest concealment of ladies' bosoms and men's calves. In manners, it stressed the pleasures of evening coffee or chocolate around the family's round parlour table, of Sunday walks in the local park, of a leisurely clay pipe smoked over the books and magazines of the town's public reading room.

In the case of romanticism too, we can use a set of stylistic assertions and applications to recapture other parts of Europe's varied cultural life, as long as we recognize the immense range of individual traits displayed by the romantics themselves. Just as writers such as Shelley, Keats and, later, Heine, would be impossible to equate with a Wordsworth, a Novalis, or a Chateaubriand, in terms of political and religious attitudes, so in visual art, the mystical genius of William Blake (1757–1827), painter, engraver and poet, had little save mystery itself in common with the eerie seascapes and dark woods of his fellow-countryman J. M. W. Turner (1775–1851) or the terrifying 'Black Studies' of Goya in the years of madness before his death in 1828. Yet Blake, Turner and Goya all expressed the rejection of measured, classical rationalism. So did several Germans, including the romantic landscape painter, Caspar David Friedrich (1774–1840), and the rebellious student of Schadow, Adolf Schroedter (1805–75), in his jumbled medieval vision of Don Quixote poring over manuscript volumes with a lance tilted against the table next to him.

Nevertheless, the full efflorescence of romanticism in painting—the pre-Raphaelites in England, for example, or the medieval scenes of Moritz von Schwind (1804–71) in Germany—still lay ahead in 1830. So did the bulk of Honoré Daumier's (1810–79) very unromantic but equally anticlassical caricatures of ancient myths and heroes. Since the Gothic revival in architecture was also impending, but no more than that, at the close of our period, it seems fair to say that neoclassicism, challenged on several sides as it had often been in the past, still held the central ground on the battlefield of plastic and graphic taste.

A considerably different conclusion imposes itself when one turns to music. Even allowing for the mixture, earlier noted, of neoclassical and romantic elements in the corpus of Ludwig van Beethoven's works, musical composition during our fifty-year time span showed an undeniable movement away from abstract rules governing form, towards more personal and often more passionate self-expression by the composer and the performer alike. It was also, be it noted, an era of larger and larger, but not necessarily more sophisticated, audiences, a time of proliferation of musical societies and spacious, permanent concert halls and opera houses. Like newspapers, journals of opinion and the flood of new novels, to which we shall turn in a moment, the musical performances of the early nineteenth century appealed increasingly to large urban gatherings.

At the beginning of the century, F. J. Haydn (1732–1809), *Kapellmeister* to successive princes Esterházy in Vienna, was Europe's reigning orchestral composer. His early works, like most of Mozart's, might seem too stylized, too reminiscent of the Old Régime to have given him this place of honour. Since the 1790s, however, Haydn had been producing symphonies, such as the 'Surprise' and the 'Clock', for London audiences and choral masterpieces for performance primarily in Austria. Both sets of works delighted new masses of admirers. Many of the symphonies were actually amusing; and the oratorios were popular in subject and in appeal—'The Seasons', for instance, was based on a romantic poem by James Thomson presenting idyllic scenes of peasant life.

It must not be assumed that in becoming broader and more accessible, Haydn's work became less important as an influence on other German musicians who followed him. It had been his identification with Vienna that in 1792 drew Beethoven from Bonn to the Habsburgs' capital, there to live for the rest of his life. In 1830 Beethoven had been dead for three years; but his music continued to excite sharp controversy. In particular, his Ninth Symphony, first performed in 1824, seemed to many of the cognoscenti too elaborate, even wild, to qualify as a great achievement. Yet both the music and the words of the 'Ninth', the final movement of which introduces a chorus singing Schiller's 'Ode to Joy', stirred powerful emotions in countless listeners. Just as his overture to Goethe's *Egmont* in 1811 had caught the spirit of political freedom from that drama of Dutch resistance to sixteenth-century Spanish rule, so now the composer's use of Schiller permitted him to apotheosize the ideal of brotherhood among free men. Though Beethoven's string quartets of the 1820s were generally, though mistakenly, assumed at the time to be formalistic reversions to the chamber music of the Old Régime, his symphonies and overtures already exercised a powerful hold on public taste.

If Haydn and, somewhat less obviously, Mozart had given Beethoven a basis of form on which to build his original structures of genius, another German composer owed the late eighteenth-century masters a different kind of debt: the ability to elaborate simple melodies into complex vocal arrangements with instrumental accompaniment. This was Franz Schubert (1797–1828), the first and the greatest writer of *Lieder*. The hold of these dramatic and often exceedingly difficult songs on presentday audiences springs both from admiration for the performers' virtuosity and from fascination with the stories being told. Drawing on poems by Goethe and others, Schubert composed hundreds of *Lieder*, including the haunting *Erlkönig* of 1815; but neither these works nor his 'Unfinished Symphony' (1822) had won full recognition at the time of his death. It was rather as the harbinger of new extensions of romanticism that he figured in the history of our period as such. The same could be said of Louis Hector Berlioz (1803–69) whose *Symphonie fantastique*, the first major work of the French romantic school, was completed in 1830.

A word more must be said about music, specifically about the continuing success of the opera. This was the age of G. Rossini's (1792–1868) greatest successes: *Tancred* (1813), *The Barber of Seville* (1816), *William Tell* (1829). It was also the age of Karl Maria von Weber (1786–1826), whose *Der Freischütz* in 1821 and *Oberon* in 1826 really started the development of nineteenth-century German opera—as Beethoven's popular, but musically less successful, *Fidelio* in 1805 had not. Considering that earlier works, especially those of Mozart and Gluck, continued to be performed on dozens of stages to ever growing audiences, it is easy to appreciate the importance of the opera, viewed as a social institution. On the Continent, with Germany a partial exception, it was doubtless the most beloved of all musical forms.

As in the case of music, so too in that of literature the historian must discuss aesthetic achievements partly in terms of their relevance to a changing society. This is true of the influence on public taste and attitudes exercised by romantic poetry in the 1820s, when the lyrics of Keats (1795–1821) and Shelley (1792–1822) in England, like the translations of Ludwig Tieck (1773–1853) and August Wilhelm von Schlegel (1767–1845) in Germany, were opening new vistas of imagination, while the name of Lord Byron (1788–1824) became a household word in some amazingly remote corners of Europe. It is perhaps still more emphatically true of a genre which in 1830 was approaching its zenith of popularity and power, namely, the novel.

The rise of the novel to pre-eminence as the mid-nineteenth century's most significant contribution to world literature has been explained in various ways. As regards the audience, for example, it is doubtless true that an expanding literate public—produced by the relative democratization of at least elementary education in many countries and fed by circulating libraries and journals of serialized fiction—was a major influence. To some devotees of eighteenth-century novelists, of Defoe, Fielding and Richardson in England, or Prévost and Diderot in France, the emergence of mass readership and the growing responsiveness of authors and publishers to the demands of mass taste seem in retrospect to have augured ill for literary quality. As of 1830, however, and indeed for some decades thereafter, it seems hard to challenge the claims of the best in novel-writing as an enrichment of European letters.

Among all the causes that can be cited for the novel's immense popularity during the nineteenth century, two seem particularly interesting for our purposes. The first has to do with the rise of historical awareness, under the dual influence of romanticism and nationalism. Sir Walter Scott (1771–1832), whose *Waverley* appeared in 1814, produced a literally epoch-making series of historical romances, including *Kenilworth* (1821), *Quentin Durward* (1823) and *Ivanhoe* (1825). Across the Channel in France, Prosper Mérimée (1803–70), who was destined to write *Carmen* at mid-century, had in 1828 already published his first historical novel, *La Jacquerie*. Not all historico-nationalist enthusiasm was expressed in prose, as witness Alexander Pushkin's epic poem in Russian, *Ruslan and Liudmila* (1820) and his tragedy, *Boris Godunov* (1825), frankly modelled on Shakespeare's history plays. Probably the very best product of this whole movement, however, *was* a novel, Italy's finest drawn from history: *I Promessi sposi* (*The Betrothed*) by Alessandro Manzoni (1785–1873), published in 1825–27. It is in essence a tender love story, but the rich background of seventeenth-century Lombardy under Spanish domination makes it a classic of its kind.

Other countries, lacking a Manzoni, were less fortunate than Italy, perhaps because imitation of Scott could not alone substitute for originality and authenticity. Thus several emulators of *Waverley* failed in Spain; Tieck's historical novels fell short of real success in Germany; and even some intrinsically better works, such as the Polish historical romance, *Jan z Tęczyna* (1825) by J. U. Niemcewicz (1757–1841), and the Hungarian drama of the thirteenth century, *Bánk Bán* (1820) by József Katona (1798–1830), are less interesting as literature than as statements of their authors' intense patriotism. The same was to hold true of the Belgian Hendrik Conscience's Flemish romances in the 1830s and following. Yet the volume of such efforts is in itself significant.

A wholly different type of novel, concerned with introspection, manners and interpersonal tensions, was also coming into its own in our period—not, be it said at once, without precursors in the eighteenth century and even earlier. This brings us to the second cause for the novel's popularity, having special relevance to general history. The nineteenth century was a time when society was changing in certain obvious respects, but when numerous other features, including older notions of decorum and group relationships, still hung on from the past. Thus the evolution of personality, within itself and in its social setting, held a fascination which should not be hard for us to appreciate. The novel of personality and of manners employed, usually at any rate, a style that was detached, sometimes almost clinical, rather than empathetic or sentimental. Author joined reader as a cool and often amused, albeit keenly interested, observer of the human condition.

This style Jane Austen (1775–1832) carried to an unrivalled state of polish in her portrayals of middle-class English provincial life: *Pride and Prejudice* (written in 1796–7, but published only in 1813), *Sense and Sensibility* (1797–8, published in 1811), and several later novels, including perhaps her subtlest and best, *Emma* (1816). There is no thrilling action in her works, as there is in Scott's, and none of Manzoni's historical tapestry, but instead the patient dissection of moods and motives achieved by meticulously chronicling the details of daily life. The reader is held by a lucid style and the ripple of quiet wit. On the Continent, Goethe had focused on an individual's education in *Wilhelm Meisters Lehrjahre* (1795–6); in *Wilhelm Meisters Wanderjahre* (1821–1829), he concentrated on the same hero's later travels and more mature development. Between these novels, in 1809, he produced a truly psychological drama of love and renunciation, *Elective Affinities* (*Die Wahlverwandtschaften*). And in 1830, almost unnoticed for the moment but in due course to be hailed as one of Europe's most brilliant novels, appeared *Le Rouge et le noir* by a Frenchman from Dauphiné, Marie-Henri Beyle (1783–1842), whose *nom de plume* was Stendhal and whose theme was the mixture of religion, ambition, passion and violence in the downfall of young Julien Sorel.

The role of nationalism, of pride in a 'fatherland' politically defined, has here been stressed in discussing historical novels and plays, as it was earlier in relation to the rise of history itself as a discipline. One other aspect of patriotism in the record of European letters has still to be noted. This was the early nineteenth century's enthusiasm for folklore, for dialects, for vernacular literature. Scott's *Lay of the Last Minstrel* (1805) breathed fervent Lowland Scottish sentiments, couched in colourful local expressions. In 1806–8, Achim von Arnim (1781–1831), his wife Bettina (1785–1859) and her brother, Clemens Brentano (1778–1842), published the first of many versions of romantic German songs of magic, *Des Knaben Wunderhorn*. Even more important for the future, Jakob Grimm (1785–1863) and his brother Wilhelm (1786–1859), both of them destined for international renown as philologists, in 1812–15 issued the first edition of their collected German fairy tales, *Kinder- und Hausmärchen*.

Interest in folklore and vernacular dialects was not exclusively self-centred. The Grimms, for example, wrote on Irish, Scandinavian and Slavic legends, as well as on those of their native Germany; and in 1824 Jacob Grimm translated into German the first Serbian grammar to receive such recognition. Nevertheless, the patriotic impulse to glorify one's own people's tongue and traditions was as powerful as it was widespread. For obvious reasons, this was especially true of spokesmen for nationalities living under what seemed to them alien rule. Consider for example the *Historical Songs of the Poles* (1816) by Niemcewicz, (*see above*, p. 384) and the inspirational *Poems* (1822–3) of Adam Mickiewicz (1798–1855), or Henrik Anker Bjerregaard's (1792–1842) anthem, 'Sons of Norway' (*Sönner ab Norge*), written in defiance of the Swedes in 1820. The first published story in Flemish prose, *Jellen en Mietje* by Karel Broeckaert (1767–1826), first appeared in 1811, when Belgium was under French rule; but it retained its popularity during the years of Dutch domination after 1815. Nowhere was the mounting interest in vernacular literature and in local chronicles stronger than in the Balkans, where Vuk Karadžić (1787–1864) had by 1830 published several of his collections of Serbo-Croatian folk poetry. In 1829 a Bulgarian scholar living in the Ukraine, Yurii Venelin, published the first comprehensive history of his people, their customs and their language, *The Bulgarians Ancient and Modern*.

This general development suggests a footnote of some importance to the history of the years between 1780 and 1830. It will be recalled that in Chapter III (*see above*, pp. 43–8) we had to distinguish between the aristocratic and remarkably cosmopolitan 'high' culture of Europe on the eve of the French Revolution and the far less widely appreciated, but more deeply rooted, 'low' culture of local traditions and popular languages. That distinction still existed in 1830, but it had become less sharp. On the one hand, we have remarked the growing popularity, in the most literal sense, of serious music, poetry and, above all, fiction. On the other hand, eminent historians, philologists and literary figures had turned to folk themes for inspiration, as well as for subject matter. Not the least significant effect of the Revolution's dual legacy of democratic ideals and nationalistic emotions was the narrowing of the gap between 'high' and 'low' cultures in the age that followed it.

Conclusion: The Balance Between Continuity and Change

In this volume's introduction the notion of a 'revolutionary-Napoleonic watershed' was put forward as a central theme for all the narrative and commentary that was to follow (see above, pp. 1–3). Now the question can at last be put directly: by 1830, how basically had Europe's situation changed from that of 1780? The question, of course, raises one of history's universal problems. As the American historian, Carl Becker, liked to point out, two truths about human affairs must always be kept in sight, however much strain may arise from the fact that both are equally true. One is that the world may change, but it changes slowly. The other is that while the world may change slowly, it does change.[1]

Let us consider some of the arguments *against* the idea of a sharp break between the Old Régime and post-Napoleonic Europe. They are substantial, and they rightly oppose any simplistic thesis of a total break in continuity. In the realm of ideas, for example, it can be maintained with considerable justice that both the end of the seventeenth century, with Locke, Newton, Bayle and Leibniz, or the turn of the nineteenth, with Einstein, Freud, Pareto and Lenin, represented far deeper shifts in conceptions of man and his world than did the period we have been examining. Thinkers who reached their maturity just before or after 1830—Auguste Comte, Karl Marx, John Stuart Mill—have all been called eighteenth-century *philosophes* in spirit, because of their rationalistic and utilitarian assumptions. Even Hegel seems in most respects more the culminator of earlier rational, idealistic and progressive traditions than the inventor of a wholly new philosophy. Similarly,

---

[1] For an essay devoted to the theme of this section, see F. L. Ford, 'The revolutionary-Napoleonic era: How much of a watershed?' *American Historical Review*, vol. LXIX (1963), pp. 18–29.

in literature and art it will be remembered that, on the one hand, well before 1780, first Rousseau and then the young Germans of the *Sturm und Drang* had espoused values which would later be called 'romantic' while, on the other hand, an older 'classicism' was still powerful in 1830, especially in architecture and the visual arts.

Other strands of continuity either were unbroken by the Revolution or were quickly reconnected in 1815. Dynastic diplomacy, like the cosmopolitan fraternity of diplomats, dominated international relations in 1830, when Metternich still had eighteen years more of power before him in Vienna, as surely as it had a half-century earlier. Strategic and tactical theories of warfare, whether on land or at sea, had not been revolutionized by the struggles from Valmy to Waterloo, at least so far as most holders of actual commands were concerned, however earnestly such writers as Clausewitz and Jomini lectured the future about 'new' ideas. As for the political map of Europe in the 1820s, while the Holy Roman Empire had vanished, its successor, the German Confederation, showed a number of strikingly familiar features; Italy remained splintered and Poland divided under Russian-Prussian control; Norway had simply passed from Danish to Swedish overlordship and Belgium from Austrian to Dutch; a Bourbon sat once more on the throne of France and another on that of Spain. Even at the level of economic development, the Industrial Revolution, though already under way in Britain before 1780, was by 1830 only beginning to make its full impact felt on the Continent.

Together, these and other possible reflections might appear to prove that there was no historic watershed cutting across late eighteenth- and early nineteenth-century Europe—that instead, as can happen in nature, clouds of dust whipped up by a sudden wind were mistaken for mountain ranges, until the dust settled. Such a conclusion seems consistent with the obvious biological facts that 'life goes on' and that generations do not 'break', but overlap endlessly. Nevertheless, to settle for such a bland flattening-out of the history of this period would leave us with only a poor and distorted conception of what it actually represents as a part of Europe's past.

Here again, we should recall some important features of our story and of the era with which it dealt. We saw not just modification but in many instances fundamental reorganization of major governments. The administrative convulsions produced by efforts to meet revolutionary France on something like its own terms produced changes in state structure all the way from Russia and Alexander I's new central ministries, through Prussia with its reforms of 1807–8, to the England of Addington's income tax. In warfare, while theory might remain conservative, the realities of battle between hordes of citizen-soldiers were never again, after the *levée en masse*, to resemble those of the eighteenth century. In politics, the introduction of democratic demands, supported by popular patriotism and focused on the making of written constitutions, brought alterations in both the tone and the content of public life which the Restoration struggled vainly to reverse or to thrust out of sight. As for the aesthetic realm, despite the difficulty of imposing clear stylistic breaks, there can be no denying the change of atmosphere, the heightening of the emotional atmosphere of European culture that came with the full onset of romanticism.

All these features of our period deserve to be considered at least as important as the lines of continuity we have also traced. Still, it might be suggested at this point, the balance between continuity and change comes out about even, a roughly equal combination of the old and the new, no more significant one way or the other than one would expect in any other half-century of human history. Just here, however, a further and, it can be argued, a decisive element of difference between 1780 and 1830 must be taken into account. This is the matter, emphasized in Chapter III (*see above*, pp. 21–7) of social structure—of how people were sorted out, in their own and in others' minds, as well as how they were grouped for action within the population as a whole.

Using the simplest possible terms, but yet seeking to avoid misleading oversimplification, it is possible to contrast European society of the 1830s with that of the 1780s on the basis of the marked degrees to which the concept of *orders* (nobility, clergy, bourgeoisie) as the primary subdivisions among men had been overshadowed by *parties* and *classes*. As usual in history, the change was not without its precursors and was not total when it came. In the very first decade of our period, we saw political parties in action—Patriots and Orangists in the United Provinces, Republicans, Moderates and Patriots in Poland, and so on. We also saw class conflict appear explicitly in 1789 with the *affaire Reveillon* at Paris in April of that year (*see above*, p. 105). Conversely, nobility, clergy and, to a much more limited degree, bourgeoisie survived well beyond 1830 as legally defined orders; and in some countries, of course, they still do. In short, we are talking about a change which was neither completely unheralded nor lacking in exceptions and nuances. It was nonetheless of crucial importance.

One way to gauge the shift is to note the prestige which the revived

Roman title of 'citizen', at once pre- and post-medieval, has never lost since the French Revolution. To be a citizen is to be something that makes noble birth or religious ordination, if not irrelevant, certainly not decisive. Another index is the shift in the basis for honorific status, particularly for what some modern sociologists call generalized status, as distinct from the specialized status one earns by acquired knowledge or skills. The holder of generalized status honour is deferred to by large numbers of people either because of some factor other than specific, acquired ability or because of some such ability which nevertheless has little to do with wide areas in which his opinion is, often puzzlingly, revered. Under the Old Régime a noble, *any* noble, enjoyed this kind of status to some degree. Today we accord it to, among others, war heroes, astronauts, film and sport stars, scientists—and the rich. Men of the mid-nineteenth century, dazzled by new fortunes and by industrial and commercial ingenuity, honoured *especially* the rich, regardless of birth, far more willingly than had men of the eighteenth.

It is interesting to recall that Napoleon himself, in a portentous linking of attributes, had signalled the new day with his decree of 1808 establishing the Imperial Nobility (*see above*, pp. 184–5). Remember that titles could be conferred by the emperor on anyone; but in order to be passed along by inheritance, every such title had to be accompanied by a minimum financial legacy as well. Nobility thus was rejuvenated, but on the basis of service and of wealth, not of ancient family claims.

Does the rise in absolute importance of economic gradations among men signify the complete triumph of classes as the only authentic units of social conflict and political action? Not necessarily. It is now common in both Europe and the United States for historians and others to insist rather vehemently that men do not act at all consistently in terms of their economic interests, rationally perceived, or in groups defined by shared economic stakes, be the latter wealth, insecurity or poverty. The mixed and shifting composition of revolutionary mobs, for example, can be cited to upset the more simple-minded forms of Marxist analysis. This new scepticism may serve a useful purpose in warning us not to see class struggle, among self-conscious economic interest groups, in all the other kinds of conflict known to history. Here too, however, a doctrinaire tendency to oversimplify in the other direction can become dangerous. After all, poor men and rich men *have* struggled against one another for advantage, with just that difference in mind.

The significant shift between 1780 and 1830, the true basis for speaking of a revolutionary-Napoleonic watershed, was in any case more complex than any mechanical replacement of orders by classes or parties. It can be seen in two developments. The first, which we have been discussing, was the *relative* increase in the role of wealth, at the expense of birth, calling or religious affiliation, as a factor determining status. The second, unblinkable by the 1820s and still more so in the revolutions of 1830, was the triumph of party, sometimes admittedly combining well-to-do citizens and poor ones, but just as often linking noblemen and commoners, as the critical unit of public action. Living within a society thus conceived and a political order thus constructed, preoccupied with such issues as national unification, constitutional democracy, the division of industrial production, Europeans in 1830 already stood a long way from the world of their eighteenth-century forebears. It was in fact a longer way than the passage of just any half-century might have been expected to carry them. In a very real sense, they looked back to the Old Régime across a historic watershed—and so do we today.

Bibliographical Note

In addition to the works cited in footnotes throughout the preceding text, there are certain titles deserving of mention for their importance to an understanding of the entire period here discussed. The *New Cambridge Modern History* now includes vol. VIII, *The American and French Revolutions, 1763–93*, and vol. IX, *War and Peace in an Age of Upheaval, 1793–1830* (both Cambridge, 1965). Less recent but still very useful are the four corresponding volumes in W. L. Langer's series, *The Rise of Modern Europe*: L. Gershoy, *From Despotism to Revolution, 1763–89* (New York–London 1944); C. Brinton, *A Decade of Revolution, 1789–99* (New York–London, 1934); G. Bruun, *Europe and the French Imperium, 1799–1814* (New York–London, 1938); F. B. Artz, *Reaction and Revolution, 1814–1832* (New York–London, 1934). Of three competing French series, the most highly compressed is *Clio: Introduction aux études historiques*, which includes E. Préclin, *Le Xviii^e siècle*, 2 vols. (Paris, 1952); L. Villat, *La Révolution et l'Empire*, 2 vols. (2nd edn., Paris, 1940–2); and J. Droz, L. Genet and J. Vidalenc, *Le Xix^e siècle*, part I: *Restaurations et révolutions, 1815–71* (2nd edn., Paris, 1963). More expansive, but less detailed as regards bibliographical guidance, are two volumes of the *Histoire générale des civilisations*: R. Mousnier, E. Labrousse and M. Bouloiseau, *Le Xviii^e siècle: Révolution intellectuelle, technique et politique, 1715–1815* (Paris, 1953), and R. Schnerb, *Le Xix^e siècle, 1815–1914* (Paris, 1955). The third of these collaborative enterprises, *Peuples et civilisations*, while more readable than *Clio*, is rather more conservative than the *Histoire générale* in its definition of coverage. The four volumes applicable to our period, however, have benefited from particularly frequent and diligent revision: P. Sagnac, *La Fin de l'Ancien régime et la Révolution américaine, 1763–1789* (3rd edn, Paris, 1952); G. Lefebvre, *La Révolution française* (3rd edn, Paris, 1963); the same author's *Napoléon* (5th edn, Paris, 1965); and F. Ponteil, *L'Eveil des nationalités et le mouvement libéral*,

1815–1848 (Paris, 1960, superseding the previous volume of the same title, written by G. Weill).

Two major collections deal with special aspects of general history. The *Histoire des relations internationales* edited by P. Renouvin offers as vols. III, IV and V (part one): G. Zeller, *De Louis XIV à 1789* (Paris, 1955); A. Fugier, *La Révolution française et l'Empire napoléonien* (Paris, 1954); and P. Renouvin, *Le Xix^e siècle: De 1815 à 1871* (Paris, 1954). In another field, the *Cambridge Economic History of Europe*, vol. VI, *The Industrial Revolutions and After*, ed. H. J. Habakkuk and M. Postan (Cambridge, 1965), is well worth consulting, not least for the remarkable 328-page chapter on 'Technological change and industrial development in western Europe, 1750–1914' by D. Landes.

Turning to major national histories, we have two volumes of the *Oxford History of England*: J. S. Watson, *The Reign of George III, 1760–1820* (Oxford, 1960), and E. L. Woodward, *The Age of Reform, 1815–1870* (Oxford, 1938). The participants in the general French series mentioned above naturally give particularly full treatment to their own country's history. In addition, for the first years of our period there is vol. IX, part I of the magisterial *Histoire de France des origines jusqu'à la Révolution* edited by E. Lavisse: H. Carré, P. Sagnac and E. Lavisse, *Le Règne de Louis XVI* (Paris, 1911). The best introduction to Germany is the 8th revised edition of B. Gebhardt's *Handbuch der deutschen Geschichte*, ed. H. Grundmann, vols. II–III (Stuttgart, 1955–60), or the briefer *Deutsche Geschichte im Überblick* edited by P. Rassow (2nd edn, Stuttgart, 1962). A survey in English by a distinguished German émigré to America is H. Holborn, *History of Modern Germany*, vol. II, *1648–1840* (New York, 1964); but at once the most profound and the most original treatment of the pre- and post-Napoleonic scene is F. Schnabel, *Deutsche Geschichte im neunzehnten Jahrhundert*, 4 vols. (rev. edn, Freiburg im Breisgau, 1948–51). Austria's past is reviewed less brilliantly, but very solidly, by H. Hantsch, *Die Geschichte Oesterreichs*, vol. II beginning in 1648 (3rd edn, Graz-Vienna, 1962). Among several full histories of Spain, one of the most judicious and surely the most handsomely illustrated is A. Ballesteros y Beretta, *Historia de España y su influencia en la historia universal*, vols. IX–X (rev. edn, Barcelona–Buenos Aires, 1956–8); but F. Soldevila, *Historia de España*, vols. VI–VII (Barcelona, 1958–9), also should be mentioned, especially for its fine bibliographies. Quite different in scope and purpose is the penetrating interpretive essay by J. Vicens Vives, *Aproximación a la historia de España* (3rd edn, Barcelona, 1962).

In rather puzzling contrast to Spain and Germany, not to mention England and France, Italy continues to lack any large corpus of truly general national history. However, appropriate chapters from L. Salvatorelli, *A Concise History of Italy*, trans. B. Miall (New York, 1940) may be usefully supplemented by A. J. Whyte, *The Evolution of Modern Italy, 1715–1922* (Oxford, 1944). Most of Europe's smaller nations have also been subject to very uneven treatment. B. J. Hovde, for example, in his two-volume work, *The Scandinavian Countries* (Ithaca, 1948), limits himself entirely to internal history, while B. H. M. Vlekke's *The Evolution of the Dutch Nation* (New York, 1945) is scarcely more than a short manual. A welcome exception to this general pattern is H. Pirenne, *Histoire de Belgique*, published since the early twentieth century in various editions, most recently with beautiful illustrations (Brussels, 1950); vol. III is relevant here.

If one looks towards eastern Europe, one finds Polish historical studies well synthesized in W. H. Reddaway *et al.*, *The Cambridge History of Poland*, vol. II (Cambridge, 1941). In the vast Russian field, we should note that G. Vernadsky, *A History of Russia* (New Haven, 1929), and N. V. Riasanovsky's later, as well as much more detailed, work under the same title (New York, 1963) may serve to introduce the reader to more detailed surveys by continental scholars, including P. Milyukov, C. Seignobos and L. Eisenmann, *Histoire de Russie* vols. II–III (Paris, 1932–3), and V. Gitermann, *Geschichte Russlands*, vols. II–III (Zurich, 1945–9), the latter made attractive by its excellent maps and illustrations. For the Ottoman Empire, we must still rely heavily on J. W. Zinkeisen, *Geschichte des osmanischen Reiches in Europe*, vols. VI–VII (Hamburg, 1859–63); but important facets of that area's history are very ably dealt with by L. S. Stavrianos, *The Balkans since 1453* (New York, 1958).

Index

For rulers the dates given are those of their reigns, save in certain cases where it has seemed advisable to include birth and death dates as well. For other persons birth and death dates only are given. These dates are omitted for individuals whose importance for the present volume is marginal.

162, 163, 197, 318–20; Irish Parliament, 87–88, 197, 313; Irish Volunteers in 1770s and 1780s, 87–88; franchise, 88, 152, 163, 197–98, 318, 320; United Irishmen (1791), 141, 162; relations with French Republic, 152, 155, 162, 252; revolt of 1798, 162–63, 197, 244; Act of Union (1800–01), 197, 296, 318; population, 291; Catholic Association (1823 ff.), 319–20; emigration, 373

Islam, 41, 54, 160, 277, 278–80, 297, 309, 379

Istanbul, 40, 41, 59, 70, 73, 220, 281, 309, 325, 327, 328

Italian Republic, 200, 204

Italy, 2, 14, 16, 38, 47, 51, 56, 80, 232, 239, 269, 354, 356, 363, 369, 376, 388; reformers and revolutionaries, 10, 271–75, 287–88, 296–97, 305–308, 324, 328; Restoration and Austrian domination, 17, 257, 261–264, 302, 328; art and architecture, 18, 379–80; Catholic Church in, 22, 160, 296, 305; society, 32–33, 291; literature, drama and opera, 46, 47, 81, 383–84; individual states, 57, 58, 59, 144, 283, 290, 295, 305–08; effects of French Revolution, 130–131, 139, 144, 148–49, 153, 155–63, 288; and Napoleon, 131, 177–78, 180, 187, 191–93, 196, 198–200, 202, 204–05, 212, 219–20, 222–24, 228, 252; Kingdom of Italy (1805–1814), 204–05, 212

Jacobi, Karl, 355, 356

Jacobins, 117–128, 129, 131–32, 133, 136, 147, 153, 166, 171, 173, 234, 251, 286, 288, 332, 338, 340; outside France, 153–54, 159, 163; 'Jacobinism' as political epithet, 197–98, 270, 286–87, 322

Jahn, Friedrich Ludwig, 303

Janissaries, 277, 309; massacred (1826), 325, 326

Jassy, treaty (1792), 74

Jay, John, 66

Jebb, John, 140

Jefferson, Thomas, 80, 81

Jemappes, battle (1792), 148, 252

Jena, battle (1806), 206, 217, 228, 229, 233, 238, 239, 245, 250; university, 303, 366

Jerome, King of Westphalia, see Bonaparte, Jerome

Jesuits, 296

Jews and Judaism, 24, 26, 35, 40, 42, 261, 270, 296, 334, 347, 349, 350; effects of French Revolution, 159–160; treatment by Napoleon, 176–78, 186

Joachim, King of Naples, see Murat

John, Archduke (Habsburg), 193

John VI, King of Portugal (1821–26), 274, 275

Jomini, Antoine Henri, Baron de, 253, 388

Joseph II, Holy Roman Emperor (1765–90), 51, 163, 169, 334; domestic policies, 35, 39, 82; political opposition, 90–93, 145, 299; foreign policies, 70–74, 82, 283

Joseph, King of Naples and of Spain, see Bonaparte, Joseph

Josephine, Empress of the French, see Beauharnais, Josephine

Jourdan, Jean Baptiste, Comte, 129, 135, 148, 150, 155, 157, 161, 221

Jovellanos, Gaspar Melchor de (1744–1811), 97, 145, 334

Judges and law courts, 26, 34, 84, 96, 98–100, 105, 109, 111, 123, 126–28, 152, 159, 171, 173, 185–86, 314–15, 348–49

Junkers, 36–37, 217–19, 238, 376

Junot, Andoche, Duke of Abrantès, 208, 209

Kamptz, Karl Christoph Albert Heinrich, 369

Kant, Immanuel (1724–1804), 45; and the French Revolution, 15, 142, 340, 352; political theories, 332, 340–41; ethical doctrines, 349, 351–353; views on history, 365–67